Edward Palmer's
ARKANSAW MOUNDS

Arkansas and Regional Studies Series
volume five

Edward Palmer's

ARKANSAW MOUNDS

∿ ∿ ∿

EDITED BY
Marvin D. Jeter

Contributions by
Ian W. Brown, Ann M. Early, Mary Farmer,
Dan F. Morse, Martha Ann Rolingson, and Bruce D. Smith

THE UNIVERSITY OF ARKANSAS PRESS
Fayetteville London
1990

The editor wishes to thank the Arkansas Archeological Survey,
whose assistance has brought this project
to its successful realization.

Designer: B. J. Zodrow
Typeface: Linotron 202 Sabon
Typesetter: G & S Typesetters, Inc.

The paper used in this publication meets the minimum requirements
of the American National Standard for Permanence of Paper
for Printed Library Materials Z39.48-1984. ∞

Library of Congress Cataloging-in-Publication Data

Palmer, Edward, 1831–1911.
    [Arkansas mounds]
    Edward Palmer's Arkansaw mounds / edited by Marvin D. Jeter;
contributions by Ian W. Brown . . . [et al.].
      p.   cm.
    Includes bibliographical references.
    ISBN 1-55728-074-6 (alk. paper).—ISBN 1-55728-075-4 (pbk. :
alk. paper)
      1. Indians of North America—Arkansas—Antiquities. 2. Mound-
builders—Arkansas. 3. Arkansas—Antiquities. I. Jeter, Marvin
D. II. Brown, Ian W. III. Title.
E78.A8P35 1990
976.7' 01—dc20   89-20226
                                        CIP

This project was funded in part by a grant
from the Arkansas Endowment for the Humanities.

To the memory of
Edward Palmer and Henry Jackson Lewis,
who preserved some of the heritage
of the American Indian for the future.

Contents

Figures

Tables

Preface and Acknowledgments

Edward Palmer's 1881–84 work at numerous Indian mounds in Arkansas has been my major research project through most of the 1980s. Here I will summarize in more or less chronological order the extensive, and intermittently intensive, researches that have resulted in this book and will acknowledge the contributions of numerous individuals and institutions.

In 1980 I was the Arkansas Archeological Survey's station archeologist at the University of Arkansas at Monticello (UAM) Station. I had some knowledge of Edward Palmer's work in that territory but had no real appreciation for his total accomplishment in Arkansas and elsewhere. Bruce D. Smith, curator of North American archeology at the Smithsonian Institution (SI), and Stephen Williams, director of the Lower Mississippi Survey (LMS), Peabody Museum, Harvard University, invited me to participate in two meetings that year that marked the beginnings of my interest in this project.

The first of these meetings was the SI/LMS Conference on the centennial of the Mound Exploration Division of the Bureau of Ethnology, held in Washington, D.C., at the Smithsonian's National Museum of Natural History in January 1980 and co-hosted by Bruce and Steve. During a preview session, Bruce and I opened the Drew County, Arkansas, file folder, prepared by the staff of the Smithsonian's National Anthropological Archives, and were startled and elated to find the Lewis drawing (fig. 7.16) of the skeletons and artifacts excavated by Palmer at the Tillar site in 1882. During the course of this conference, I learned much about the Mound Survey in general and about the potentials of the Smithsonian's archives and artifact collections.

The second meeting was a symposium, entitled "New Perspectives on the Mound Exploration Division, Bureau of (American) Ethnology" and chaired by Smith, presented at the thirty-seventh annual meeting of the Southeastern Archaeological Conference (SEAC), at New Orleans in November 1980. I have incorporated in this book material from several papers presented at that symposium, including an expanded version of Smith's paper and a slightly revised version of a paper by Ian W. Brown of the LMS, plus excerpts from papers by Survey archeologists. I have also adapted material from my own paper on Palmer's work at the remarkable Tillar mound site.

Dr. James B. Griffin, emeritus director of the Museum of Anthropology at the University of Michigan, "dean" of eastern U.S. archeologists, and a participant in the SI/LMS Conference, got me off to a good start by referring me to the 1956 biography of Palmer by his colleague Rogers McVaugh, former director of the herbarium at the University of Michigan. He also furnished several other useful leads as the research progressed.

James R. Glenn, archivist of the National Anthropological Archives at the Smithsonian, gave us an excellent orientation at the 1980 conference and helped me in subsequent correspondence and visits. It has been a pleasure to work with Jim and his cooperative staff, especially Paula Fleming, then, during my 1983 and 1985 visits, and in obtaining photographs during 1988. Margaret Lethbridge and Felicia Pickering of the Smithsonian Anthropology Laboratory, Harry G. Heiss and Susan Glenn of the Smithsonian Institution Archives, and Joyce Goulait of the Smithsonian Department of Printing and Photographic Services also provided much valuable assistance.

On the Arkansas front, Dr. John L. Ferguson, the state historian, granted me permission to use the Arkansas History Commission's archives in Little Rock, the repository for the original notes which were the basis of the 1917 *Arkansas Mounds* publication. Frances Valescu of the Commission's staff (and a member of the Arkansas Archeological Society) enthusiastically helped me by locating these notes and in guiding me to some of the Commission's other resources during my 1981 visit, and Russell Baker helped during my 1988 visit. One of the most gratifying aspects of this project has been the way that the Commission's notes complement the notes and drawings from the National Anthropological Archives.

An invaluable resource has been the regional expertise of the Arkansas Archeological Survey's station archeologists, several of whom freely shared their knowledge in a variety of ways. The Survey's support staff at the stations and the Fayetteville headquarters also made several significant contributions.

Although Palmer's investigations did not encroach upon what was to become Frank Schambach's southwest Arkansas station territory, Frank's expertise extends well beyond that boundary. He provided much useful information as we examined Palmer's collections at the 1980 conference and subsequently as I analyzed the Tillar artifacts.

Dan Morse's northeast Arkansas territory was extensively investigated by Palmer, and I greatly enjoyed some memorable visits to Mound Survey sites with Dan in June 1983. Dan and Phyllis Morse also generously shared the maps they had prepared for their 1980 symposium paper, plus some suggestions for references. The Morse family also graciously provided hospitality and excellent home cooking for me and my children.

Martha Rolingson's ongoing researches at Toltec Mounds State Park have significantly cleared up Palmer's somewhat mysterious investigations at that spectacular site. University of Arkansas at Pine Bluff (UAPB) Station Secretary Mary Farmer and John House, working at both UAPB and UAM furnished comments and basic descriptive data on Palmer's east-central Arkansas sites; Mary also discovered new information, both published and archival, on Lewis and Palmer. Although Ann Early was not at the 1980 conference, several sites in her south-central Arkansas territory were visited by Palmer, and she generously provided comments on these sites and some of the artifacts from them.

Henry S. McKelway, my former assistant at the UAM Station, researched land-ownership records that cleared up some uncertainties about the location of Palmer's Tillar site. His parents, Mr. and Mrs. John McKelway of Kensington, Maryland, provided hospitality during my May 1983 visit to the Smithsonian. In addition, later in 1983, Hank went to the Smithsonian on my behalf to document and photograph some collections that I had not had time to see, including those from Early's territory. Joyce Abney, UAM Station Secretary, did her usual excellent job of typing draft after draft of my Palmer manuscripts and also cheerfully took on the horrendous task of transcribing the handwritten notes of Palmer and his scribes.

S. D. Dickinson of Prescott, Arkansas, John Solomon Otto, a one-time Arkansawyer now at the University of Maryland, and William Shea of the University of Arkansas at Monticello shared a number of interesting insights into Arkansas history and folklore. Another UAM faculty colleague, Eric Sundell, commented on some of Palmer's botanical references and visited the Arkansas City Cemetery Mound with me in August 1983 to verify Palmer's 1882 report of *Ailanthus* trees growing on the mound.

This project, or at least my contributions to it, languished after I left the Survey for an administrative position in western Illinois between mid-1983 and the end of 1985. My "St. Louis support group," Leonard W. Blake, Patti O'Connor, and Margaret Serrano, made numerous contributions toward preserving my sanity during those difficult times and have given me encouragement and hospitality since then. In particular, Leonard shared his personal archeobotanical library and his intimate knowledge of St. Louis, which helped me explore connections between Palmer's notes and that city's contemporary residents.

During the 1983–85 period, Survey Editor Mary Lynn Kennedy and her helpers got my Palmer manuscripts "up" on word-processor files. When I made a brief visit to Survey headquarters in Fayetteville, Arkansas, in October 1984, she straightened me out on the matter of editorial procedures for dealing with Palmer's documents. I had had visions of correcting Palmer's eccentric and idiosyncratic spelling, grammar, and syntax, but Mary Lynn knew that major battles in the field of editing historical documents had been fought during recent decades and requested that I look into a landmark volume summing up the situation (Vogt and Jones 1981). I found that my major arguments and others along the same lines had all been defeated by better arguments on the "literary editing" side.

I revisited the Smithsonian briefly in early 1985, and gave a colloquium on my Palmer research for the anthropology department. I again received encouragement and assistance from Smith, Griffin, J. Glenn, and Fleming, and from Mary Lucas Powell and Joseph Ewan, who were then at the Smithsonian.

In January 1986 I escaped the flooded and frozen tundra of Illinois, and made a beeline for the high ground of Fayetteville. I received a welcome back to the fold from Survey Director Charles R. McGimsey III, Assistant Director W. Fredrick Limp (who was then also in charge of the Survey's publications program and made the word-processing facilities available to me), and State Archeologist Hester A. Davis (who also made her "wandering archeologists' safe house" apartment available to me during January and February).

The generosity of my late aunt, Miss Kumi Jeter of Birmingham, Alabama, made it possible for me to spend the better part of the period from January through June 1986 working solely on this project. Aunt Kumi was a fine teacher and a frustrated scholar, and I know she would have greatly enjoyed this kind of research. At last having the time and library resources that the project deserved, I discovered the great mass of undigested information available on Palmer's earlier archeological work and began to gain some awareness of what H. J. Lewis had accomplished. My manuscript expanded in several unexpected directions, leaving a number of unanswered questions at the end of June.

From July 1986 through December 1987, I worked most of the time on a variety of contract archeological editing and writing projects for the Survey and as a consultant on several contract projects in New Orleans. Between projects and during breaks in them, I continued to research the Palmer volume, at various libraries, via correspondence, and through personal communications, gradually finding the answers to my leftover questions.

I received valuable help from the staff members of the Mullins Library, University of Arkansas, Fayetteville; the Howard-Tilton Library, Tulane University, New Orleans; the St. Louis Public Library; the Indiana University Library in Bloomington; the Watson Library, Northwestern State University, Natchitoches, Louisiana; and the University of Arkansas at Monticello Library.

Also furnishing useful information, most of which is specifically cited at various places in this volume, were: Larry Banks of the U.S. Army Corps of Engineers, Southwestern Division; John S. Belmont, formerly of the LMS; Henry F. Dobyns of Tucson, Arizona; John Connaway of the Mississippi Archeological Survey; Wilma Dulin of the Indiana Historical Society; Robert C. Euler of Prescott, Arizona; Chris Goodwin of Goodwin and Associates in New Orleans; Hiram F. "Pete" Gregory of Northwestern State University in Natchitoches; Patricia Harpole of the Minnesota Historical Society; Curtis "Kit" Hinsley of the Department of History, Colgate University, and author of *Savages and Scientists*, a history of early anthropology at the Smithsonian; Edie Jeter of the Valentine Museum in Richmond, Virginia; William F. Keegan of the Florida Museum of Natural History; Vernon J. Knight of the University of Alabama; Col. Howard Mac-Cord of Richmond; Robert C. Mainfort, Jr., of Pinson Mounds State Park, Tennessee; Tim Perttula of North Texas State University in Denton; Jerome C. Rose of the University of Arkansas in Fayetteville; and Dee Ann Story of the University of Texas in Austin.

Special mention should be made of the contributions of several individuals. Robert A. Bye, Jr., of the Jardin Botanico, Universidad Nacional Autónoma de México in Mexico City, is the most active researcher into Palmer's ethnobotanical collections and documents, which he still finds very useful in his work on plant germ-plasm conservation. Bob supplied me with numerous reprints of articles and some very encouraging correspondence.

David H. Dye of the Department of Anthropology, Memphis State University, found the first clue that Palmer's artist-assistant H. J. Lewis was also the man who was called the first black political cartoonist. And, in April 1986, David gave me a guided tour of the Bradley mound site, where Lewis first worked with Palmer in Arkansas.

Joseph Ewan, scholar in residence at the Missouri Botanical Garden in St. Louis and emeritus professor of botany at Tulane University, is the country's leading authority on the history of natural history and of botany. Joe and his wife Nesta have been on Palmer's trail since 1946. They provided gracious hospitality and generously shared his Palmer file and reference works from his superb library with me. I visited them briefly in New Orleans in late 1986, at the Garden in early 1987, and again in March 1988.

We are living in an age of remarkable but eccentric electronic devices. Due to changes in equipment and my semi-nomadic lifestyle, portions of the manuscript for this book have been in and out of as many as seven different computers and their word-processing or translating programs. It would have been impossible to maintain any semblance of order without the help of several staff experts, including Mary Lynn Kennedy, Karen Wagner, Ian Johnson, and Jim Farley. Finally, during my temporary return to the UAM Station in early 1988, the electronic manuscript wound up on disks for my own microcomputer, but I was only able to access and deal with it because of the absolutely indispensable expertise of Patricia Kay Galloway of the Mississippi Department of Archives and History.

Meanwhile, in mid-1987, Mary Lynn Kennedy convinced me to inquire about the possibilities of having this volume published by the University of Arkansas Press. I received a warm welcome at the Press from Director Miller Williams, Brenda Zodrow (then assistant director), and Martha Estes (then managing editor). Subsequently, the manuscript was significantly improved by Editor Sandra Frierson, Designer Brenda Zodrow, and Artist Jim Scott.

My early 1988 researches were partially supported by a grant from the Arkansas Endowment for the Humanities, as were the photographs of drawings and artifacts made at the Smithsonian. AEH Director Jane Browning and Assistant Director Donna Champ provided me with generous support.

I offer my warmest thanks to all of the above-named persons and institutions for their numerous contributions. Any mistakes or misrepresentations of their data and opinions are, of course, my responsibility. I also apologize to any contributors whose names were inadvertently omitted.

This project has been unduly prolonged but has had numerous gratifying aspects. It is difficult to express my admiration for Edward Palmer and H. J. Lewis, but at least I've walked a few miles along their trails. In particular, I have developed a sense of personal empathy with Palmer, falling somewhere short of a belief in reincarnation. It is, after all, merely coincidental that we both worked at Fort Toulouse, Alabama, in the Prescott region of Arizona, and in southeast Arkansas; that we both hired assistants named Henry in the Memphis vicinity for our Arkansas work and lost our assistants due to budgetary problems; and that we were temporarily married to women with similar names. Beyond the coincidences there has been the perhaps eccentric pleasure of working with century-old documents and associated collections, correcting long-standing mistakes, and at last making a greater semblance of sense and archeological significance out of the whole business.

Finally, one last glance at the past, and a hopeful look toward the future. The Survey's motto, after all, is "Preserving the Past for the Future." I hope this book will contribute to general consciousness-raising about the still rich but heavily damaged and endangered archeological resources of Arkansas. And in particular, this study of the past is presented to my own major contributions to the future, Amanda and Daniel. They're both excellent readers; I hope you enjoy it, kids.

Marvin D. Jeter

Edward Palmer's
ARKANSAW MOUNDS

Introduction

Between 1881 and 1884, a remarkable man worked in eastern Arkansas on an unprecedented archeological project. Edward Palmer (1830?-1911) was perhaps the nineteenth century's greatest botanical and natural history field collector. By the 1880s he had also made quite a name for himself as a collector of ethnological and archeological specimens for major museums. He had been recruited by the Smithsonian Institution early in the planning stages of this project, which has been called the birth of modern American archeology.

Funds were authorized by Congress for the formation of a Mound Exploration Division within the Smithsonian's Bureau of Ethnology. For the first time, a massive, sustained, and controlled scientific effort was mounted in an attempt to solve an archeological problem. In this case it was a long-standing and vexing question: who had built the prehistoric mounds of the eastern United States?

Then, as now, Arkansas was unusually rich in prehistoric remains, especially mounds. Palmer had some prior knowledge of this and appears to have influenced the decision to explore and excavate here. Arkansas became one of the most intensively investigated states in the entire project, and the great majority of the work done here was done by Palmer. His colleagues continued sending reports and artifacts to the Smithsonian over more than a decade of field work.

The lengthy final report on the great mound survey, written by the Division's director, Cyrus Thomas, and published in 1894 in the Bureau's *Twelfth Annual Report*, demolished the theory of a lost race of non-Indian Mound-Builders, which had become popular as eighteenth- and nineteenth-century American settlers had spread westward onto lands recently expropriated from their aboriginal occupants. Now, in a triumph of nineteenth-century scientific and historical research, the myth was shattered; the mounds had been built by the ancestors of the historic eastern North American Indians.

Palmer produced three kinds of documents related to his Arkansas work: diary-like notes, letters to his superiors at the Smithsonian, and reports, usually on a monthly basis. After having been separated and scrambled for more than a century, these documents are reassembled here, essentially in chronological order. All are written in his inimitable and idiosyncratic, but ultimately quite appealing, style: the style of a somewhat crusty and eccentric Victorian Anglo-American who was well-traveled and thoroughly imbued with the work ethic and a sense of fair play.

Palmer's notes primarily record incidents of travel and are often informative about the Arkansas scene of the 1880s; they are sometimes poignant and sometimes quite humorous. The letters include much archeological information but also often deal with the logistics of Palmer's investigations, including some of the kinds of problems that bedevil field archeologists to this day—they're funny only in retrospect. Finally, the reports contain most of the descriptive archeological information that was used by Thomas and is still of great value to Lower Mississippi Valley archeologists. All too often, this is the only information we have about sites, or parts of sites, that have been destroyed.

For about two months, from early November 1882 to early January 1883, Palmer was assisted by an equally remarkable man. Henry J. Lewis was a talented black artist, who had been born a slave in Mississippi. He had never been formally schooled but had somehow learned to read, and at some time he had moved to Pine Bluff, Arkansas. He developed his talents to the point that he won the praise of white contemporaries and sold sketches of Arkansas and Mississippi River scenes to major Eastern magazines. For the Mound Survey project, he made some thirty-eight drawings of mound sites in eastern and central Arkansas, most of which are still curated by the Smithsonian and are reproduced herein.

I began this research believing that Palmer had been a botanical collector who suddenly found himself doing archeology in Arkansas. But, in reading his long-forgotten publications and other documents of his day, I found that he had already been involved in the beginnings of American archeology in the U.S. Southwest and Great Basin, and in Mexico. Furthermore, it became clear that the full story of Palmer's involvement in archeology across the Sun Belt and south of the border had never really been told. Much less was known about Lewis, and the little that could be found was buried in old newspapers and periodicals and a few other obscure sources. Only gradually did it become apparent that he had led a fascinating and significant life himself, again an untold story.

This book tells of Palmer's and Lewis's work in Arkansas for the mound survey, in Palmer's words and Lewis's pictures insofar as possible, augmented by notes provided by present-day archeologists. It also attempts to place that work in the contexts of late nineteenth-century archeology, their careers, and late nineteenth-century Arkansas.

PART ONE

Contexts,
Personalities,
and Beginnings

CHAPTER ONE

The Mound Survey
and Its Contexts

. . . the remains of the mound section are due
to the ancestors of the Indians of that section. . . .

—Cyrus Thomas

With this statement, the director of the Mound Exploration Division of the Smithsonian Institution's Bureau of Ethnology sounded the death-knell for the belief that the ancient earthworks of eastern North America had been built by a "lost race" who were not Native American Indians. It came at the end of his now-classic 1894 final report on a massive project that had begun some thirteen years before.

Thomas not only rang out the old; he also rang in the new. His project, often called the "Mound Survey" today, has been hailed as "the birth of modern American archeology."

It might better be characterized as the grand culmination of an early series of multiple births. American archeology has been born again and again, in terms of concepts and methods, and in different regions, over the years. A close examination of the history of American archeology in region after region, especially in what is now called the Sun Belt, reveals that again and again the first, or some of the earliest, "scientific" archeology was done by a man named Edward Palmer, who worked for the Mound Survey in Arkansas.

Palmer was basically a botanical and natural history collector. His archeological concepts were often questionable, and his methods were often crude, but there can be little question about his dedication to science as he saw it. Like all good scientific field workers, he kept records and made reports that permit us to understand and evaluate his work.

The Mound Survey covered much of the eastern U.S., in a sort of cluster-sampling pattern (see figure 1.6). One of the most intensively sampled states was Arkansas, and most of the Arkansas work was done by Palmer, between 1881 and 1884. He concentrated on the alluvial lowlands where the mounds were most common: the delta country of the Mississippi Valley, and the Arkansas Valley as far up as Little Rock, with occasional forays into lesser valleys such as those of the St. Francis, White, and Ouachita rivers.

The Problem of the Mounds

Americans first became interested in the riddle of the mounds in eastern North America in the late eighteenth century (Silverberg 1968; Willey and Sabloff 1980:20–43; Hinsley 1981:23). Thomas Jefferson opened a mound on his Virginia property in 1784, in what has been called "the first scientific excavation in the history of archaeology," but unfortunately his work "had no immediate intellectual offspring" (Willey and Sabloff 1980:28–29).

Instead, speculation ran rife, especially in the nineteenth century. The process of westward expansion increased, and the Native Americans were moved out of their ancestral lands, but the mounds and other earthworks remained and were discovered in great numbers as the land was cleared. Many of them were massive, and some were laid out in curious geometrical or naturalistic (animal effigy) patterns. Who had built them?

The answer to this question had more than academic implications. The analogy of the fall of Rome to the barbarians was not overlooked. If the Indians had not built the mounds but were merely savage squatters in a land formerly occupied by relatively civilized (and possibly white) peoples, here was a rationale for dispossessing them. As Silverberg has summarized the situation, "The controversy over the origin of the mounds was not merely an abstract scholarly debate, but had its roots in the great 19th-century campaign of extermination waged against the American Indian"(1968:159–60).

In this atmosphere, one major answer gained credence: the mounds had not been built by the Indians of the eastern United States or their ancestors, but by a lost race. Variations on this theme identified the Mound-Builders as Danes, Vikings, Mexican "Toltecs" (a notion to which Palmer himself, ironically, subscribed), Lost Tribes of Israel, or simply an unknown but noble and civilized non-Indian race (Willey and Sabloff 1980:20–31). Prophetic voices such as those of the Reverend James Madison and the naturalist William Bartram, arguing in favor of the Indian explanation and even offering evidence of Indian mound-building or use, were generally drowned out, and volumes supporting the lost race theory began to appear.

The first systematic mound study was by Caleb Atwater in his "Description of the Antiquities of Ohio and Other Western States"(1820). He carefully described some of the "Ancient Works" but suggested that they had been made by Hindus from India who had been displaced by later immigrants from Asia, the ancestors of modern American Indians, and had themselves moved to Mexico (Willey and Sabloff 1980:29–30).

The major argument in favor of the mound-builders theory, though, was published by the Smithsonian Institution itself, shortly after its establishment in 1846. *Ancient Monuments of the Mississippi Valley,* by Ephraim G. Squier and Edwin H. Davis (1848), was the first volume in the *Smithsonian Contributions to Knowledge* series and as such carried an aura of authority. Again this was reinforced by a generally well-done and lengthy descriptive section, but they "adhered to the great race of Moundbuilders theory" (Willey and Sabloff 1980:36).

Pressures had been building for some such official solution to the problem. Joel R. Poinsett, an influential statesman and amateur scientist from South Carolina for whom Poinsett County, Arkansas, and the poinsettia are named, argued in a discourse commemorating the first anniversary of the Smithsonian's predecessor, the National Institution for the Promotion of Science, that the Institution had "a special duty to inquire into the history of the people we have dispossessed" and specifically referred to "the Indian races, now fading from the earth; their mounds and pyramids" (Poinsett 1841 : 19–20, 42).

The first secretary (director) of the Smithsonian, Joseph Henry (1797–1878), in his "Programme of Organization" written just before he was elected in 1846, had "proposed to increase knowledge of man in North America through surveys and explorations of mounds and other remains" (Hinsley 1981 : 34). And in August 1846 the pioneering ethnologist Henry Rowe Schoolcraft had sent a "Plan for the Investigation of American Ethnology" to the board of regents of the new Smithsonian Institution. The plan was presented at the board's first meeting, in September. Among the activities suggested was "archaeological investigation, particularly of the ancient earthworks of the Mississippi Valley" (Hinsley 1981 : 20). The Squier and Davis (1848) publication answered such proposals, for a while.

But dissenting voices were heard, and the debate resumed. Samuel F. Haven of the American Antiquarian Society, in his *Archaeology of the United States* (1856), which was published in the same Smithsonian series, argued cogently against the lost race hypothesis. And Schoolcraft, "who was generally sympathetic toward the Indians, decided that there were cultural continuities" between the builders of the mounds and the Native Americans (Willey and Sabloff 1980 : 39), although, as Willey and Sabloff noted, his views were buried deeply in an unindexed six-volume work (Schoolcraft 1851–57).

The Civil War brought archeological field work and scholarly research to a virtual halt, but in a broader sense provided the impetus for a great reorganization of American science in general and government-sponsored science in particular:

> Before the Civil War, government science had tended to be ancillary and ad hoc, uncertain in both constitutional footing and bureaucratic tenure. By 1880 Congress had established permanent scientific bureaus, secure in their legitimacy and missions.
>
> Where did the Smithsonian fit in the taxonomy of scientific institutions? The question sometimes arose in Congress but with no clear answer. The Smithsonian was neither fish nor fowl. . . . Part private, part governmental, it was an improbable hybrid—or to borrow one of Joseph Henry's favorite words, a chimera.
>
> In origin and law the Smithsonian was a private institution. Yet Congress had established it and now was funding its National Museum. . . . (Bruce 1987 : 323–24)

It was in this context, and amidst once-again mounting pressures to address the problem of the mounds, that the leaders of the Smithsonian brought the Mound Survey into existence.

The Great Collector at Washington: Spencer Fullerton Baird

If Edward Palmer had one major patron, that man was Spencer Fullerton Baird (fig. 1.1). Their association began indirectly in 1853, with Palmer's first collecting trip as a member of an expedition outfitted by Baird (McVaugh 1956 : 9–11; Bruce 1987 : 210). It continued in the late 1850s as Palmer began to send Baird specimens from his western explo-

FIGURE 1.1

Spencer Fullerton Baird (1823–1887), second secretary of the Smithsonian Institution and Edward Palmer's major patron, c. 1878. (Smithsonian Institution Archives, Record Unit 95, #10737)

rations, and during and after the war years as Palmer made collections around military posts. In 1869 Baird commissioned Palmer as a general collector in the West, and the relationship intensified through various projects in the 1870s, though Palmer also worked for others (including Frederic Ward Putnam of the Peabody Museum at Harvard, for whom Palmer made some investigations into the mound problem in 1879). When Baird became the second secretary of the Smithsonian upon Joseph Henry's death in May 1878, Palmer had a congenial friend—or at least patron (McVaugh 1956:86)—in a very high place.

Baird certainly deserves a new biography. The standard volume by the naturalist William H. Dall presents the basic facts of his life thoroughly and reproduces numerous letters, but it does not venture much into interpretation and scarcely mentions the Bureau of Ethnology (1915:387–88). A recent study of the Smithsonian's role in the development of American anthropology (Hinsley 1981), on the other hand, has relatively little to say about Baird—understandably, since Baird was primarily a zoologist—and again virtually nothing about his relationship with the Bureau. Instead, the best insights into Baird's motivations in general and his motives with regard to the Bureau and its Mound Survey in particular may be derived from a recent study of the "launching of modern American science" (Bruce 1987) and an article about early North American archeology and archeologists (Meltzer 1985).

Baird was born in 1823 in Reading, Pennsylvania. In 1836, at the age of thirteen, he entered Dickinson College in Carlisle, Pennsylvania, from which he graduated in 1840. As a young man he collected an astonishing number of bird specimens and began a correspondence with John J. Audubon that continued until the latter's death. After further studies in medicine and natural history, and private teaching, he was elected full professor of natural history at Dickinson College in 1846, "a tall, energetic young man with an insatiable passion for the slaughter, stuffing, and storing of specimens" (Bruce 1987:49).

After months of preliminary negotiations with Joseph Henry and others, Baird was named assistant secretary of the Smithsonian in July 1850. In October of that year, he moved to Washington, bringing two railroad boxcars of his own specimens with him.

Henry, a prominent physicist, had all along insisted that the Smithsonian's primary roles were and should be scientific research, exploration, and publication. He strongly resisted any proposals that the Institution should become involved in museology and the accumulation of collections (Hinsley 1981:34–75). Yet, with the hiring of Baird, the battle was joined, albeit among mutually respectful colleagues; time and the tides of natural history were on Baird's side.

The tireless Baird was soon working twelve- and fifteen-hour days organizing a network of field collectors and administering the receiving end at the Smithsonian:

> Baird rejoiced in every new correspondent who might feed specimens into his insatiable collections. Travellers . . . army officers . . . amateur naturalists, all were advised and cultivated by the great collector at Washington.
> . . . he surely meant for the Smithsonian's holdings to become definitive for the natural history of the entire continent. And in realizing his imperial dream, Baird had a military strategy. The army and to some extent the navy were to be enlisted.
> . . . he wrote his ally and confidant George Marsh [in July 1853], "I have had no less than 19 [expeditions, including that of the *Water Witch* with Palmer aboard] to

equip and fit out . . . I expect [them] to have the effect of forcing our government into establishing a National Museum, of which (let me whisper it) *I* hope to be director." (Bruce 1987:198–99)

Baird's forces on land, sea, and the home front continued their efforts through the 1850s, leading to the publication of his 1859 classic *Mammals of North America* and numerous taxonomic articles. Even during the Civil War, the onslaught continued.

Ultimately, Baird got his National Museum. Although an unofficial guidebook, privately printed in 1859, had been entitled "Guide to the Smithsonian Institution and National Museum," and the words "National Museum of the United States" were painted over the entrance to the Smithsonian's Exhibition Hall about this time, it was fifteen years later that Congress officially sanctioned the use of this name. In 1874 an appropriation bill for 1875 included an item, "For official postage stamps for the National Museum in the Smithsonian Institution, $1000.00" (Dall 1915:409). And it was not until 1877 that a resolution was presented to the Institution's board of regents proposing the erection of a suitable National Museum building (1915:410).

Another aspect of this protracted war of administrative attrition was indeed the issue of government support:

> [Henry] steadfastly denied that the Smithsonian was or ought to be a government agency. He considered dependence on government to be incompatible with the Institution's first duty, that of giving scientists support without strings. . . . After the war he managed to unload the library . . . the herbarium and insect collections . . . the art collection . . . the weather bureau . . . and the human skulls and bones. . . . But these divestitures fell far short of making up for the uncontrollable growth of Spencer Baird's National Museum.
>
> Baird could not be checked by withholding money for acquisitions. Free of charge, they tumbled in like a confluence of avalanches. . . . At Baird's urging, seventy-eight freight cars full of Centennial Exhibition specimens and artifacts . . . arrived in 1876 for permanent deposit.
>
> In the face of Henry's public reproaches, Baird remained calm—and collected. (Bruce 1987:324–25)

Henry died in May 1878, and Baird was immediately confirmed as his successor. The next year, "Congress appropriated $250,000 for a new museum building on the Smithsonian grounds. Baird was delighted" (Bruce 1987:325). This, then, was one major aspect of the Smithsonian's context on the eve of the Mound Survey.

Baird had become interested in fish and other marine life quite early in his career. In 1863 he had visited Woods Hole, Massachusetts, for the first time and became quite excited by the rich and varied marine life there (Dall 1915:416). He also became interested in the development of fisheries as food sources, and in 1871 he was named as U.S. Commissioner of Fish and Fisheries, without additional salary (1915:416–23). He continued working at Woods Hole, where he was assisted by Palmer in the summer of 1871 (McVaugh 1956:53–54). The Commission is now the U.S. Fish and Wildlife Service, and his Woods Hole research station eventually became the present Woods Hole Oceanographic Institute (Bruce 1987:324).

Baird retired from the Smithsonian in 1887 due to failing health. Samuel P. Langley, an astronomer and physicist, was named as his successor. Baird died at Woods Hole on August 17, 1887.

John Wesley Powell: Surveyor, Geologist, Ethnologist, Organizer

It is probably futile, if not ludicrous, to try to sum up the human torrent that was John Wesley Powell in a few words, or a few thousand. Several full-length biographies are readily available; the task has been performed thoroughly and in an orderly manner by Darrah (1951) and eloquently by Stegner (1954). His roles in creating and running the Bureau of Ethnology, which became the Bureau of American Ethnology in 1894, have been summarized by Judd (1967:3–22) and scrutinized by Hinsley (1981:125–289).

One key to understanding Powell has been emphasized by Bernard De Voto:

> Powell's importance is that . . . he pierced through [misconceptions about the West] to the realities. His career was an indomitable effort to substitute knowledge for the misconceptions and get it acted on . . . writers of history have . . . long failed to understand the massive figure of John Wesley Powell, and therefore have failed, rather disastrously, to understand the fundamental meaning of the West in American history. (De Voto 1954:xvi–xvii)

Powell's roots were in the Midwest, his base was in Washington, but he looked west—and beyond. He was born in 1834 in upstate New York. His father was a Methodist minister who had emigrated from England in 1830. A pattern of westward movement was established early, as the family moved along the Erie Canal from town to town, then to Ohio, Wisconsin, and Illinois. By the age of twelve, Powell was managing the family farm. He also developed an interest in natural history, collecting all sorts of specimens and digging in mounds for Indian artifacts.

Powell became a country schoolteacher in 1851. In 1855 he entered Illinois College at Jacksonville. He also made his first long-distance trip that year, gathering specimens of mollusks from the Mississippi drainage basin. In 1858 he began a "barnstorming tour" of Illinois to urge the inclusion of science in common school curriculums. Powell made a lecture tour in 1860 through Kentucky and Tennessee into Mississippi and was named school principal in Hennepin, Illinois.

On May 8, 1861, Powell joined the Twentieth Illinois Volunteer Infantry as a private. He received several promotions during the war, eventually to the rank of major. In April 1862 he lost his arm at the battle of Shiloh, but he returned to active duty and took part in the siege of Vicksburg, studying the local geology during the ordeal.

After the war, he resumed working with his collections and, in the fall of 1865, took a position as professor of geology at Illinois Wesleyan University at Bloomington. Again he "barnstormed" the state, speaking on behalf of science education. He also spoke to the state legislature in Springfield on behalf of the Illinois Natural History Society and was named curator of its museum. He then immediately organized a collecting expedition to Colorado, which took place in the summer and fall of 1867.

Powell continued teaching, but by now he was fascinated by the West and the possi-

FIGURE 1.2

John Wesley Powell (1834–1902), director of the Bureau of Ethnology and orga-
nizer of American government anthropology, c. 1880. (National Anthropological
Archives, Smithsonian Institution)

CONTEXTS, PERSONALITIES, AND BEGINNINGS

bilities of government-sponsored science. In early 1868 he began intensively politicking on behalf of a major expedition to obtain geological information from the Grand Canyon and survey that region and its Indian occupants. He obtained Congressional funding for the expedition, which left in June as a party of twenty-one.

In reconnoitering the wild terrain, Powell soon concluded that the only way to explore the Colorado was by boat (Darrah 1951:108–43; Stegner 1954:42–115). In early 1869 they entered the Green River in southwest Wyoming, finally reaching the Colorado in July. After an incredible series of rapids, portages, side-trips, and mishaps, they survived the Grand Canyon and disbanded the expedition on September 1.

Powell returned to the East as "Powell of the Colorado" and went on a lecture tour. He immediately began planning a second expedition to make up for the scientific shortcomings of the first exploration. In March 1870 he went to Washington, consulted with Joseph Henry, Spencer F. Baird, and influential politicians, eventually obtaining ten thousand dollars from Congress with good prospects for a similar amount the next year. This time the goal was to be a survey of the lands within fifteen miles of the river, officially designated as the "Geological and Topographical Survey of the Colorado River of the West."

On May 22, 1871, they embarked again from Green River Station, in improved boats, and began the work of recording, surveying, and mapping, which continued into 1872 (Darrah 1951:160–76; Stegner 1954:116–98). But,

> The work of 1871, instead of solving the geology of the Colorado River, suggested greater problems. Ten years of exploration would not be enough to describe even the chief features of this wonderful region.
> The more Powell weighed his data, the more he determined to do the job right. . . . Suppose the federal government could be persuaded to finance the entire program? (Darrah 1951:177–78)

In a decisive series of moves, Powell went to Washington with his wife and infant daughter, bought a house there, lobbied congressmen, and resigned his Illinois position. Funding was obtained, and the "Powell Expedition" continued in the field until 1875.

Powell repeatedly contacted the Indians of this region. He obtained a special commission to visit the Indians of Utah and Nevada, study their situation, and make recommendations about their relocation on reservations. Unlike the political appointees in the Indian bureau, Powell sympathized with the Indians and had some understanding of their cultures and intergroup relationships. Some of the commission's practical suggestions were implemented, with promising results, but "the fundamental recommendations, [the] appeal for greater justice to the Indians, went unheeded" (Darrah 1951:204).

On his new home front in Washington, Powell prospered. A "happy clerical error" had taken his Western activities out of the Department of the Interior and placed them under the shelter of "the learned and non-political Smithsonian Institution" (Stegner 1954:123; cf. Darrah 1951:204). He usually worked at home, but had a very small office in the Smithsonian "Castle" and often conferred with Henry and Baird. And he completed his 1875 *Report on the Exploration of the Colorado River of the West and its Tributaries* and his 1876 *Report on the Geology of the Eastern Portion of the Uinta Mountains.*

FIGURE 1.3

John Wesley Powell with an Indian guide near the Grand Canyon, c. 1873. (National Anthropological Archives, Smithsonian Institution)

Although he was capable of doing detailed field work, Powell was ultimately a synthesizer and generalizer on a grand scale. He also had intuitive grand visions of problems to be solved and learned to delegate the details to capable subordinates such as the geologist G. K. Gilbert and, in the case of the Mound Survey, Cyrus Thomas.

In his other major field, ethnology, Powell studied some 670 Indian vocabularies on file at the Smithsonian. He added some of his own data and published his *Introduction to the Study of Indian Languages* in pamphlet form in 1877 as a guide to field workers. It was a major factor in winning Baird's support when the Bureau of Ethnology was created in 1879 (Darrah 1951:261). Powell put together a reorganized and much longer second edition in 1880, "a portable course in ethnology" (Hinsley 1981:161).

Powell and the results of his research also became more deeply involved in Washington politics. In early 1878 he hastily put together portions of his uncompleted report on the public-domain lands of the West and presented them to the progressive new secretary of the interior, Carl Schurz. This document was immediately published as his *Report on the Arid Region of the United States, with a More Detailed Account of the Lands of Utah* and is regarded by some as his magnum opus. It caused a furor.

Powell had concluded that these lands were being parceled out in ways that had worked in the East but made no sense when applied to arid lands. He proposed different recommendations for different land uses such as mining, timbering, and farming. His own background perhaps influenced him to focus on pasture lands and irrigation. He recommended eighty-acre units for irrigable homesteads, based on his observations among the Utah Mormons. For pasture farms, though, he recommended 2,560-acre (four-section) units, to forestall the effects of overgrazing.

Even more radically, with regard to water, the most precious resource in these lands, he argued against the traditional General Land Office rectangular grid system for parceling out the land. Instead he proposed irregular parcels based on topographic surveys, with water frontage and irrigable soil on each parcel. And further still, he offered Congress two revolutionary sample bills providing for the formation of communal irrigation and pasturage districts.

Beginning in 1872, Powell had lobbied for the consolidation of the various rival geological surveys that were operating in the West under different Federal departments. In a May 1878 letter to Secretary Schurz, he had suggested that he would be willing to leave the embattled field of geological surveying and concentrate on ethnology (which in those days encompassed all kinds of anthropological research; Judd 1967:7). In November, following "a tight inside job" heavily influenced by Powell (Stegner 1954:234), the National Academy of Sciences recommended to Congress that the competing surveys be consolidated. In December, at Schurz's request, Powell drafted a bill and three riders for larger bills, proposing to implement the recommendation and reform the land laws.

After protracted debates and maneuvers, the land reforms were lost, but on March 3, 1879, Congress created the United States Geological Survey and tucked into the same "Sundry Civil Expenses Bill" a provision that changed the Powell Survey into the Bureau of Ethnology, under the Smithsonian, provided that "all of the archives, records, and material relating to the Indians of North America [by the old Survey and the new Bureau] shall be turned over to the Institution." Powell was named director of the Bureau, sheltered to some degree from politics by the Smithsonian umbrella. It will be recalled that about this time new Smithsonian Secretary Baird was about to get his new National Museum building. The circumstances that would lead to the Mound Survey in 1881 were definitely taking shape in 1879.

The highly political position of first director of the Geological Survey went to Clarence King, a brilliant geologist and raconteur who favored the mining interests rather than pure research. Powell had dropped out of the running for this hotly contested job; instead, he lobbied intensively on King's behalf and against an old surveying rival, Ferdinand Hayden.

In the 1879–81 period, Powell held only the Bureau position and concentrated on organizing the chaotic field of ethnology. His message appears explicitly in his "Report of the Director" in the Bureau's *First Annual Report:*

> It has been the effort of the Bureau to prosecute work in the various branches of North American anthropology on a systematic plan. . . . (Powell 1881a:xiv)

> It is the purpose of the Bureau of Ethnology to organize anthropologic research in America. (Powell 1881a:xxxiii)

The first four "accompanying papers" in this volume were written by Powell himself, and in one of them he indicated that he had already solved the "Mound-Builder" riddle, at least to his own satisfaction:

> With regard to the mounds so widely scattered between the two oceans, it may also be said that mound-building tribes were known in the early history of discovery of this continent, and that the vestiges of art discovered do not excel in any respect the arts of the Indian tribes known to history. There is, therefore, no reason for us to search for an extra-limital origin through lost tribes for the arts discovered in the mounds of North America. (Powell 1881b:74)

Instead of addressing this non-question, Powell's Bureau probably would have focused on the West, which "was in 1879 still the home of tribes with some of their traditional culture left" (Stegner 1954:261). There were also basic tasks to be accomplished, beginning with a complete bibliography of works about the American Indians. For this task, Powell selected one of his closest companions from the Western adventures, the meticulous court stenographer James C. Pilling (Hinsley 1981:164–67).

> It was characteristic of Powell's labors that a preliminary job designed to prepare the way for future important research should itself become a major area of research, should consume twenty years of diligent labor and remain unfinished at the end. . . . Almost every project he began ended the same way. . . . The only thing clearer than the failure of his grandiose schemes of study is the compelling weight of their partial accomplishment.
>
> Whether or not his plans were scheduled for completion, it is a beautiful thing to watch so capable an administrator set up and activate a bureau. . . . By providing a center, an organization, and a system of study he channeled enthusiasms that had formerly frittered themselves away, and steered them until their results could prove valuable. (Stegner 1954:264–65).

But the "mound problem" did intrude itself into Powell's Bureau, and his own energies were deflected—no doubt willingly—back into geology. A "surprise" amendment to the Bureau's budget, mandating research on the mounds, was introduced on the House floor on February 24, 1881.

> Baird did not share Powell's view of the importance of abstract science. He viewed the BAE as a source of museum collections. This difference of opinion led on occasion to administrative friction . . . and may have prompted Baird to force Powell to undertake large-scale archaeological research.
>
> In the initial plans of the BAE, archaeology was neglected. [It is in fact not mentioned, except with regard to "picture writing" at Mesoamerican ruins, in Powell's

(1881a) first Report.] It became a focus of inquiry after an 1881 budget amendment. . . . Powell afterward (1894) claimed that the rider was suggested by "certain archaeologists" [i.e., Wills de Hass; cf. Smith, below], and had caught him by surprise.

Given Powell's notable skill at manipulating Congressmen, and the watchful eye he kept on his budget as it passed through the Congress . . . [it] seems more likely that amendments to Powell's bill would have to come from an inside source, say the person who introduced Powell's budget on the hill: Spencer Baird. (Meltzer 1985:250–51)

At this point, Meltzer briefly summarizes Baird's early 1881 correspondence with "the peripatetic collector" Edward Palmer, who was then winding down a tour of duty with the Peabody Museum at Harvard. That correspondence is reproduced in full at the beginning of chapter 3. It indicates that Baird was anticipating the amendment as early as January 13, whether or not Powell knew anything about it. Meltzer concludes, "The evidence is clear. Baird had motive (desire to use archaeology to develop museum collections) but no means; Powell had the means but no motivation. Spencer Baird provided the motivation" (1985: 251). Or at least the "mandate," as Meltzer notes later. But Meltzer does not remark upon what may well have been Powell's real motivation, namely a new chance to head the U.S. Geological Survey, nor upon Baird's supporting role in that affair.

Clarence King, the Survey's first director, had expensive tastes and soon became frustrated by the limitations of his salary. Less than a year and a half after taking office, he became ill (probably depressed); he took a leave in September 1880 and went west to recuperate. Somewhat recovered, he extended his leave and went to Mexico to inspect a gold mine with his personal benefit in mind. It is not known whether he communicated his plans at this point to Powell, but in 1879 he had written Powell thanking him for his support and stating "it will be one of my greatest pleasures to forward your scientific work and to advance your personal interest" (Stegner 1954:241).

King returned to his office in February 1881 but ignored its business while organizing a mining company. On March 11 he gave President Garfield his letter of resignation. As noted by Stegner, King may or may not have recommended Powell to Garfield as his successor, and it might not have been necessary: "Garfield himself told the National Academy . . . that he consulted only one man about a successor to King. The man was not King, but Spencer Baird, Secretary of the Smithsonian, who recommended Powell" (1954:248). Coincidentally or not, on March 18 Baird wrote Palmer, "I am now prepared, I think, to arrange, before long for some explorations in archaeological work under your charge."

Powell turned the major portion of his attention and energies once again to geology and the arid West. As described in detail by Darrah (1951:270–84) and Stegner (1954:269–93), he eagerly set about reorganizing the U.S. Geological Survey, set up the modern system of mapping conventions, cleverly expanded the Survey's authorized mapping territory to include the whole country, and steadily jumped its budget appropriations to "fabulous" levels. As for the Mound Survey, as detailed later in this chapter by Brown and Smith, he employed and then got rid of his critic Wills de Hass, defined a problem orientation in order to overshadow Baird's obsession with amassing artifact collections, and hired Cyrus Thomas to execute his plan.

For the remainder of Powell's life and career he continued his battles for rational land

and water use in the West and for government sponsorship of ethnological researches. His own writings became increasingly philosophical and wide-ranging and were criticized harshly.

In the 1890s he was surrounded and ultimately beaten by his enemies among the Western developers and their Congressional cohorts. He resigned from the Survey in 1894 but held his title as nominal and unsalaried Director of the Bureau until his death on September 23, 1902. He was buried with military honors in Arlington National Cemetery. Congress had just passed the Newlands Act, "putting the United States government in the business of reclaiming the arid region according to principles that Powell himself had first suggested" (Stegner 1954:366).

The Artistic Archeologist: William Henry Holmes

A generally peripheral but occasionally significant role in the Arkansas investigations by the Mound Survey was played by another important Smithsonian figure. William Henry Holmes (1846–1933) was first and last an artist, but since he "does not figure in the art histories or the galleries at all, he must be viewed entirely in the government publications for which he drew" (Stegner 1954:187).

Born in Ohio, Holmes came to Washington in 1871 to continue his art studies. He became acquainted with Joseph Henry's daughter, visited the Smithsonian, and immediately found employment there drawing specimens (Stegner 1954:156). In 1872 he joined Hayden's geological survey as a staff artist, working in Wyoming, Colorado, New Mexico, and Arizona. In the process, he became something of a geologist. Then, according to Judd,

> In 1875 while surveying the southern border of what is now Mesa Verde National Park, southwestern Colorado, Holmes saw his first cliff dwellings, and the experience abruptly changed his second major interest from geology to archaeology. . . . During the next twenty years he wrote eleven archaeological monographs for the Bureau of American Ethnology *Annual Reports* and three *Bulletins*. (1967:23)

His road to the Bureau was not a direct one, though. In 1875 he supervised archeological work in and near southwestern Colorado and published a brief report on that project in the Hayden Survey's *Annual Report* for that year.

As noted above, Hayden's survey was absorbed into Clarence King's U.S. Geological Survey (USGS) in 1879. Holmes went to Europe and studied art during the next year. After his return, he joined King's survey in July 1880 and was immediately dispatched to the Grand Canyon, where he made his classic drawings for the geologist Clarence Dutton, "the highest point to which geological or topographical illustration ever reached in this country" (Stegner 1954:189; cf. drawings following 1954:92).

Holmes continued with the reorganizing USGS under Powell in 1881. Although he was technically a Survey employee until 1889, when he moved over to the Bureau, Powell used his talents in both organizations (Judd 1967:23–24). Particularly relevant here are his "Art in Shell of the Ancient Americans," (1883), which appeared in the Bureau's

FIGURE 1.4

William Henry Holmes (1846–1933), artist, archeologist, geologist, and second chief of the Bureau of American Ethnology, c. 1905. (National Anthropological Archives, Smithsonian Institution)

Second Annual Report and included a number of Palmer's 1881 finds from eastern Tennessee plus Palmer's 1882 "Akron shell" from the White River valley of northeast Arkansas, and his longer "Illustrated Catalogue of a Portion of the Collections Made by the Bureau of Ethnology during the Field Season of 1881" (1884), which appeared in the *Third Annual Report* and was dominated by Palmer's Tennessee shell and stone artifacts and Arkansas pottery vessels.

Holmes also published two major ceramic summaries in the *Fourth Annual Report:* his "Pottery of the Ancient Pueblos" (1886a) illustrated and discussed not only his own Colorado finds but also numerous examples obtained by Palmer in Utah, and his "Ancient Pottery of the Mississippi Valley" (1886b) included several of Palmer's Arkansas specimens. The latter study was merely a preliminary to his synthesis of Eastern U.S. ceramics (1903), which, among other contributions, established the name and basic ceramic assemblage of the "Mississippian" culture. As Judd noted, "Holmes was a master of the English language; he wrote with a clarity and readability unsurpassed in anthropological literature. His contributions . . . added greatly to the fame of the Smithsonian Institution and the Bureau . . ." (1967:25).

From the mid-1880s on, and especially after his direct employment by the Bureau, Holmes became increasingly involved in the controversy over the antiquity of the earliest arrivals to the New World. This took him into studies of preceramic remains, which were almost exclusively stone artifacts, and into dealing with claims that naturally modified stones were artifacts (Willey and Sabloff 1980:49–50; Hinsley 1981:105–08). His geological background fitted him admirably for this task. Between 1889 and 1892, he worked with alleged paleoliths found near Washington, and his experimental replication studies showed these to be what are now called "blanks" and "preforms" (and "rejects") from relatively recent (Archaic) prehistoric Indian stone tool-making processes.

Holmes also visited Arkansas in the course of this work. In 1890 he traveled to the Hot Springs–Magnet Cove vicinity to study the novaculite outcrops, which had been heavily used as quarry and tool manufacturing sites in prehistoric times. He published an article about the Arkansas quarries in the *American Anthropologist* (Holmes 1891). En route he stopped at the Knapp Mounds site, now known as Toltec Mounds, near Little Rock to remeasure the large mounds which Palmer had failed to measure accurately in 1882–83 and again in 1884 (Rolingson 1982:74).

It appears that between the middle 1880s and early 1890s Holmes prepared most of the illustrations that eventually appeared in Cyrus Thomas's 1894 final report on the Mound Survey. In the case of Arkansas mounds, he worked with pencil sketches prepared by H. J. Lewis, the black artist who had worked with Palmer in late 1882 and very early 1883. In addition to the published results, some of Holmes's unpublished revisions of Lewis's drawings have been curated in the Smithsonian's National Anthropological Archives. They are presented here in a later chapter and throw some light on the editorial decision-making processes that went into the preparation of Thomas's final report.

In 1893 Holmes prepared an exhibit for the World's Columbian Exposition at Chicago. This led to his taking a position as curator of anthropology at the Field Columbian Museum in Chicago, but he left for a similar post in the National Museum in 1896. Upon Powell's death in 1902, Holmes was named as his successor, but instead of adopting the title "director" chose "chief" (Judd 1967:24). However, "Holmes had scant capability as an administrator. He lacked the necessary firmness and resolution; he was too gentle and considerate of others; he disliked giving orders" (1967:24). Under Holmes, and with the rise of academic anthropology under Franz Boas at Columbia University, Smithsonian anthropology went into decline (Hinsley 1981:262–89). He stepped down at the end of 1909 and returned to the National Museum. There he not only resumed his former title of Head Curator of Anthropology but also became the first director of the new National Gallery of Art, a position that truly suited him (Hinsley 1981:100).

Cyrus Thomas and the Mound Explorations of the Bureau of Ethnology

IAN W. BROWN
Lower Mississippi Survey, Peabody Museum, Harvard University

In February of 1881, Congress appropriated five thousand dollars for the investigation of the prehistoric mounds of North America. The Mound Exploration Division was set up as an adjunct of the Bureau of Ethnology. Cyrus Thomas (fig 1.5) was not the initial head of the Division, but he has come to be the one individual most associated with the mound research. Here I will examine his role in what turned out to be the most extensive archeological survey ever conducted in North America.

For a man who was to lead such an ambitious archeological project, Thomas had a rather inauspicious beginning. He was born in Kingsport, in the northeast corner of Tennessee, on June 26, 1825. He continued to live there for the next twenty-four years, receiving a rather minimal educational background at the nearby academy at Jonesboro. Although initially apprenticed to a doctor, Thomas soon switched to law. He moved to Illinois and continued in the legal profession until 1865. Thomas must not have felt comfortable in law, because at the age of forty he again changed his vocation. For the next two or three years, he was put in charge of the schools of the DeSoto community in Jackson County, southern Illinois, just north of Carbondale. Still not finding his niche in life, he subsequently joined the ministry of the Evangelical Church, but he abandoned this religious calling several years later.

One interest that Thomas developed very early in his career was the study of natural history. He helped found the Illinois Natural History Society in 1858 [Powell joined shortly thereafter; Darrah 1951:40–41], and his doctorate, received from Gettysburg College, was apparently in the natural sciences. In 1869 he was made an assistant in entomology for the U.S. Geological and Geographical Survey of the Territories known as the Hayden Survey. Four years later he was appointed professor of natural science at Southern Illinois Normal University, at Carbondale.

Thomas held this professorship until 1877, when he became state entomologist of Illinois. Finally, in 1882 at the age of fifty-seven, he was put in charge of the Mound Survey of the Bureau of Ethnology. This job with the Smithsonian was his last professional position (Anonymous 1910; Keel 1970). Thomas replaced Wills de Hass, the first director of the Mound Exploration Division. He accused De Hass of having no comprehensive plan of operations (Thomas 1894:19), but according to Williams (1980), De Hass did indeed set up a strategy for the operation of the survey. After all, De Hass was instrumental in getting Congress to allocate money to set up the mound investigations in

FIGURE 1.5

Cyrus Thomas (1825–1910), director of the Mound Exploration Division, Bureau of Ethnology, and author of the final report on the Mound Survey, c. 1890. (National Anthropological Archives, Smithsonian Institution)

1881 (Powell 1894:xl–xli), and he certainly had a great interest in seeing the work carried out. There is some suggestion of political intrigue in the replacement of De Hass by Thomas, and John Wesley Powell appears to have been the major force in the transition of power.

When Powell became director of the Bureau of Ethnology in 1879, his appointment may in part have been the result of an association with Gen. John A. "Black Jack" Logan of Illinois. During the Civil War, Major Powell served under Logan at the siege of Vicksburg (Goetzmann 1966:533). After the war, Logan was a freshman congressman from Illinois and had very close contacts with Baird. As Powell had previously held professorial positions in Illinois, it is probable that he was quite familiar to the congressman. Logan undoubtedly had some influence on Baird's decision to appoint Powell director of the Bureau of Ethnology.

Powell may have thanked Logan by appointing Thomas head of the Mound Exploration Division. Powell already knew Thomas, as they had both taught in Illinois, and they were both involved in the various surveys of the Territories. The primary factor supporting the appointment may, however, have been Thomas's close personal relationship with Logan, who was the brother of Thomas's first wife, Dorothy (Anonymous 1910:338). It is well known that Thomas became a member of the Geological Survey of Nebraska in 1867 because he was John Logan's relative (Goetzmann 1966:495–96, 514). Perhaps this same relationship contributed to his receiving the directorship of the Mound Exploration Division.

Powell may have found it difficult to push De Hass immediately to the side, as De Hass had played such an integral role in the founding of the Mound Exploration Division, but within a year Thomas was in and De Hass was out. Powell claimed to have been amazed by the act of Congress appropriating money for the mound investigations (1894:xl–xli), but in view of Powell's interest in archeology (1894:xxxix–xl) and his obvious inclination to political intrigue, it is highly unlikely that the action of Congress was a true surprise. For some reason, however, Powell obviously did not want the creation of the Mound Exploration Division to be attributed to himself.

Cyrus Thomas may not have been the most appropriate choice for such an important position as director of the Mound Exploration Division, but there can be no question that he did an excellent job in running the organization. Although he did have some background in archeological field work (Thomas 1873), he was for the most part an armchair archeologist. The actual field work conducted by the Mound Exploration Division was performed by Thomas's assistants.

It is quite clear from his correspondence that Thomas was in strict control of the activities of these assistants. He often wrote weekly to his staff, telling them that their reports were sloppy, more detail was needed, or their budget was not in order. Strong organization was absolutely necessary to complete the goals of the project.

As the area of mound distribution was so large, and the mounds themselves so numerous, Thomas decided to obtain as wide a coverage as possible. Even as early as the late nineteenth century, site destruction was a constant threat. Mounds were being destroyed daily by agricultural activities and various commercial enterprises (Thomas 1894:20), including vast pot-hunting endeavors in regions such as southeast Missouri (1894:183). As a result, Thomas decided that thorough investigations of a single area, or even a single site, should be left for the future. The purpose of the Mound Survey was to make as extensive an archeological study as possible, by examining typical structures throughout the East.

Particular attention was given to the mode of mound construction and, more specifically, to the methods of burial in the conical tumuli (Thomas 1894:23). Thomas was a stickler for accuracy. Much of the Ohio section of the *Twelfth Annual Report* is a detailed listing of measurements (1894:452–89), essentially correcting the inaccuracies of Squier and Davis's earlier survey. Thomas demanded the same excellence of detail from his staff. He wanted full and complete reports on the various sites investigated. Condensed reports were inadequate, and Thomas did not hesitate to speak of his dissatisfaction in such cases. He wanted to be able to publish the reports verbatim, if need be. We know that Thomas was guilty to some extent of nepotism, but being a relative did not necessarily ensure a permanent position. John Rogan, a "cousin" to Thomas, did not write a good report on his work in east Tennessee. He therefore suffered a salary cut, an action which eventually forced him to resign from the staff, as indicated by his 1886 letters to Thomas.

Those who could not, or would not, shape up eventually left. [Palmer left in 1884 and returned to the less strenuous work of natural history and botanical collecting; his problems with Thomas may well have been a factor.] Thomas was on an extremely limited budget, and he had no time for individuals who were getting in the way of the project's objectives. He was constantly concerned with money and how it was being spent. Thomas himself did not receive a salary while he was on assignment, but he was reimbursed for travel expenses (Judd 1967:13). A considerable portion of the Bureau of Ethnology's total expenses under Powell's tenure was taken up by railway passes (1967:20), suggesting that the selection of areas surveyed by the Mound Division members may, to some extent, have been affected by the railroad routes of the period. [This is certainly true in the case of Palmer.] The lack of adequate funding necessitated small crews (Brose 1973:88) and extremely mobile assistants. The latter rarely stayed in any one place for long periods of time.

As an able administrator, Thomas was severe to those who were not doing their jobs, but their principal task was not simply one of finding artifacts, as suggested by some of the Bureau's critics (e.g., Peet 1883:333). Artifacts were indeed important, as they provided visible proof of the archeological investigations to the public (Thomas 1894:22–24), but as long as his assistants did the best work they could, Thomas seems to have been satisfied: "I know that the results of your examination in Michigan and the northwest were, as a rule, negative, nevertheless it is necessary to know the area hunted over and the efforts made in order to determine the value of this negative testimony" (Thomas, letter to Gerard Fowke, October 31, 1887, Smithsonian Institution Archives).

Although Thomas made use of his assistants' reports in their original form, he does not appear to have been overly protective of publication rights. It is clear from his correspondence that Thomas had no real objection to his assistants' writing independently on their field work and artifact studies. He even encouraged it, but he was concerned about the waste involved in duplicating published information. He also insisted that the Bureau of Ethnology be given full credit for sponsoring the work. Overall, he was quite proud of his staff and the Mound Exploration Division, as he indicated in his letter of October 31, 1887, to Gerard Fowke, asking the latter to accompany him at a meeting: " . . . I would be glad to have you with me as I propose to give the people a taste of the '*New Archaeol-*

ogy' of the Bureau, and wish a witness on hand whose character 'for truth & veracity' is unimpeachable." It should be noted that "New Archaeology"—a phrase indicating a "revolutionary" movement in the 1960s and 1970s (cf. Binford 1968, 1972)—was capitalized, in quotes, and underlined in the letter. For its day, the Mound Survey surely was the New Archaeology (Jennings 1974:39).

Eastern North America still has not dealt adequately with the vast amount of data produced by the Bureau between 1881 and 1890. Although the contributions were many, Thomas felt that one of the main benefits of the survey for future archeology was the correct description of the various mounds, including the numerous figures and diagrams. Thomas even visited a number of the larger sites in 1888 to recheck the observations of his assistants. The forty-thousand artifacts collected by the Division were also obviously of immense value to future archeological investigations in eastern North America (Thomas 1894:22).

The main contribution of the Mound Survey was the putting to rest of the notion that a mythical race was responsible for the mounds. Thomas's report was the final confirmation that the ancestors of the historic Indians were responsible for the construction of the mounds of eastern North America. With such an immense accomplishment, one might have thought that Thomas, at the ripe age of sixty-nine, would have retired. However, the last years of his life were spent writing three books and over a dozen articles (Brown and Williams 1980).

When Thomas died on June 26, 1910, at the age of eighty-five, the scientific community lost one of its major figures. He is most remembered for his archeological work in North America, but it must not be forgotten that Thomas also made vast and outstanding contributions to entomology and to the study of Mayan hieroglyphs during his long and eclectic career. The following passage is from his obituary in the *American Anthropologist:* "Dr. Thomas' career was typically American, but of a kind which will scarcely find future duplication. The complete story of his life and times would throw an interesting light on the upgrowth of higher education and modern science on purely American soil" (Anonymous 1910:339). I can think of no finer epitaph for the man who destroyed the Myth of the Mound-Builders.

The Division of Mound Exploration of the Bureau of Ethnology and the Birth of Modern American Archeology

BRUCE D. SMITH
Smithsonian Institution

On February 24, 1881, the annual appropriation for the Bureau of Ethnology of the Smithsonian Institution for the coming fiscal year (1882) was considered by the House of Representatives. The proposed appropriation read, "For the purpose of continuing ethnological researches among the North American Indians, under the direction of the Smithsonian Institution, $25,000" (Rhees 1901:863). When the clerk had finished reading this, Mr. J. Warren Keifer, from Ohio, offered an amendment stating, "five thousand dollars of which shall be expended in continuing archaeological investigations relating to mound-builders, and prehistoric mounds" (Rhees 1901:863).

From some of Mr. Keifer's remarks in the subsequent debate, it is clear that his proposed amendment was motivated by John Wesley Powell's resistance the previous year to using any of the Bureau's appropriation for the investigation of mounds in the eastern United States. Powell himself further clarified the origin of Congressman Keifer's amendment in the following passage from the Bureau's *Twelfth Annual Report:*

> When the Bureau of Ethnology was first organized the energies of its members were devoted exclusively to the study of the North American Indians, and the general subject of archeology was neglected, it being the dominant purpose and preference of the Director to investigate the languages, arts, institutions, and mythologies of extant tribes rather than prehistoric antiquities; but certain archeologists, by petition, asked Congress to so enlarge the scope of the Bureau as to include a study of the archeology of the United States. . . . (Powell 1894:xl)

By his own account, Powell was not aware that "such a movement was on foot" (Powell 1894:xli), and, when Keifer's amendment passed fifty-one to twenty-one (Rhees 1901: 865), it apparently came as a distinct surprise to him, and not a very pleasant one.

Powell was not exactly inept at administrative tactics, however, and responded to this turn of events in predictable fashion:

> In compliance with the terms of the statute the work of investigating the mounds of the eastern half of the United States was at once organized, and Mr. Wills de Hass was placed in charge, as he was one of the men who had interested himself to have the investigation enlarged. (Powell 1894:xli)

By placing one of the most outspoken of his critics in charge of the newly formed Division of Mound Exploration, Powell appears to have effectively headed off any further congressional criticism of his administration of the Bureau of Ethnology, and there is no evidence of their meddling in its appropriation in subsequent years.

At the same time, Powell brought one of the archeologist petitioners, Wills de Hass, inside his tent, so to speak, and under his thumb. Not surprisingly, De Hass just didn't seem to work out, and he resigned within a year. In his place, Powell appointed Cyrus Thomas, and the research program of the Division of Mound Exploration began in earnest.

Problem Orientation

When Congress earmarked five thousand dollars for mound explorations, they did not provide even the most general guidelines as to what kinds of research questions should be pursued under the appropriation—only that prehistoric mounds and Mound-Builders should be investigated. A general problem orientation was quickly provided, however, by Powell, who instructed Thomas to settle the then still unresolved debate over the identity of the Mound-Builders:

> The most important question to be settled is, "were the mounds built by the Indians?" (Thomas 1894:21)

The Director of the Bureau of Ethnology was desirous, therefore, that this important question, the origin of the mounds, should if possible be definitely settled, as it is the pivot on which all the other problems must turn. (Thomas 1894 : 21)

It is important to emphasize that Powell clearly did not consider the mound-builder debate as an isolated issue that should be addressed solely because of its wide popularity. He placed the mound-builder identity question within the larger context of the cultural development of the historically described Indian groups of the eastern United States. When viewed in this context, the mound-builder debate represented a major roadblock to Powell's driving interest in obtaining an accurate and detailed picture of North American Indians. It not only attracted too much of the time and efforts of the researchers in eastern North America, but it also served to scatter their lines of investigation far too widely, and often in unproductive directions.

It was Powell's hope that the Mound Exploration Division could break this roadblock by once and for all demonstrating that the prehistoric Mound-Builders and the historic tribes were part of the same fabric of unbroken cultural development. If it could be proven that the prehistoric mounds had been constructed by the ancestors of the Indians, then

> . . . the questions relating to the objects and uses of these ancient works would be merged into the study of the customs and arts of the Indians. There would then be no more blind groping by archeologists for the thread to lead them out of the mysterious labyrinth. The chain which links together the historic and prehistoric ages of our continent would be complete; the thousand and one wild theories and romances would be permanently disposed of; and the relations of all the lines of investigation to one another being known, they would aid in the solution of many of the problems which hitherto have seemed involved in complete obscurity. (Thomas 1894 : 21)

It is evident, then, that even as Powell shaped the general problem orientation of Thomas's research he was looking beyond the mound-builder issue itself to the potential beneficial impact that its resolution would have on North American Indian studies in general.

Although it is difficult to determine the degree to which Powell provided the Division of Mound Exploration with subsequent advice or direction beyond his initial general instructions concerning resolution of the mound-builder identity question, he appears to have given Thomas free rein and to have left him pretty much alone: "General lines of investigation were adopted by the Director and the details were entrusted to selected persons skilled in their pursuits" (Powell 1894 : XXI). Thomas considered the overall general goal of the Mound Exploration Division to be "the collection of data necessary to an understanding of the more general and important problems relating to the mounds and the mound-builders" (Thomas 1894 : 20). He was clear and explicit concerning what these more general and important research problems were and expanded the Division's problem orientation beyond Powell's primary goal to include a number of related questions.

The "imperfect and faulty" (Thomas 1894 : 27) mound classification scheme developed by Squier and Davis (1848), with its inherent function attributions (e.g., "mounds of sacrifice") was still widely used in the 1880s, and Thomas hoped that the Division's work would produce a more comprehensive classification system for prehistoric mound sites—one based on observed and documented characteristics that would "group the individual monuments according to types of form and external characters, reference being made to uses only where these were obvious" (Thomas 1894:28). There was also an explicit interest in determining the geographical range of occurrence of the various "types" of mounds, with the aim of defining different archeological districts (Thomas 1894:23).

In addition, Thomas was very concerned with accurately determining the mode of construction of mounds, not only in the hope of "acquiring a clear insight into the character and methods of mound-building and into the purpose of their builders" (Thomas 1894:20), but also to provide further information on geographical variation in the occurrence of the various mound types:

> Particular attention has been paid to the mode of construction and methods of burial in the ordinary conical tumuli, because these furnish valuable evidence in regard to the customs of the builders and aid in determining the different archeological districts. (Thomas 1894:23)

This concern with developing a comprehensive taxonomy of mound types also applied to the artifactual assemblages recovered during the exploration of mounds. It was hoped that subsequent detailed analysis of the various classes of artifacts by specialists would produce the ordered descriptive classification schemes that were so badly needed (Thomas 1894:19, 25; see chapter 10).

The research of the Division of Mound Exploration thus became explicitly problem-oriented. Powell identified the primary goal of resolving the mound-builder debate, and Thomas provided an interrelated set of four secondary objectives. These were to identify the full range of variation in the form or external shape of prehistoric mounds and develop a comprehensive mound classification system; to investigate and accurately describe the mode of construction of mounds of various types; to establish a system of regional archeological districts that reflected the geographical range of the various mound types; and to obtain representative artifact assemblages from prehistoric mounds, not only for distinguishing various mound categories and archeological districts, but also to allow subsequent taxonomic analysis of the various classes of artifacts.

In addition to these problem-oriented goals, Thomas established another, equally important goal: he was determined that the work of the Mound Exploration Division would result in a detailed and objective data base that would be available and of value to future generations of archeologists.

> By following the plan adopted and using proper care to note the facts ascertained, without bias, not only would the facts bearing on this important question be ascertained, but the data would be preserved for the use of the archeological students without prejudice to any theory. (Thomas 1894:21)

Research Design

The research design or data recovery plan of the Division of Mound Exploration was a logical extension of the Powell and Thomas problem orientation and can be seen to have been carefully and deliberately tailored to obtain information relevant to the research questions that had been defined.

The most obvious problem faced by Thomas in developing a research design was one of simple geography; prehistoric mounds were scattered in great numbers over most of the eastern United States. The limited financial resources available to the Division of Mound Exploration made it obvious from the start that it was not feasible to thoroughly examine all, or even a large number, of the mounds. Thomas rejected the option of thoroughly investigating the mounds of a smaller and more manageable geographical area because it would not yield the information necessary to answer several of the defined research questions. Instead, a research design was instituted that involved the selection and detailed examination of a sample of mounds that represented the full range of known variation in form and mode of construction, and which were distributed over a wide geographical area:

> . . . such mounds and groups as are believed to be typical of their class have been examined with care and thoroughness. By the method of a careful examination of typical structures in the various districts it is thought that the end aimed at has been secured—that is, the collection of data necessary to an understanding of the more general and important problems relating to the mounds and the mound builders. (Thomas 1894:20)

The process of selecting the prehistoric mounds to be examined, described, and possibly excavated was initially based on background research carried out by Thomas, who drew on published accounts of mounds, including newspaper articles, as well as the extensive correspondence concerning mounds, both solicited and unsolicited, that had accumulated at the Smithsonian Institution over the years. *Bulletin* 12 of the Bureau of Ethnology, "Catalogue of Prehistoric Works East of the Rocky Mountains," by Thomas (1891), provides a good indication of the total known universe of prehistoric mounds from which Thomas's sample was drawn. In addition, promising mound groups located during the course of field investigations were quite often added to Thomas's original sample.

In extending the research design down to the actual process of data recovery, Thomas continued to keep the problem orientation of the Division clearly in mind. Each mound or mound group selected for examination was first described in a detailed manner: "The topography of the immediate locality, the form, characters, and dimensions of the works and their relations to one another was written out, accompanied by diagrams and figures illustrating these descriptions" (Thomas 1894:21). These descriptions were often accompanied by horizontal and vertical sections showing the locations of skeletons and artifacts.

Specimens recovered during excavations were in turn assigned field numbers and were packed and shipped, accompanied by a descriptive list with corresponding numbers, to the Washington offices of the Bureau of Ethnology. The Bureau was an independent research branch of the Smithsonian Institution, separate from the National Museum, with no storage facilities of its own. Division of Mound Exploration specimens were, as a result, subsequently transferred to the old National Museum (now the Museum of Arts and Industries), adjacent to the Smithsonian Institution "Castle." When these field collections were unpacked in Washington, each specimen received a Bureau of Ethnology catalog number, and this number was entered into the Division's catalog ledger, along with the specimen's field number, the collector, the locality from which it was collected, provenience information, and a description of the object. This information was actually recorded twice. A dual ledger system was maintained, one set for the National Museum, where all of the specimens eventually ended up. Since each specimen was also assigned a

National Museum catalog number, most ended up with three separate catalog numbers, often accompanied by the collector's name and site name.

The research design of the Division of Mound Exploration was formulated entirely by Cyrus Thomas. The sampling strategy was on the one hand designed to obtain a systematic geographic coverage of mounds in the eastern United States and was, at the same time, stratified in an attempt to obtain "classes" or taxonomic categories of mounds. Procedures of data recovery were standardized and involved detailed descriptions and plans of mound sites, descriptions and section drawings of the internal composition of mounds, and descriptions of the location of recovered materials. Collections management procedures involved the field numbering and cataloging of recovered specimens, followed by their rapid shipment to Washington, where a detailed project catalog was maintained.

Field Operations

In setting up the field operations of the Division of Mound Exploration, Thomas faced a variety of problems. The most obvious problem involved the sheer size of the defined geographical study area, which stretched from the Dakotas to Florida and from Texas to New York.

One way to approach the vast expanse of territory that needed coverage would have been to engage for short periods of time a variety of local researchers to investigate nearby mound sites. Thomas did in fact do this to a rather limited degree, but this approach had the obvious drawback of having to deal with and rely upon, individuals of varied qualifications, levels of competence, and trustworthiness.

Largely for this reason, I suspect, Thomas channeled most of the funds and research efforts of the Division into the three permanent field assistant positions that he established. Although it has recently been proposed that a dark cloud of nepotism and cronyism surrounded Thomas's selection of his field assistants, I think this is an unfair assessment of his choices. Thomas needed field assistants that were willing to put up with constant travel, difficult logistical problems, and hard, dirty excavation work, and who would at the same time meet his high standards of accurate and detailed descriptions of mound sites, excavations, and artifacts. It is thus not too surprising that Thomas hired people that he knew well, or whose work he admired. Table 1.1 lists the different individuals who filled, at one time or another, one of the three permanent field assistant positions. Also listed are those individuals who were temporarily engaged by the Division of Mound Exploration.

Except for an occasional foray into the field, Thomas stayed in Washington and directed the activities and movements of the three field assistants by mail.

To judge from the correspondence between Thomas and his men in the field, he was not exactly an easy man to work for. His outgoing letters invariably contain comments, corrections, and admonitions concerning the last batch of artifacts or mound descriptions received from a particular field assistant, as well as instructions as to where the field assistant should next proceed. The incoming letters from field assistants (cf. Palmer's of January 10, 1883, in chapter 7) similarly share several common themes: responses to Thomas's most recent comments concerning the quality of their work, explanations as to why they were not proceeding as quickly as Thomas wanted, and requests for both the vouchers and money owed them. Thomas was clearly tight-fisted with the funds of the Division, sending out the field assistants' salaries on a month-by-month basis and making

Table 1.1.
Duration of Employment of Regular Field Assistants
(Division of Mound Exploration)

July 1882	Dr. Edward Palmer Washington, D.C.	Col. P. W. Norris Norris, Michigan	James D. Middleton Carbondale, Illinois
July 1883			
July 1884	John P. Rogan Bristol, Tennessee		
July 1885		J. W. Emmert Kingsport, Tennessee	
July 1886			
July 1887	Gerard Fowke New Madison, Ohio		
July 1888		Henry Reynolds Washington, D.C.	
July 1889			
July 1890			

Individuals "Engaged for Short Periods"

Rev. W. M. Beauchamp, Baldwinsville, New York
F. S. Earle, Cobden, Illinois
Gerard Fowke (also known as Charles M. Smith and Kentucky Q. Smith), New Madison, Ohio (became a regular field assistant)
William McAdams, Otterville, Illinois
Rev. J. P. McLean, Hamilton, Ohio
Rev. Stephen D. Peet, Clinton, Wisconsin
Henry L. Reynolds, Washington, D.C. (became a regular field assistant)
John P. Rogan, Bristol, Tennessee (became a regular field assistant)
L. H. Thing, Cobden, Illinois

it clear that next month's check was dependent on continuing adequate performance. He was constantly pushing the field assistants to keep more detailed and accurate mound description and excavation records, to find more and better artifacts, and to cover more territory in a shorter period of time. This stick and carrot relationship between Thomas and his field assistants is, I think, the key to understanding their astounding accomplishments.

There are a number of ways of unraveling the movements of the field assistants, one of which is shown in table 1.2. By going through the Division of Mound Exploration's artifact ledger, I was able to determine the geographical sources of collections sent in by the different field assistants on a year-by-year basis. Table 1.2 does not tell the whole story, however, since field assistants often visited and described sites without sending back artifacts to Washington. The 1882–83 column of this table indicates that in a twelve-month period Edward Palmer sent back specimens from eight different states. During the same fiscal year, P. W. Norris visited eleven different states. Clearly, Thomas did not allow his field assistants to dawdle too long in one place.

The bottom row of table 1.2 lists the total number of catalog numbers assigned each

Table 1-2.
Sources of Specimens Obtained by Field Assistants or from Other Parties, 1882–90 (Division of Mound Exploration)

	July 1882 to June 1883	July 1883 to June 1884	July 1884 to June 1885	July 1885 to June 1886	July 1886 to June 1887	July 1887 to June 1888	July 1888 to June 1889	July 1889 to June 1890
Alabama	Palmer L. C. Jones	Palmer Norris	Burns Rogan Johnson Thibault					
Arkansas	Palmer Norris Thing Middleton	Palmer	Thing Middleton Norris Derositt	Derositt				
Dakotas	Norris	Norris						Reynolds
Florida	Rogan	Rogan	Babcock					
Georgia	Rogan Palmer	Rogan Palmer	Rogan	Rogan	McGlasham (collection)			Reynolds
Kentucky	Norris	Norris				Middleton Fowke	Middleton	
Louisiana								Smith Waddell
Illinois	Thing Middleton			Middleton		Fowke	Middleton	
Indiana	Palmer							Reynolds
Iowa	Norris							Reynolds
Michigan	Allis							
Minnesota	Norris							
Mississippi	Palmer		Smith			Rogan		
Missouri	Thing Baird Norris							
New York						Reynolds		
North Carolina	Palmer Emmert Rogan Spain Hour	Palmer Rogan						
Ohio	Norris	Norris	Rogan Smith Middleton			Fowke	Reynolds Fowke	
Pennsylvania			Thomas	Smith				
South Carolina	Palmer			J. W. Earle				Reynolds
Tennessee	Palmer Emmert Middleton	Palmer	Middleton Emmert Rogan	Emmert Rogan	McGill (collection)	Emmert	Emmert	
Texas	Norris	Norris						
West Virginia	Norris	Norris	Norris (Death 1-85)					
Wisconsin	Norris Middleton	Norris			Emmert Middleton			
Number of catalog numbers assigned	2168	2164	1175	1153	296	144	376	127

year and provides a rough index of the level of activity of the field assistants. The number of assigned catalog numbers drops by almost half after the first two years and then to almost nothing after the spring of 1886. This clearly indicates that in terms of excavation and collection acquisition the Division of Mound Exploration was active only during the four-year span 1882–86. Although some mounds were excavated after 1886, mostly to fill in obvious gaps in their geographical coverage, field assistants in these later years (Middleton and Reynolds) were primarily engaged in mapping mound sites and rechecking the accuracy of previous descriptions.

Figure 1.6 shows the 130 counties from which over forty-thousand specimens were obtained by the Division of Mound Exploration and provides a general picture of the geographical coverage of their excavation activities. The field assistants of the Division managed to visit over 140 counties and to investigate over two-thousand mounds:

> Over 2,000 mounds have been explored, including almost every known type of form, from the low diminutive, circular burial tumulus of the north to the huge truncated earthen pyramid of the south, the embankment, the stone cairn, the house site, etc. Every variety of construction hitherto known, as well as a number decidedly different in detail, have been examined. (Thomas 1894:23)

Preparation of the Twelfth Annual Report

The research results of the Division of Mound Exploration were presented as a lengthy "accompanying paper" to the *Twelfth Annual Report* of the Bureau of Ethnology, published in 1894 and reprinted in 1985 by the Smithsonian. The brief abstract, preface, and introduction by Thomas were followed by a 486-page descriptive section on field operations composed of annual reports written and submitted to Thomas by each of the various field assistants (Thomas 1894:24). These field reports were then edited and sometimes revised by Thomas, Holmes, and others and finally organized and consolidated by state and county. Almost all of the 344 figures presented in this descriptive section were the work of Holmes.

Following the field operations section of the paper are two sections written entirely by Thomas. The first outlines his division of the Eastern "mound area" into eight archeological districts, while in the second he marshalls the evidence collected during the field operations of the Division and addresses the question of the identity of the Mound-Builders.

Discussion

Historians of American archeology have invariably recognized that the Division of Mound Exploration played a prominent role in the development of American archeology. While they tend to view the world through Harvard Crimson–tinted glasses, Willey and Sabloff nevertheless do allow Thomas and his assistants to share the stage with Frederic Ward Putnam and his Peabody Museum during the "dawning age of professional archeology in the 19th century" (1980:41). Both Hallowell and Jennings, however, clearly give Thomas top billing:

> It was under the auspices of the Bureau of American Ethnology, in short, that, through a series of widely gauged programs, the empirical foundations of archeology in the United States were established on a broad geographical scale. (Hallowell 1960:84)

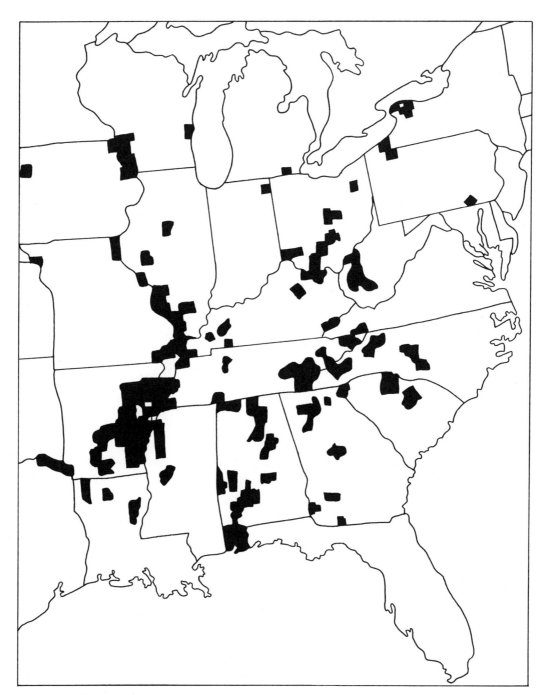

FIGURE 1.6

Eastern United States counties from which collections were made by field assistants
of the Division of Mound Exploration. (After Smith 1981: Figure 1)

Thomas' huge report of a decade of mound exploration by the Bureau of American Ethnology can be thought of as marking the birth of modern American archeology. (Jennings 1974:39)

Although both Jennings and Hallowell mention the broad geographic coverage of Thomas's mound research, they emphasize the results of the project, the resolution of the identity of the mound-builders issue, as their primary reason for marking it as the beginning of modern archeology.

While I would certainly agree that the resolution of this stubborn issue was of great importance, I think that it was the methodology employed by Thomas in formulating and carrying out the mound survey that in fact sets it apart as the first modern archeology carried out in America. It is, I would propose, not so much the results as the process by which they were reached that is the key.

If the work of the Division of Mound Exploration is analyzed within the conceptual framework of present-day archeology, as I have tried to do here, it turns out to be surprisingly modern, even though it was carried out almost a century ago.

It was a long-term regional research program and had a larger regional focus than any subsequent archeological undertaking in North America. It was explicitly problem-oriented, and the research questions that were addressed were among the most important ones facing eastern North American archeology in the nineteenth century.

There was also a clear and direct relationship between this problem orientation and the research design developed by Thomas. The sampling strategy for selecting sites to be investigated and the kinds and level of specificity dictated by Thomas's plan of standardized data recovery were carefully tailored to produce the information relevant to the research questions being addressed.

CHAPTER TWO

Edward Palmer
and H. J. Lewis

The archeological and ethnological work accomplished by Edward Palmer before he came to Arkansas has been underemphasized by his previous, botanically-oriented biographers—and often ignored or inadequately treated in the archeological and ethnological literature. Again and again, however, we find that Palmer was the first more or less controlled and scientific archeological or ethnological collector in a given region or area.

I have made a particular effort to examine Palmer's own publications, especially his archeological articles, which have languished for a century or more, buried in rare or nonarcheological publications. Individual articles have rarely been consulted first-hand by archeologists and have been misread in some cases, nor have they been studied collectively. Yet they have some potential for contributing to certain archeological data bases and to the history of archeology. Together they reveal some useful insights into Palmer's general *modus operandi* and his strengths and limitations in relation to contemporary anthropology and archeology.

Though he only worked with Palmer for about two months, H. J. Lewis made a significant contribution to Arkansas archeology with his drawings and maps of mound sites. Apparently the whole story of his life has never been pieced together before, but it is an amazing story, even in outline form. Born a slave in Mississippi, he taught himself to read, write, and draw. He was working in the Arkansas and Mississippi valleys as a freelance artist when Palmer met him in late 1882. In late 1888 he moved to Indianapolis and became the first black political cartoonist. His premature death in 1891 cut short a career that, as one of his colleagues put it, "biography would not have spurned."

Edward Palmer

> Than longen folk to gon on pilgrimages,
> And *palmers* for to seken straunge strondes.
>
> —Chaucer, *Canterbury Tales*

With this epigraph, William E. Safford, a botanist with the U.S. Department of Agriculture, began his lengthy but unpublished biography of his late colleague, Edward Palmer. By way of explication, Safford commented:

> Edward Palmer was a man well named. A palmer of the olden time was one who travelled to the Holy Land in fulfillment of a vow, and brought back with him a palm branch to be placed on the altar of his parish church. Afterwards, the name was applied to pilgrims who travelled from land to land under a perpetual vow of poverty and celibacy. This is what Edward Palmer did. From the age of early manhood until the winter of his life, never content to remain inactive even for a short time, he set out upon one pilgrimage after another, bringing back with him many palm branches and other strange and beautiful products of distant climes, reverently to lay them on the altar of Science. (1926:1)

Although this biography was unfinished when Safford died in 1926, its length alone gives one a good impression of Palmer's extraordinarily eventful and peripatetic life. Its twenty-four chapters cover Palmer's life from birth around 1830 to the year 1889, at which time he still had more than twenty-two years to live, and during those years he made more than a dozen trips abroad (McVaugh 1956:ix, 96–102, 106, 415–16).

The author of the published biography of Palmer, botanist Rogers McVaugh, has summed up the man as follows:

> Beyond the mere facts of Palmer's life, . . . consider the setting of that life, and the romance of it. Palmer's days began in the time of sailing vessels, and continued until the airplane was a curiosity; he went west across the Great Plains before the railroads had left Kansas City; he took part in the Pikes Peak stampede, one of the great gold rushes in our history; he was in mortal danger from the Comanches and Apaches who are peaceful citizens today; he saw Brigham Young and he knew Joseph Henry; Mexico was his second home in the days of the Díaz regime, when the stagecoach was the only means of transportation and the pines grew uncut on the great haciendas where the goats now graze; he was with the first party of scientists to penetrate the wilderness of Lake Okeechobee, and the first to call the attention of scientists to the destructive habits of the cotton boll weevil . . . most rewarding after all has been a vicarious acquaintance with this amazing man who, although small and frail, a hypochondriac, and often unfortunate in his dealings with other people, nonetheless overcame barriers of language and time and transportation in a fashion that has rarely been surpassed. (McVaugh 1956:v–ix)

The following sections will present a chronological summary of Palmer's life. The major source used has been McVaugh's (1956) biography, which emphasizes Palmer's botanical activities but generally gives rather short shrift to Palmer's ethnological and archeological pursuits, which will be expanded upon in this volume.

FIGURE 2.1

Edward Palmer. This was once thought to have been his earliest portrait but is now believed to have been made in late 1867 in the studio of A. Zenow Shindler, a Washington, D.C., photographer. (Smithsonian Institution Photo No. SA-41)

Early Years (1830?–52)

Edward Palmer was born in England, near Wilton and Hockwold in southwestern County Norfolk. The year of his birth is uncertain. Palmer himself gave his date of birth or age on several documents that state or imply various years as early as 1830 and as late as 1839. I believe 1830 to be the most likely year, since the two earliest available records, entered when he was twenty-four and twenty-six, both imply a year no later than 1830 (McVaugh 1956:8). His birthday was invariably stated to be January 12.

According to Safford (1926:2), Palmer's father was a commercial gardener or florist named William Palmer. However, McVaugh (1956:7) found that when Edward Palmer married in London in 1856, he gave his father's name as Robert and occupation as farmer. Little information is available about any other relatives, except that his mother's maiden name was Mary Ann Armiger. Essentially nothing definite seems to be known about Palmer's youth in England. McVaugh has noted that "tradition has it that young Edward was interested in plants from earliest youth and worked in his own garden under his father's tutelage" (1956:7). In addition to his father's interests, Palmer's home county certainly had a rich heritage in natural history, especially in botany. Norfolk claimed many varieties of flora, and numerous distinguished botanists were born or lived in the county in the late eighteenth and nineteenth centuries (Geldart 1901:40).

Palmer's home locality also included some resources of archeological significance. Hockwold and Wilton are only a few miles from the "Grime's Graves" Neolithic flint-quarry site, and from Brandon and other centers of the historic British black-gunflint-knapping industry (Clinch 1901:258; Woodward 1901:9–10).

It also seems likely that the work ethic displayed so consistently throughout Palmer's career was derived from the predominant attitudes of his home county. Norfolk was regarded as England's "leading agricultural area" at the end of the eighteenth century, according to Horn (1981:23); this was attributed to child-rearing practices by a contemporary observer: "While a boy, [the worker] is accustomed to run by the side of the horses while they trot with the harrows.—When he becomes a plowman, he is accustomed to step out at the rate of three to four miles an hour . . ." (Marshall 1795; quoted by Horn 981:23).

Despite this tradition, Norfolk became caught up with the other English counties in the increase of rural poverty in the 1830s and 1840s (Horn 1981:97). In fact Norfolk had more people defined as paupers between 1840 and 1845 than any other rural county tabulated by Horn (1981: Table 3), and the number of Norfolk paupers increased steadily from 31,076 in 1840 to 42,161 in 1845.

In 1849 Palmer came to America, "with a family of friends" (McVaugh 1956:9). His biographers provide no reasons for his emigration, but the agricultural situation in Norfolk seems a likely explanation, especially considering that " . . . the consensus of opinion from 1848 to 1850 was that every English landowner, tenant and agricultural laborer was headed for ruin. . . . In these two years the volume of the departing English and Scots probably exceeded that of the Irish" (Hansen 1940:265–66).

Palmer landed in New York and soon afterward moved to Cleveland, Ohio. There he became the personal attendant of John W. Taylor and studied biological and medical subjects in the library of Dr. Jared Kirtland. Obviously, both men influenced him significantly. Taylor (1784–1854) had been a U.S. congressman from New York, was Speaker of the House twice, and had been an active opponent of slavery, but had become paralyzed. Through him, Palmer met Kirtland (1793–1877), a highly respected doctor and biologist; the scholarly journal *Kirtlandia*, named after him, is still published by the Cleveland Museum of Natural History. He was also an accomplished botanist and horticulturist who "found a willing disciple in young Palmer, whom he invited to his home and, inspiring him with the display of his zoological collections and herbarium, taught him to prepare bird skins and to dry and press plants, thus laying the foundation for his future career" (Safford 1911a:341, 343).

The Voyage of the Water Witch (1852–55)

In late 1852, Palmer came to a significant turning point in his life. According to Safford's biographical sketch (1911a:343), the United States wished to open Paraguay to the outside world, as Commodore Perry's expedition had opened Japan. Palmer enlisted as an apparently civilian member of the U.S. Navy expedition to South America. His duties included working as a hospital steward and collecting and curating biological specimens. The party was commanded by a navy officer named Thomas Jefferson Page, whose ship, the *Water Witch*, left Norfolk, Virginia, in February 1853 (Wood 1985).

The unpublished biography by Safford recounts details of the expedition from Palmer's diaries (1926: chapters I–V); here, a summary will suffice. The expedition was delayed at Montevideo, Uruguay, due to political problems in Argentina but finally ascended the Parana River northward to Corrientes, Argentina. From there they ascended the Paraguay River to Asuncion, the Paraguayan capital, and eventually across the Brazilian border, turning back at Corumba. They made collecting forays during sojourns at all of the river ports and along the river banks, and the explorers contacted a number of local Indian groups. Palmer's characteristic "supreme detachment and naivete" were evident, when he "had some trouble persuading the Paraguayan Indian women to let him measure their enormous breasts, which far exceeded anything of which he had previous knowledge" (McVaugh 1956:11).

The *Water Witch* then returned to Montevideo, came back to Asuncion, and became caught up in diplomatic problems between the U.S. and Paraguay. Another return to Montevideo was followed by another to Paraguay; the *Water Witch* was fired upon from a Paraguayan fort, killing the helmsman. At this point, the ship returned to Montevideo. Palmer, who had been seriously ill—probably from malaria—for several months, left the expedition at Montevideo in April 1855 and returned to the U.S. at his own expense. Far from discouraging him, however, the trip "had confirmed his liking for travel, and set him upon the career that was to be his life for the next fifty-five years" (McVaugh 1956:11).

Palmer made this offer in the first of many letters he was to write to Joseph Henry and Spencer Baird at the Smithsonian:

> Washington City June 13th—1855
>
> Dear Sir
>
> I beg to lay before you an application for an appointment in any expedition that may be formed.
>
> I have just returned from the Exploriseing expedition to the Laplat River and the success which have attended my labours may be judged from the quality of the specimens collected. In the preservation of birds—insects—fish quadrupeds and botanical specimens I take great interest.
>
> Intending to spend my life in the prosecution of science and trusting my qualifications be found sufficient to meet with your favourable consideration.
>
> I remain, your obedient survent
> *Edward Palmer*
>
> To Professor Henry of the Smithsonian Institue

Commenting on this letter, McVaugh remarked:

> . . . it shows its writer exactly as he was to remain: anxious for opportunities to travel and collect, but without organizing ability to direct his own expeditions; sincere in his devotion to the prosecution of science, but not realizing his own limitations; willing to let his work as a collector speak for itself, and proud of the work, without understanding that the collections in themselves were not enough to make him the intellectual equal of such men as Henry and Baird. (1956:11–12)

Digressions (1855–56)

Palmer was not hired immediately by the Smithsonian, however. He went back to Cleveland for the summer, worked in Kirtland's library, and "collected a few grasshoppers" (McVaugh 1956:12).

In September 1855 he returned to England for six months, visited his mother, and brought back a twenty-year-old bride whose maiden name had been Dinah Riches. However, according to McVaugh, his young wife "vanishes from view" after their arrival at New York in April 1856, and she probably "came to an early and untimely end, for certainly she did not accompany her husband on his later wanderings" (1951:13).

Medical Training and Practice (1856–59)

Palmer's own whereabouts during the next half-year are uncertain; then, from November 1856 to at least February 1857, he attended lectures, but apparently never completed any formal curriculum, at Cleveland Homeopathic College; afterwards he moved to Kansas to practice medicine, though "actually we are not even sure that he did practice the profession. . . . It was common at this period, however, for medical men to assume the title (and the profession) of 'Doctor' with no more training than Palmer had experienced aboard the navy vessel" (McVaugh 1956:13).

Palmer may not have been very busy as a doctor. During the winter of 1857–58, he made a long trip through northeast Kansas and into Nebraska, of which he wrote, "A more inhospitable country was never seen," but was able to collect only minerals and fossils due to bad weather. During these years, he did send some boxes of specimens and a few letters to Baird at the Smithsonian.

The Gold Rush and the Civil War (1859–65)

During the summer of 1859, Palmer left Kansas to join the Pikes Peak gold rush, which had been going on for about a year. He lived in Denver until August 1861. He probably did very little prospecting but may have continued his medical practice to some extent and definitely made some collections of minerals, fossils, plants, and animals. On August 6, he left Denver by stagecoach for San Francisco; then he worked for the Geological Survey of California collecting marine invertebrates near San Diego. The Civil War had started, and in early 1862 he decided to join the Union side; he sailed to New York, then went to Washington and joined the Union Army, as a volunteer assistant surgeon in the Second Colorado Regiment. Many of his former steps were retraced, as he joined the regiment at Fort Leavenworth, Kansas, and traveled with the troops to Denver, arriving on June 2, 1862, "after an absence of only ten months, but after more than 8,000 miles

FIGURE 2.2

Edward Palmer in his Union Army uniform, from a photo taken in Kansas City in
early 1865. This is now believed to be his earliest known portrait.
(National Anthropological Archives, Smithsonian Institution)

and nearly five months of travel!" (McVaugh 1956:19–20).

Palmer worked in hospitals and other medical facilities at various posts in Colorado and Kansas during the rest of 1862 and early 1863, making occasional small collections of plant and animal specimens. In May and June 1863 he took part in a march to Fort Scott, Kansas.

From there his regiment left in late June on a march across Oklahoma toward Fort Smith, Arkansas, in a little-known phase of the war that involved skirmishes against Cherokee guerillas aligned with the Confederacy. After a culminating victory at Honey Springs, Oklahoma, the regiment was able to reach Fort Smith. After about two months, his unit marched from there to St. Louis, arriving on December 17. This trip, however, did not take Palmer into the regions of eastern Arkansas in which he later made his mound investigations. Instead it went northward through the Ozarks to Springfield, Missouri, thence to St. Louis (Dyer 1909:1006).

On January 4, 1864, Palmer formally enlisted as a private at Leavenworth, Kansas. His induction papers describe him as 28 years old, 5'6" tall, with brown eyes, black hair, and dark complexion, a nurseryman by occupation.

Palmer next worked in various hospitals in Kansas and Missouri but soon became ill himself. He was hospitalized in May and June 1864, and again during September and October. "Certified as disabled because of rheumatism and heart disease contracted during the march from Arkansas" (McVaugh 1956:23), he accepted a civilian contract position as an acting assistant surgeon and was placed in charge of wounded Confederate prisoners at the Kansas City General Hospital. He served in this capacity from November 17, 1864, to March 31, 1865, when he resigned.

The Southwest and Anthropological Interests (1865–67)

Arizona had been given Territorial status on February 24, 1863 (Faulk 1970:113–17). In the spring of that year, the Walker Party had ascended to the montane conifer forests of west-central Arizona, staking mining claims and establishing the settlement that became known as Prescott (Conner 1956). Here, as elsewhere in the Southwest, the Indians had been antagonized and military posts were established.

In late July 1865, after a long stagecoach trip from Kansas City, Palmer arrived at Fort Whipple, near what is now Prescott, Arizona, to resume his career as a collector. He worked closely with Dr. Elliott Coues (1842–1899), a surgeon at the fort, who became one of the leading naturalists of the American West, but the exact nature of their agreement is not known. In the autumn, Coues left for the East and presented their collections to Dr. George Engelmann, whose herbarium was the forerunner of the present Missouri Botanical Garden, in St. Louis.

In October 1865 Palmer re-enlisted in the Army, as acting assistant surgeon at Camp Lincoln on the Verde River in central Arizona. His salary was $125 per month, and his weight was given as 143 pounds. He went along on scouting parties and raids against the Indians, who were most likely Yavapai (Gifford 1932, 1936), although they were generally called Apaches by the soldiers and settlers; the true Apaches occupied territory to the east (Goodwin 1942). At all times he thought as a collector, exhibiting what McVaugh called a "curious detachment" (1956:30). When an Indian child died after being wounded in a raid, Palmer wrote,

The females of the camp laid it out after their custom & covered it with wild flowers and carried it to a grave. . . . They hid it so completely that its body could not be found, as I had a wish to have it for a specimen . . . no persuasion could induce them to tell the secret, so I did not get the specimen. (quoted by McVaugh 1956:30)

This was an especially difficult tour of duty, due to rationing of food, and malaria, and danger from the Indians. Palmer was thrown from a mule in late May 1866 receiving head injuries from which he never fully recovered. He became seriously ill with malaria during the summer and was hospitalized at Fort Whipple, probably from September to November.

Nevertheless, Palmer made a number of collections, which were unfortunately lost. In his illness he had entrusted his collection to an officer at Camp Lincoln, who failed to forward it. In an account written several years later, Palmer remarked on this loss, "I was told that the things had been thrown away and the only thing that was recovered was a scrap book, so that the collection made around the Post and on 7 foot scouts, under adverse circumstances, was all lost by carelessness . . ." (quoted by McVaugh 1956:31).

Most of the ruins that Palmer saw were probably those of the late prehistoric period, c. A.D. 1150–1400, which include easily visible pueblo-like structures, such as Tuzigoot, and cliff dwellings, such as the misnamed Montezuma Castle. The earlier prehistoric remains of the region are less easily recognizable, having only filled-in subsurface structural remains if any, and low trash mounds (Jeter 1982c).

It appears that not quite all of Palmer's archeological collections were lost at Camp Lincoln and that he did visit some of the "cavate rooms" of the Verde Valley in 1865. As will be seen, his later work in southwestern Utah has been claimed by some as the first scientific work in Southwestern archeology; however, this 1865–66 exploration should perhaps be given that honor. In his first published paper, he stated,

> When stationed at Camp Lincoln, Arizona, as post surgeon, the writer explored some ancient rock caves near by, which were plastered in the interior, and obtained several corn-cobs, two of which were preserved, and are now in the museum of the Smithsonian Institution. One is slender and narrow, being five and one-quarter inches long; the other is thicker, but its length is only four and one-half inches. The former had ten and the latter eight rows of grains, with no more difference discernible than exists among the corn raised by all the Pueblo Indians of to-day, and which certainly is the kind grown by them at the Spanish conquest of Mexico. The ruins in which the cobs were found have not been inhabited by the present Indians of the country, who are Apaches, as they believe that evil spirits hover about them, and therefore will not enter them. (Palmer 1871:420)

Late in 1866 Palmer was released from the hospital and went to Camp Grant, Arizona, on the San Pedro River north of Tucson. He continued to suffer from malaria and was described by a military doctor as "a very sick man." Even while bedridden, he managed to make collections, as noted by Safford (1911a:344–45):

> . . . He did not on that account cease to add to his collection, but while he lay in the little hut that served as his dispensary he was aided by a cat that brought in small animals to her kittens. He would seize her gently, take away her prey, and after removing the skull and skin of the animal, allow her to proceed with its body to her little ones. In this way he secured specimens of several new rodents.

FIGURE 2.3

Edward Palmer, from a photograph thought to have been made soon after the Civil War. (National Anthropological Archives, Smithsonian Institution)

On March 31, 1867, he requested a release from his contract due to ill health; it was granted, but he stayed at the camp until August and collected botanical and zoological specimens from that vicinity. He then went to Tucson, and from there to Yuma and Los Angeles via the Southern Pacific Mail Stage (the Butterfield Stage route), arriving around mid-September. According to McVaugh (1956:34), "Palmer's first important ethnological collections were made in this year, especially near Tucson and Yuma, from the Apache, Pima, and Papago Indians."

In late September, Palmer went by boat from Los Angeles to San Francisco, where his contract was annulled. During October he visited Sonoma, in the California wine country, to take the "grape cure" that was then believed to be effective against malaria. On October 25 he departed San Francisco for New York, via Nicaragua, on a series of steamers. Before the year's end, he was back in Washington.

Transition in Oklahoma (1868)

The year 1868 saw Palmer through a crucial time in his transition from medical duties to a career as a full-time collector. Early in the year he was appointed as an Indian Agency doctor and traveled to the Kiowa and Comanche Agency in the Washita Valley of southwestern Oklahoma, then known as Indian Territory. But, after less than a month, his commanding officer expressed disappointment due to Palmer's "lack of interest in his Indian charges, and his great absorption in collecting specimens" (McVaugh 1956:36). Despite counter-arguments by Palmer and Maj. Henry Shanklin of the adjoining Wichita Agency, Palmer was discharged on May 4. He moved to the Wichita Agency and continued collecting, probably without doing much medical work, if any.

During June Palmer learned of a plot by Kiowas and Comanches to burn the agency and kill him; he may have been warned by Black Beaver, a Delaware Indian whom he acknowledged, along with Major Shanklin, many years later in his last will and testament (1956:37, 401). He left the agency and retreated to the vicinity of Cherokee Town, in the Washita Valley of southern Oklahoma, and made extensive collections of botanical, zoological and ethnological specimens, despite ill health.

Safford relates an incident that probably occurred during this period in which a group of Indians "were about to destroy his collections, but stopped short at the sight of snakeskins, evidently recognizing them as the property of a medicine man with whom it was dangerous to trifle" (Safford 1911a:345).

In October Palmer returned to Leavenworth, perhaps to recuperate. Early in November he went to Washington and remained there until the next spring; during this stay, he negotiated the kind of arrangement he had obviously been dreaming of.

Full-time Collecting in the Southwest (1869–70)

The completion of Palmer's transition from amateur to full-time collector has been summarized by McVaugh:

> It was apparent to men like Spencer Baird that a multiple purpose was to be served by botanical, ethnobotanical, and purely ethnological work in the Southwest: new crops or new areas suitable for familiar crops might be discovered, but most important of all was to record the vanishing culture of the Indians before it was modified or extinguished by the culture of the Europeans. With these purposes in mind, Palmer set out for Arizona in mid-March [1869], as a general agricultural explorer, under the auspices of the United States Department of Agriculture, the Smithsonian Institution, and the Army Medical Museum. (1956:41)

Palmer traveled from Washington by train to northwestern Kansas. From there he went by stage to Santa Fe, Albuquerque, and Fort Wingate, New Mexico, which became his headquarters from mid-April to the first of June. From Fort Wingate he visited the Navajo Agency and "nearby Pueblo Indian villages," including Acoma and almost certainly Zuni as well.

In early June Palmer joined President Grant's special Indian Commissioner, Vincent Colyer (1825–1888), who was controversial because of his sympathies with black soldiers and Indians, for something of a whirlwind tour into Arizona and back. Their main objective was the Hopi mesas; they arrived at Oraibi about June 9 and returned via Canyon de Chelly to Fort Wingate on June 18. Palmer shipped a large collection of Hopi materials, along with botanical and zoological specimens, to Washington.

Palmer also appears to have made a minor contribution to linguistic anthropology at this time. Fowler and Matley (1978:20) stated that he sent Hopi, Tewa, and Zuni vocabulary lists to the Smithsonian during his 1865–67 Southwestern tour of duty, but it is more likely that these lists were compiled during the spring of 1869.

On June 22 Palmer left Fort Wingate with an army-escorted wagon train, heading west. They visited the San Francisco Peaks, near Flagstaff, Arizona, ascending to the snow line on July 4, and arrived at his former post, Fort Whipple, on July 9. He made it his base again for more than a month, with excursions to Bill Williams Mountain, west of Flagstaff near Williams, Arizona, and to his other former base, Camp Lincoln, where he searched for his earlier lost collections and explored "Astect" ruins. Fowler and Matley (1978:20) indicated that Palmer had contributed "maps, drawings, and photographs from the Verde Valley . . . including some of the earliest photographs of Montezuma's Castle" to the Smithsonian during his earlier stay at Camp Lincoln, but it seems much more likely that this work was done during this 1869 Smithsonian-sponsored expedition.

He then, in the heat of August, crossed the desert west of the Prescott uplands to the Colorado River and went downriver by boat to Yuma, where he visited the agricultural Cocopa Indians, and beyond to the head of the Gulf of California. He took a steamer back upstream to the Pima villages near Sacaton, which is southeast of Phoenix between the prehistoric Hohokam sites of Snaketown and Casa Grande (cf. Haury 1976; Wilcox and Shenk 1977). From there he traveled overland back to Fort Whipple, thence southwest through chaparral and grasslands to Camp Date Creek at the northwestern margin of the Sonoran Desert. After further trips to Yuma, the Gulf of California, and Baja California, he went by stage to Tucson and south into the Mexican state of Sonora, where he continued his collecting in November and December 1869. His unflagging energy at this point is clear: "he chartered a dugout to take him and his collections to Guaymas; for nine days he walked along the shore, collecting as he went, while the boat kept pace with him offshore; how his boatman must have marveled at the demented ways of the gringo!" (McVaugh 1956:44).

In early January, 1870, Palmer took a steamer to San Francisco. After a month there, he left for New York with twenty boxes of specimens.

First Expedition to Utah (1870).

Palmer's enthusiasm for his new line of work clearly continued as he immediately planned another trip. After two months he left for Utah, traveling to Salt Lake City on the new transcontinental railroad. From there he began his expeditions south, stopping for about ten days at St. George.

St. George is on the Virgin River in extreme southwestern Utah, just north of the Arizona state line, in what might be termed the interface zone between two great aboriginal culture areas: the Southwest and the Great Basin. Culturally, this region was the scene of a short-lived (c. A.D. 800–1150) expansion by a variant of the Anasazi tradition that dominated the Plateau regions to the east (Euler et al. 1979:1089–91). It is generally believed that, around A.D. 1150, the ancestors of the Southern Paiute moved eastward into this region from adjacent portions of Nevada, perhaps ultimately from southeastern California (Fowler and Fowler 1981:131–32).

The St. George locality is significant in the history of archeology. Several previous authors (e.g., Holmes 1886a:287–91, 307–11; Judd 1926:40–43; McVaugh 1956: 67–68; Fowler and Fowler 1981:141; Fowler and Jennings 1982:106) have credited Palmer with the first scientific or significant recovery of data by excavations in the Great Basin, or even in the "Puebloan" Southwest, during his 1875 stay there. However, they seem to have overlooked Palmer's own published reference to an archeological investigation he made during this 1870 visit: "The past summer the writer opened a mound near St. George, Utah, in which several nicely made and well-burnt earthen pots were found, full of human ashes, charcoal, and several pieces of charred corn-cob" (1871:420). On the same page of this publication, Palmer had also referred to his work in the "ancient rock caves" of the Verde Valley in central Arizona. It is not clear whether those investigations involved excavations or merely surface collections, but they might be claimed to push the beginnings of scientific archeology and/or archeobotany in the Southwest back to 1865, since they produced archeobotanical specimens for the Smithsonian and resulted in a published description and interpretation. Palmer's reference to human ashes probably means just that, rather than ashes from cooking fires; the brief report on his 1875 excavation described several cremated Indian remains (Anonymous 1876).

From St. George, Palmer traveled southwest to St. Thomas, Nevada, with a party transporting a threshing machine. The road ended there; he bought a mule, made an extremely difficult journey to the Colorado River valley, and crossed into Arizona. He collected specimens up and down the valley, in heat as high as 117° F., revisited Yuma and the Gulf of California, returned upvalley to Ehrenburg, and traveled by stage across the Mojave Desert to Los Angeles, a route slightly north of that taken in 1867. He returned to Washington by an overland route for the first time, arriving in early November 1870.

During this year, Palmer wrote at least a few short notes on his observations of the Paiute Indians. Some, if not all, of these were assembled and published "without comment as a minor contribution to Utah ethnology" by Heizer (1954). One of the entries is indicated as having been made at Fort Union, New Mexico, in 1866, but McVaugh's (1956) summaries do not show that he was in that state during that year; perhaps it dates to his 1869 visit to northwestern New Mexico instead. Most of the published entries appear to date to this 1870 expedition. One briefly describes his dealings with the "Pah Ute" Indians at St. Thomas (Heizer 1954:2).

Eastern Interludes (1871–74)

McVaugh characterized the years 1871–73 as an interlude during which Palmer "made no important natural history collections" (1956:53–55). He lived in Washington and spent the summers on the New England coast assisting Baird in the collection and preparation of marine animal specimens.

At least one noteworthy archeological find resulted from this tour of duty. During the summer of 1873, while working at Peak's Island off the coast of southern Maine, Palmer visited the nearby village of Harpswell and excavated an Indian burial. He recovered a number of corroded copper tubular beads, with fragments of a belt made of buckskin and vegetal cordage that had been preserved by the copper salts. These materials were donated to the Peabody Museum in 1877 (Putnam 1878:215) and were described in an article on the Museum's "copper objects from North and South America" by Frederic Ward Putnam (1882b:88–89). Putnam stated that the find was made in 1868, but this seems unlikely, especially since McVaugh (1956:249, 272) found records of Palmer's having been in Maine only in 1872 and 1873 and specifically having visited Harpswell in 1873.

In October of 1873, Palmer began working on collections of marine animals for the famous naturalist Louis Agassiz (1807–1873) at the Harvard Museum of Comparative Zoology. Agassiz and Baird had been sharing their numerous mutual interests since 1846 (Herber 1963:11), so it is likely that this was the key to Palmer's obtaining this new position. It apparently was also about this time that Palmer became acquainted with Frederic Ward Putnam, who was a former student and long-time associate of Agassiz, thus beginning "a connection that continued for some years to the profit of both parties" (McVaugh 1956:68). The first tangible results of their collaboration appear to be two brief articles by Palmer (1873, 1874a) in Putnam's *American Naturalist*. Dexter (1987) has recently summarized the Putnam-Palmer relationship as related to the early development of American ethnobotany.

Agassiz died on December 14; foreseeing the end of his funding, Palmer arranged to join a private expedition to Lake Okeechobee in southern Florida in early 1874. He thus returned to collecting plants, but conditions were difficult, and he was not satisfied with the results. He extended his stay in Florida through early September, then returned to Cambridge and remained there until late December 1874. In all likelihood, he wrote three more short articles for the *American Naturalist,* based on his most recent trip, at this time.

Publications (1871–75)

Curiously, McVaugh's biographical sketch of these "interlude" years failed to mention Palmer's publications. At least one of these has a legitimate claim to significance, as McVaugh noted in passing elsewhere (1956:6). In a U.S. Department of Agriculture publication, the *Report of the Commissioner of Agriculture for 1870,* Palmer authored "Food Products of the North American Indians" (1871:404–28), which has been called "the first ethnobotanical [article] in the United States" (Bye 1972:100). It drew primarily on his own Southwestern field work but also included some information gathered by himself and others in other areas.

Also during these years, Palmer began publishing a series of shorter notes in the *American Naturalist.* The first of these notes drew upon his Southwestern observations; three notes published in 1875 were based on the trip to Florida and the Bahamas.

"Indian Rope and Cloth" (Palmer 1873) discussed the processing and use of *Apocynum cannabinum* (Indian hemp or dogbane) by contemporary Southwestern and Great Basin Indians for twine, fishing lines and nets, rope and cloth, and medicinal purposes. He noted that he had given the Department of Agriculture "a fine specimen of rope made of this fibre by the Ute Indians," and that the Smithsonian had "good specimens of strings and a fishing net made of this plant by the Indians of Arizona." He also stated that "Near Camp Lincoln in Arizona we obtained, from some old Aztec ruins, cloth that had been manufactured by hand from this plant" (1873:755).

"The Manufacture of Pottery by the Indians" (Palmer 1874a) is a brief summary of his observations of Indian potters in the Southwest and California. At the end he suggested that round stones found with prehistoric burials were analogous to those he had seen used to smooth vessels before firing.

"The Berries of Rhamnus as Indian Food" (Palmer 1874b) essentially reiterated, and added slightly to, one of the entries in his "Food Products" article (1871:414). This was a discussion of *Rhamnus croceus* (hollyleaf buckthorn, now *Rhamnus crocea;* Little 1950:84), an evergreen shrub with "showy" and edible red berries. One reason for this selective republication may have been to expose a wider audience to Palmer's rather gory account of his examination of the bodies of twenty-two Apaches who had recently eaten "greedily of these berries and other coarse substances" before being killed by soldiers in the Mogollon Rim country of east-central Arizona.

"Clay-balls as Slung Shot or Cooking Stones" (Palmer 1875a) was inspired by Palmer's observation of "round balls of clay as hard as that material could be made" in the museum at Nassau in the Bahamas. He compared them to stone balls he had seen Indians in Arizona, New Mexico, Utah, and California use in two ways: as hide-wrapped "slung shot" by Apaches; and in boiling food, in the absence of pottery, by heating the balls redhot and dropping them into water-tight baskets containing the food and water.

This rather imaginative little article was one of Palmer's better efforts in the use of ethnographic analogy. He anticipated by many years a similar discussion of the functions of the variously (and sometimes elaborately) shaped clay "Poverty Point objects" in the Lower Mississippi Valley (Ford et al. 1955:55–57). The later authors also discussed California clay balls, quoted an 1889 ethnographic paper on the use of clay "nodules" in baking pits by Australian Aborigines, and even cited C. B. Moore's second-hand information to the effect that "double cones of fired clay were obtained by Edward Palmer from the Paiute in 1875 and were said to have been used in a hand game," but did not cite Palmer's (1875a) paper.

However, Palmer was wrong about the composition of the Bahamian objects, and they are probably not artifacts at all. They are not made of fired clay but are caliche (calcium carbonate) nodules which probably formed during the last three hundred years due to drier conditions brought on by deforestation (Sealey 1985:75–76, Figure 6.3; William F. Keegan, 1987 personal communication). Although it is believed by some that they were made or used by the Indians of these islands (hence their display in the museum during Palmer's visit), there is no ethnohistoric documentation for this, and none have yet been found in controlled archeological investigations.

"An Indian Mill Seen in the Museum of Nassau, New Providence" (Palmer 1875b) similarly used a Nassau museum specimen as a basis for an analogy. This time a wooden item labeled "Indian idol or stool" in the museum was compared to similarly-shaped stone *metates* he had seen used by "the poor people and Indians of Mexico." Palmer was definitely off the mark here; small wooden ceremonial stools, known as *dujos* or *duhos,* are well-documented ethnographically as having been used by "big men" of the Caribbean islands (R. Christopher Goodwin, 1986 personal communcation; Fewkes 1907: 202–07, Figures 39 and 40)

"The Starch of Zamia" (Palmer 1875c) was a slightly longer, and more useful, discussion of *Zamia pumila* or "Compte," which he had observed in Florida, especially around the head of Biscayne Bay. Swanton (1946:271, 361–62) stated that a related species, *Zamia integrifolia,* was used by the Creeks and Seminoles and known as *kunti* or *koonti;* perhaps "Compte" was Palmer's rendering of the same word. Sturtevant (1969:189–92) noted that more than twenty species of *Zamia* were used by Indians from the Southeast through the Antilles and southern Mexico to northern South America.

Return to the West (1874–75)

During late 1874, Palmer had been contacted by Baird, who was beginning to plan, along with John Wesley Powell and others, the exhibits for the 1876 Centennial Exposition in Philadelphia (Fowler and Matley 1978:20). However, the congressional appropriation was delayed, and Palmer arranged for an alternative expedition to Guadalupe, an isolated island off the coast of Baja California where no biological collection had ever been made. The flora there was being threatened by commercially bred goats. Palmer was supported in this venture by Sereno Watson (1826–1892), who was curator of the Gray Herbarium at Harvard from 1874 until his death and one of Palmer's major patrons (McVaugh 1956:4, 60). Although Fowler and Matley (1978:20) implied that Palmer went to the West "in the early fall of 1874," that is incorrect; he stayed in Cambridge from mid-September through most of December (McVaugh 1956:159).

Palmer left Cambridge by train for New Haven, arriving and departing around December 22, 1874. From there he took the transcontinental railway to San Francisco, arriving on January 3, 1875. On January 14 and 15 he took another train to San Diego, remaining there until late January and arranging to be left on Guadalupe Island. Due to a missed boat connection, he was forced to remain there, living on goat meat and wild plants, until mid-May before being rescued by friends from San Diego. Safford described the difficulty of Palmer's life and work on the island:

> . . . he lived in a dug-out with a roof of poles covered with dirt. His explorations were attended with much difficulty and for several weeks he was seriously ill. Sometimes in order to secure plants growing on the faces of cliffs, which had been preserved on account of their inaccessible position from the greed of goats, he made use of a noose at the end of a long pole, much to the amusement of the herders, who laughed at the doctor's attempts to "lasoo plants." Many of the species could have been secured in no other way. "Goats," he says, "were my only rivals; but they made a clean sweep of everything in reach, not discriminating between what was common and what was rare." (1911a:347)

Palmer's work on the island was among the most important of his career; according to Safford,

> The bearing upon evolution of the remarkable fauna and flora of this island . . . is almost as important as that of the animals and plants of the Galapagos Archipelago, as demonstrated by Darwin. Every bird in his collection from Guadelupe, except a single sea bird, proved to be new to science; and among the plants col-

EDWARD PALMER AND H. J. LEWIS   53

lected at this time there were 21 new species, the greater part of which have never since been found elsewhere. (1911b:62)

Back on the mainland, Palmer worked extensively in southern California and northern Baja California, through September. His work emphasized botanical and zoological specimens, but he also made ethnological collections from the desert Indians. Bye (1980) has compiled data on his ethnobotanical collections from these regions during this year and the next.

Utah Archeology, Other Collecting Ventures, and Speculations (1875–77)

The Centennial appropriation was finally approved by Congress, and, in the fall of 1875, Baird wrote Palmer to assure him of funding for "explorations in Utah" that should be "thorough and exhaustive" and to encourage him to "pay particular attention to the subject of foods of the Indians" (Fowler and Matley 1978:20). In October Palmer left San Francisco and returned to St. George to resume his archeological excavations and other work near there. He stayed at the home of Joseph Ellis Johnson (1817–1882), a Mormon pioneer who had developed an outstanding garden there and had corresponded with leading botanists of the day.

Palmer's 1875 work at St. George was summarized in an unsigned article entitled "Exploration of a Mound in Utah" (Anonymous 1876), which appeared in the July 1876 issue of *American Naturalist*. The article began by noting that "information [had] been received that a mound existed on Santa Clara River, a few miles from . . . St. George" and that Palmer, who had "been in that neighborhood last fall," had directed an investigation for the National Museum there. The source of the information was not indicated, but, as noted previously, Palmer (1871:420) had "opened a mound near St. George" in 1870. This may well have been a return to the same site, or it may have been a new site that he learned about by correspondence from Joseph Ellis Johnson or some other local acquaintance.

Alternatively, he may have learned about the site from Dr. Charles Christopher Parry (1823–1890), a well-known botanist from Davenport, Iowa. Palmer and Parry had known each other at least since 1870 and would work together in Mexico in 1877–78, but had not met in the field before 1875 (McVaugh 1956:27, 69). Parry had come to Utah in the summer of 1875 and had made "special explorations" on behalf of the Peabody Museum, including the opening of "an ancient mound, on the Santa Clara River," recovering pottery and other artifacts "characteristic of the ancient Pueblos" (Putnam 1876:12–13, 17–18). There seems to be no report on this excavation; as McVaugh noted (1956:27), Parry published little, even in his principal field of botany.

Excavation Methods. Palmer's methods of excavating at this site are of some interest. Fowler and Jennings stated that "Reputedly, the Santa Clara site was 'dug' by diverting an irrigation ditch through the 'mound' and collecting the out-washed artifacts on the downstream side" (1982:106). This is probably an exaggeration: Fowler and Matley stated that the excavation was done only "in part" by diverting the ditch (1978:22), which is more in line with eyewitness and hearsay accounts.

The earliest published report stated that "with the necessary workmen and tools he proceeded to the mound in question" (Anonymous 1876:410) and that groups of pots were found with burials as house floors were "dug up and cleared away" (1876:412). It also furnished details of house construction and feature locations (1876:410–11), burial positions (1876:412), and such details as "specimens of food (such as corn and pine nuts) discovered near the skeletons" (1876:412–13), "fragments of charred textile fabric" found in a "stratum of ashes" (1876:413), and seven pottery vessels "in connection with one skeleton, associated with some very neatly made arrowheads" and other artifacts (1876:413). Some of the "better forms and finer kinds of pottery" were found "near children's skeletons" (1876:414), and the better-preserved vessels tended to be "extricated from near the interior" of houses rather than from exposed proveniences (1876:414). All of this sounds as though a fair amount of hand excavation was done and at least minimal controls were maintained over proveniences.

Further insights were provided by a later Smithsonian archeologist, Neil Judd, who made an "inquiry at St. George" which resulted in

> a chance meeting with Mr. R. A. Morris, one of the three men who assisted Doctor Palmer in 1875. Mr. Morris's memory is quite clear on certain phases of these early excavations. . . . With further reference to the Santa Clara mound, Mr. Morris recalls that in addition to adobe houses others were exposed which seemed to be semisubterranean and whose low earth walls were plastered with about 1 inch of clay. (1926:41)

Judd furnished further details of house construction from Morris's recollections and stated that similar techniques had been disclosed during his own excavations in 1917 at Paragonah, Utah (1926:41–42). He also noted that, according to Morris, "one or two mounds which Doctor Palmer opened in the immediate vicinity of St. George possessed the same characteristic features of construction" (1926:42) and remarked, "The one regrettable thing in connection with these early explorations is that Palmer's notes have been widely scattered, if not, indeed, utterly lost to science" (1926:41).

William Henry Holmes, who had quite possibly talked to Palmer about this project, reported that "The work of exhumation was most successfully accomplished by means of water. A small stream was made to play upon the soft alluvium, of which the mound was chiefly composed. The sensations of the collector, as skeleton after skeleton and vase after vase appeared, must have been highly pleasurable" (1886a:288).

This confirms the use of water in the excavation but implies that it was not the only means used, merely the most successful or efficient, and that the water was applied under at least some semblance of control. Curiously, Holmes did not mention Palmer by name in this article and got the year wrong, stating that "in 1876 a collector was sent out to make an investigation" (1886a:287).

Artifacts and Cultural Affiliation. Holmes's descriptions and illustrations of selected specimens of the coiled ware (1886a:288–91, Figures 241–44), plain ware (1886a:299–301, Figures 255–57), and painted ware (1886a:307–15, Figures 258–61, 266–67, 269–71) from the "tumulus at St. George" indicated clear relationships to vessels from other Anasazi regions. This had also been apparent to Palmer; the original report on this excavation, based on his observations and impressions, stated that "certainly they must be classed with the Pueblo tribes," calling attention to "the quality of the pottery and its ornamentation" (Anonymous 1876:412).

These insights were confirmed by Fowler and Matley (1978:25−32, Figures 1−6), who provided a detailed typological and technological analysis of the entire collection, with abundant photographs. They did not explicitly suggest a cultural affiliation or chronological placement, but most of the apparently indigenous ceramics were classed in the "Virgin Series" of Tusayan Gray or White wares, implying affiliation with the Virgin-Anasazi subtradition. Several of the intrusive pottery types are well-dated by tree-ring associations (Breternitz 1966) and are consistent with the generally accepted Virgin span of A.D. 800−1150.

The general consensus of this literature is that these "mounds" were tell-like heaps formed by reoccupation of former house sites, with accumulations of wall and roof rubble, refuse, and fill dirt (Anonymous 1876:412; Palmer 1880:170−71; Putnam 1878:198). Judd stated that this "obviously conveys Doctor Palmer's conclusion after several years' explorations throughout western Utah" (1926:14).

Other Collections. Palmer also collected materials from the local Indians, who were Southern Paiutes. The artifacts included five whole pots and an unfired clay figurine self-portrait bust of a local Paiute named Shem. Three of the vessels, the figurine, a hafted bone "mescal knife," and other items went to the Smithsonian and were described and illustrated by Fowler and Matley (1978:32, Figures 2, 5, 6; see also Fowler and Fowler 1981:141, Figure 1). Two vessels went to the Peabody Museum (1981:141).

As Baird had suggested, Palmer's collection included Southern Paiute food plants; here again he made a small contribution to linguistics by recording the Paiute names for these plants. Palmer himself used some of this information in a follow-up to his original (1871) publication on Indian use of plants (Palmer 1878e). His plant specimens have been reexamined as the basis of a modern ethnobotanical study (Bye 1972). Fowler and Matley (1978:40−41) added some minor details from Palmer's original descriptions and a clarification of his linguistic transcriptions.

Palmer's collections from these and other Native Americans were also used extensively in two classic monographs by Smithsonian anthropologists, "Primitive Travel and Transportation" by Otis T. Mason (1896) and "Games of the North American Indians" by Stewart Culin (1907). In particular, Mason (1896:357−58, Plates 5 and 6) cited specimens of Paiute sandals; Culin's index gave twenty-six citations to materials collected by Palmer and cited him ten times on the rules of various Southwestern and Great Basin Indian games (1907:835).

At some time during his stay at St. George, Palmer traveled about ninety kilometers (or sixty miles) east to the vicinity of Kanab, Utah, and obtained additional archeological materials. Information about the sites he investigated has apparently not been preserved, but Holmes (1886a:310−11, Figures 262−65) did describe and illustrate two bowls, probably from Palmer's Kanab collection, which appear to be attributable to the Virgin-Anasazi subtradition. Palmer revisited this locality in March 1877 and excavated in a small cave.

A Venture into Nevada Archeology. At some time between October 1875 and January 1876, Palmer made a second trip to the vicinity of the abandoned St. Thomas settlement in southeastern Nevada, this time primarily for archeological collecting in the Moapa or Muddy River valley (McVaugh 1956:68, 260). This is a significant locality for prehistoric remains (Harrington 1930:6), and again it appears that Palmer may have been the first archeologist there, although he has not been credited for it.

Harrington (1930:15–16) noted that the "mountain man" Jedediah Smith may have been the first to report the presence of prehistoric remains in this vicinity, as early as 1827, but stated that the next real explorations known to him had not occurred until the twentieth century. Fowler, Madsen, and Hattori (1973:4), in a summary of southeastern Nevada prehistory, cited Palmer's 1875 work in Utah but did not mention this venture into Nevada. They stated that the earliest reports of sites in this region were 1869 newspaper accounts; however, Harrington dismissed those reports as "plainly more or less a bit of fiction" (1930:15). The next accounts they cited were from an 1881 publication.

The Muddy River is a tributary of the Virgin River; according to Harrington, the Virgin was generally too "intractable," with high banks and a swift, flood-prone current, to attract much in the way of prehistoric settlement (1930:5–6). But " . . . when we come to the Moapa or Muddy . . . we find an almost unbroken line of ancient villages of various periods from the Muddy's junction with the Virgin to the large springs forming its source some 30 miles to the north" (1930:6).

The sites of this locality include a major Puebloan complex known as Lost City (Harrington 1927; Shutler 1961), a smaller village called Mesa House (Hayden 1930), and numerous other open and cave sites (Fowler, Madsen, and Hattori 1973:5–7). Palmer's collections could have come from any of these and might be especially difficult to assign correctly; McVaugh stated that his numbering system for this year was "to say the least, somewhat confusing" (1956:68). Nevertheless, they might be of at least historical value, especially since his locality may well have been submerged by Lake Mead (McVaugh 1956:259–60).

Collections in Arizona and California. On January 5, 1876, Palmer left St. George and began an extremely wide-ranging campaign in western Arizona and California, with emphasis on collecting ethnographic materials from the riverine Yuman Indians. At some time during this period, probably in March, he visited the Mojave reservation on the Colorado River in southwestern Arizona. During that stay, he hired an Indian potter to demonstrate her manufacturing techniques for him (Palmer 1877a). Probably also at this time, he bargained with an Indian man to show him how to make fishhooks from cactus spines (Palmer 1878e).

Palmer rejoined C. C. Parry in May for explorations in the Mojave Desert and San Bernardino Mountains but was thrown from his horse on the return trip. His injury was severe enough to force him to forgo plans for more "heavy work" in archeology; instead he collected plants in California, ranging northward as far as the redwood forests north of San Francisco. In September he went to Parry's home in Davenport with his specimens. He left for Cambridge on October 5.

Palmer on Pottery-Making and Indian "Divisions". Palmer returned to Davenport, Iowa, via New Haven, New York, and the Centennial Exposition at Philadelphia, arriving on November 5, 1876. At the November 23 meeting of the Davenport Academy of Natural Sciences, he read his paper on "Manufacture of Pottery by Mojave Indian Women," which was subsequently published in the Academy's *Proceedings* (Palmer 1877a). This article exhibited several of Palmer's characteristic traits, both positive and negative, and is therefore worthy of some consideration here.

After noting that the first European explorers had "found the native Indians in possession of pottery . . . all over the American continent, that of Chilli and Peru being of superior quality," Palmer stated,

> There seems to be two divisions of the American Indians, the Toltecs and Aztecs
> . . . The Toltecs are makers of the superior pottery, and are represented by the Pimo
> Indians of Arizona, the Moqui and Rio Grande Indians of New Mexico. This divi-
> sion is distinguished . . . also by their superior dwellings and the manner of dispos-
> ing of the dead, by burying instead of burning, as is practiced by the Aztecs. The
> pottery of the Aztecs is very inferior. . . . (1877a:32)

These ideas were elaborated upon in another article, probably written, or at least, conceived, at about the same time (Palmer 1877b). That article, which will be discussed in some detail later in this chapter, made it clear that he considered the Mojave Indians to be in the "Aztec" category (1877b:736).

In the "Manufacture of Pottery" article, Palmer continued,

> The [Indian] women have always been superior to the men in their knowledge
> and successful prosecution of the domestic arts and manufactures, and have always
> been the sole pottery makers. If a man or his children depended upon *him* to make
> a pot to cook or eat from, they would starve before they would have one. As the
> female artists of both divisions use the same means of constructing pottery, it may
> be interesting to many to know how pottery is made by the native women of our
> continent.
> Last summer I visited the Mojave Indian reservation. . . . Wishing a set of dishes
> of their make, I engaged the services of a native woman. . . . The next day she ap-
> peared, as desired, accompanied by an assistant. They were somewhat aged, ap-
> proaching to four score years, and possessed of many wrinkles. . . . (1877a:32–33)

Palmer went on to describe the forming of the pots by use of wooden paddles and stone anvils, drying in the sun, firing, and in some cases, glazing with salt water. He concluded:

> These artists, though homely and plainly clad and besmeared with dirt, had per-
> formed their work well. Judging them by their works, it must be acknowledged
> they had done as well as most men and women of the paler and better-to-do race
> could have done with like materials. Dire necessity and compulsion would be nec-
> essary to compel most of us to attempt the task. Considering the beauty of the pot-
> tery, its symmetry of form, quality of workmanship, the rude tools, the kind of ma-
> terials used, and also that necessity had been their only teacher, these female artists,
> though Indians, had, by their works, proven themselves heroines in domestic art,
> challenging competition by either sex of Americans under like conditions. Credit
> must be given to the female for her good works, let her be of whatsoever race or
> color. (1877a:34)

Return to Utah. Palmer stayed in Davenport until December 18, when he departed for St. George once again. He arrived around Christmas and made his headquarters there until June 22, 1877. According to McVaugh (1956:71; cf. Putnam 1878:198–99, 213) he excavated in Washington and Kane counties for the Peabody Museum, with several side trips for botanical collecting. Around March 12, he visited southwestern Kane County and excavated in a cave near the town of Johnson (McVaugh 1956:234). Fowler and Matley stated that this took place "sometime during October or November of 1875" (1978:21) during an earlier stay at St. George, but it seems more likely that most, if not all, of this work was done during this visit (cf. Putnam 1878:199). Palmer (1878a) published a brief report on this cave excavation in the Peabody Museum's *Annual Report* for 1877.

In this report, he summarized finds of: several pottery vessels with resemblances to "Ancient Pueblo" ceramics, one of them containing a string made of *Apocynum cannabinum* fibers (cf. Palmer 1873); wooden tongs, which he interpreted by analogy to have been used for gathering cactus fruits or moving hot articles; a probable hair brush made of grass stems; preserved food items, including an *Agave* leaf, a pinyon pine cone (which furnishes edible nuts), and several corncobs; and a small basket. His "most interesting" and only illustrated find was an item interpreted as a shovel (Palmer 1878a:272, Figure 1), with a fourteen inch blade made from the horn of a mountain sheep, fastened with sinews to a wooden handle five feet long. He stated,

> Altogether the implement is a very handy one for use in a light soil, and would prove of great service in planting, cutting up weeds, ditching, etc. Several old Indians of different tribes have told me of such implements having been used for agricultural purposes before they obtained iron tools. They stated that the blades were made of horn, bone or stone, and, by the outlines they would draw on the ground, they showed that the general shape of the shovels they described was like this interesting and probably unique specimen. On showing this implement to some old Pah Utes, they said at once that it was of Moqui make, and was used to make ditches and plant corn. (1878a:272)

He then worked his way northward toward Salt Lake City, making more biological collections, with additional archeological researches at Red Creek (Paragonah), Beaver, Fillmore, Payson, and Spring Lake Villa (Springville); Judd provides a map that includes these localities (1919: Plate 1). Another informative and amusing recollection of Palmer at work was related in a footnote by Judd:

> Mr. John J. Starley, chief informant during our observations near Fillmore, pointed out the former locations of numerous mounds. Mr. Starley recalls vividly a brief visit made by Dr. Edward Palmer and an escort of soldiers from Fort Douglas about 1874 [Starley's memory was obviously imprecise here], when two or three small mounds were opened. In one of these an earthen jar was found; the vessel was half filled with sunflower seeds, and these in turn were covered by a layer of corn or broken corncobs. Both corn and seeds were charred. Despite these excavations, Starley remembers Doctor Palmer as "a collector of bugs and grass," who "nailed every lizard he saw and grabbed every insect, and usually had his pockets bulging with such stuff." (1919:63)

Palmer arrived at Salt Lake City on August 13. From there he made one more apparently brief and inconsequential investigation of reported mounds at Tooele and returned. Overall this had been a productive trip; in addition to his usual botanical collections, his entomological specimens, especially butterflies, were noteworthy (Brown 1967), and "the archaeological collections of 1877 were large ones; Palmer noted the shipment of nine boxes and four bales from Salt Lake City. The catalog of this collection, in the files of the Peabody Museum, includes 186 individual items" (McVaugh 1956:71).

Debunking at Davenport. Palmer left Salt Lake City for Davenport in late August and arrived on September 1, 1877. He probably attended the regular meeting of the Davenport Academy on September 28. The Academy's *Proceedings* published a paper by him which was read at that meeting, entitled "A Review of the Published Statements regarding the Mounds at Payson, Utah, with an Account of Their Structure and Origin" (Palmer 1880).

At the meeting on October 27, 1876, Parry had read some letters from a Utah correspondent, Miss Julia J. Wirt. The gist of those letters was subsequently published in the Academy's *Proceedings* under the title "Exploration of a Mound near Utah Lake, Utah" (Parry 1877). This brief note alleged that a skeleton "six feet seven inches in length" had been found, with "a stone pipe weighing five ounces between its teeth," in a mound on the farm of a Mr. Amasa Potter, near Payson in central Utah. It added that further investigation had produced "an air-tight stone box" containing another box, which contained "about a quart of light, mouldy wheat, a few of the best grains of which were planted and grew," and that one of the "numerous pieces of pottery" found had "painted upon it a quite recognizable sketch of a range of mountains visible from the locality of the mounds." Parry later read another letter from Miss Wirt into the record, retracting the claims about the box and the wheat (1877: 29, 82).

In his paper, Palmer successively attacked these claims. His strongest arguments, although not recognized as such by himself, were that neither Amasa Potter nor his neighbors had been able to show him any direct evidence for these fantastic finds and that some of the claims appeared very unlikely, e.g.:

> How it happened that several feet of earth and rubbish could fall upon that skeleton without breaking or displacing the pipe is somewhat surprising! . . .
> I was shown some of the cement said to have come from around the box. In my opinion it is not cement, but grooved pieces of clay, that once formed part of the roof covering of a house. . . . In constructing a roof, small poles and sticks were used, over which wet mud was thickly plastered. . . . (1880: 167–68)

Palmer recognized that the remains were those of prehistoric Indians rather than any lost races. But he was not able to free himself completely from his prejudices:

> . . . The most conclusive evidence against the matter is that the Indians who left these ruins behind, like the present races, did not work for the sake of work, but only did what labor the collecting, preparing and preservation of native animal and vegetable substances required to convert them into articles of food and clothing. (1880: 168)

Having addressed the statements made in the Davenport Academy's *Proceedings*, Palmer moved on to some additional claims made by Potter in a letter to a Nevada newspaper (the Eureka *Sentinel*, date not given; reprinted in *Popular Science Monthly* for November 1877, Vol. 7, p. 123):

> . . . He says, "in the right hand" of the large skeleton "was a huge iron or steel weapon which had been buried with the body, but which crumbled to pieces on handling." Mr. Potter, it seems to me, must have mistaken a piece of juniper wood that had decayed to dust . . . for his supposed "iron or steel weapon." The color

would be the same, and to one ready to draw conclusions to suit his preconceived desire to have his explanations verify the book of Mormon, this would be sufficient. (1880:169)

After attacking several other new claims made by Potter, Palmer remarked,

> As Mr. Potter's letter does not explain the formation of these mounds, I will do so in order to give a better idea of the simple habitations of the people that once inhabited Payson. The mounds prove on examination to be debris of many dwellings successively built in the same location. (1880:170)

Palmer then went on to describe the construction of typical pueblo-style buildings, and concluded:

> It may be asked, "Who were the Ancient People of Utah?" From the evidence left behind in their ruined dwellings, they appear to belong to the same class of Indians as the Moquis of Arizona, a people simple in all their wants and habits, yet plain Indians. This is evident by the materials taken out of their ruined dwellings. . . .
> In reviewing Miss Wirt's letters to the Davenport Academy of Sciences and Mr. Potter's letter . . . I have done so, not with the view of showing their statements intentionally false, but to correct the errors . . . Mr. Potter is alone responsible for all the statements, which were evidently made with the idea of proving that these ruins belonged to the ancient race known to the Mormons as Nephites, said to have been a great people, cultivating wheat and acquainted with the use of iron. Miss Wirt derived her information wholly from Mr. Potter. Various persons in Utah, Latter Day Saints, spoke to me freely regarding these discoveries and regretted that the statements should have been made in the proceedings of the Academy, or that they should in any sense be regarded as gotten up in the interests of the Mormon church, inasmuch as none of them concur with Mr. Potter in his extravagant, and as we have shown, absurd views. (1880:171–72)

Additional Publications (1877–78)

Palmer left Davenport for Cambridge on October 8, 1877, and stayed in Massachusetts until early December. It may have been during the early portion of this interval that he wrote a curious article, "Remarks Concerning Two Divisions of Indians Inhabiting Arizona, New Mexico, Utah, and California" (Palmer 1877b), which was published in the December 1877 issue of the *American Naturalist*.

This was one of Palmer's longer articles (about twelve pages); it certainly must rank as one of his worst efforts, and makes a strange contrast with his critical debunking of the Payson claims. It is replete with stereotypes, overgeneralizations, prejudices, and leaps to wrong conclusions.

His basic thesis was still that two divisions could be classed, in their "pure" form, as Aztecs and Toltecs. This notion goes back at least to the views promoted around 1800 by Rev. Thaddeus M. Harris of Massachusetts (Thomas 1894:598) and to those of the pioneering physical anthropologist Samuel G. Morton in the mid-1800s (Hinsley 1981: 25–27). Morton had postulated, within a single but "separate and peculiar" race of Native Americans, two "families": superior, mound-building "Toltecan" and inferior, "Barbarous (American)" Indians. A secondary theme that frequently emerged was Palmer's prejudice—perhaps understandable in a transplanted Englishman—against the Spanish Catholic conquerors of the Mexican and Southwestern Indians.

In summary, Palmer characterized the Aztecs as warlike, roving hunters who built flimsy houses, made crude pottery, cremated their dead and left few or no grave goods with them, and tended to have "little power of thinking." Typical "pure Aztec" groups in the Southwest were said to include the Apache, Mojave, Yuma, Cocopa, and the "Diggers" of Nevada, plus "many of the Texas Indians." In contrast, the Toltecs were alleged to be relatively peaceful, settled agriculturalists who built substantial structures such as pueblos and mounds, made elaborate pottery, buried their dead with grave goods, and were more industrious and intelligent, with a "systematic form of government." As typical "Toltecans" he listed the "Puma" or "Pimo" (Pima), "Moqui" (Hopi), Zuni, and "Rio Grande Indians" of New Mexico, plus the Mandans and the "so-called mound-builders." Going even further afield, Palmer claimed that " . . . the cremationists or Aztecs look like Japanese, while the Toltecs or burying Indians look more like Chinese, not only in similarity of features but in manners and customs" (1877b:744).

Palmer attempted to explain instances of mixed traits by the influences of the Spanish soldiers and priests or by situations in which members of the two divisions had been forced to live together. He began to take a more promising line of reasoning, which could have led to some useful cultural-ecological insights, but soon became mired in a morass of overgeneralized environmental and economic determinism:

> It must be evident that the nature of the country which is occupied by a nation influences the manners, habits, and intelligence of the people. The ever-craving appetites of life, especially that of hunger, operating upon each individual cannot fail to give direction to his inventive habits, determine his pursuits, and impress upon him a character for all time. . . . The course of an Indian's life day after day is thereby established permanently, for the wants of nature compel him to one fixed system of procuring food. (1877b:739)

Here Palmer ignored his own observation that "Aztecs or Apaches" had taken over a territory (the Verde Valley) formerly occupied by "Toltec" Puebloans with a very different means of subsistence (1877b:741). He also clearly lacked any real anthropological concepts of culture and cultural change or evolution, thinking instead mainly on the level of individuals and their brief life-spans, or at best, in terms of a static ranking of various ethnic groups in categories more or less corresponding to the stages of a very influential unilinear evolutionary scheme of classification that had just been published in Lewis Henry Morgan's *Ancient Society* (1877).

But, of course, it is difficult to fault Palmer for not breaking through the dominant theoretical orientations of the professional anthropologists of his day, who had some racist tendencies themselves (cf. Harris 1968:142–216). It is of at least passing interest that the so-called "neoevolutionary" movement that occurred in American anthropology more than a half-century later (1968:634–87) was led by men who had done field work in and comparative studies on some of these same regions that Palmer had traversed. Julian Steward (1955) based his theory of multilinear evolution on his concept of the cultural core of subsistence-related practices, as illustrated by his major comparative studies of Southwestern and Great Basin sociopolitical groups (1937, 1938). And Leslie A. White, who did field work at the Rio Grande pueblos (e.g., 1942), devised a general scheme of cultural evolution (1943, 1949, 1959), although it was not explicitly grounded in his field experiences.

Some of Palmer's notions prove to be ironic mistakes. Although he classed both the Pima and Hopi as "Toltecans," both groups have been classed by linguistic anthropologists as speakers of "Uto-Aztecan" languages (Hale and Harris 1979:170–71). And the prehistoric Hohokam, generally regarded to have been the direct ancestors of the Pima (Haury 1976:357), predominantly disposed of their dead by cremation (1976:164–72). On the other hand, the Apache, far from being related to the Mexican Aztecs, are recent (c. A.D. 1500) immigrants to the Southwest from the north and speak an Athapaskan language related to those of the Indians of western Canada (Hale and Harris 1979: 171–72; Wilcox 1981). Finally, Palmer's attempt to deny the Spanish achievement in subduing the Aztecs led him to denigrate Aztec culture beyond the point of absurdity; the achievements and wealth of Aztec culture have been described in a recent survey by Fagan (1984).

It was probably during his late 1877 stay in Cambridge that Palmer also completed four more articles that were published in various issues of the *American Naturalist* in 1878. In these he returned to the firmer ground of his own observations.

"Notes on Indian Manners and Customs" (Palmer 1878b) was simply a collection of anecdotal information on a rather mixed bag of subjects: Navajos in the presence of death, Navajo women gambling, Apache playing cards made of horsehide, an Apache medicine man, Apache rat-catchers, Apache marriage, his 1869 visit to the Moqui or Hopi with Vincent Colyer, and "eating customs in several tribes."

"Indian Food Customs" (Palmer 1878c) was a short note that touched on food-sharing, collecting, and bread-baking. "Fishhooks of the Mohave Indians" (Palmer 1878d) was another brief note, describing his bargain with an old Mojave man who showed Palmer how to make fishhooks by wetting, bending and heating cactus spines. Photographs of such fishhooks, stated to have been collected by Palmer in 1871, have been published in a recent article on the Mojave (Stewart 1983: Figure 6e); however, Palmer spent 1871 in the Northeast, and it is likely that these were made and collected during the 1876 visit that also produced his (1877a) article on Mojave pottery-making.

"Plants Used by the Indians of the United States" (Palmer 1878e), a much longer article, was a supplement to his well-received (1871) "Food Products" publication, including "all the additional matter that has since come under [Palmer's] observation." More than 125 species were mentioned, with a heavy emphasis on Southwestern, Great Basin, and California plants. Again, descriptions of the ways plants were used as foods predominated, but discussions of textiles, medicines, and dyestuffs were also included.

This brief flurry of writing seems to have satisfied Palmer's need to get his thoughts and observations on paper. He did not publish again until 1881.

Collections in Mexico and Texas (1877–80)

The Palmer-Parry Expedition. During late 1877, Parry and Palmer put together a plan which "developed into one of the most important collecting trips ever made to northern Mexico" (McVaugh 1956:74). Parry was to concentrate on and manage the botanical collecting. They obtained advances, to be repaid from their Mexican plant specimen sales, from several sponsors. One of these, the Peabody Museum, also engaged Palmer to collect from mounds and Indian villages, in addition to his botanical and zoological work. On December 5–6, 1877, Palmer went from Cambridge to New York; from there, he left by steamer for Veracruz on December 8, arriving on December 21.

Palmer's complex itinerary in Mexico during 1878 and early 1879, mainly in the state of San Luis Potosi but also involving visits to Mexico City, Teotihuacan, Tula, and other archeologically noteworthy places, has been detailed by McVaugh (1956:74–78, 307–09). Parry and Palmer apparently were less than perfectly compatible; perhaps Palmer's emphasis on ethnological and archeological collecting was a factor. Parry returned to Davenport in August 1878 and began cataloging his own botanical collections. Palmer remained in San Luis Potosi for several months, then sent his plant collections to Parry, who gave away some of Palmer's specimens and made other arrangements that made Palmer "a financial loser in the whole affair" (McVaugh 1956:77).

But in other aspects the expedition was a huge success. Bye has reexamined Palmer's 1878 plant collection from San Luis Potosi and called it "the basis of the first modern ethnobotanical study in Mexico" (1979a:135). Bye's article also included two excellent ethnological photographs (1979a: Figures 1 and 2) made by or for Palmer during this trip, reprinted Palmer's cover letter to Putnam and three excerpts from Palmer's manuscript on collection and preparation of plant foods by the natives of San Luis Potosi (1979a:151–62), and reproduced two sketches from Palmer's field notebook (1979a: Figures 3 and 4).

From San Luis Potosi, Palmer made a circuitous journey to Tampico, Tamaulipas, where he spent most of February 1879. From there he went by steamer to New York, arriving on March 17, and immediately went to Cambridge, where he was greeted with open arms.

It took over eight hundred entries to catalog his collection, of which Putnam wrote:

> The articles which Dr. Palmer obtained from the Indians of Mexico illustrate the customs and arts of the tribes in a very perfect and comprehensive manner, and are of great importance in showing the methods of savage art and its connection with that of prehistoric times. Of the collection of antiquities, it can be said that it is the first we have received from Mexico of which the exact condition under which each object was found is known. The care with which the excavations were made and every associated object secured and properly labelled, gives the first clue we have had at the Museum for the proper understanding of the different periods of prehistoric time in Mexico. (Putnam 1880b:716–17)

Putnam's description of this "magnificent collection," which consisted of over fifteen hundred specimens, shows the wide variety of items Palmer retrieved:

> It may give some idea of the size and range of this collection to say that in articles of modern pottery alone, it numbers over five hundred specimens. . . . In it may be found . . . a large and varied assortment of all the articles of native manufacture in earthen-ware, that are found in an Indian village of to-day . . . With these are samples of the clay in different stages of preparation, with the moulds, dies, paints, polishing stones, and scrapers of wood, bone and corncob, so that it is possible to follow the native potter through all the various processes of manufacture from the crude clay to the perfect vase. . . . The collection of articles made from vegetable and animal substances is also complete, though of course they are neither so numerous nor in such great variety. In it there are specimens of cloth, blankets, etc., of

wool; bottles of pig-skin, or rather an entire skin used as a vessel; dishes, spoons, musical instruments, and bows and wooden pointed arrows of wood; cups, bottles and spoons of gourd; nets, fans, mats, baskets, rope, twine, thread, brushes, bags, brooms, paper, etc., made from rushes, canes, palm leaf, agave and yucca; medicines, distilled liquors, and various articles of fruit and other vegetable food, raw and prepared, with the loom, earthen-still, and mortars, pestles, metate, grinding and other implements of stone, used in their manufacture.

Among the articles possessing a distinctive archaeological interest and of which the antiquity cannot be doubted, there are earthen jars, vases, dishes, cups, spoons, tubes, pipes, spindlewhorls, and numerous fragments of pottery, painted, plain and polished, in human and animal forms; beads, arrowheads, axes and polishing implements of stone; obsidian cores, flakes, knives and arrowheads, and worked shells, from ruins at Tezcuco [Texcoco] and Teotihuacan. . . . (Putnam 1880b: 733–34)

Putnam also acknowledged, among the additions to the Museum's Library for 1879, a set of "Stereoscopic views of Mexico" from Palmer (Putnam 1880:750), plus a pamphlet which appears to have been a reprint of Palmer's (1878c) "Notes on Indian Manners and Customs."

Expedition to Texas and Northern Mexico. In a short time, Palmer arranged for another trip, this time to Texas and adjacent northern Mexico. Again he was to collect archeological materials for the Peabody Museum; this time he was to sell his plant collections himself, thus averting the problem he had encountered with Parry. In late June 1879, he left Massachusetts by boat for Norfolk, Virginia, then traveled by rail across the middle South, reaching Longview, Texas, on July 3. He set up his base of operations in San Antonio and traveled widely in eastern and central Texas using a railroad pass. McVaugh noted, "His archaeological work, which was the primary purpose of his visit to Texas, kept him fully occupied, even though he found few ancient remains at many of the localities. . . . His most satisfactory sites were at Longview, which he worked in July, and near Georgetown, in October" (1956:79).

Putnam reported that Palmer observed no mounds in eastern Texas of the type found in the Mississippi Valley and no evidence of occupation by people other than recent Indian tribes. Palmer believed that several of the so-called Indian mounds were actually natural hills. He did find piles of burnt stone, about which Putnam quotes him as having written:

These piles of stone are found in many places in Texas where flint is abundant, the most noted place being Georgetown. In the ploughed field at Georgetown, where I obtained the large number of flint implements sent to you, there were formerly several of these piles, which were described as similar to those at Comfort, from which I have sent you specimens. Outside of the flint regions these stone piles are not found. I have concluded that the Indians made brush fires on the limestone rock containing the masses of flint which they desired to split. The limestone becoming heated, imparted its heat to the flint and thus in time, the continued heat of the brush fire, caused the flint to split into pieces various shapes and sizes convenient for use in the manufacture of implements. Perhaps the splitting of the flint was aided by throwing water on the rock while heated. I cannot attribute these piles of stone to any other cause than that here suggested. The fact that they are only found in the flint region and that they contain so many pieces and flakes of flint of all sizes, when considered in connection with the amount of labor saved by such a method of procuring flint of proper size for making implements, seems to me to warrant my conclusion that these piles of burnt stones show where and how the Indians of Texas obtained their flint. (Putnam 1880b:719–20)

Palmer and Putnam were wrong in their premature conclusion about a lack of mounds in eastern Texas. A number of Caddoan mounds have been excavated in the northeastern counties of the state, the best-known and most intensively investigated being at the George C. Davis site in Cherokee County (Newell and Krieger 1949; Story and Valastro 1977). Also, there are mounds in the Longview vicinity (Larry Banks, Hiram F. Gregory, and Timothy Perttula, 1986 personal communications).

Palmer's explanation of what are now called "Texas burnt rock middens" is almost certainly erroneous. Georgetown is on the eastern margin of the Edwards Plateau, which contains numerous outcrops of Cretaceous chert-bearing limestones, as he noted. Cherts are obtainable without going to the effort of fire-cracking limestone blocks, and they are of good quality, so that heat-treating is not necessary to make them knappable. Also, heat-treated artifacts are relatively rare in this region. These middens occur on alluvial terraces as well as limestone plateaus here, and although they were once collectively called "Archaic," they may also be much later, perhaps even protohistoric. Although there is still no consensus explanation of these features, many archeologists now think they were associated with preparation of vegetal foods (Larry Banks, 1986 personal communication).

It is curious that Palmer did not suggest the vegetal-food-preparation explanation, given his general interest in this subject and the fact that one of his notes on the Paiutes had dealt with hot-rock cooking of "greens or native plants," concluding that "piles of stones that have been used for this heating process are often met with in Utah and Nevada" (Heizer 1954:5).

Despite the erroneous conclusions, Palmer's work here represents yet another first; it was the earliest scientific archeology in these regions of Texas (Dee Ann Story, 1987 personal communication). No restudies of his collections or attempts to reidentify his sites have yet been accomplished.

Early in 1880, Palmer and others hired a coach for a trip to Monterrey, Mexico, which became his headquarters until mid-March, when he moved west to a base at Saltillo, Coahuila, for the rest of the summer. Much of this trip was concerned with botanical collections, especially in the mountains, but he also investigated prehistoric burial caves in Coahuila. Soon afterward, he summarized his observations in a six-page *American Naturalist* article, "Mexican Caves with Human Remains" (Palmer 1882), and the skeletal remains were described in a Peabody Museum *Annual Report* by Cordelia A. Studley (1884). Some of the preserved sandals from these caves were further described and illustrated by Mason (1896:358–61, Plates 7 and 9).

Palmer's (1882) paper began with a summary of the physical and biological environment, then described the mummified remains: their tightly flexed positions, preserved wrappings, clothing, sandals, ornaments, hair styles, wooden tools, basketry, bedding, and sparse (perhaps due to looting) pottery and bows and arrows. He paid particular attention to the uses of local plants and concluded that, although the contemporary Indians of that locality had been influenced "to some extent" by European culture, "one comes to the conclusion that they are the descendants of the cave people" (1882:308–09). He further stated, in a burst of enthusiasm:

> We are astounded in beholding their workmanship, they simply took nature's gifts and made the best of them. Comparing the cave clothing with that of the ancient Peruvians, we find a close alliance; both made by a hand-loom, the same as is used by the Indians of Peru, Mexico, Arizona, New Mexico and Southern California today. The rude Navajo Indian makes a blanket upon one of these hand-looms, which commands not only a good price from white men, but their admiration—yet he is considered a savage—lives in a hut. It is not necessary to live in palaces, in order to perform great works, and it is shown by our ancient and modern American Indians, that they were equal to emergencies, until compelled to face Europeans with their civilization. (1882:310)

In his concluding paragraphs, however, Palmer (1882:310–11) shifted to a discussion of his notions about "two races of Indians to-day, as there were in ancient times," though without specifically mentioning the Toltec-Aztec dichotomy. He made no reference to his (1877b) paper on this subject, and his remarks here would be difficult for the modern reader to follow without knowing that this is what he had in mind.

Studley's (1884) longer paper is a very thorough and competent report on the skeletal remains. She provided some additional details on the cave sites, including the information that Palmer had had to descend into the first cave "through a hole in the roof, by means of a rope." Studley's major emphasis was on the twenty-five crania that Palmer had recovered from the four caves, and she provided tables of detailed measurements of them. A pioneering woman in the fields of physical anthropology and archeology, she appears to have mastered the state-of-the-art craniological literature of the day, namely that of Paul Broca (1824–1880) and his students in France, and to have been well ahead of other American physical anthropologists, including Aleš Hrdlička (Jerome C. Rose, 1986 personal communication).

Palmer's work for the Peabody Museum was cut short by pecuniary problems; after summarizing Palmer's 1879 work in Mexico and Texas, Putnam had noted, "It is to be regretted that, for want of funds, Dr. Palmer will be obliged to discontinue his investigations when so much of importance could be obtained by extending his field work into southwestern Texas and the adjoining parts of Mexico, a region of which the archaeology is yet unknown" (1880:720).

Return to Cambridge. In late September 1880, Palmer left Coahuila for Texas; he spent most of October there, and returned to Cambridge in mid-November. He remained there over the winter and through the spring of 1881, working with his collections. According to Putnam (1882a:69–70), during this period Palmer gave a talk to the Natural History Society of Boston about the materials recovered from the Mexican caves. It was almost certainly during this period that he wrote his article about the caves.

It must have also been at this time that Palmer wrote a brief note entitled "The Sacrificial Stone of the City of Mexico, is it Genuine or Not?" which was published in the September 1881 issue of *American Naturalist*. This was another example of his penchant for proposing alternative explanations for artifacts on public display (cf. Palmer 1875a, 1875b). The stone in question was said by Palmer to have been crudely altered by the Spanish. Once again his notions about the Aztecs, and his prejudices against them and the Spanish, came to the fore when he wrote that the Aztecs were, like "their kin the Apache, the Yuma, Mojave and others, plain, simple Indians, not fond of the pageantry attributed to them by the conquerors, who must fictitiously give them importance in order to throw reflected greatness upon their conquest" (Palmer 1881:753–54).

Meanwhile, in early 1881, Spencer Baird of the Smithsonian Institution began corresponding with Palmer about the plans for the Mound Survey and the possibilities of Palmer's employment on that project. The surviving documents from that correspondence are presented in the next chapter.

It is important to note that at this point, just before his Mound Survey employment, Palmer was at his peak, with a generally excellent reputation as a collector and pioneering investigator (but perhaps not as a critical scholar) among botanists, zoologists, and archeologists (McVaugh 1956:84). McVaugh reports that Palmer was the first to point out the destructive potential of the boll weevil (1956:81). An additional perspective on his achievements can be derived from McVaugh's summary of the major results of the expedition:

> The collections of 1879–80 are of primary importance. The archaeological materials, especially those from Coahuila, remain among the most important series ever to have come from this area. A total of 1,446 specimens was collected in 1879, and the collections of 1880 included 259 specimens from Coahuila (localities given are San Lorenzo Cave, Monclova Cave, Acatita Cave, and Coyote Cave) and 295 specimens from Texas. In addition to this imposing series of 2,000 specimens, Palmer collected approximately 17,000 specimens of plants. . . . (1956:81)

The Mound Survey Years (1881–84)

This period is, of course, the major subject of the present volume and will be examined in detail in later chapters. Here some general perspectives from his biographers will suffice. McVaugh was, as a biographer, disappointed in this period of Palmer's life, because Palmer wrote few letters. Though McVaugh stated that Palmer sent to Washington approximately two thousand individual collections, many of considerable interest, he called Palmer's work for the Bureau of Ethnology "haphazard" and said that it

> . . . for the most part was that of a preliminary or exploratory investigator. . . . He had neither the strength for excavation nor the patience and technical skill required for the meticulous dismemberment of the mounds according to the most approved practices, and so most of the mounds . . . were subsequently studied in detail by other workers. . . . Palmer's work is occasionally referred to (it seems to me without much warmth) in the comprehensive reports . . . by Professor Cyrus Thomas. . . . From comparison of Palmer's notes with published accounts of certain sites mentioned by Thomas, it is evident that the field work was done by Palmer although in most cases no credit is given him. (1956:85)

Safford called the results "satisfactory" but pointed out the financial and physical limitations Palmer worked under. He quotes Palmer:

> On my botanical excursions . . . I managed to get along with one assistant who helped me to collect and also to dry my plants. At the end of the day I could go over my collections, catalogue the plants by numbers, noting their color, odor or taste while still fresh, record their habitats, local names, and, if they were of economic

value, the uses to which they were applied. In my mound work I had to pay my diggers by the day out of my allowance, and I could not afford to suspend the work in order to make plats and descriptive notes of the articles unearthed; nor could I go over my specimens each night as I had done with my plants, for many of them were in fragments or so fragile that I dared not unwrap them after they had once been packed. I therefore shipped the cases to Washington, hoping to unpack them there and to make a descriptive catalogue of the specimens. In forwarding them I begged that the cases might be allowed to remain unpacked [*sic*] until my arrival, but my request met with a curt refusal from Mr. Cyrus Thomas, who had been put by Major Powell in charge of mound excavations, and who was most exacting in his requirements, expecting me alone to do work which would require a whole party of explorers including a surveyor and draughtsman. In acknowledging the arrival of my boxes he wrote to me as follows: "Notwithstanding your protests to the contrary (your boxes) have been opened, the contents properly cared for, marked with your name and the localities as far as known. You may be assured that in making up my annual report full and proper credit will be given in it for all that is collected or communicated by you. In fact I shall use your reports as far as they can be adapted to the plan of the work." Notwithstanding this assurance the result was as I feared. Instead of giving an account of my work as Professor Holmes [1884] had done in his admirable paper on my collection of 1881, which illustrated the handicraft and customs of the people found in the graves, the results of my work during the following year were referred to in scant, introductory paragraphs, in subsequent publications of the Bureau of Ethnology, and the specimens, distributed before my arrival, used to illustrate dissertations on various arts and in most cases without indication of the exact locality of their origin or an acknowledgement to their collector. This treatment contrasted sharply with that accorded me by distinguished botanists under whom I had served, who, in their published accounts of my collections, had not failed to pay a kindly tribute to my work, adding an incentive to my efforts and my enthusiasm by naming new species in my honor. (Safford 1926:479–81)

Aftermath (1884–85)

Palmer's work for the Mound Survey was effectively completed in May of 1884. On the twenty-sixth of that month, he arrived in Washington after four months of work in Alabama, Georgia, and South Carolina (McVaugh 1956:88, 345). The length of his stay in Washington is uncertain but may have been virtually a full month. On June 30, he arrived in Little Rock again for a final attempt to obtain the correct measurements of the major Knapp mounds (1956:345). This last task for the Mound Survey was done on the first day of the new fiscal year, July 1, with only limited success; the mounds had to be remeasured by W. H. Holmes (Rolingson 1982:72, 74).

Probably during his May-June stay in Washington, Palmer wrote another short note, which was published in the August 1885 issue of *American Naturalist*. It was entitled "Burnt Clay in the Mounds," and appears to have been his only publication drawing on his Mound Survey experiences, other than the posthumous 1917 publication of some of his Arkansas notes. The article is another example of misplaced analogy, in which he attempted to interpret Mississippi Valley prehistoric house remains by comparisons with house construction techniques he had seen Indians using in the Southwest. His Arkansas notes also contain repeated examples of this fallacy.

Palmer's activities after leaving the Mound Survey are generally less relevant for the purposes of this volume than those of his earlier years. Almost immediately after leaving Arkansas, he began working for Baird in another branch of the Smithsonian, to collect numerous specimens of "the varied animal resources of the coral reef and sponge regions of Southern and Western Florida" for the World's Industrial and Cotton Centennial Exposition, which was to open in December in New Orleans. He worked on this project from July to October, returned to Washington, and set up an ethnological collecting trip to the Southwest. From December 1884 to March 1885, he worked primarily among the Pima and other Indians of southern Arizona and adjacent Sonora. Bahr (1983: Figures 6 and 8) has recently published photographs of items—some balls used in kick-ball races and a basket—collected by Palmer from the Pima at this time.

Return to Botany (1885–93)

During the rest of 1885, 1886, and 1887, Palmer made three major trips to Mexico, primarily making botanical collections. He ranged over portions of Chihuahua, remote sections of Jalisco, and ended in the vicinity of Guaymas, Sonora. The Chihuahua expedition was conceived by Baird, who wanted Palmer to study the Tarahumara Indians, "an interesting tribe inhabiting caves and dwellings of the most primitive kind; with the object of comparing them with the Cliff Dwellers of Arizona and New Mexico" (Safford 1911a:351).

No comparative ethnological study seems to have come directly from this project, but it was ultimately quite significant in ethnobotanical, ethnomedical, and ethnopharmacological terms. In making plant collections in such situations, and in general,

> . . . his specimens [were] remarkable . . . for their completeness, showing when possible bark, root, wood and seed-pods or fruit, as well as leaves and flowers. He did not content himself with a single example, but in spite of difficulties would often bring a whole series, . . . knowing that the aspect of the foliage might vary on different parts of the same plant, and that entire plants might differ according to their situation. He accompanied the specimens by accurate notes as to locality, habitat and season, not disdaining to give local names however barbarous they might sound to ears tolerant only of classic Greek and Latin; and he noted the taste and odor of bark and wood and leaves as well as the color of flowers and the uses of fruits, seeds, herbs and roots, together with the virtues attributed to them by the simple natives, no matter how foolish such information might appear to the eyes of the learned. (Safford 1911a:353–54)

Robert Bye has used Palmer's data in a comparative study of Tarahumara and urban Mexican uses of plants sold in Mexican markets—where Palmer did much of his collecting and interviewing (Bye 1979a:135)—noting that plants that are effectively used by two cultural groups with different ethnomedical concepts "may be of interest for intensive research" (1986:103). And Bye noted that during this trip Palmer collected some of the earliest information from the Tarahumara on the use of the most famous North American hallucinogenic plant, peyote (1979b; cf. Safford 1911a:352).

Palmer's work around Guaymas was done for the U.S. Department of Agriculture, and as a result he obtained appointments to work as a field botanical collector for the Department's Division of Botany during the years from 1888 through 1893. His travels carried him to the mountains of California and eastern Arizona, and again into Baja

California and Sonora, plus the poorly known west Mexican states of Colima, Nayarit, and Sinaloa. A photograph of Palmer collecting in the latter state in 1891 was published by McVaugh (1956: facing page 335). His last field season under these auspices took him to a really new environment far to the north, on the Snake River Plains of southern Idaho.

Palmer's Last Years (1894–1911)

By this time, Palmer was approaching what is now widely considered mandatory retirement age. He made eleven more trips to Mexico, where he spent an increasing amount of time studying the plants available in the city markets, as well as one short trip to Cuba, but lived primarily in Washington.

McVaugh also quoted one of Palmer's younger colleagues, who was with him in Acapulco in the winter of 1894–95, who described him as "not strong but active, and continuously at work, pressing and changing blotters during long hours, joking and talking with the other guests at the hotel" (1956:109).

Between trips to the south Palmer found temporary employment before and after the turn of the century as an "expert" with the Department of Agriculture and the Bureau of Plant Industry in Washington, primarily working with his own collections and notes. He also continued to sell specimens from his expedition collections to various institutions.

On May 14, 1904, just before leaving on another trip to San Luis Potosi, Palmer signed and filed his last will and testament. The complete text is given by McVaugh (1956:400–02).

From March to September 1906, Palmer was in the Mexican state of Durango:

> . . . His collections and travels in Durango were remarkable ones for a man seventy-five years old; the former in fact have not been surpassed in interest by any other collections from that part of Mexico. As soon as he reached the city of Durango he made plans to go to Tepehuanes, at the end of the railroad about 150 kilometers northwest of Durango, "to see what is there." From Tepehuanes he made a strenuous trip to the mine called San Ramon, a project which entailed a four-day ride on horseback each way. On his return he was enthusiastic, and ready for another excursion: "I returned two days ago . . . the only way to get to that place is on horse back four long days ride each way . . . am going by team to morrow to a box canyon 9 miles." (McVaugh 1956:117)

Palmer's next trip was to Tamaulipas, from January to June 1907. He spent the summer in Washington and again worked as an "expert" with the Bureau of Plant Industry from late October until the end of January 1908. This may have been his last official employment in such a capacity. From late March to late June 1908, he worked in Chihuahua, especially at the city market. He probably was back in Washington for most of the rest of that year and 1909.

In December 1909 Palmer began his last collecting trip, from Washington to Tampico, Tamaulipas. He stayed there until June 1910, having collected nearly six hundred specimens. Little is known of his final months, as McVaugh noted, since he wrote very few letters (1956:122).

On January 10, 1911, the Botanical Society of Washington met to celebrate Palmer's eightieth birthday. At the meeting, Palmer's colleague and biographer William E. Safford read the biographical sketch that was published at about the time of Palmer's death (Safford 1911a). In an obituary, he noted that:

> During the meeting of the society Dr. Palmer was seated in the place of honor, and at the close of the exercises he was presented with an appropriate birthday gift as a token of the appreciation of the members of the society of his important life-work. The venerable traveler received the congratulations of those present with tears streaming down his cheeks, doubtless realizing that this must be his valedictory. (1911b:62)

A somewhat romanticized—if not maudlin—description of Palmer's last days appears to have been added to the version of the biographical sketch Safford published:

> And now, as his busy life is nearing its close, enfeebled by hardships and almost incessant physical suffering, he sits close to the fire with his great coat around him. His last set of plants has been disposed of. Is his task finished? He can not bear to think so. He had planned to do so much more. As he closes his eyes he has visions of palm trees reflecting their crests in the still lagoon; or perhaps he hears the tinkling of bells as flocks of goats wander across the sunny plain and climb rocky hillsides dotted with cactus, maguey and yuccas; or perhaps he is once more among pines and oaks on a mountain top, or in moist forests gathering orchids and creeping arums. His old enthusiasm comes back; his pulse throbs with renewed vigor. No, the end is not yet. Once more he prepares his pack; his staff stands in the corner. He unfolds the map. To-morrow he will start off, but to what fresh field he can not yet decide. (1911a:354)

Edward Palmer died in Washington on April 10, 1911. He was buried in Rock Creek Cemetery (McVaugh 1956:400). Of Safford's three obituary notices published in scientific journals that year (1911a, 1911b, 1911c), the first two were accompanied by an excellent photograph of Palmer as a kindly-looking old man (McVaugh 1956: facing p. 302).

Palmer's death was not overlooked by the anthropological profession. The *American Anthropologist* published an obituary notice, written by Smithsonian anthropologist Walter Hough (1911), in its "Anthropologic Miscellanea" section. It contained a brief summary of Palmer's career:

> **Edward Palmer.**—Dr Edward Palmer, for more than two generations an assiduous collector in ethnology and natural history, died on April 10, 1911. His work was confined principally to the Southwestern United States and Mexico, although during his long period of service he gleaned in many fields. The value of his collections lies in the early period of their acquisition and the care with which the data and the method of securing them were recorded.
>
> Dr Palmer made the first exploration of an ancient pueblo ruin, in 1873, a mound at St George, Utah, which he thoroughly searched, preserving every fragment of evidence that came under his trowel and carrying out the exploration with a skill and perfection of method that have not been surpassed in that field. This work was followed by archeological excavations on the lower Verde River in Arizona. His connection with the United States army in the west as Assistant Surgeon took him among the wilder tribes of the frontier and at this period he collected some of the most unique specimens ever obtained from the Apache.
>
> Many branches of biology are indebted to Dr Palmer for first class material and

the number of new species that rewarded his zeal is surprising. His ethnological material, to which he constantly added, is accounted among the most valuable in the United States National Museum.

Except in the earlier years, he did not publish his researches, being satisfied with the rewards of a diligent collector, who does his part well in adding to the stores of science.

It is perhaps noteworthy that once again Palmer's contributions to the Mound Survey were not mentioned. Hough was certainly well qualified to evaluate Palmer's ethnological collections, though; he had served from 1884 to 1908 as assistant to the curator of the Division of Ethnology in the Smithsonian's National Museum (Hinsley 1981:84, 94).

But the final words should be reserved for Palmer's botanical colleagues and successors. Safford noted that "scarcely a monograph of a family or genus appears, including representatives in Mexico and the southwestern United States, but among the species described are new ones based upon types collected by Edward Palmer" (1911:354). And McVaugh concluded that "he added no small amount to the total of scientific knowledge, and we may hope that he was sufficiently repaid for the decision he made in his youth, to 'spend his life in the prosecution of science' in the ways for which he was best fitted" (1956:122).

H. J. Lewis

For about two months at the end of 1882 (and the first few days of 1883), Edward Palmer was assisted in his work for the Mound Survey by a black artist named Henry Jackson Lewis. Little is known about Lewis, but that little suffices to demonstrate that he was a remarkable man in his own right. A very brief summary statement about him was included in a May 26, 1883, *Frank Leslie's Illustrated Newspaper* article about Palmer's work in Arkansas (see chapter 9).

Although the text of the article states that the sketches were made *by* Lewis, the caption reads "From Sketches by H. J. Lewis," and it is clear that the latter wording is correct. It is also obvious from an examination of Lewis's surviving original drawings that the redrawing was done in a more sensational manner. The most blatant example is the impossible exaggeration of the vertical dimension of Menard Mound A in the re-drawing by *Leslie's* anonymous artist; this and the other drawings in that article will be discussed in a later chapter.

Early Life

The year of Lewis's birth is every bit as uncertain as Palmer's, and the month and day are completely unknown. About all that can be concluded at this point, lacking a birth certificate or census data, is that Lewis was most probably born in the mid- to late 1840s, but possibly in the early to mid-1850s.

It is quite likely that he was born in the delta country of northwest Mississippi, which had a large black slave population and is near the lower Arkansas River and Memphis regions, which he appears to have frequented before meeting Palmer. Nothing is known of his early life, but at least by the mid- to late 1870s, he appears to have moved to Pine Bluff, in eastern Arkansas.

Early Published Work

The earliest example I have found of Lewis's work was in the January 11, 1879, issue of *Harper's Weekly,* which published (on p. 25) an engraving of a "Scene at Pine Bluff Station, Arkansas" and credited it as derived from a sketch by H. J. Lewis. The brief accompanying text stated that the drawing showed "the accumulation of cotton at a railway station in Arkansas since the raising of the recent fever quarantine."

Four more illustrations based on Lewis sketches were published in the March 8, 1879, issue of *Harper's* (on p. 187) and collectively labeled "Scenes at Pine Bluff, Arkansas.—From Sketches by H. J. Lewis." Three of these four illustrations were reproduced in a recent history of Pine Bluff and Jefferson County by a regional historian, James W. Leslie (1981:59).

At least one more widely-known *Harper's* 1879 illustration was derived from a Lewis original. It appeared in the August 16 issue, was captioned "En Route For Kansas—Fleeing From The Yellow Fever—Drawn by Sol Eytinge, Jun., from a sketch by H. J. Lewis" and was not accompanied by any text. It depicts a black extended family proceeding westward with a mule and wagon and a cow. This illustration was also reproduced (without attribution to either Lewis or Eytinge) in *A Pictorial History of Blackamericans,* by Langston Hughes et al. (1983:217), who added the information that the travelers were "Louisiana freedmen." It is also the earliest Lewis-derived work cited by Igoe's bibliography (1981:217).

No drawings by Lewis or based on his work have been found for the period between late 1879 and late 1882. But, virtually on the eve of his association with Palmer, on October 25, 1882, the *Pine Bluff Commercial* published the following brief item as one of a series of one-paragraph entries under the heading "Additional Local News" on page 4: "J. H. Lewis, the caricaturist and pencil artist is still aboard in Pine Bluff. His sketches of both imaginary and real scenes, are wonderfully correct and we bespeak for him a brilliant and successful future in his line of business."

Work with Palmer

Although none of the studies of black artists I have consulted mention Lewis's work for Palmer and the Mound Survey, this collection, now curated in the Smithsonian's National Anthropological Archives, probably constitutes the major extant set of Lewis originals.

It is not clear precisely how Lewis came to work with Palmer, but it may be at least conjectured that they met in or near Memphis on or shortly after November 6, 1882. Palmer had traveled from Forrest City, Arkansas, by mule team and boat to Memphis, probably on November 6. From all indications Lewis's first work for Palmer was done at the Bradley's Landing site, just upstream and across the Mississippi from Memphis, most likely late in the first week of November. Palmer, and probably Lewis, then traveled by rail from Memphis to Little Rock, thence to Pine Bluff, arriving perhaps as early as November 11.

On or about November 13, 1882, Palmer wrote, "Henry J. Lewis is entitled to the thanks of the Bureau of Ethnology." Palmer usually used the phrase "entitled to thanks" to suggest official acknowledgment of gifts of artifacts, but there is no indication that Lewis had made any such gift.

Palmer appears to have been in and around Pine Bluff for about ten days, from about November 11 to about November 21. However, no site visits at all are recorded for that period in his notes, and there are no Lewis drawings of sites in the Pine Bluff vicinity. This lengthy and unproductive stay was apparently due to bad weather.

Palmer's last entry for this stay in Pine Bluff was dated November 20; he and Lewis may have left by train as early as the next day for southeast Arkansas. Palmer's next dated entry documents his arrival on November 22 at Winchester Station with "my colored man." However, undated entries describe test excavations at the Walnut Lake and Choctaw mounds on the railroad line between Pine Bluff and Winchester. Lewis drew both of these mounds, and it is likely that he and Palmer spent November 21 there.

The last week of November was taken up by the investigations at the Taylor and Tillar mound sites, which were highly productive in terms of drawings. On November 29 Palmer sent Powell four boxes of Tillar and Taylor specimens, promising the drawings later. On December 2 he sent a fifth box of specimens and a brief letter to Powell from Pine Bluff.

Palmer's travels during December are difficult to reconstruct, due to undated entries, but it is certain that during the first week he and Lewis traveled to Arkansas City. From or en route to that base, they visited several Desha County sites, which they described and illustrated.

There are no dated entries at all by Palmer between December 6 and December 25. At least a week or so of this time span, though, must have been taken up by Palmer's fairly extensive investigations and test excavations, plus at least six Lewis drawings, at the Menard and Wallace mound sites in southern Arkansas County.

On Christmas Day 1882 Palmer arrived at the Knapp or Toltec Mounds southeast of North Little Rock, beginning an investigation that may have lasted about four days. Lewis produced another five drawings there, one of which has been lost.

An engraving of Lewis and Palmer, "Assorting the Relics of Knapp Mound's," appeared in the 1883 Leslie's article. It has been published by Rolingson in her recent volume on the Toltec Mounds site (1982: Figure 48). The Leslie's artist probably worked from a Lewis sketch that included a self-portrait, but the original has not been found. The Leslie's version, however, does not resemble an 1889 self-portrait of Lewis very closely (fig. 2.5).

On December 29, again from Pine Bluff, Palmer sent a letter to Thomas, stating that he was sending "by Express" a package containing "numerous mound drawings & notes." He added that " . . . many mound pictures [along the St. Francis and Mississippi rivers] could be made provided you desire me to continue the man that makes the drawings." With regard to his immediate plans, Palmer stated that he wished to visit "one place more on the Arkansaw [River]" and that he could be written to at Arkansas City.

While awaiting Thomas's reply, Palmer and Lewis traveled southeast of Pine Bluff, arriving at Heckatoo on the Arkansas River on January 3, 1883. They stayed there at least until January 8, losing about three days to "wet & miserable" weather. Nevertheless, they made brief visits to Smith's Mound, the Adams Mound, and Sarassa Mounds; Lewis made drawings of the latter two. It appears that from Heckatoo they went upstream to Garretson's Landing on or about January 8. From that base, they made brief forays to the Howson Mounds and Smuggs Mound; Lewis produced drawings of each.

Apparently on January 9, they went a short distance inland to Linwood Station, probably visiting the Waldstein Mounds en route. An unlabeled drawing by Lewis fits Palmer's description of these mounds and is therefore probably the last drawing Lewis made for Palmer. From the Linwood-Garretson's Landing locality, they traveled by freight train in cold winter weather to Arkansas City, arriving at one a.m. on January 10. Later that day Palmer received "letters relating to discontinueing my man" from Cyrus Thomas, plus a telegram apparently to the same effect. He replied, "I pay him off tomorrow. My object in having him was to try and show clearly the mounds and their surroundings."

In summary, Lewis was associated with Palmer in Arkansas over a period of slightly more than two months, during which he produced at least thirty-eight pencil drawings. Thirty-one of these have survived; the general nature of five others is known from surviving versions re-drawn by Holmes. It is not clear whether or not Lewis did much work for Palmer other than drawings; there seems to be no indication of this in Palmer's notes, which only refer to him as "my colored artist," "the man that makes the drawings," etc.

Baird, in his report as secretary of the Smithsonian Institution for 1882, remarked, "Dr. Palmer had with him for a month an excellent artist who has furnished a number of very valuable drawings of mounds and other works . . ." (1884:44).

Later Work

After being paid off by Palmer, Lewis appears to have traveled down the Mississippi and resumed his former trade of doing free-lance drawings for submission to various publications. At this writing I have found only three additional pictures from this phase of his life, despite an intensive search. All three were published by *Frank Leslie's Illustrated Newspaper,* even before the publication of the article about Palmer's work.

Two engraved illustrations "from sketches by H. J. Lewis" were published in the April 14, 1883, issue of *Leslie's,* accompanied by a brief story under the headline "The Mississippi Floods" and depicting the inundation of Water Proof, Louisiana, and Greenville, Mississippi.

The next issue of *Leslie's* (April 21, 1883) included another engraving (fig. 2.4) based on a Lewis sketch, with another brief article, headed "Another Louisiana Town Inundated." The text described the flooding of Troyville, Louisiana, now known as Jonesville, and pointed out six Indian mounds rising above the water. This drawing of the famous Troyville mound group has apparently never been republished in an archeological report before now (Robert W. Neuman, 1987 personal communication). The "great mound" at Troyville, shown looming behind the flooded buildings, was destroyed in 1931–32 but was partly salvaged by Winslow Walker, whose (1936) report remains the basic data source.

The mound used as a cemetery was measured in 1896 as being two hundred feet long and ninety feet wide (1936:12). The "great mound" had been described by early nineteenth-century explorers as a "stupendous turret" capped by a "great cone" and totaling about eighty feet in height (1936:6). It was severely damaged during the Civil War "by having the summit cone virtually cut down to provide space for a rifle pit" (1936:9).

It is quite possible that Palmer accompanied Lewis to the Troyville site, even though they were no longer officially working together. According to McVaugh (1956:248), Palmer went by steamboat from Natchez, during a flood period in February or early March

FIGURE 2.4

The 1883 flood at Troyville, Louisiana, showing the prehistoric mounds (engraving, after a sketch by H. J. Lewis, from Frank Leslie's Illustrated Newspaper, *April 21, 1883).*

1883, to the "Junction of Black Washita and the Tensaw Rivers" and sent materials to the Smithsonian from the Troyville site. It is also possible that Palmer and Lewis joined forces again at Greenville; Palmer was there about March 19–20, 1883 (1956:215, 340), or immediately before the levee broke, according to the April 14 *Leslie's* article.

One additional picture published in *Leslie's* was based on a Lewis drawing. This engraving immediately followed the pictures of mound explorations in the May 26, 1883, issue but had its own accompanying text, headed "An Arkansas River Tow," which described a ferry boat towing a barge at Rob Roy Ferry. Rob Roy is a community that still exists on the north margin of the Arkansas River flood plain, a few miles downstream from Pine Bluff. It is not mentioned in Palmer's extant notes. This nonarcheological drawing is reminiscent of Lewis's earlier work for *Harper's* and may indicate that he had returned to free-lance work from his Pine Bluff home base.

The 1883–88 Lost Years

There is virtually no evidence of Lewis's activities over the next five years. It does appear that he continued to live in Pine Bluff, probably until late 1888. The 1883–84 edition of the Pine Bluff city directory listed "Lewis, Henry J., colored. Residence N.W. corner Sevier." And his obituary in the *Indianapolis Journal* (April 11, 1891 issue) stated that he "came to this city from Pine Bluff, Ark., two and a half years ago."

Lewis's obituaries stated that he had sold drawings to periodicals such as *Puck* and *Judge* during his career. But an intensive search of these journals and *Leslie's* for these "lost years" has failed to locate any more examples of his work.

The First Black Political Cartoonist:
Work for The Freeman, *1888–91*

Two of Lewis's obituaries stated that he left Arkansas in late 1888 and went to work as a cartoonist and artist for *The Freeman,* a black weekly newspaper in Indianapolis. He has been called the "first Black political cartoonist" (Spradling 1980:593) on the basis of this work.

The Freeman had been founded in 1886; in this first incarnation, it appeared rather staid, with neat columns of type and essentially no illustrations. In mid-1888 it was taken over by Edward E. Cooper, who set about converting it into "A National Illustrated Colored Newspaper," which he described as "the Harper's Weekly of the Colored Race" (Gatewood 1979:223). Hiring Lewis was clearly in line with his plans.

The earliest surviving *Freeman* work signed by Lewis was a two-panel cartoon that appeared at the top of page 8 in the February 2, 1889, issue. It depicted scenes in Washington, D.C., including Uncle Sam, the newly inaugurated President Benjamin Harrison, a black office-seeker, and two white racists. The caption, quite probably written by Cooper, said that the artist "doesn't think it too soon for the Negro to have a place in the Cabin(et) or any other part of the ship of State. . . . He does not like to see first class colored men put off while third rate people of other races are rewarded."

Lewis's cartoons and other artwork appeared regularly in *The Freeman* during the remainder of 1889. Outstanding examples include a sequence entitled "Time and Prejudice," in which Father Time removes the devilish figure of Prejudice from black-white social relations; depictions of lynchings and other atrocities in the South; portraits, including a remarkable self-portrait in the July 13 issue (fig. 2.5); a rebus; cartoons poking fun at the foibles of "colored" folk; and, perhaps most significantly, a number of cartoons attacking the racial policies of the newly elected President Benjamin Harrison and his administration. His last cartoon of 1889, in the December 21 issue, depicted a black Santa Claus bearing gifts and holiday greetings.

However, Lewis apparently did not have any further work published by *The Freeman* for about the next seven months. The reasons for this gap are undocumented and uncertain at this writing, but circumstantial evidence suggests that political and economic factors may have been involved. The 1890 work of Lewis's successor as *The Freeman's* principal artist, Moses Tucker, was politically innocuous as far as the Harrison administration was concerned. And, after Lewis's work reappeared in August 1890, it also tended to be noncontroversial with regard to national politics. It is certainly not beyond the realm of possibility that political-economic pressures had been brought to bear on the financially troubled *Freeman* by friends of the Harrison administration (Harrison himself, of course, was from Indiana).

Lewis's work continued to appear regularly in *The Freeman* through the end of 1890 and the first three months of 1891. One two-panel cartoon, in the January 10, 1891, issue, did depict a black man, "The People's Embassador," being kept away from the White House by "Prejudice," shown as a huge, vicious dog. Perhaps significantly, the White House's occupant was drawn as Uncle Sam, rather than Benjamin Harrison.

Lewis's last published work for *The Freeman,* and quite possibly the last work of his life, was an excellent architectural drawing of the then-new St. Paul A.M.E. Church in St. Louis, which appeared on page 3 of the March 28, 1891, issue.

FIGURE 2.5

H. J. Lewis (self-portrait), from The Freeman, *July 13, 1889, page 2.*

Obituaries

H. J. Lewis died in Indianapolis, on the morning of April 9 or 10, 1891. The cause of death was given as "pneumanitus" on his death certificate (Marion County, Indiana, Division of Public Health, Death Record Volume 6, p. 195). The death certificate also stated that he was buried in Mt. Jackson, Indiana.

Several Indianapolis newspapers published obituaries that generously assessed his work. Both the *Indianapolis Journal* (April 11, 1891) and *The Freeman* (April 18,1891) called Lewis a genius. *The Freeman* also stated:

> Mr. Lewis, in many respects, was a remarkable man, and had his lines been cast in different places, and his earlier years been spent under different skies, surrounded by other influences and aids, the space he would have filled in the world's notice might have been one that biography would not have spurned, and without the record of which, future encyclopedias would be incomplete.

CHAPTER THREE

The Early Stages
of the Mound Survey

Preliminary Correspondence (January–June 1881)

Edward Palmer spent the period from mid-November of 1880 through the spring of 1881 in and around Cambridge, Massachusetts, mainly assisting the Peabody Museum staff in the cataloging of his collections from Mexico and Texas. Just as funding was exhausted for this project (Putnam 1880b:720; 1881:21), a prospect for federal funding appeared. Spencer F. Baird, who had been receiving specimens from Palmer since at least 1857 (McVaugh 1956:14), and who had seized the opportunity to turn Palmer into a full-time, all-purpose collector in the Southwest in 1869 (1956:41), had become the second secretary of the Smithsonian Institution in 1878. As discussed in chapter 1, he now took the opportunity to expand the Smithsonian's National Museum of Natural History collections and clearly saw Palmer as a potential key member of his collecting team.

The Baird letters are quoted here not from the originals themselves but from typed copies on file at the National Anthropological Archives. They do not bear Baird's signature, and in several cases his middle initial is mistyped as "W." Palmer's replies to Baird's letters have not been found, but his major points can be at least partially inferred from Baird's responses. Palmer's first notice of the new opportunity came in the following letter:

SMITHSONIAN INSTITUTION

Washington, D. C. Jan. 13, 1881

Dear Doctor.

I am very strongly inclined to avail myself of your services as an explorer of antiquities, whenever the funds are at my command, & I have asked for an appropriation from Congress, to enable this work to be done. If you can stave off a decision in the matter until about the 4th of March, I can tell you exactly what I can do, during the present year.

Of course, if the Peabody Academy wants to keep you going, I have no right to interfere, as they have the first claim. But I should be sorry to have you take service with any other parties until I can say positively whether I can give you a commission.

In view of the increased scope of our museum, I shall want not simply antiquities & illustrations of modern life, & food, but also all the industrial products derived from the vegetable kingdom in the way of gums, roots, dyes, etc.

Sincerely yours,

Spencer W. Baird

Dr. Edward Palmer,
    Peabody Museum,
      Cambridge.

The actual decision-making progress extended well beyond March 4 and was not finally settled until June. Palmer did not start his field work until early July, just after the beginning of the next fiscal year. Baird's concept of multi-purpose collecting, similar to that which Palmer had done for him in the Southwest and for the Peabody Museum in Mexico, was followed only during Palmer's earliest work in this new position in the Cherokee country and was abandoned as the research focused on prehistoric mounds in regions where the Indians had been moved out.

The next Baird letter on file is dated more than a month after the first:

SMITHSONIAN INSTITUTION

Washington, D. C., Feb. 23, 1881.

Dear Dr. Palmer:

I have been too busy to answer your last letter earlier, and even now I cannot do it very well, as I must wait to see the action of Congress in reference to the appropriation. Should I be able to employ you as an explorer, I should, of course want to control the collections of archaeology and zoology.

I do not think the Agricultural Department would insist on controlling everything; but while wanting the best series would be willing to share the surplus with others; especially as I would secure to you a better return for your labor. It will be quite in accordance with the necessity of the case to defer any positive action until April; & this might give time to discuss the whole subject very fully. In the meantime, please give me a sketch of several of the different regions you would like to explore, either singly or successively, the object being in the first place, to increase our important archaeological collections; & then the botanical and zoological.

There is some prospect that Dr. Belding will go to Lower California, partly in the interest of the Smithsonian, & partly on his own account.

Very truly yours,

Spencer F. Baird,

Dr. Edward Palmer,
    Peabody Museum,
      Cambridge,
        Mass.

As noted in chapter 1, the appropriation for the Bureau of Ethnology was considered by the House of Representatives on February 24—the day after this letter was written—

and in an amendment five thousand dollars of the Bureau's twenty-five thousand dollar appropriation was set aside for "archaeological investigations relating to mound-builders, and prehistoric mounds." It is of some interest that, in this letter at least, Baird presented the major goal of the project as increasing archeological collections, rather than solving the riddle of the Mound-Builders. Baird's request that Palmer should suggest regions for exploration was reemphasized in his next letter.

The Department of Agriculture, whatever its interests in this potential project may have been, seems to have dropped out of the picture as the emphasis on archeology became more definite. Palmer may have been negotiating with this department in the hope of augmenting his income by dealing with multiple sponsors, as he had done successfully in Mexico after his unfortunate experience with Parry. The "Dr. Belding" Baird referred to was Lyman Belding (1829–1917), an eminent California ornithologist and naturalist (Joseph Ewan, 1986 personal communication). Palmer probably knew Belding from his work in that state.

Within a month, Baird wrote Palmer again:

SMITHSONIAN INSTITUTION

Washington, D. C. March 18, 1881.

Dear Dr. Palmer.

I am now prepared, I think, to arrange, before long for some explorations in archaeological work under your charge, & would like to know something of the character of your previous financial relations to the Peabody Museum. If I am not mistaken, they gave you a certain sum of money which was to last as long as it would go, in the way of personal salary, travelling expenses, hire of labor, etc. Will you tell me just how this is & how long a given sum met your requirements?

I am inclined, for various reasons that I can explain hereafter, to have you go into some state, say Tennessee & carry on researches among the mounds, as diligently & sedulously as possible, making notes of what you find as you go along. With this, possibly you might combine the work of picking up suitable specimens of forest timber for the collection which Prof. Sargent is making for the New York Museum.

The appropriation out of which the cost of your work would be paid is specifically for the exploration of mounds. If you know any better locality for mounds than that suggested, let me hear from you in regard to it.

Yours very truly,

Spencer W. Baird.

Dr. Edward Palmer,
     Peabody Museum,
          Cambridge, Mass.

By this time, of course, the congressional appropriation had been approved. Here the focus on a specific kind of archeology, "the exploration of mounds," has become explicit, and botanical collections are fading into the status of something that might "possibly" be done. "Prof. Sargent" was Charles Sprague Sargent (1841–1927), who was then director of the Arnold Arboretum at Harvard and had previously paid Palmer for specimens from Mexico (McVaugh 1956:74).

It is probably quite significant that Baird asked the well-traveled Palmer to suggest a "better locality for mounds" than Tennessee. Since none of the correspondence to this point had mentioned Arkansas, it is very likely that Palmer's response did, particularly in view of Baird's next letter:

SMITHSONIAN INSTITUTION

Washington, D. C., April 12, 1881

Dear Doctor Palmer:

I have been talking over, with Major Powell, the matter of your engagement, & we propose to assign to you one thousand dollars from the funds at our command, for which you are to give, say eight months of services, in exploring mounds. This amount would include your own pay and the expenses of the work. We would like you to go to Tennessee as soon as you can get away conveniently, & stay there until the weather is sufficiently healthy in Arkansas to proceed to work. If you find you can remain through the winter in Arkansas, then we will make an additional grant. Please let us know if this is satisfactory to you. If you think eight months' service is too much we will call it seven; but I would like to have something definite.

We propose to make a somewhat similar arrangement with another explorer who has been very eloquent as to what he can do. We shall assign him to another field, so as to have the benefit of a comparison of results, which I have no doubt will be in your favor. It will be perfectly agreeable to me to have you combine with these operations, the gathering of samples of wood for Prof. Sargent, with the understanding that you do not allow the new venture to materially interfere with your work in the old. Between the two I think you could make a comfortable support. We will consider the matter further in regard to operations in other sections; but we now wish to simply make a beginning at some point and see how much of a result we can command.

I think we can arrange matters to have you begin, say the early part of May. For the sake of saving trouble in regard to accounts, we would pay you a monthly salary of $125 for the eight months.

I do not know that it will be necessary for you to come to Washington. You need no instruction from us beyond that, to make careful notes of all the mounds you examine, so as to furnish data for an article, making diagrams illustrating the relative positions of the relics, & of the different strata,—being careful to note their relation to the remains you may detect.

We shall wish you to use your best endeavors to obtain any specimens you may find in the hands of the people, with the privilege of paying moderate sums for single series or specimens; this to be in addition to your allowance; & to notify us of the extent and character, with the price of any collections you may find that are purchaseable.

Very truly yours,

Spencer F. Baird.

Dr. Edward Palmer,
   Cambridge,
      Mass.

This letter is the first record of Powell's involvement with Palmer's prospective employment. If the "mound amendment" to the congressional appropriation was indeed something of a surprise to him, perhaps he took all of March and the first portion of April to adjust and reach an agreement with Baird as to how to carry out the congressional mandate.

It is quite probable that Palmer himself was responsible for selecting Arkansas as an especially promising area for mound explorations. He certainly would have been aware of the numerous finds that had just been made in Arkansas mounds by Edwin Curtis for the Peabody Museum. Palmer's and Curtis's finds for the Peabody during 1879 had been described in successive paragraphs of the curator's report for that year (Putnam 1880b: 716–20), as would be their 1880 collections (Putnam 1881:18–22). Curtis had just died in December 1880 (1881:12); this, coupled with the Peabody's problems in funding such expeditions, would have created a vacuum to be filled in this archeological land of opportunity. Baird's mention of waiting for the weather to become "healthy" in Arkansas probably referred to both the oppressive summer heat in the delta country and the prevalence of malaria during the hot months.

The "eloquent" other explorer may have been Col. Philetus W. Norris or, less probably, James D. Middleton; both were eventually hired, along with Palmer, as regular assistants, and as Smith notes in chapter 1, Norris was actually paid more than Palmer for the 1882–83 fiscal year. Norris died in the line of duty, in early 1885, as a result of the malaria he had contracted in northeast Arkansas in 1882 (Baird 1885:68; Perttula and Price 1984:11).

Baird's suggestion of a sort of competition between field assistants points up his overweening interest in amassing collections—of artifacts in this case—and was followed up by a letter of December 17, 1881, in which he informed Palmer that ". . . so far, you lead the entire force of mound explorers." Palmer, in turn, used this as leverage to obtain additional reimbursement for some of his expenses (see the letters in chapter 6).

Baird's willingness—even eagerness—to purchase private collections of prehistoric artifacts is a reminder that we are here dealing with the nineteenth-century museum mentality that emphasized relics as ends in themselves. Archeologists have long since come to emphasize the painstaking recording of information about the stratigraphic and associational contexts of artifacts, as Baird was beginning to do. The purchase of private collections is now seriously denounced by professional archeologists, as it leads only to the destruction of sites and contexts by grave robbers and other untrained collectors.

Baird's instructions for notes and diagrams explicitly recognized publication, though only of "an article," as the ultimate goal. He clearly recognized the concepts of stratification and association, and these are also reflected in a number of Palmer's notes. Palmer tried to provide better diagrams by hiring H. J. Lewis in late 1882 but was ordered by Thomas to let Lewis go after only two months, apparently due to budgetary considerations.

Although the wood-collecting project for Sargent was still considered a definite possibility by Baird at this time, McVaugh found "no record that he actually carried on such work in addition to his regular duties" (1956:85).

Palmer replied immediately and received a prompt response:

SMITHSONIAN INSTITUTION

Washington, D. C., April 18, 1881.

Dear Doctor:

Yours of the 15th is to hand. I will write you before long more definitely about the plans of exploration and I can give you letters to parties in Tennessee who will tell you more about what can be done. I do not think it makes any difference where you go in that region, so that you do not take in any mound previously explored. Of any six mounds you may work at five and find nothing, while the sixth will be full of interesting things.

Yours truly,

S. F. Baird.

Dr. Edward Palmer,
    Peabody Museum,
       Cambridge,
          Mass.

Here Baird's emphasis is still on the things that might be found in the mounds, rather than on the mound-builder question. If Baird wrote Palmer "before long," the evidence is not in the "2400" file. Instead, the next communications that have been found, which may well have been the next that were sent, took place nearly two months later:

WESTERN UNION TELEGRAPH COMPANY.

Dated Washington D. C.   June 14 188
Received at Camb. Mass 15 via Boston 15
To Dr. Edward Palmer
        Peabody Museum

Come on whenever you are ready matter all arranged for the exploration.

S. F. Baird.

16 Dst.
   Collect 50¢ via Boston.

SMITHSONIAN INSTITUTION,

Washington, D. C. June 15, 1881.

Dear Doctor;

I telegraphed you last night to say that I am now ready to start on your work, and as now arranged with Major Powell, I propose to pay you $125 a month, and incidentals, this to include eight months' work. You can come on any time you please and discuss the plan of work. A single day here will answer the purpose.

Yours truly,

Spencer W. Baird.

Dr. Edward Palmer,
    Cambridge,
       Mass.

According to McVaugh (1956:159), Palmer left Cambridge for Washington around June 20. A week later, he received his letter of employment:

SMITHSONIAN INSTITUTION,

Bureau of Ethnology,
J.W. Powell, Director,
Washington, D. C., June 27, 1881.

Dr. Edward Palmer,
    Washington, D. C.

Sir:

You are hereby appointed a temporary Assistant of the Bureau of Ethnology at a monthly compensation of One hundred and twenty-five ($125.00) dollars, to date from June 1, 1881. This amount is to include your salary, expenses for traveling, cost of excavations and all incidental expenses; and the appointment will extend to January 31, 1882.—

Your field of investigation will be the mounds of Tennessee and Arkansas. Within the area thus designated you will select such districts as you may deem wise.

In making researches the following objects should be held in view:

1. To make a collection of skeletons, especially crania found entombed in the mounds or stone graves.

2. To make a collection of all works of art in stone, copper, clay, or other material.

3. To give a description of the mounds, including size, form and topographic position.

As fast as collections are made they shold be carefully packed in boxes accompanied by labels giving a sufficient description of each find, and the boxes should be forwarded as freight or express to J. W. Powell, Director of the Bureau of Ethnology, Smithsonian Institution, Washington, D.C.

At each shipment a catalogue of the collection sent should be transmitted by mail to the same address.

At the end of each month a report of progress should be made to this office.—

Enclosed I send a copy of General Orders, No 65, Headquarters of the Army, Series of 1879, in reference to the shipment of specimens, &c.—

I am.

Yours respectfully,

J. W. Powell,
Director.

(One enclosure).

Ethnological Collections from the Cherokees (July 1881)

Palmer left Washington around June 30 (McVaugh 1956:344). Despite Powell's specification of mounds as his "field of investigation," his first collecting stop, around July 10, was at one of the principal "council house" villages of the Cherokees. This was Yellow Hill, which is now Cherokee, the site of the Cherokee Reservation headquarters, at the eastern margin of the Great Smoky Mountains in southwestern North Carolina (1956:86, 265, 350). McVaugh only noted that he "secured a number of examples of [Cherokee] handiwork" and "a few plants," but Safford provides details of the many items Palmer collected, including cane baskets and sieves, hickory bowls and arrows, magnolia spoons and bowls, blow guns, stone axe heads, pipes and pottery, and balls and racquets (1926:471–74).

Palmer's collection from the Cherokees was summarized by raw material categories and catalog numbers by Holmes (1884:434–37).

Mound Excavations in Tennessee (July–October 1881)

About July 15, Palmer crossed into Tennessee (possibly going down the valley of the French Broad River) and began his mound excavations in earnest. His work here could be summarized succinctly by quoting Safford (1926:471) who said that " . . . he opened many mounds, some of them containing remarkable objects." Holmes (1883:214–303), in his *magnum opus* on "Art in Shell of the Ancient Americans," described and illustrated a number of Palmer's Tennessee finds. The next year, Holmes devoted some thirty pages to summarizing Palmer's work and findings in Tennessee (1884:438–67).

Cyrus Thomas, however, appears generally to have ignored or downplayed the work Palmer did before Thomas joined the Bureau of Ethnology in 1882. Palmer had been officially designated by Powell to investigate "the mounds of Tennessee and Arkansas" on behalf of the Bureau and had been commended by Holmes in the Bureau's *Third Annual Report* for his "marked success" and "fine collection" in his 1881 mound investigations (1884:433). But, although Thomas's "Catalogue of Prehistoric Works" (1891) often included summary statements such as "Reported by Dr. Edward Palmer," his 1894 final report discussions seem at times to have studiously avoided any mention of Palmer and his first-season finds.

A summary of Palmer's 1881 itinerary has been provided by McVaugh (1956:330–31):

> . . . Palmer investigated aboriginal mounds at Newport (about July 15–25), and Greeneville (July 29–August 8), visited Bakersville, North Carolina (about August 10), worked at Sevierville, Tennessee (August ?15–31), visited Dandridge (September 2), Jacksboro, Paint Rock Ferry, Kingston (September 26), Niles Ferry and Taylor's Bend (all in September). He was at Loudon about September 30, and probably spent some time in September at the junction of Poplar Creek and the Tennessee River, near the mouth of the Clinch River. Most of October was spent near Kingston, Roane County; early in November [actually in mid- to late October, as noted by McVaugh 1956:140, 254; but not in September as stated by Holmes 1884:433] Palmer moved his headquarters to Arkansas. . . .

Newport is in Cocke County, just north of the Great Smoky Mountains, near the junction of the Pigeon and French Broad rivers. Although Holmes had explicitly stated that Palmer "began work by opening a number of mounds in Cocke County" (1884:433), he only described a single mound, in which Palmer found three hearths or cooking pits and associated potsherds (1884:440–41). Thomas (1891:202) listed several mounds in this county, including one a mile from the Pigeon-French Broad junction, but did not mention Palmer. In the final report (Thomas 1894:356), he stated that "but one mound in [Cocke] county was examined . . . on Vincent Island, Pigeon River." That mound was excavated by another of the field assistants, J. W. Emmert (Thomas 1891:202). Emmert was from nearby Kingsport, Thomas's home town, and figured prominently in the later years of the Mound Survey.

Greeneville is in Greene County, immediately north of Cocke County. Neither Holmes (1884) nor Thomas (1894) mentioned any sites or finds from this county. Thomas's catalog (1891:204) listed three mounds but did not mention Palmer.

Bakersville, Mitchell County, North Carolina, is in the Blue Ridge Mountains north of Mt. Mitchell, the highest point in the eastern United States. Thomas did not include this county in his listings (1891, 1894), and there is no indication from other sources that Palmer investigated a mound there. McVaugh (1956:265) stated that his purpose was to visit a mica mine. This may have been for the purpose of obtaining documented samples to compare to the well-known Hopewellian mica artifacts.

Sevierville is in Sevier County, north of the Great Smoky Mountains on a tributary of the French Broad River. Thomas stated that "two mounds on the west bank of Little Pigeon River, just opposite Sevierville" had been "explored by Dr. Edward Palmer" (1891:213). His 1894 final report, however, did not mention this county at all. This seems very odd, given Thomas's general emphasis on his east Tennessee homeland in this report (Jeter 1986b:149), and in light of Palmer's finds and Holmes's repeated mentions of them (1883:214, 292, 301, 303; 1884:442, 446). Holmes's (1883) report on shell artifacts was liberally sprinkled with descriptions and illustrations of Palmer's finds from the McMahan Mound and other Tennessee sites. His general report on the 1881 collections gave about ten pages to the mound and its artifacts and another four to collections from the surrounding fields (1884:442–56).

Taylor's Bend and Dandridge are in Jefferson County, about ten miles apart on the French Broad River. Thomas (1891:205–06) listed five mounds in this county but did not mention Palmer, although Emmert was cited twice (1891:205–06). In the final report (1894:357), he stated that the examinations in this county "were hasty and incomplete. The agent was, at the time of his visit, simply on a prospecting tour, expecting to return to those works which he thought worthy of special investigation." Without mentioning Palmer by name, he reported two mounds near Taylor's Bend and stated that no artifacts or burials were found in the test excavations there (1894:357–58). Holmes reported on excavations by Palmer of two burials and a few artifacts from a single mound and collections from the surrounding fields at Taylor's Bend (1884:457–60). This site does not match the description of either of Thomas's mounds at Taylor's Bend. It would appear that Thomas ignored the Palmer-Holmes mound and artifacts and reported instead on later work by Emmert, who was credited with having investigated "two mounds immediately below Taylor's bend" in the preliminary catalog (1891:206).

Fain's Island is in the French Broad River, about three miles below Dandridge in Jefferson County, and was almost certainly the object of Palmer's visit to Dandridge mentioned by McVaugh, although more than a single day's stay must have been required. Holmes (1884:463–65) described Palmer's finds in the mound, which yielded the remains of a burned building that may have been a charnel house, at least thirty-two burials, and some "unusually large and well preserved" fragments of both Mississippian and earlier, cord-marked pottery. Several shell items were also recovered, probably from the mound (Holmes 1883:215, 272), although Holmes's later publication perhaps inadvertently included them under a list of artifacts "from the fields of Fain's Island" (1884: 466–67). Thomas (1891:205) listed a mound on the south end of this island but did not cite Palmer. In his final report, Thomas (1894:358) reported briefly on what appears to have been the same mound but did not mention Palmer by name or refer to Holmes's reports. Instead he stated, "As a shaft had been sunk in the center by a previous explorer a broad trench was cut on each side," and described only the similar but less abundant findings of the later excavations.

Kingston is in Roane County, at the junction of the Clinch and Tennessee rivers. Holmes mentioned sixteen mounds (1884:460)—probably accounting for Palmer's return visit and the "most of October" statement by McVaugh—on three farms near Kingston, which were at least tested by Palmer, with generally negative results. Possibly, one of these sites was at the Poplar Creek locality mentioned by McVaugh, although Holmes did not use that name. Paint Rock Ferry is also near Kingston in Roane County; Palmer's finds here were sparse but did include several noteworthy shell artifacts and were summarized by Holmes (1883:223, 258; 1884:461–62). Thomas (1891:211–12) listed numerous mounds in this county, citing Emmert eight times and Palmer thrice. In the final report (1894:358–66), he mentioned none of Palmer's sites but did describe several which had been investigated by Emmert or others.

Jacksboro is in Campbell County, well to the northwest of Palmer's other east Tennessee explorations. Thomas (1891:201) listed only a single entry for this county, a "mound near Jacksboro," and did credit the report of its existence to Palmer. He did not mention this county in his final report, nor did Holmes in his summaries of Palmer's work.

It is not at all clear what, if anything, Palmer did at Loudon. McVaugh merely mentions it as a place in "Loudon County" (1956:247, 331), but Palmer may have been referring to Fort Loudon (or Loudoun; cf. Chapman 1985:104), a British fort site (1757–60) in Monroe County near Niles Ferry. Thomas listed eleven multi-mound sites in Loudon County (1891:207), crediting eight of them to Emmert. One two-mound site "about a mile from the village of Loudon" was not credited to an assistant.

In his work at Niles Ferry and elsewhere on the lower Little Tennessee River, Palmer played a role that was to become rather characteristic for him in this position: that of "a preliminary or exploratory investigator" of mounds or other remains that were to be "subsequently studied in detail by other workers" (McVaugh 1956:85). Holmes, perhaps inadvertently, or perhaps due to problems with Palmer's notes, erroneously included Palmer's Niles Ferry work, which produced essentially "nothing of interest," in his Roane County section (1884:461). Thomas listed numerous mounds reported by Emmert in Monroe County but did not mention Palmer (Thomas 1891:209–10). He did mention "two mounds on the south side of the Little Tennessee River at the upper end of Big Island near Niles's Ferry" but did not credit an assistant, and it may be that Palmer worked there. However, the "Niles Ferry mounds" site on the north side of the Little Tennessee was the only place in Tennessee where Thomas's (1894) final report mentioned Palmer by name, and Holmes's description of "a large mound that has the appearance of a Creek or Cherokee ball-ground" adequately matches Thomas's description of the largest mound in this group. According to Thomas, the Niles Ferry group included three mounds:

> . . . Nos. 2 and 3, which are comparatively small and of the usual conical type, stand on a timbered ridge which comes to the river immediately below the blockhouse opposite old Fort Loudon. No. 1 is a very large mound. . . . A single shaft was sunk part way down in it some years ago by Dr. Palmer, but it has never been thoroughly explored. . . . The Bureau agent, expecting to return to the group the following season, took no other notes than the courses and distances of the mounds from one to another and from the river. (1894:388–89)

Thomas's (1891:210) preliminary catalog, however, listed only two mounds in this location, crediting them to Emmert. It seems likely that his (1894) "Niles Ferry Mounds" may have been a composite of the large Mound 1, investigated by Palmer, and the two smaller mounds, reported by Emmert.

The valley of the Little Tennessee, between the Great Smoky Mountains and its juncture with the Tennessee River in Loudon County, was characterized (correctly, according to Chapman 1985:16) by Thomas as "undoubtedly the most interesting archeological section in the entire Appalachian district" (1894:366). After Palmer's brief visit, it was intensively investigated for the Mound Survey by Emmert, who worked at fifty-three mounds between 1885 and 1889 (Chapman 1985:14, 16).

Emmert's project was probably conceived by Thomas, who had just broken openly with theories about Mound-Builders who were not North American Indians (Jeter 1986b:148–49). Otis T. Mason, the first curator of ethnology in the Smithsonian's National Museum, reported (1884:745–46) that on February 5, 1884, Thomas had read a paper before the Washington Anthropological Society, entitled "Were the Cherokees Mound-Builders?" He then published an article in the May 1884 *Magazine of American History* entitled "Cherokees probably Mound-Builders." And, in the Bureau of Ethnology's *Fifth Annual Report* (for 1883–84, but delayed in publication), Thomas again proclaimed "The Cherokees Probably Mound-Builders" (1887:87). He quite possibly intended Emmert's work as a field test of his new ideas, as he stressed that

> . . . whether the "Indian theory" proves to be correct or not, I wish to obtain for it at least a fair consideration. I believe the latter ["Indian"] theory to be the correct one, as the facts so far ascertained appear to point in that direction, but I am not wedded to it; on the contrary, I am willing to follow the facts wherever they lead. (Thomas 1887:80)

In his final report, Thomas (1894:366–404) devoted a substantial amount of space to a summary of his assistants' findings in this valley, especially those of Emmert, carefully mapped their mound and village site locations (1894: Plate XXV), and explicitly correlated these with the locations of Overhill Cherokee towns mapped by British Lt. Henry Timberlake in 1762 (1894:367–89, Plate XXVI).

In subsequent decades, a number of archeological investigations were made in the Little Tennessee Valley. Most recently, an intensive fourteen-year project has been conducted by the University of Tennessee department of anthropology, under contracts in mitigation of flooding by the waters of Tellico Reservoir. A report summarizing the findings, from Paleo-Indian through historic Cherokee and Euro-American remains, has recently been published (Chapman 1985).

Palmer's last work done in Tennessee in 1881 appears to have been his extended and relatively fruitless return visit to the mounds near Kingston, as summarized above. (He did return to eastern Tennessee in the spring of 1882; see chapter 6.) According to McVaugh (1956:86, 140, 254), during mid-October Palmer moved his base of operations from east Tennessee to Osceola, Arkansas, arriving on or about October 20. His method of travel is uncertain; although he apparently preferred railroads, he could have easily traveled by boat from Kingston down the Tennessee, Ohio, and Mississippi rivers to Osceola.

CHAPTER FOUR

Archeological Concepts and Arkansas Prehistory

The archeologists of Palmer's and Thomas's day, and for decades afterward, did not know or were only beginning to grasp the answers to numerous questions about the mounds. Today we can see that the most glaring gap was their lack of an absolute chronology, a matter that only began to be resolved in the eastern U.S. after 1950. Other problems that are much better understood now include cultural (or at least, artifactual) relationships, subsistence, settlement patterning, and the nature of the sociopolitical systems that produced the mounds and affiliated sites.

These problems have begun to be resolved not only by the application of scientific and technological innovations such as radiocarbon dating but also through the gradual development of archeological methods and concepts. Archeologists working in and near the Mississippi Valley have long been in the forefront of such efforts, especially building upon the work of James A. Ford and his associates such as Gordon R. Willey, Philip Phillips, and James B. Griffin (Ford 1936; Ford and Willey 1941; Phillips, Ford, and Griffin 1951; Phillips 1970). Their work has emphasized the building of culture-historical sequences, an approach that continues to dominate much of Mississippi Valley archeology (Williams and Brain 1983).

Another approach, which characterized the New Archeology movement beginning in the 1960s, emphasizes cultural ecology and processual explanations of cultural change and continuity (Binford 1964, 1968, 1972, 1983). The application of this approach requires an "explicitly scientific" approach to research design and hypothesis testing, implemented by recovery techniques, such as flotation of dirt-matrix samples, that recover large quantities of small-scale ecofacts, such as charred seeds, in addition to the usual artifacts. Analyses by specialists in fields such as archeobotany (which was pioneered by Palmer), archeozoology, pollen analysis, soil chemistry, etc., must be integrated by project archeologists, often on a regional scale.

The development of these and other approaches has been summarized in a general history of American archeology by Willey and Sabloff (1980). I have contributed a brief critique of the situation in the Mississippi Valley (Jeter 1982a:110–19). Virtually all archeologists working in this area use a set of spatial, cultural, and temporal concepts that were formally proposed by Willey and Phillips (1958), and a conceptually related artifact classification system that was brought into this area by Phillips (1970).

These concepts have been modified or augmented by later researchers, as will be noted. Also, there is some dispute as to their usefulness for processual studies or their relationship to ethnohistorical reality. But, in practice, even the archeologists who criticize these concepts use them at least as a convenient means of communication.

Artifact Classification and Typology

This is the most basic conceptual step in the building of cultural sequences. Two general classes of artifacts, ceramics (pottery) and lithics (stone), have been subjected to the most intensive general attention in this regard. In the present case, given the nature of Palmer's collections, only the ceramics are relevant.

Prehistoric ceramics have long been emphasized in Mississippi Valley archeology, for a number of reasons. First, pottery is relatively common in this area, unlike stone, and is often of good to high quality—museum quality, in fact. This was known to local and regional collectors long before Palmer and his associates began obtaining specimens for institutions such as the Peabody Museum and the Smithsonian and is the primary reason that site destruction by pot-hunting continues unabated today. A synthesis of the early collections, written by Holmes (1903), and subsequent collections by a wealthy Philadelphian, Clarence B. Moore (1908, 1909, 1910, 1911, 1913), who plied the Southern streams in his steamboat the *Gopher* (Morse and Morse 1983:21–22, Figure 2.1), brought national attention to these artifacts.

It was not until the pioneering work of Ford, though, that ceramics, including potsherds or fragments as well as complete vessels, were shown to be of great use in constructing cultural sequences. Ford (1935, 1936) at first experimented with numerical typologies but, lacking computers, was overwhelmed by their complexity. He then turned to a binomial system (Ford and Willey 1940), in which a combination of proper names and descriptive terms was used (e.g., Coles Creek Incised; Marksville Incised; Marksville Stamped; Wilkinson Punctated).

This system was used in a number of subsequent reports, most notably in the first major synthesis of Lower Mississippi Valley prehistoric archeology (Phillips, Ford, and Griffin 1951). However, it was revised significantly by Phillips (1970), who brought in the type-variety system that had been developed in Mesoamerican archeology and applied it in an even larger scale synthesis. In this system, whenever possible, the types are subdivided into varieties, and the names of the latter are underscored or italicized (e.g., Coles Creek Incised, *var. Coles Creek*; Marksville Stamped, *var. Mabin*). Variety names may be used alone (e.g., *Coles Creek; Mabin*) if the context is clear.

This system has been criticized on general conceptual grounds (Gibson 1979; Jeter 1982a:116–19) and on grounds of inapplicability to certain ceramic collections (Schambach 1981 has proposed an alternative system), but it is now the *lingua franca* of Mississippi Valley archeology. It has recently been revised and augmented by Williams and

Brain (1983:87–212) and will be applied here to Palmer's ceramic collections when possible.

Synthesizing Concepts

In order to understand the archeological literature, one must be familiar with several kinds of concepts that have been developed to assist comparisons. They involve the spatial, cultural, and temporal dimensions of the bygone social units or societies under study. The following summaries are based on longer discussions by Willey and Phillips (1958) and by others, as cited.

Spatial Concepts.   The *site* is a fundamental concept of archeology. Definition of its spatial extent may be simple or quite difficult (especially if it has buried portions). In the Arkansas Archeological Survey's (AAS) records, sites are numbered according to the "Smithsonian system" developed in the 1930s. The Menard site, for example, is numbered 3AR4. The "3" stands for Arkansas (Alaska was not a state when the system was established). The "AR" stands for Arkansas County, and the "4" indicates that this was the fourth site recorded in that county. Many of the sites visited by Palmer have also been assigned numbers by a research organization that works in several states, the Lower Mississippi Survey (LMS) of the Peabody Museum, Harvard University. LMS site numbers (cf. Phillips 1970) are based on a grid of fifteen-minute quadrangle maps, each map being assigned a number in a north-south series and a letter in a west-east series. In this system, the Menard site is numbered 17-K-1, the final "1" indicating that it was the first site recorded by the LMS on map 17-K. In the following pages, both AAS and LMS site numbers will be given where relevant.

The *locality* is the next spatial unit above the level of the site. It is variable in size, but generally not larger than the space that might have been occupied by a single local group or community. Examples in Arkansas often include a major site and its immediate surroundings, perhaps a small drainage basin or part of a larger one.

A *region* is considerably larger than a locality, often covering as much space as several modern counties. It is roughly equivalent to the territory that might be occupied by a social unit such as a tribe. In Arkansas, regions often consist of portions of major drainage basins or of major upland zones and may include several major contemporary sites.

An *area* is a much larger spatial unit, which may include several modern states or portions of them. Areas often coincide with major geographic divisions, such as the American Southwest or Southeast. Arkansas is sometimes considered as at least partially in the archeological-ethnological Southeast (Smith 1986), but it is definitely on the western margin of that area. More frequently, Arkansas archeologists divide the state among what might be called *subareas,* such as the Lower (or Central) Mississippi Valley, the Trans-Mississippi South (Schambach 1970; also sometimes called the "Caddoan area"), and the Ozarks.

Almost all of Palmer's work in Arkansas was done in what is here regarded as the Lower Mississippi Valley (following Phillips, Ford, and Griffin 1951; Phillips 1970; Saucier 1974). It should be noted, though, that Morse and Morse (1983) have referred to northeast Arkansas and adjoining regions between the Ohio and Arkansas rivers as the central Mississippi Valley; here that territory is regarded as the northern part of the lower valley. Palmer did make a few brief ventures into the Trans-Mississippi South, in south-central Arkansas, and approached but did not work in the Ozarks.

Cultural Concepts.   The cultural units used by archeologists have historically been mixed or loaded with spatial and temporal implications. This has been decried (Spaulding 1957; Gibson 1979; Jeter 1982:113) but is almost unavoidable, inasmuch as the former so-cieties existed in specific places during specific times. Two basic cultural units, the com-ponent and the phase, are commonly used, and a third, a modification of the culture concept, has been proposed.

A *component* is the sum total of evidence for a specific cultural occupation at a specific site. A site that produces evidence of only one occupation is called a single-component site; one that shows evidence of more than one occupation is called a two-component or multiple-component site.

A *phase* is defined on the basis of related components from several sites in a locality or region. The components need not be similar in all ways: a complex society may leave very different remains at its major ceremonial centers, minor centers, large and small villages, single-family farmsteads, and hunting camps. However, the components must be demonstrably related, usually on the basis of shared artifact types and styles. A phase is usually temporally restricted from as little as fifty years to a few hundred years. Phases are often named after a key site, e.g., the Nodena, Parkin, Kent, and Tillar phases in eastern Arkansas.

In recent years, a number of attempts have been made to identify archeological phases with ethnohistorically described tribes or other ethnic groups, especially with regard to the Native American "provinces" described by chroniclers of the Hernando de Soto *en-trada* in 1541–43, and the "Quapaw phase" of the Lower Arkansas Valley. A great deal of scholarly controversy has raged, and continues, with regard to various aspects of these questions (Swanton 1939; Phillips, Ford, and Griffin 1951; Brain, Toth, and Rodriguez-Buckingham 1974; Brain 1978, 1985; P. Morse 1981:61–72; Jeter 1982:113–15; Morse and Morse 1983:305–15; Hudson 1985).

The concept of the *culture* has recently been redefined for archeological purposes by Belmont as "a set of phases, contiguous in space and time, sharing substantial similarities in artifact content, settlement pattern and adaptational systems, and differing in the same criteria from surrounding phases or cultures" (1982b:77). This appears to be a useful "big picture" synthesizing concept (cf. Jeter et al. 1989), and it will be used in some of the discussions that follow.

Temporal Concepts.   Archeologists have combined their spatial and cultural concepts with chronological information to produce a set of temporal concepts. These include the local sequence, the regional sequence, and areal sequences of culture periods. Some, in-cluding myself, have argued in favor of replacing the culture periods whenever possible by pure time periods.

A *local sequence* is one of the fundamental building blocks of the archeological study of cultural stability and change. It is basically a chronological sequence of components within a locality.

A *regional sequence* is a chronological sequence of phases, within a region. It is usu-ally built up over an extended period of research, by correlating the local sequences of the region in question.

An *areal* sequence of *culture periods* has been proposed for the Lower Mississippi Valley by Phillips (1970). His scheme is depicted in table 4.1. However, it could be argued that a number of his period names were extended beyond their geographic limits of usefulness. For instance, his "Coles Creek period" is not really applicable to northeast Arkansas, which was not occupied by the Coles Creek culture, but by a contemporary "emergent" or "frontier" Mississippian culture in its northern portions (Morse and Morse 1983:200–33) and by the newly defined Plum Bayou culture (Rolingson 1982) in its southern part.

Table 4.1.
*Native American Culture Periods
in the Lower Mississippi Valley and Eastern U.S.*

Dates & General Terms	LMV Terms (Phillips 1970)	Eastern U.S. Terms (Griffin 1967)	(Willey 1966)
Historic	Quapaw, Tunica, Natchez, Yazoo, etc.	Various Tribes	
1700			
Protohistoric			
1500			
Prehistoric	Mississippi	Mississippian	Temple Mound II
1000			
	Coles Creek		Temple Mound I
500	Baytown	Late Woodland	
A.D. / B.C.	Marksville/Hopewellian	Middle Woodland	Burial Mound II
500	Tchula	Early Woodland	Burial Mound I
	Poverty Point		
1500			
		Late Archaic	
3000			
		Middle Archaic	
7000			
		Early Archaic	
9000			
		Paleo-Indian	

The Biases and Contexts of Palmer's Collections

It should be noted that Palmer, like most of his predecessors and successors until well into the twentieth century, was primarily looking for museum-quality specimens, especially of pottery. Most such specimens are to be found in sites of the later prehistoric, protohistoric, and early historic Native American groups, especially those of the Mississippian and Caddoan cultures. Palmer did not do much work at Caddoan sites, but he did a great deal of work on classic Mississippian sites.

The southward spread of Mississippian culture during the late centuries of prehistory (Phillips 1970; Morse and Morse 1983; Jeter et al. 1989) should provide some comprehension of the major phenomenon that Palmer and his associates were investigating without really understanding. In brief, it is a saga of the rise of higher levels of social organization among peoples who were intensive agriculturalists after about A.D. 1000. These peoples achieved the "chiefdom" or "paramount chiefdom" level in portions of northeast Arkansas, along the Mississippi and St. Francis rivers, in the Nodena, Parkin, and Kent phases, at least. Their major settlements had hundreds, and probably thousands, of residents, and some are now archeological sites with deposits up to three meters (about ten feet) deep, analogous to Near Eastern *tells* formed over the decades and centuries by superimposed layers of house rubble and associated debris.

These were the most impressive settlements and societies encountered by the De Soto *entrada* of the early 1540s, but paradoxically they were the most vulnerable. Old World acute viral diseases, such as smallpox, measles, and many others, thrived on crowded settlement patterns, and the Native Americans had no resistance to them. Whole societies were literally decimated (Ramenofsky 1985), and northeast Arkansas was essentially abandoned. There are probably some connections between remnants of these former chiefdoms and protohistoric phases such as the Quapaw phase of the Lower Arkansas Valley and the Tillar phase of southeast Arkansas, but archeologists are still wrestling with these difficult questions (Morse and Morse 1983:271–320; Hoffman 1986; Jeter 1986a; House 1987), and they probably will not be resolved soon. These researches begin with the controlled and documented collection of data, and in many if not most cases, the first man on the trail was Edward Palmer.

PART TWO

Palmer in Arkansas

CHAPTER FIVE

Editor's Introduction to the Documents

Palmer's Primary Arkansas Documents

During Edward Palmer's 1881–84 employment by the Bureau of Ethnology, he produced three types of handwritten primary documents relating to his archeological investigations in Arkansas. These can be classed as notes, letters, and monthly reports; each is worthy of some discussion.

Notes.   The most immediate and intimate of Palmer's Arkansas documents are the notes he wrote in the manner of a diary or personal journal. These appear to have been written at irregular intervals, on whatever kind of paper was available. They sometimes bear dates or partial dates but sometimes do not. Their subject matter tends to include impressions of places, people, and incidents of travel. Less frequently, they include references to the archeological sites; when these are present, they tend to be general rather than specifically descriptive of either the sites or the work he did at them.

It appears that these notes remained in Palmer's possession until his death in 1911. After the settlement of his estate, such documents were sold at a public auction in 1914 by the Merwin Sales Co. of New York (McVaugh 1956:ix), and some of them found their way to Arkansas and eventual publication (Palmer 1917).

These notes do indeed reveal something of the writer's psychology and personality, and they also tell us a great deal about the appearance of portions of Arkansas and the highly variable behaviors of Arkansawyers in the early 1880s. A more or less typical note, summarizing Palmer's October 13, 1882, journey from Osceola to the B. F. Jackson (Wildy) Mounds site in Mississippi County, northeast Arkansas, is illustrated in figure 5.1.

Palmer's handwritten originals of most of these notes, or copies of some of them made by anonymous "scribes," are in the archives of the Arkansas History Commission in Little Rock.

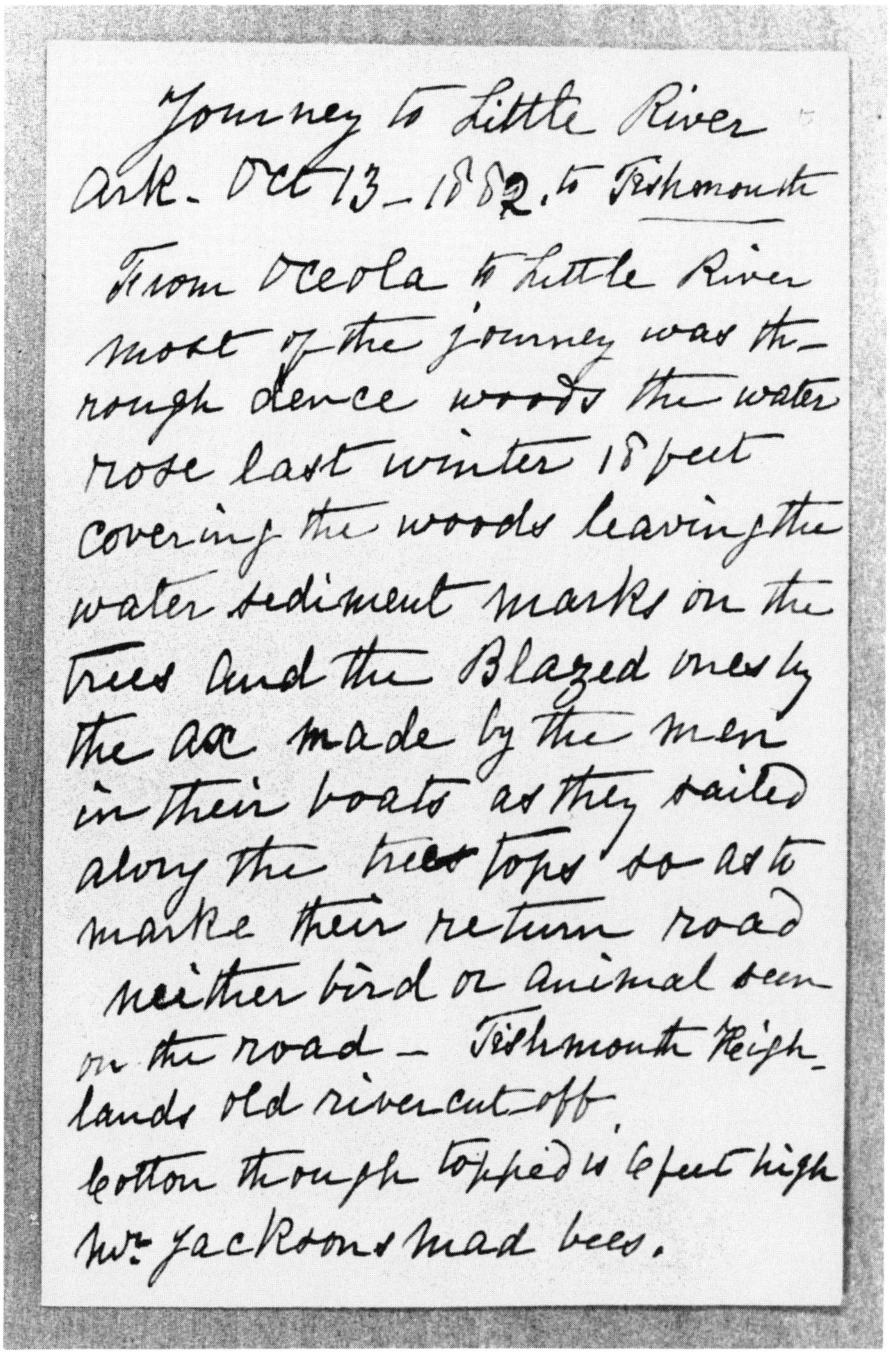
Journey to Little River
Ark- Oct 13 - 1882. to Fishmouth

From Oceola to Little River
most of the journey was through dence woods the water
rose last winter 18 feet
covering the woods leaving the
water sediment marks on the
trees and the Blazed ones by
the ax made by the men
in their boats as they sailed
along the trees tops so as to
marke their return road
neither bird or animal seen
on the road - Fishmouth Highlands old river cut-off.
Cotton though topped is 6 feet high
Mr Jacksons mad bees.

FIGURE 5.1

Palmer's note summarizing his October 13, 1882, trip from Osceola to the B. F. Jackson Mounds, northeast Arkansas. (From Arkansas History Commission Small Manuscript Collection, Box XIII, No. 9, Item No. 1.)

Letters.   Palmer was "a confirmed and verbose letter writer" (McVaugh 1956:x), but he wrote significantly fewer letters during his years with the Bureau of Ethnology than during his earlier and later years as a botanical collector (1956:85–86). His letters about his Arkansas investigations are usually specific as to the place and date of writing. They were usually addressed to his superiors at the Smithsonian Institution and tend to be much more businesslike than his personal notes. Some of them are brief progress reports (cf. the monthly reports, below) describing sites visited and the work done at them, summarizing information from people contacted or remarking about people to be contacted, mentioning plans for site visits in the immediate future, etc. Others are more concerned with logistical matters, such as shipments of boxed specimens and/or notes and drawings, problems with the weather or his health, and, not infrequently, financial problems.

The letters and postcards in Palmer's own hand are in one or another of the Smithsonian's archival facilities or files and were not included in the 1917 publication. A reproduction of a letter written by Palmer to Thomas is presented near the end of chapter 7 (figure 7.67).

Only one partial (and variant) scribe's copy of a letter (from Palmer to Thomas, dated October 1, 1883) was included in the 1914 acquisition by the Arkansas archives and was published (Palmer 1917:393–94). We now have Palmer's original (see chapter 8). Other apparent letters in the 1917 publication are actually scattered portions of scribes' copies of monthly reports.

Monthly Reports.   Palmer's June 27, 1881, letter of employment from Powell (transcribed in chapter 3) explicitly stated, "At the end of each month a report of progress should be made to this office." When available, these reports furnish our best and most detailed information about the archeological sites (including crude sketches by Palmer in some cases), his work at them, and his findings. An added bonus in some cases is information, not available elsewhere, about the sequence of Palmer's visits to the various sites.

Unfortunately, this is a feast or famine situation. For a few months, generally early ones in the overall picture, we have not only Palmer's original (often heavily marked editorially, perhaps by Thomas), but also revised versions by a scribe or scribes.

For too many other months, though, we have nothing. The most tantalizing and frustrating such case is perhaps that of the report for November 1882, which probably would have included additional details on the excavations at the Tillar Mound in southeast Arkansas. In his December 2, 1882, letter to Powell (see chapter 7), Palmer concluded, "Wil forward Report for November to morrow." Yet it is nowhere to be found in any of the archives visited.

All of the monthly reports in Palmer's own hand and most of the copies by the scribes are in the "2400" file at the Smithsonian's National Anthropological Archives. The materials that went to Arkansas in 1914 included some second-generation scribes' copies of the reports for November and December 1881. The November report was actually two separate documents; the first covered work in northeast Arkansas, including some done in late October, and the second summarized his first investigations at the Menard site. The December report covered most of the month and discussed work done in east-central Arkansas. Only the second November report was presented as a coherent document in the earlier publication (Palmer 1917:445–47). The others were wildly scattered.

Secondary Documents

In addition to the primary documents produced by Palmer in the field, we have three kinds of secondary sources. The first such case is that in which Palmer's original has been lost or discarded, and we have only a scribe's copy. The second is the occurrence of explanatory notations that appear to have been written by Palmer on other documents. The third class consists of letters from others to Palmer. Again, all are worthy of additional discussion.

Copies by Scribes.   Much of the 1917 publication of Palmer's notes was based not on Palmer's original documents but on copies produced by unidentified persons, referred to here as "scribes." There are also numerous examples of scribes' copies, with and without Palmer originals for comparison, in the previously unpublished documents at the Smithsonian.

An example of a scribe's handwritten version of Palmer's now-missing description of his initial work at the B. F. Jackson Mounds site is illustrated in figure 5.2. The 1917 publication made no distinction between the primary source and the secondary one, and both were "corrected" by the Arkansas editors.

In the present publication, a typographic distinction will be made. Palmer's own handwritten documents will be set in italics, and documents produced by scribes will be set in roman. In our cursory studies of these cursive styles, it appears that the handwriting of at least two different scribes could be discerned. That distinction appears to be irrelevant for the present purposes, however, so any and all scribes have been lumped together and appear in the same typeface.

Additional Notes by Palmer.   Palmer's additions to pre-existing documents also occur in several varieties. Probably the most significant are the cases in which Palmer's handwriting was added to a scribe's on the same page. An example is illustrated in figure 5.3, showing the account of Palmer's continuing investigation at the B. F. Jackson site as begun by a scribe, then taken over in mid-sentence by Palmer.

The significance of such examples is their proof that Palmer worked closely with the scribes, at least some of the time and apparently on repeated occasions. A number of such instances have been indicated typographically herein. This work with the scribes was almost certainly done by Palmer at the Smithsonian after his return from field seasons.

Palmer also added written captions, labels, and notes to the drawings made by H. J. Lewis and occasionally added written afterthoughts or explanatory remarks to his own notes. It is not at all clear whether these additions were made in the field or in Washington, or how much time elapsed. In the case of additions to his own notes, the main indications are the use of obviously different writing implements or inks and the use of margins or interlinear spaces. Such instances will be noted in the accompanying text or notes.

Letters to Palmer.   The various Smithsonian archives contain copies of several letters to or about Palmer, mainly from Baird. Most of these deal with the preliminary organizational and recruiting stages of the Mound Survey during the first half of 1881. Chapter 3 reproduces several such letters from Baird, plus Palmer's letter of employment from John Wesley Powell. None of Palmer's replies to these preliminary letters have been found, but their general nature may be inferred. Probably the most nearly complete exchange of

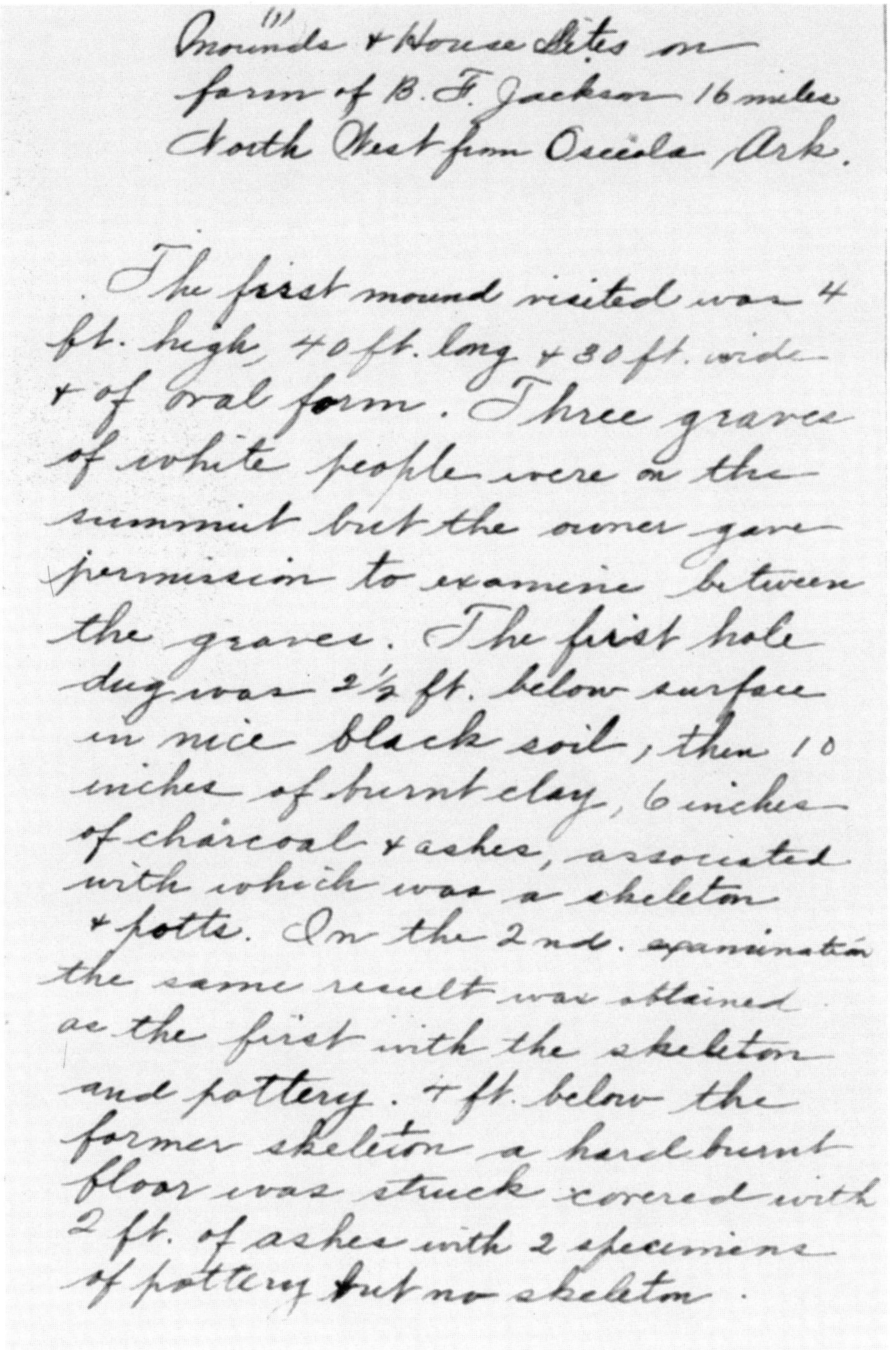

"Mounds & House Sites on
farm of B. F. Jackson 16 miles
North West from Osceola, Ark.

The first mound visited was 4
ft. high, 40 ft. long & 30 ft. wide
& of oval form. Three graves
of white people were on the
summit but the owner gave
permission to examine between
the graves. The first hole
dug was 2½ ft. below surface
in nice black soil, then 10
inches of burnt clay, 6 inches
of charcoal & ashes, associated
with which was a skeleton
& potts. In the 2nd. examination
the same result was obtained
as the first with the skeleton
and pottery. 4 ft. below the
former skeleton a hard burnt
floor was struck covered with
2 ft. of ashes with 2 specimens
of pottery but no skeleton.

FIGURE 5.2

Scribe's version of note describing Palmer's work at the B. F. Jackson
Mounds. (From Arkansas History Commission Small Manuscript Collec-
tion, Box XIII, No. 9, Item No. 1.)

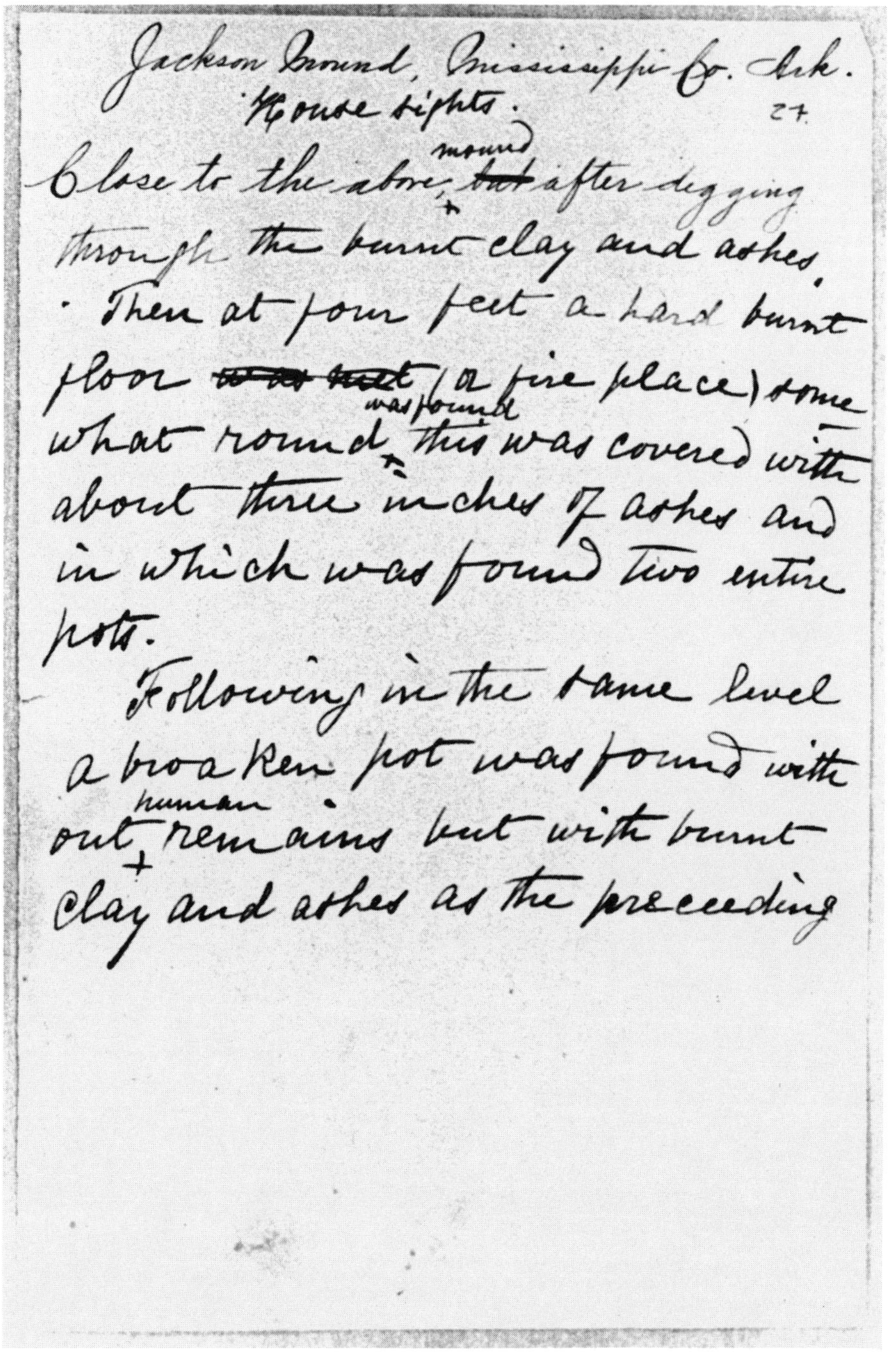

Jackson Mound, Mississippi Co. Ark.
House sights. 27.

Close to the above mound ~~but~~ after digging through the burnt clay and ashes. Then at four feet a hard burnt floor ~~was met~~ (a fire place) some what round was found this was covered with about three inches of ashes and in which was found two entire pots.

Following in the same level a broaken pot was found with out human remains but with burnt clay and ashes as the preceding

FIGURE 5.3

Scribe's version of note on work at the Jackson Mounds, interrupted by Palmer's handwriting. (From Arkansas History Commission Small Manuscript Collection, Box XIII, No. 9, Item No. 1.)

letters is that among Palmer, Baird, and Powell toward the end of Palmer's first field season, beginning with Baird's letter of December 17, 1881, to Palmer and ending with Baird's letter of February 9, 1882, to Powell (see chapter 6).

There is one major gap in the record of correspondence. No copies of letters from Cyrus Thomas to Palmer have been found in the Arkansas or Smithsonian archives. Also, neither Bruce D. Smith nor Ian W. Brown, both of whom have worked with Thomas's documents (see chapter 1), have seen any Thomas-to-Palmer correspondence (1982–85 personal communications). This is quite unfortunate, as the relationship between Palmer and Thomas appears to have been rather strained and mutually unsatisfactory. It would be useful to have more details of Thomas's side of various issues. In at least some cases, the nature of Thomas's letters is relatively easy to infer from Palmer's reply (e.g., Palmer's letter of January 10, 1883, in chapter 7).

Palmer's Style and Related Matters

Palmer was characterized as a man whose writing style "was, to say the least, highly original" and who "could neither express himself clearly nor spell his words consistently" (McVaugh 1956: xi, 3). He was certainly a creative and inconsistent speller, but the implication of total lack of clarity is something of an exaggeration. It would be more accurate to say that at times, some of them critical for archeological interpretation, Palmer's meanings are not clear.

Adding to the difficulty of expression are Palmer's other eccentricities. Palmer often used dashes instead of periods, invented odd abbreviations, and began sentences with lowercase letters. But after a while the effect on the reader often becomes that of a letter from an eccentric and amusing friend. Indeed, it would be wrong for an editor to deprive the readers of this source of almost constant enjoyment in reading Palmer's documents.

The scribes, by the way, had their own brands of creativity, such as introducing "staid" for stayed, "cyprus" for cypress, and otherwise occasionally botching a word that Palmer had somehow gotten right.

One canard, from a source generally sympathetic to Palmer (cf. Judd 1926: 40–41, 1968: 62–66), should be rebutted. Judd stated, "Palmer was one of those busy individuals who trusted his memory. Such notes as he kept were scrawled on scraps of paper—any handy scrap—and were absolutely illegible. When he and his memory passed on, such notes as were made . . . passed on also, and only the pottery now remains" (1968: 66). Although Palmer's handwriting is certainly no model of legibility, a little practice suffices to make it readable. Even some of his most unusual writing habits, such as his "x," which often looks for all the world like a cursive "sc," become familiar. As noted by a well-known authority on such matters,

> . . . the editor's task, viewed in this light, does not simply become a mechanical one. The fact that editors pledge themselves to report all textual details of the documents does not mean that no judgment is involved . . . it is a rare case in which the editor's judgment is not called upon to determine exactly what the author wrote at particular points. The editor, as an expert in the handwriting of a given author and period, is in a better position than most other people to read that handwriting accurately, and one of the great contributions of an editor's transcription is the authority it represents in the deciphering of the hand. (Tanselle 1981: 43)

Lewis's Drawings and Derivative Engravings

The other major documents produced during Palmer's sojourn in Arkansas were some thirty-eight drawings and maps of mound sites, made by his artist-assistant, H. J. Lewis, during the last two months of 1882 and the first few days of 1883. The thirty-one surviving original drawings and maps of Arkansas mound sites by Lewis are all in the "2400" file in the National Anthropological Archives. None of them were used in the 1917 publication, wherein most of the references to them were systematically edited out, as will be seen. They are all reproduced in chapter 7, in conjunction with the relevant notes, in chronological order, as closely as it can be ascertained.

Eight of Lewis's drawings were redrawn as engravings, which were published in Cyrus Thomas's 1894 final report on the Mound Survey. The published versions were probably done by William Henry Holmes (as noted by Bruce Smith in chapter 1). All of these are also reproduced in chapter 7 (figs. 7.15–7.18, 7.26, 7.27, 7.32, 7.33). In five of these cases, the original Lewis drawing is missing, and we have only the published version to suggest its nature.

Four other Lewis drawings were redrawn, again probably by Holmes, with publication in the final report obviously in mind, but the engravings were never published. Apparently, considerations of space, esthetics or archeological judgment were the deciding factors. In all four cases, the original Lewis drawings are still on file and provide means of evaluating the general resemblance of the derivative engravings to the originals. Both the originals and the engravings are reproduced in chapter 7.

There are also two missing Lewis drawings that were apparently not redrawn. One was his "Plate A" of the Tillar Mound before excavation. The other was a view of Mound B at the Knapp Mounds. The only indication of these drawings' former existence is Palmer's references to them (see chapter 7).

Less reliable derivative engravings are available from a popular publication of the day, *Frank Leslie's Illustrated Newspaper*. The May 26, 1883, issue of that New York journal carried nine engravings derived from original drawings by Lewis (see chapter 9). Five of these engravings depict mound sites; for all five, the originals are available, affording some humorous comparisons with the products of somewhat sensationalized journalism.

No Lewis originals have been found for the other four *Leslie's* engravings. Two depict incidents of travel and two emphasize relic collections. The former two could well be fairly accurate renditions of Lewis originals. In the latter two, the artifacts are not accurately depicted, but one of them (figure 7.52) includes a likeness of Lewis, shown working on the collections with Palmer.

The 1917 Publication

Several references have already been made to the previous publication of *Arkansas Mounds* by the Arkansas Historical Association. Although it was published some six years after Palmer's death, and he had nothing to do with its editing or assembling ("randomizing" might be a more appropriate word), it is generally cited as "Palmer 1917," and this practice will be continued here.

The editors of the 1917 publication deviated from the document texts in a number of ways, some of them much more significant than simple "corrections." They also systematically deleted certain kinds of passages and introduced several egregious errors, due to lack of knowledge about archeology, lack of information, or simple carelessness. Before discussing these problems more fully, it may be of some relevance and interest to examine just how they came into possession of these documents in the first place.

Transmittal of Documents to Arkansas.   Though the path of the documents themselves appears to be fairly clear, the human motivations involved are open to some conjecture. After Palmer's death in 1911, the Merwin Sales Company of New York auctioned off (in 1914) the documents that had been in his possession. Some three hundred separate lots were sold for a total of about $450, but the sales records, if any, have long since been destroyed, according to McVaugh (1956:x). It seems quite likely, though, that the papers dealing with Arkansas were purchased directly by a resident of St. Louis who soon, if not immediately, sent them on to the Arkansas state historian.

Included with the Palmer documents at the archives in Little Rock is the envelope in which they were sent to Arkansas via the United States Express Company. That company's prepaid shipment label is stamped "APR 18 1914," and the envelope is addressed to "Mr. Dallas T. Herndon, Sec'y Arkansas History Commission, Little Rock, Ark." Dr. Herndon (1878–1953) was the first secretary of the Arkansas History Commission, having been named to that post in 1911 (Simpson 1973:252). The holder of this position also holds the title of state historian.

The envelope also bears a note written in the same hand, "Mss Value $10.00," and has embossed on its lower left portion, "American Art Galleries, Madison Square South, New York." The relevance of that institution is unclear: perhaps it was connected in some way with the Merwin Sales Co. More obviously relevant is the envelope's printed return address: "The Henry Graves Noel Co., Municipal Bonds, 408 Olive St., St. Louis, Mo." The address on Olive St. is in downtown St. Louis, but the Noel business is no longer there and is not listed in modern directories.

An effort has been made to learn something about Mr. Noel, beginning with the assumption that he may have been an antiquarian with interests in prehistoric archeology. Leonard W. Blake, who has been active in archeological circles in St. Louis and Missouri since the 1930s, had not heard of him and found no mention of him in a variety of archeo-historical sources. However, I found some relevant and intriguing information in two biographical dictionaries published by the now-defunct newspaper the *St. Louis Republic* (1906, 1912).

The later of these was consulted first, since it was closer in time to the 1914 transactions. It contains the following information: "NOEL, Henry Graves, bonds and stocks; born St. Louis, Aug. 18, 1868 . . . Princeton Univ., A.B., 1889. . . . Has been in the bond and stock business since 1890. . . . Recreations: golf and music . . ." (*St. Louis Republic* 1912:447–48).

The biographical notice also stated that the bond and stock business had been founded by Noel's father, Henry Martyn Noel, around 1879. The elder Noel was listed in the 1906 volume.

A brief digression is in order here. There was only one other tenuous (and seemingly completely unrelated) connection between Palmer's Arkansas investigations and St. Louis. In his note on the mound at Akron, Independence County, northeast Arkansas, visited in mid- to late October 1882 (see chapter 7), Palmer stated, "A figure of clay was taken out at the same time with the shells. It was sold to Dodd, Brown & Co. cor. 5th & St.

Charles st. St. Louis Mo." This entry had been included in the 1917 publication (Palmer 1917:420); Dan Morse and Leonard Blake had already attempted to locate the figurine, a century after its removal to St. Louis, without success.

The earlier biographical volume stated that Henry Martyn Noel "was the first salesman employed by Dodd, Brown & Co., wholesale dry goods, when that firm was organized, 1866, remaining until 1876, when was elected cashier of Security Bank" (*St. Louis Republic* 1906:436).

No further connections with antiquarianism were listed for Noel the elder. About a dozen Browns were listed in each of the volumes, none of them having any obvious connections with Dodd, Brown & Co. The later volume listed Samuel Morris Dodd only as "merchant; 1832–1912" (1912:158). The earlier one stated, "in 1865 the firm of Dodd, Brown & Co. was established, continuing in mercantile business until 1885, when retired" (1906:158).

These rather obscure and peripheral research trails have, for the moment and perhaps forever, ended. We have not found the missing figurine or effigy vessel and probably never will. All we have is a brief, partly factual and partly conjectural reconstruction: Henry Graves Noel, a forty-five-year-old, prosperous and well-educated man, whose father had been connected with people who had at least some antiquarian interests in Arkansas archeology, may have bought some of Palmer's papers directly from the Merwin Sales Co. in 1914 and definitely did send them to the Arkansas state historian in April of that year.

The Arkansas History Commission's microfilmed official correspondence records do contain six letters relating to the sending of the documents to Arkansas. The correspondence began with a letter from Henry Graves Noel. The addressee is not indicated in the surviving files, but it is clear that it was sent to Dr. David Yancey Thomas in Fayetteville. Thomas (1872–1943) had obtained a PhD at Columbia University in 1903 and was professor of history at the University of Arkansas from 1907 to 1940. He was the author of numerous articles and four books, including the four-volume *Arkansas and Its People*. The correspondence began with this letter to him:

HENRY GRAVES NOEL
507 MERCHANTS-LACLEDE BLDG.
ST. LOUIS

St.Louis, April 10,1914.

Dear Sir:-

I have for sale a valuable manuscript by the late Dr. Edward Palmer,U.S.A.who spent 60 years, from 1853 onwards,in constant travel and observation in the West, Mexico,and other points in the U.S.

The MSS is entitled

Arkansas Mounds. Observations and Results of excavations made among the mounds in various parts of the State. Slat wells, Filler Mounds, Journey From Osceola, Remains of Old Fortification on the Arkansas River, etc. etc. made in various years. by Dr. Edward Palmer. Most of the notes are dated 1881 to 1883.

About 150 pp.8vo size. Price $10.00

If you are interested in the purchase,kindly advise me promptly, as I am offering the item to several persons.

Yours very truly,

H. G. Noel [signed]

This letter bears a marginal note in pencil: "This was sent to me. Perhaps it will interest you. Appears to me as worth investigating. D.Y.T." The next letter in the Commission's "Noel" file makes it clear that Thomas had promptly passed the letter along to Herndon:

April 17, 1914.

Mr. H. G. Noel,
    507 Merchants-Laclede Bldg.,
      St. Louis, Mo.

    Dear Sir:

      Your letter of April 10th to Dr. D. Y. Thomas of Fayetteville has been referred to me and I write to inform you of my interest in the manuscript described therein.

      However I should like to know more of its contents and the nature of the treatise before making an offer of purchase. I shall be very glad to hear from you on the subject.

Yours very truly,

[copy is unsigned]

Secretary.

Since the manuscripts were sent by Noel to Herndon by express on or about April 18, it would appear unlikely that their shipment was prompted by Herndon's April 17 letter. Probably, Thomas had replied to Noel's letter of April 10, suggesting that he send the documents to Herndon for examination. In any event, Graves made a prompt response to Herndon:

HENRY GRAVES NOEL

Municipal Bonds and Highgrade Investment Securities
of the
Central West, South and Southwest

507 Merchants-Laclede Building   408 Olive Street
Telephone, Olive 1265
St. Louis

April 24, 1914

Mr.Dallas T.Herndon,Sec'y
    Little Rock, Akr.

Dear Sir -

    Your favor of the 23rd [*sic*; perhaps Herndon's letter of the 17th arrived on the 23rd] is at hand and noted. As far as I have been able to learn,the Palmer manuscript sent you has not been published.I do not find it in the index of Government scientific publications,- Smithsonian Reports,etc-.

Very truly yours,

H. G. Noel

[signed]

The next letter in the files is dated more than a month later and suggests that at least one letter from Noel is missing:

June 12, 1914.

Mr. Henry Graves Noel,
408 Olive Street,
St. Louis, Mo.

Dear Sir:

Your letter of recent date has been received. In reply, I beg to say that I have drawn a warrant against the funds of this department to pay you for the Palmer manuscript. However, I have been unable so far to cash the warrant, on account of the fact that the State of Arkansas is without funds in the State Treasury. Within the next few days I hope to be able to receive pay on it, and as soon as I succeed, I will forward to you my personal check for the amount.

Yours very truly,
[copy is unsigned]
Secretary.

Graves replied by return mail:

[letterhead truncated]
St. Louis
June 16, 1914.

Mr. Dallas T. Herndon, Sec.
  Arkansas Hist. Commission.
    Little Rock, Ark.

Dear Sir:-

I am in receipt of your favor of the 12th and am glad to note that you have accepted the Palmer manuscript, and thank you for your attention to the matter.

I shall be pleased to submit any rarities in the way of historical items which might be of interest to your history commission at any time I come across such items.

If you have prepared a list of books or pamphlets wanted by your commission I should like to have a copy of it, as I frequently see good Arkansas items. The only one I have on hand pertaining to Arkansas, which is of any rarity, is Bishop's "Loyalty on the Frontier", published in St. Louis 1863, but you doubtless have a copy of this item.

Yours truly,
H. G. Noel

The "Noel" file closes with an apparently incomplete copy of a brief note from Herndon:

Aug. 8, 1914.

Mr. Henry G. Noel
507 Lacledge Bldg.
St. Louis, Mo.

Dear Sir:-

You will please find enclosed my personal check for $10.00 as payment in full for the Palmer manuscript, purchased of you some two months ago, and oblige,

Secretary.

The Arkansas Editorial Situation. The papers were published in 1917 in volume 4 of the publications of the Arkansas Historical Association. That volume's editor was John Hugh Reynolds (1869–1954), the Association's secretary (cf. Simpson 1973:242–53). In the preface to the volume, he noted:

> The delay in printing this volume is due to the inadequacy of the printing fund in 1913 and to executive vetoes of later appropriations for this purpose. The expenses of issuing the publications are jointly borne by the state and by the sale of the volumes. The failure of either makes impossible the printing and distribution of the publications. In the meantime, however, the state has provided the means for carrying on in an effective way the work of the Arkansas History Commission. Its secretary, Dallas T. Herndon, for the last six years has done a classical piece of work in collecting, arranging and making available source material of the state's history. The editor is under obligations to Mr. Herndon for his cooperation in editing this volume.

It is unclear whether Herndon, Reynolds, or anonymous assistants edited the Palmer papers. What is clear is that certain kinds of information were systematically edited out, and a number of errors and confusing statements were introduced.

The confusion began on the first page (Palmer 1917:390), which started abruptly with some of Palmer's February 1883 (erroneously printed as "1882") notes on his observations at Arkadelphia, then jumped to his January 1883 arrival at Heckatoo. The only "explanatory" material was a brief footnote, the only editorial entry in the entire fifty-nine-page publication, summarizing the contents as "observations and results of excavations made around the mounds in various parts of the State: Salt wells, filler mounds, journey from Osceola, remains of old fortification on the Arkansas river, etc., etc., made in various years."

The mysterious-sounding "filler mounds" turn out to be an editorial absurdity: a new genus of mounds, as it were, derived ultimately from Palmer's misspelling of "Tillar" as "Tiller," followed by a scribe's misrendering of "Tiller" as "Filler" and a careless labeling job by someone at the Merwin Sales Co. (cf. Noel's letter of April 10 to Thomas). Clearly the editors did not compare this label to the actual notes. Numerous other specific cases of editorial malpractice could be cited.

Deletion of References to Drawings. Since the Arkansas editors did not have copies of Lewis's drawings and presumably did not even know of their whereabouts (or existence), virtually all references to them were systematically edited out of the notes.

The unavailability of the drawings and the lack of knowledge about archeological stratigraphy on the part of the editors, plus carelessness, led to an absurd passage in the 1917 publication. Lewis's "Plate 3" drawing of the Menard Mounds (fig. 7.37) included a stratigraphic profile cut into what Palmer called the west wing of the main mound. Three strata were numbered, and Palmer's original notes summarized the predominant deposits of each stratum. The scribe's version reads:

Plate 3
Is a view of the north side of the mound showing the section view of west.
Wing No (1). is composed of 6 inches of sandy loam,
Wing No (2)—6 inches of burnt clay -
" No (3) 3 " of matting & corn.

This grossly distorts what Palmer must have had in mind; perhaps the scribe was led astray by Palmer's hectic handwriting and poorly organized tabulation in the now-missing original. Taking the drawing and the total archeological context into account, it is clear that what Palmer meant to say was something like:

Plate 3
Is a view of the north side of the mound [Mound A], showing the section view of the west wing [Mound B]:
Stratum No. 1 is composed of 6 inches of sandy loam.
Stratum No. 2 is composed of 6 inches of burnt clay.
Stratum No. 3 is composed of 3 inches of matting and corn.

Lacking Palmer's original, Lewis's drawing, and archeological insight, the editors of the 1917 publication compounded the scribe's error. Although the previous paragraph in the published version had begun, "This mound has two wings," and went on to describe them as twenty and seven feet high, respectively, the description of the strata became transmuted into the ridiculous statement, "One wing is composed of six inches of sandy loam, another of six inches of burnt clay, and the third of three inches of matting and corn" (Palmer 1917:431).

Deletion and Confusion of Specimen Numbers. Another example of the confusion that was edited into the 1917 publication is illustrated in a scribe's version of Palmer's account of his November 1881 investigations at the Pecan Point site in northeast Arkansas, which includes a five-line insertion in Palmer's handwriting, and Palmer's own handwritten note about his July 1882 return visit to Pecan Point.

Page 410 from the 1917 publication shows that the two accounts from separate field seasons were juxtaposed. (See below for additional remarks on chronological problems.) It also shows that "corrections" were again made in both versions. Two of these changes introduced an unnecessary confusion into the published text. Two of Palmer's field specimen numbers (numbering systems are discussed below), 131 and 132, were spelled out, so that they appear at first glance to be counts of artifact packages. His remaining specimen numbers (133 through 136, and 122) were simply deleted. The latter, by the way, was the usual way the editors dealt with specimen numbers and descriptions, again indicating that they had no appreciation of the existence, let alone the potentials, of the collections at the Smithsonian.

Chronological Disorder. The most obvious shortcoming of the 1917 publication is its almost completely haphazard chronological order ("disorder" would be more accurate). As noted above, Palmer himself seems to have used whatever loose paper was at hand for his intermittent note-writing. These papers, and those he retained from the scribes, may well have become mixed during the thirty-odd years between his Arkansas work and his death.

Whether or not this was the case, the published result is in an order that might have been produced by throwing the papers into the air, picking them up, and publishing them. A not atypical example is seen on pages 412 and 413 of the 1917 volume, showing jumps from 1883 back to December 1881, to December 1882, and January 1883, thence to a marginal reference to May 1883, and finally back to 1882.

Editorial Practices for This Volume

Chronological Order. The documents dealing with Palmer's Arkansas mound investigations will be presented in chronological order, as nearly as that can be determined and accomplished. One of the really gratifying aspects of this research has been the repeated neat dovetailing of the long-separated elements: notes and fragments of other documents from the Arkansas archives on the one hand; letters, monthly reports, and drawings from the various Smithsonian files on the other.

The monthly reports have been particularly useful in assigning at least approximate dates to previously isolated and undated notes. This has been done both by positive assignment to a specific month and a specific place in that month's sequence, and by elimination of certain undated notes from certain months on the grounds of lack of mention in the monthly reports.

Various other techniques have been useful in assigning either absolute dates or relative places in the overall sequence to undated entries. Many of the pages bear handwritten numbers. These are often floating sequences beginning with numbers greater than one; one sequence for Palmer's undated notes on eastern Desha County sites begins with a page numbered 80.

Undated notes may contain internal evidence, such as references to previous or planned future visits to sites or places for which dates are available. Or places described in undated notes may be referred to in other entries which do have a datable context.

The plate numbers and letters assigned by Palmer to the drawings made by Lewis constitute an important sequence or set of sequences. In some cases Palmer used a self-contained series for drawings of an individual site; in others he started the series at one site and continued it at one or more other sites. He appears to have made these assignments and written the captions and accompanying notes some time after the field work was done.

Less reliable are the specimen number sequences. Palmer's surviving entries occasionally include lists of his own field specimen numbers, which are probably the most nearly chronological numbers for his Arkansas specimens. Although Palmer's collections were kept in better order than those of most other natural-history collectors of his day (McVaugh 1956:v–viii), his system was by no means rigorous. His basic, botanically oriented numbering system has been summarized by McVaugh:

> Palmer's collections before 1885 were usually numbered by him in the field, in more or less chronological sequence. Later they were sorted by those to whom they were sent for determination, the original species renumbered arbitrarily, after their rearrangement in some systematic order. . . .
>
> Even in later years, however, there is little continuity expressed by the serial numbers of the specimens, even though they may be approximately chronological in order. This is primarily because of Palmer's method of "cataloguing," that is, of numbering his collections and writing up his notes upon them. His notes were usually rather complete, but were often written up from memory some time after the actual specimens were dried. His practice was to collect a number of specimens at a locality, keeping these in the order of drying, or in no particular order, then to write up the "catalogue" for these before collecting more. (1956:131–32)

As previously noted, the Mound Survey specimens received not only field numbers but also Bureau of Ethnology numbers (which Palmer sometimes called "Thomas numbers") and finally, since the Bureau had no storage facilities of its own, National Museum of Natural History numbers (or Smithsonian numbers). The latter two sets of numbers were, of course, assigned in Washington and are of even less utility in suggesting the sequence of Palmer's site visits. Palmer himself was quite unhappy with Thomas for having his shipping boxes opened before he could return to Washington and participate in the cataloguing (see chapter 2).

It does appear that Palmer was often, if not always, careful enough to specify at least something of the contexts of his archeological specimens. Examples can be found in the field numbers in his reports of excavations at mounds in northeast Arkansas and at the Menard site and in the "House Sites" vs. "Mound Pottery" distinction made in his list of Smithsonian numbers for the specimens from his work at the B. F. Jackson site, and elsewhere.

In reassembling the whole chronological sequence, of course, the various techniques have been combined. This has also been done on a smaller scale in several more or less self-contained instances. One example is the early December 1882 eastern Desha County sequence, alluded to above. The pages numbered by Palmer include only a part of the sequence: 80 for the Wynn site, 81 for the Franklin site, 82 for the J. P. Clayton Mound, 83 and 84 missing, and 85 for the Arkansas City Cemetery Mound. Other notes and figure captions, though, connect the J. P. Clayton Mound closely to the De Soto or De-Priest Mound, and yet another note states that Palmer traveled to Arkansas City from the De Soto Mound on December 6, 1882. So the De Soto Mound visit can be interpolated into the sequence with some confidence; conversely, it provides a definite date, whereas the "page 80–82, 85" entries bear no dates.

The remaining undated and unattached entries have been tentatively assigned to places in the overall sequence, primarily on the basis of factors such as geography and likely or available means of transportation. Consistency with geography and knowledge of the history of railroad lines were factors in the Walnut Lake Station and De Soto Mound interpolations, for instance.

A more complex case is that of the scribe's undated note about the "Remains of Old Fortification" (called "Old French Fort Desha" by Thomas 1894: Figure 148; actually, it was a temporary location of Arkansas Post, as discussed by Arnold 1983). It was at first tentatively placed before the visit to the Wynn Mounds, simply because the fort site is only about ten airline kilometers (or six miles) east-southeast of Wynn. However, the most direct practical route between these two sites in extremely flood-prone country would have been about twice that far on the winding Arkansas River. And, since Palmer had come from the northwest (Pine Bluff), it seemed unlikely that he would have overshot Wynn, visited the fort site, then backtracked to Wynn and proceeded in a generally southerly direction from there to Arkansas City. As it became apparent that Palmer's return visit to Menard had taken place in mid-December 1882 rather than in early 1883, a more likely scenario for the fort site visit suggested itself: perhaps Palmer had traveled by steamboat up the Mississippi and Arkansas rivers from Arkansas City to Menard and stopped en route at the fort site. A weak, but still gratifying, bit of supporting evidence for the reassignment came from the observation that Palmer had assigned his field number 422 to specimens from the fort site, and numbers 423, 424, and 425 to specimens from the Menard visit.

A generally critical approach was taken, and entries of dates on the documents were not automatically accepted as representing the actual dates of field work. In some cases they are self-contradictory, e.g., the scribe's change from "83" to two "82" entries on a single page summarizing Palmer's observations in Arkadelphia on February 6, 8, and 10, 1883. In the 1917 publication the editorial choice was 1882. That is obviously the wrong year, as Palmer had been driven from Arkansas by "excessive rains" and arrived in Washington, D.C., on February 2, 1882, as noted at the end of chapter 6. This information was available to the editors, who published it (Palmer 1917:418) but did not appreciate its implication.

A final example suggests that Palmer himself was not completely rigorous in keeping track of daily details. Although his monthly report for the first portion of November 1881 begins with the "Pemiscott" Mound (as do the scribes' copies), a scribe's version of a note in the Arkansas files indicates that this mound was actually visited on October 31 (Palmer 1917:400; cf. chapter 6 of the present volume).

Order of Presentation of Document Types. It was stated above that Palmer's diary-like notes appear to be the most immediate documents relating to first impressions of sites, their surroundings, incidents of travel, and people contacted. It is usually possible to date the site visits, at least approximately, and in such cases the relevant notes will be presented before the letters and monthly reports that refer to a given site. The letters, which tend to be precisely dated and contain some references to just-completed work at various sites, will be presented next. Notes and letters that do not refer to work at sites will be placed according to the evidence for their dates, between the site discussions.

The monthly reports, though, often combine reports of work done at several sites over extended periods into single, more or less coherent documents. They will not be broken up, even though a strictly chronological account could be produced by doing this. Instead, they will be inserted *in toto* immediately after whatever notes and letters related to the contents of a given monthly report have been presented.

Multiple Documents. In some cases, particularly those involving monthly reports, we now have more than one version of essentially the same document. A good example is the case of late September 1883, for which we have two versions by Palmer describing his work in the Arkadelphia vicinity. The wordings differ slightly in places, some reordering of paragraphs was done, and they include two sets of Palmer's rough sketches of several mound sites.

Another kind of case is the December 1881 monthly report, for which we have not only Palmer's original but also versions by two different scribes. The original appears to have been lightly edited by Palmer himself, mainly by adding or changing words or phrases, and has been more heavily edited by someone who appears to have been fond of deletions. The scribes' versions both appear to have been derived from the original rather than one from the other, as both contain words or passages that are present in the original but not in the other scribe's copy. One of the scribe's versions was broken up, apparently by chance, and published on several far-flung pages of the 1917 publication, which introduced yet a few more changes.

To handle such hectic situations, one looks for general principles, such as those discussed by Tanselle:

The point of view I have been outlining here is, in its essentials, simple to state. It begins with the premise that the serious study of a text depends on access to the documentary evidence (whether the documents are manuscripts or printed) and that the process of editing therefore should not be one that conceals such evidence. It moves on to recognize that for writings not intended for publication the surviving documents are the end products, which should be reproduced with as much fidelity as possible . . . [A] critical approach—when it involves editorial judgment directed toward establishing what the author wished, not merely what the editor prefers, and when it entails the recording of the evidence (variant readings, emendations) for assessing that judgment—at once shows respect for the historical record and for the work as a completed intellectual production. (1981:53–54)

In the first case of duplication noted above, one of the documents was probably produced by Palmer in the field. The handwriting is somewhat more careless, and no specimen numbers are given. The other is more neatly organized and includes some Smithsonian specimen numbers. Clearly, the latter version is closer to what the author wished, and it has been used as the copy-text in chapter 8. Notes have been used to indicate variant readings in the earlier field version. Since the field version's drawings were apparently done at the sites and are therefore presumably somewhat more accurate (all of Palmer's drawings are rather crude), they are presented.

The starting point taken for the second case is that the most basic documents to be presented herein are those produced by Palmer himself. He, not the scribes and editors, gathered the data in the field and had the most complete understanding of contexts. So the copy-texts published herein for these monthly reports will be those written by Palmer, with the deletions restored. Indications of significant deletions and other changes made by the scribes and editors will be relegated to notes.

Selective Deletions and Deviations. It is hardly possible, barring complete photo-reproduction or costly typographic devices, to produce an absolutely faithful reproduction of documents such as these. Certain compromises must be made, and probably the best approach is to be selective, systematic, and explicit about them.

A trivial example is that no attempt has been made to make the line breaks match those of the written originals, but an effort has been made to emulate the originals in either indenting or not indenting the beginnings of paragraphs. In many cases, though, the indentions on the originals are less than half-hearted, and judgment calls must be made.

Marginal additions and interlinear insertions that clearly flow into the adjacent text have simply been included in the printed text. Interruptive marginal additions and insertions, however, are indicated by notes or, in the case of Palmer's additions to the scribes' texts, by a distinctive typeface.

Although many of the documents were given page numbers by Palmer or a scribe, these page numbers have been systematically deleted from the present printed version. Their inclusion would have interrupted the flow of the text without adding information useful to the reader. Similarly, the running heads used by Palmer and his scribes at the tops of pages following the first page of a continued text have also been deleted.

Separation of Entries. Individual documents, from one-line or one-sentence notes to multi-page monthly reports, will be considered as self-contained entries and indicated as such by double lines between entries.

Indications of Sources. The repository and file reference for an individual entry will be indicated immediately below the horizontal line marking that entry's beginning.

Documents from three archives have been used. These archives, and the respective abbreviations used for them and their files, are as follows:

The Arkansas History Commission, Little Rock, Arkansas, will be abbreviated "AHC." All of the Palmer documents are in the Small Manuscript Collection, Box XIII, No. 9. They are subdivided into item numbers from 1 to 30, approximately in chronological order. An indication will also be given as to the pages of the 1917 publication on which a given entry appeared. Thus, a complete citation might read, "AHC Item 21 (1917:427)."

Because the 1917 publication is more accessible than the original documents, no attempt has been made to indicate all of its numerous deviations from the Palmer and scribe texts. Only its most significant changes in wording or meaning will be noted.

The National Anthropological Archives, Smithsonian Institution, Washington, D.C., will be abbreviated "NAA" and subdivided for present purposes into two files. Most of the Palmer documents are in the "2400" File. Some of Palmer's letters are in the Bureau of (American) Ethnology "Letters Received" File. Typical citations are: "NAA 2400" or "NAA BAE Letters."

Only one relevant document, a postcard from Palmer to Baird, was found in the Archives of the Smithsonian Institution, Washington, D.C. Its name and the file designation are fully written out for that entry.

Drawings. All of Lewis's drawings and the engravings derived from them have been designated as numbered figures. The same has been done for several of Palmer's better efforts. As noted above, Palmer assigned his own plate numbers for Lewis's drawings. However, his use of Roman and Arabic numbers or letter designations was inconsistent, and his sequences started over again several times and contained some gaps. So, although his designations will be included, they will be supplanted by a consistent sequence of figure numbers, inserted in editorial brackets.

Palmer and the scribes also drew a few rather crude sketches between the lines of some of the monthly reports. These are considered here to be integral parts of those documents rather than figures and have been included between the printed lines, replicating their places in the original documents as closely as practicable.

Locations of Original and Duplicate Documents. As a by-product of this research, complete sets of original and/or duplicate documents are now accessible in three locations. The Arkansas History Commission, One Capitol Mall, Little Rock, AR 72201, now has in its archives photocopies of all the relevant original documents in the Smithsonian Institution's archives, in addition to those originals (and microfilms of them) acquired in 1914. The National Anthropological Archives, in the National Museum of Natural History building, Smithsonian Institution, Washington, DC 20560, now has photocopies of all the documents from the Arkansas History Commission's Archives, in addition to its own originals in the "2400" file and the Bureau of Ethnology "letters received" file. Finally, the Arkansas Archeological Survey, P.O. Box 1249, Fayetteville, AR 72702-1249, has photocopies of all of the relevant documents.

Chapter Section Introductions and Endnotes.   After some experiments and discussions, I decided not to use same-page footnotes to explicate Palmer's documents. Instead, two means of explication and annotation are used in the chapters that contain Palmer's documents.

First, these chapters are divided into sections, which derive more or less naturally from Palmer's practices in accomplishing his field work. As in his botanical and other collecting forays, he would typically set up a field headquarters, preferably at the home of a well-to-do local amateur naturalist or at a good hotel, and explore the locality from that base. Here, the chapter sections will include a variety of such locality episodes. In the cases of his more extensive investigations at major sites, a section will include only a single site visit.

Each section has an introduction written by myself, in many cases with the collaboration of other Arkansas Archeological Survey researchers, as noted. These introductions include the lengthier or more significant background material. The major emphases will be the identification of the sites visited by Palmer and summaries of what, if anything, has been learned about them since his day. In the intervening century, the landscape, especially in the Delta farmlands, has changed dramatically (Holder 1970; Ford and Rolingson 1972); landowners have come and gone, and many site names have changed; archeological surveys, excavations, and analyses have produced much new information and many new interpretations; and many sites have been severely damaged or destroyed. In too many of the latter cases, Palmer's information is all we have.

For each site, then, an effort will be made to locate and identify it, noting its past and present names, site numbers, culture-historical position and (if particularly relevant) relationships. The section introductions will also summarize what, if anything, Thomas had to say about the site in his 1894 final report or elsewhere and will discuss significant later investigations, findings, and publications.

Endnotes, indicated by superscripted numbers in Palmer's texts, will also be used. The emphasis here will be on technical archeological discussions and scholarly minutiae that are undoubtedly of less interest to the general reader.

In addition to the archeological explication, another class of subjects will also receive attention in the section introductions and endnotes. The documents (particularly the notes) produced by Palmer also preserve some very interesting culture-historical information about the contemporary Arkansas scene. At the very least, basic identification is needed for a number of long-dead people, communities that no longer exist or have changed significantly, and various features of a landscape that has since been heavily damaged. Also, a variety of historical situations need explication, and certain "incidents of travel" or observations on customs call for it.

Measurements.   Palmer, Thomas, and their contemporaries used the English system of measurement in miles, yards, feet, etc. American archeologists have generally converted to the metric system in recent decades, and metric measurements will be given for present-day situations. But, for ease of comparison with the nineteenth-century data, and as a concession to those of us who grew up using the English system and still use it, English equivalents will also be presented. In some cases, when metric measurements are clearly irrelevant, only the English system will be used. I have previously argued for such a common-sense approach to measurements (Jeter 1977:2).

CHAPTER SIX

Arkansas Reconnaissance and Other Investigations, 1881–82

Although Palmer may have arrived in Osceola as early as October 20, 1881, the first dated entry in his Arkansas notes states that he left there on October 27 for the Little River locality. It seems unlikely that he would have waited a week before venturing into the hinterlands, but, in the absence of more detailed information, his whereabouts and activities for the October 20–26 period must remain a minor mystery.

It is clear, in the perspective of his later work, that Palmer's first few months in Arkansas served mainly as a reconnaissance. He later revisited most of the same regions and some of the same sites.

Palmer's itinerary for this first season is detailed in table 6.1, and mapped in figure 6.1. In summary, he began in northeasternmost Arkansas near the Missouri "bootheel," which was already known in the archeological literature through the work of Swallow (1858) and an article by Putnam (1875) based on that work, and proceeded downriver to Pecan Point. He then went to Arkansas Post, on the lower Arkansas River; his most important foray from there was to the Menard Mounds, which he also revisited the next season with Lewis. Next he moved to the lower White River valley and based his operations successively at Lawrenceville, Indian Bay, and Clarendon. He then made his headquarters at Helena, on the Mississippi. His final expedition for the season was up the valley of the L'Anguille River, to Marianna and Forrest City, but bad weather curtailed his field work and forced him to return to Washington.

"The Place Beggars Description": Palmer's 1881 Investigations in Northeast Arkansas

MARVIN D. JETER AND DAN F. MORSE

Palmer's first base of operations in Arkansas was Osceola, then as now a Mississippi River port. Osceola appeared to be a pleasant enough place when we visited it in 1983 to check land-ownership records for some of Palmer's sites. However, shortly before Palmer's visit, it made an unfavorable impression on Dr. Frank Lowber James (Baird 1977), who practiced medicine there from 1877 to 1879 and sent a variety of artifacts from nearby mounds to Joseph Henry at the Smithsonian (Morse and Morse 1983:18–19).

Palmer's own rather negative impressions of Osceola are given in an entry dated November 10, 1881. One should probably read that entry first, to fully appreciate his understated decision to terminate his first Arkansas expedition and return to Osceola after his memorable October 29 breakfast at Peterson's on Pemiscot Bayou.

The overall chronological framework for this section is provided by a report from Palmer to Powell, which is transcribed at the end of the section. It was the first of two "monthly" reports that Palmer submitted for November 1881. (The second November

Table 6.1.
Palmer's Itinerary for His First Arkansas Field Season (October 1881–February 1882)

OCTOBER
20—Arrived in Osceola (McVaugh 1956:254).
27—Left Osceola for Little River; stayed with Mr. Beggs.
28—Moved on to Big Lake and Bayou Pemiscot; visited Hector's Mound; stayed at Peterson's.
29—Left Peterson's for Osceola.
31—Visited Chickasawba Mound.

NOVEMBER
?—Probably at Carson Lake Mounds during early November.
10—In Osceola.
12—Left Osceola for Pecan Point.
23—May have arrived at Arkansas Post.
24—Thanksgiving Day, at Arkansas Post. (Palmer was based at Arkansas Post at least six days, probably slightly more; he visited the Menard site, probably for at least two days, and returned to Arkansas Post.)
29—At Arkansas Post; wrote letter report to Powell about Menard Site.

DECEMBER
?—Visited Maxwell mounds, fifteen miles northwest of Arkansas Post.
7—Visited Lawrenceville-Maddox Bay locality.

8—Visited St. Charles.
12—Visited Spencer and Shipman mounds near Indian Bay.
23—Saw Bailey's Family Troupe at Indian Bay.
24—At Indian Bay; wrote letter report to Powell.
25—Christmas at Indian Bay.
26—Left Indian Bay for Holly Grove ("Holley Wood").
27—Holly Grove to East Lake; visited three mounds there.
29—Left for Clarendon.
30—Probably investigated two mounds near Clarendon.
31—In Clarendon.

JANUARY 1882
2—Arrived at Helena via rail.
3—Ferry to Mississipi; railroad to Jonestown, Mississippi.
11—Left Helena for Marianna by boat.
18—In Marianna; snow, sleet, and frozen ground.
22—At Forrest City; wrote postcard to Baird, noting sixteen days of continuous rain, followed by frost.

FEBRUARY
2—Arrived in Washington, D.C.

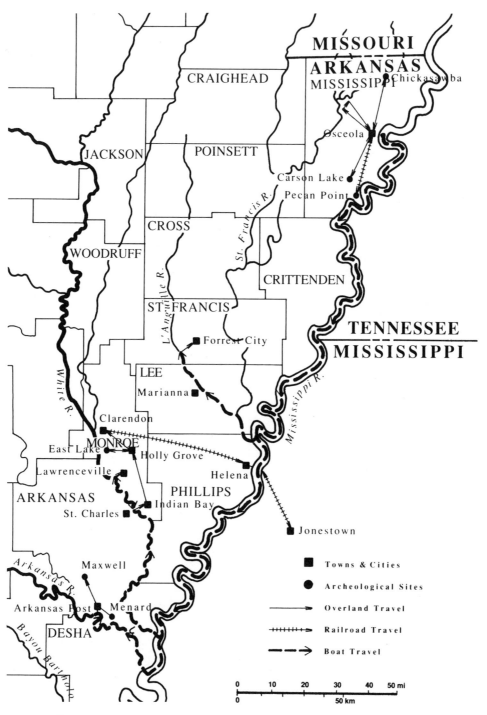

FIGURE 6.1

Map of Palmer's itinerary for the 1881–82 field season in Arkansas.

report deals with his work in the lower Arkansas River valley and is presented in the next section.) The "November" work included in the first report actually started in late October and probably continued until about November 21 or 22.

There are three handwritten versions of this report. The first, which is used here, is in Palmer's own hand but was edited by someone else who struck out many words, phrases, and sentences and rewrote some passages. All of these changes in the body of the report have been restored to Palmer's original wording here, but the unknown editor's caption and date have been retained. The second version, by a scribe, essentially follows the unknown editor's version; it has not been used here at all. The third version, by another scribe, replicates most but not all of Palmer's original. It was separated into segments that were presented in haphazard order in the 1917 publication (on pages 397–98, 400, and 410), and it remains in the Arkansas History Commission's small manuscript collection. It is not reprinted here, but several of its noteworthy textual divergences from Palmer's original will be remarked upon.

Sites Visited from Osceola

Pemiscot Mound.   It appears that the major, if not the only, site visited by Palmer during his first expedition was a mound on Pemiscot Bayou. Although no such site is mentioned in his diary-like notes, in his monthly report Palmer stated that he had visited a "Pemisscott Mound . . . 22 miles North West from Osceola [actually about twelve miles] situated on Pemisscott Bayou." Holmes reported that the mound was "20 feet in height, with a surface area of about one-fourth of an acre" and "contained no remains of interest" although charcoal and potsherds had been found when it was first plowed (1884:468). Thomas only mentioned this mound, and Palmer's visit to it, in passing in his preliminary report (1891:20) and not at all in the Mississippi County section of his final report (1894:219–23). Palmer's Pemisscott Mound has not been identified satisfactorily. One known site (3MS55) has been thought to be this mound, but Palmer's description does not fit it.

Chickasawba Mound.   Palmer's next site, however, is definitely identifiable. The Chickasawba Mound site (3MS5 or 9-Q-2) is on the northwestern outskirts of Blytheville, also on Bayou Pemiscot. This was clearly a major site, but even in Palmer's day relic collectors and farming had made a heavy impact on it. Palmer did not get permission to dig here. The site has not been studied intensively by later researchers but is known to have Early, Late, and probably Middle period Mississippian components.

Carson Lake Mounds.   Next, probably during the first week of November (which is not otherwise accounted for), Palmer traveled southwest of Osceola, to examine three mounds that have become known as the Carson Lake site (3MS13 or 10-P-1). Here, for the first time in Arkansas, he encountered fairly abundant human skeletal remains, associated with artifacts.

Palmer emphasized the effects of the great New Madrid earthquake series of 1811–12 on these remains. Similar effects have been noted during several more recent excavations in this region, e.g., at the Matthews site (23NM156 or 5-R-3) in New Madrid County, Missouri (Walker and Adams 1946:84), at the Campbell site (23PM5 or 8-Q-7) in Pemiscot County, Missouri (Chapman and Anderson 1955:72, 77, Figures 31,

33), and at the Zebree site (3MS20) in Mississippi County, Arkansas (Anderson 1977a:8–4, Figure 8–1).

Holmes (1884:468–69) briefly summarized Palmer's report on Carson Lake and did not illustrate any of the artifacts, only mentioning them in passing as "plain . . . ordinary undecorated ware" (1884:468–69). Thomas merely listed this site in his catalog (1891:21) and did not mention it in his final report (1894).

Carson Lake has never been intensively studied but, on the basis of later collections, has been included in the Late Mississippian to Protohistoric (c. A.D. 1400–1600) Nodena phase by Phillips (1970:935) and Morse (1973: Figure 40). Phillips suggested that it might belong to the earlier portion of the phase.

Pecan Point. Palmer's final foray from Osceola took him southward by train to one of the most remarkable sites in a site-rich region. Pecan Point (3MS78 or 11-P-6) was apparently one of the largest sites of the Nodena phase (Phillips 1970:447–75; Morse 1973:72–74; Morse and Morse 1983:284–87). It was never adequately mapped or measured but included a large village area and several mounds (1983:286–87). It was washed away by the floodwaters of the Mississippi River in the early twentieth century (1983:311).

Palmer's collections of numerous vessels and other artifacts from Pecan Point were described extensively, with eight illustrations, by Holmes (1884:469–75, Figures 142–49). Thomas listed Pecan Point in his catalog (1891:20) and discussed it in his final report (1894:219–22), but did not mention Palmer or refer to Holmes's publication. Palmer's collections have not been intensively studied in the light of modern archeology but have been briefly examined by Hoffman, who called them "fabulous" and strongly recommended such studies (1975:18).

Nevertheless, Palmer barely scratched the surface at Pecan Point. His notes refer to "hundreds of specimens of pottery" obtained here in the spring of 1881 by the Davenport Academy of Iowa; these included an example of the "head pot" class (Thomas 1894: Figure 130) for which this and related sites in northeast Arkansas have become famous. Two decades later, C. B. Moore (1911:447–75) excavated 349 burials there, which produced 535 ceramic vessels (see also Morse and Morse 1983:286).

Morse and Morse (1983:311–12, Figure 13.2) have suggested that Pecan Point may have been the capital of the province of Pacaha, visited by Hernando de Soto in 1541. However, they now agree with Charles Hudson's (1985:4) suggestion that Pacaha may well have been the Bradley site, which was also visited by Palmer in November 1882 and February 1883, about twenty-five kilometers (or fifteen miles) downstream.

Palmer's Speculations

In his reports on the Carson Lake and Pecan Point sites, Palmer began to make his frequently-repeated erroneous speculations about the uses of mounds and about prehistoric house construction. He repeatedly remarked on the suitability of mounds for use as observation or lookout points by prehistoric hunters. This was perhaps a possibility after the mounds had been abandoned—in fact, some mounds are now used for this purpose and as sites for deer camps, by modern hunters in Arkansas—but is quite unlikely as a primary purpose.

Unlike many of his contemporaries, Palmer correctly assumed as a matter of course that the mounds, and the house remains in and near them, had indeed been built by Indians. But, making a false analogy from his Southwestern observations of Puebloan Indians, he assumed that the Mississippi Valley Indian houses had had flat, timbered roofs plastered over with hardened clay.

Palmer may also have been familiar with, and confused by, the interpretations of C. G. Swallow, an early investigator in southeast Missouri. In 1856–57 Swallow excavated some mounds near New Madrid; he donated his collection and notes to the Peabody Museum at Harvard around 1875. In his manuscript, which was quoted by Putnam (1875a:322–23) in an article that Palmer may well have seen, he suggested that rooms had been built by setting up poles "like rafters in the roof of a house," putting split canes on the rafters, and applying a mud plastering both "above and below so as to form a solid mass, inclosing the rafters and lathing of cane." Finally, he speculated, "over this room was built the earth work of the mound."

Palmer did not understand prehistoric Southeastern house construction techniques involving vertical wattle-and-daub walls and unplastered ceilings beneath steeply pitched thatched roofs. This type of structure was also overlooked by his more famous contemporary, Lewis Henry Morgan (1881), in his classic study of Native American houses. However, Cyrus Thomas clearly understood and illustrated the basic lathing techniques used in the walls of such structures, basing his interpretations on the finds of another of his field assistants in northeast Arkansas (1894:205–06, Figure 118).

Palmer's 1881 Northeast Arkansas Documents

AHC Item 1 (1917:398–99)

Journey from Osceola.   Ark.
Oct. 27—1881—
Left Osceola Oct. 27th. 81. in a mule team for Little River over low woodlands for some miles, then through the new cut road; Trees blazed along the old road along which were a few scattering houses. Had to pass through cyprus swamps up to the knees; There was a good deal of water also—It rained all day—20 miles brought us to Arnold's but we could not stop—He had a fine cotton crop. Settlers are few & far between. Crossed Little River which was a dry sand bed, but steamboats run up it for ½ th year.
Staid all night on its bank with Mr. Beggs in a rude hut (log) & was entertained in a handsome manner. He was only temporarily here till his own house was finished. A company of log cutters arrived.
A fierce storm of wind raged all night. Falling trees kept up a noise like the roaring of many cannons, fearfully blocking the roads, which are not cleared of obstructions if they can be passed around.
We moved on to Big Lake a hunters' haven.[1]
Noticed cottonwood trees having holes cut in them for collecting water to quench the thirst of travellers.
Passed camps of hunters & a few log huts inhabited by long-haired, dirty, sickly people, who claim to live in a healthy country. On every hand is malarial fever[2] Some said they had no food but what they shot.

Pemiscott Bayou. 22 miles
S.W. of Osceola.　　Ark.

We stopped here at Peterson's an old resident. Bees, cotton, fowls, cows, corn, mules & etc, were seen in numbers. The house was poor & disordly. Three females met us with snuff sticks in their mouths. Three men with guns, just returned from the hunt, approached the house. The place beggars description. Its dirty appearance & clothing of the people would lead you to infer the people never wash.

　conversing with the owner about his fruit trees,—the owner let out a fearful tirade against the agent or nursery drummer who sold him a quantity of trees & plants. "All that lived," said he, "is 6 strawberry plants, 2 roses, & 3 fruit trees, and believe my skin," said he "if he ain't sent me a bill, all dead uns too."

Then with a threat of what he would do if another tree man came, we went to supper. The black table cloth spoke for itself as did the black coffee & plain corn bread & most abominably cooked wild goose. The Landlord was not very complimentary because of my disturbing the dead, he styling it a sin, and he could not see the use of the nonsense.[3] For his part they all belong to the church, but order or cleanliness was not a part of their religion. A horse power gin was on the place. With sufficient help about to secure his crops. He was waiting for white men to come & hire for that purpose. Suggesting we could send him black men from Osceola as they were getting through their work. With scorn & contempt on his features, he said, he would have none of the trash on his place. He did not want any of them to settle near or amoung them.

Three slept in a bed on the floor, not only dirt but bed bugs & fleas. Domestic animals, & fowls took possession of various parts of the house. At Breakfast we had Black Coffee, corn bread & Racoon very tough with a little new made stinking butter. We had seen the dogs tip of the cover from the churn and put their heads in and lick out the cream.

　We did not wait for dinner but left for Osceola.

Chickasawba. 24 miles N. of
Bayou Pemiscott,[4]　　Ark

Oct. 31st. 81—

　Visited a mound here in a team. The mound was 25 ft. high and had ¼ acre on top.[5] It had been so variously dug into that it would scarcely pay to open it, besides no men could be had. The owner did not wish to have it opened as he wanted it for a cellar for his house. For a wide distance around were the dwellings & graves of hundreds.

AHC Item 2 (1917:397–98)

Mounds on farm of Hugh Waller
In Carson Lake Township 6 miles
a little S. W. from Osceola,
Ark.

There are several mounds on this farm, all of which have been more or less changed. I am informed that the Earthquake of 1811 & 1812 cut large fissures through or ran close by all of them. Only one contained anything & that was one of the smallest. The Earthquake cut a furrow through it on one side & near the edge of this furrow were found 2 nice water vessels[6] by the side of a skull, the rest of the body being precipitated into the deep furrow. In the centre of this mound were found 6 skeletons, the bones of which, though in place, were much split & cracked by the force of the Earthquake.

AHC Item 2 (1917:398)

Osceola, Mississippi Co. Ark.

Nov 10—1881—
    The grand jury had two black men on it & gave great satisfaction.
The petite jury had one black man on it. Some strong talk by some against it.
Shoes seem to wear out very slowly—no stones.
Three cotton gins were burnt this year.
Chinnamen[7] who live here live by burning bricks. They are very industrious & dress as other men, his hair cut even all round.
Consumption in dogs & animals is caused by dampness.
Osceola is a dirty, damp expensive place to live. The buildings are small.
The grog shops outnumber any other kind of shop or business
The grand jury had 300 witnesses before it and served 60 subpoenas, so said the foriman

AHC Item 3 (1917:408–09)

Pecan Point   Ark.
Miss County

Left Osceola Nov. 12th. 1881 for Pecan Point. On the train were judges, lawyers, and many passengers all more or less connected with the circuit court. There were 6 black prisoners chained two by two & One white man. The white man sat ironed by the judge, Deputy Sheriff Lawyers & etc. to see them play cards. The white prisoner ate at a table near me, & after dinner he smoked a cigar with the clerk of the court. The black prisoners sat the whole while just inside the cabin so that their white guards could be in the cabin & look after them.

Dr. F. G. McGavock[8] who now lives contiguous to Pecan Point informs me that during the last year of the war he went to Castle Garden N.Y. and hired 86 Irish Girls at $20 per. month. with board.

All but 5 were Catholics. The negroes had left his fathers large plantation. White men had all been drafted—

Federals gunboats were in front of his house & Conferates camped in the rear who called for contributions, while the Federals had plenty. There were only 3 Old men as superintendents on the place.

Cotton was selling at from 1.40 to 1.80 per lb.

These females were hired to work the cotton for one year and they did it too. While part of the crop remained yet unpicked the floods came. The doctor promised each girl a new balmoral and a pair of shoes if all the cotton was pulled up & saved. All the teams were put in the field, 4 women on a side and the entire cotton crop (the rest) was pulled & loaded on the wagons & taken to a dry place and saved—they barefooted with dresses between their legs. Priests came every Saturday to gather money & keep them straight—He had a free ride. The year after the war only ½ remained, most of those who left received places as dometics in Memphis replacing the negroes.

The Dr. complained that he had to fee officers of both sides.

German men were hired but they were a decided failure.

Heavy rains prevented me from finishing at this place or from reaching Little River from here, so I left by steamer but waited all night for a boat, in a low wood hut on the river bank. Rain & wind made the night very unpleasant, besides it was very cold. Several others were waiting & a corpse. There was no fire which rendered it very uncomfortable.

A snag catching in a wheel & breaking it hence the delay—A telegraph along the river bank would obviate the difficulty.

Country stores—negro hands & their fondness for whisky

———————

AHC Item 3 (1917:410)

Pecan Point   Ark.

[This entry, principally in a scribe's hand but interrupted by Palmer, virtually duplicates Palmer's original "Report for November" remarks on Pecan Point and is not transcribed here. See Palmer's report, immediately below, for those remarks, and for endnotes about significant divergences in this entry.—Ed.]

NAA 2400

Palmers Report for November
Mounds of Arkansas Dec 6th 81
Major J. W. Powell
Director of Bureau of Ethnology
Smithsonion Institution
November 1881

122 Pipe found while digging near the bank of the Mississippi River, contiguous to Oseola Mississippi County, it is presented to the Smithsonion Institution by Gill Herron Esq. of Chicksawba Mississippi County. The marking now on it was thereon I am informed when found.

Pemisscott Mound

Visit to a Mound 22 miles North West from Oseola situated on Pemisscott Bayou, Mississippi County Arkansaw on the Farm of Samuel Hector, Esq

It was 20 feet high. Measured a quarter of an acre on the top and but a little larger at the base originally—since the settlement of the country the base & sides have been much enlarged by the plow and by digging after Anticquities Am informed but little was ever found in it. Its summit was untoutched so examined into it but found nothing it was composed of blueish clay & sand.

The owner informed when he first cultivated over the mound 20 years ago its sides contained three didtches all round equal distance from each other evidences of which are yet to be seen especially at one place 8 feet from sumit it was quite distinct for several feet a fence running near preserved its originality.

The situation of this mound in a region often overflowed with water, therefore may not the didtches have been dug to prevent the water from encroaching upon the mound so readily or where they to prevent enemies ascending to the sumit which affords both defensiveness and means of observation. The owner informs me that when he first plowed over its summit much ashes charcool & burnt clay with some bones and pottery was upturned.

Chickasawba Mound

Mound at Chicksawba 24 miles North of Oseola Mississippi County. This Mound is 25 feet high one part and 30 the other and one fourth of an acre on the top. It had been so much dug into during various years that to obtain anything left would require the working over of all the mound which would not pay as I was informed that only a few things was ever found and those on the surface. one party dug 16 feet down the center found nothing another dug from one side into the center and reported finding hewn timbers and quit. Now the owner does not wish to have it disturbed as he is about to have a house built on it and a celler underneath it

being the only dry spot in this locality fit for a celler. The land arround the mound is not overflowed by water. A fine view is obtained of the surrounding country and Pemiscott Bayou. Nearby is a field of several acres covered with cotton that has been cultivated for several years which is now covered with fragments of pottery bones &c. The owner informed me that when the field was first plowed quantities of ashes charcool skeletons Potts and stone impliments where turned up these where found under slight elevations only one skeleton in one place. In this large field was many of these elevations which no doubt where the destroyed houses with dead as left with their effects at death. A visit to the field convince you of that fact.

Nothing was obtained at this place. While digging a post hole at the edge of the field a small water vessel was obtained it was striped red and white.[9] The rim and bottom had been seperately made then placed in position mud was then used to attatch them as puttey does glass to the sash of a window the pot was nicely burnt and quite strong. Made an effort to obtain this specimen but failed.

Mounds that was disturbed by the Earthquake which did so much dammage at New Madrid Missouri in 1811

In Carson Lake Township six miles a little South of West from Oseola, Mississippi County Arkansas on the farm of Hugh Waller Esq is three mounds that was much disturbed by the Earthquake which did so much damage at New Madrid Mo. and to this portion of Arkansaw.

First mound visited presented this form. The earthquake changed its round form to an uneven flat surface with numerous depressions and small irregular elevations giving the sumit the appearance of having numerous potato hills thereon.[10] It is 75 feet long and 59 feet wide.

The mound is composed of clay & sand it contained no evidences of dwellings or of buriels.

Second mound visited is 100 yards in a direct line from the previous one and presents some what this form as though part of its original size had been cut off by the volcano[11] and slid downwards forming two ridges like appendages to the mound. It is now somewhat circular in the center and about 20 feet high and 23 feet accross at top. upon this sumit recent buriels have been made. Along each side is a furrow that is now five feet deep made by the Earthquake which caused the olteration to the mound, one of the end appendages is 48 feet long and 45 feet wide its surfac contain numerous small elevations more or less surrounded by depressions. The other appendage to the mound is 51 feet long 15 1/2 feet wide with a gentle slope from the center of mound. It is clay & sand but no remains.

Third mound examined was 250 yards diagnally from the preceeding one. it is six feet 5 inches high 35 feet long 35 feet wide to a furrow made on its left side by Earthquake which threw on its side 9 feet of the mound thus befor this change was made the mound was 34 feet wide & circular

In the center of this mound 6 skeletons was found associated with a strattum of ashes & charcoll above them was some ashes fine charcool and burnt clay that in all probability was the result of burning the hut down over the dead the fire must have been fierce as the bones especially the crania was much burnt and the Earthquake that plowed through the edge of the mound split the larger bones and separating the crania the bones except the burnt portions where not preservabable.

Near the edge of the earthquake furrow two peices of pottery was found the neck of one bent toward that of the other from the furrow while near them was the upper part of crania which was filled with earth on removing it fell to pieces. the rest of the body fell into the Earthquake furrow water must have overflown the mound after the flesh left the crania or it would not have filled with earth.

These mounds are in a low swampey section which overflows As the builders used to flock to these elevations to be out of the water so do Horses and cattle of to day They are admirably adabted for observation. The crockery found in this part of Arkansaw resemble closely that found at New Madrid Mo.

123   Bones from skeletons in Mound 3 showing their burnt character the unburnt portions where mostly decayed, the larger bones show old brakes as though they had been broaken by the Earthquake the crania with the skeletons was seperated and lay appart in various peices.

As Ashes and charcool was found above the skeletons may not the burning down of the hut over the dead be the cause of burning the bones so variously. If it was intended to cremate the remains then they would have all been burnt and not partially charred, as they lay lengthways which is the way fire from a roof would act upon them.
upon them.

124   Part of a small vessel found with 123 As this was the only thing found with the six skeletons may they have been drowned during the overflow, laid under the roof of a house upon this mound and the building burnt down and earth covered over. The remains lay one upon the other the crania being some inches appart they with the larger bones had been seperated by the Earthquake

125   A rude stone that have been used found contiguous to 123—they are rare hear as the soil is without gravel or rock formation.

126   Peice of charcool that belonged to a post of the house burnt down over 123

127   Burnt & unburnt clay from roof of house burnt down over 123

128   Peice of pottery found near the furrow of Mound 3 which was caused by An Earthquake

129   Two water vessels found at the edge of the furrow made by an Earthquake in Mound 3 one vessel was depressed one way the other quite opposite. close by lay Crania 130 it was in position and filled with earth it fell to peices at removel the lower part and all the body had been carried away when the Earthquake formed the furrow through the left edge of Mound 3. Nothing else was found

Mounds at Pecan Point
At Pecan Point Mississippi Co Arkansaw one mile West from the Missis-

sippi River on land owned by R. W. Friend is two mounds one 150 feet in circumference¹² and 5 feet high, nothing was found therein. The other is 4 feet high and 25 feet accross. At 16 inches from the surface was found two entirely decayed skeletons.

These mounds are near a small lake and afford an oppertunity to watch the approach of game to water Hunters to be concealed in brush hutts.

On the same estate not far from the above mentioned mounds is another one in a field of cotton: 20 feet accross and varing from 3 to 4 feet in height. It has been cultivated one year which let in the rains that destroyed completely the remains deposited therein as they where but 12 to 18 inches below the surface. The large trees that once grew upon this mound filled it with roots which broke the pottery deposited with the dead and often turning it from its original position now comes the plow and brakes and scatter it more.

131   under this number is eleven bundles of peices found more or less together and belonging to several kinds of vessels¹³

131½¹⁴   The bundles under this number where found seperate still the causes that broke them up may have some what mixed them.
        The few unbroaken specimens found in the above mound appear to have been in their original position and in various parts of the mound there being so little difference in depth of deposit and distance appart that I am of the opinion Indian brush hutts once covered it a death occurring the hut was burnt down over the remains and its household property finally a few inches of earth was covere over all. If it had been used as a burial mound only there must have been some uniformity in deposits or some marks over the graves or there would be one above the other which was not the case. If the spot was simply a buryal place then why the strattum of ashes immediately over the remains.

132   Under this number is (5) packages presented the Smithsonion Institution by Dr. J. M. Lindsley¹⁵ of Pecan Point Mississippi Co Arkansaw. They where taken from a cultivated field containing 15 acres, it is one half mile from the Mississippi river. In this field is a large mound now covered with graves of modern Inhabitants so it could not be opened
        Many years ago when the timber was cleared from this field in order to cultivate it numerous small elevations was observable scattered over the field with out any apparent order. The action of the plow in cultivating the field for years has oblitterated these former elevations but in turning up the soil the ashes that would be left by burning an Indian brush shanty is found with the clay that was the roof which the fire had burnt some what like brick. In digging three to four feet under this you come often to ashes of hard wood one foot or more in thickness a sample of which is sent under No 136 and almost invariably with these ashes is found bones of animals—birds & fish shells of land and fresh water molusks with various household articles The spot containing these deposits was undoubtedly

the slight elevations seen before cultivating the field.

A gentleman from Davenport Iowa Academy of Science last spring took from this field hundreds of specimens of pottery found by the side of skeletons It is to be regretted that no part of the skeletons was preserved.

But little can now be found in the field I found the potts under no 133 [16] Crania numbered 134 [17] Stone impliments &c numbered 135 [18]

The specimens numbered 132 and presented to the Smithsonion Institution by D J. M. Lindsley was taken from the same field as 133–134 and 135.

This gentleman proposes to run a subsoil plow to turn up what ever remains under the soil and send to the Smithsonion Institution.

Pecan Point Mississippi County
Arkansaw November   1881
Edward Palmer.

"Many Broaken Potts": Palmer's Initial Investigations at the Menard Site

MARVIN D. JETER

At some time around November 23, 1881, Palmer traveled from northeast Arkansas to the lower Arkansas River valley. He probably made the trip by steamboat, as his first notes stated that he "landed" at Arkansas Post. After a delay of about three days due to bad weather, he proceeded a short distance to the now-famous Menard site. Here he must have worked for several days, for he made a number of significant finds.

Observations at Arkansas Post

Arkansas Post, the first more or less permanent European settlement in Arkansas, was established in 1686 by Henri de Tonti, who was returning up the Mississippi valley to Illinois after an unsuccessful attempt to rescue La Salle's lost colony in Texas. He left six men at Arkansas Post, with one Jean Couture in charge, to establish a small trading post near the Quapaw Indian village of Osotouy, which is now believed to have been at the Menard site.

The first post was abandoned in 1699, but the location was reoccupied by John Law's colony from 1721 to 1749, after which the post was moved about eight airline kilometers (or five miles) upstream to Ecores Rouges, the location of the settlement visited by Palmer and of the present Arkansas Post National Memorial. In 1756 it was moved downstream to a location on the Arkansas River in northeast Desha County, which was more convenient for Mississippi River convoys. It remained there until 1779, when it was moved back to Ecores Rouges, due to decreased river traffic and intensifying floods (Arnold 1983).

Palmer did not conduct archeological investigations at Arkansas Post, which was at that time a remnant of the town that had been heavily affected by the Civil War, and was not a prehistoric mound site, in any case. Instead, it was merely his base for work at the Menard site. While waiting at Arkansas Post for the weather to improve, he did make some notes on his readings and on his observations in the town.

The 1881 Menard Investigations

All of the available information on Palmer's 1881 work at Menard is contained in his letter of November 29, 1881, to Powell. Once again, three copies of this document are extant, and again we have used Palmer's unpublished original, from the National Anthropological Archives. It had been heavily edited, but the original version is still legible and has been transcribed here. The other two versions are edited scribe's copies; one is still in the NAA and was not used here except in comparisons, and the other was used in the 1917 Arkansas publication. There (Palmer 1917:445−48), the notes from this 1881 work were followed by some, but not all, of the notes from Palmer's 1882 return visit, which were followed by the Arkansas Post notes. Here the correct chronological order has been restored, with the 1882 notes and illustrations deferred until the next chapter.

The Menard site (3AR4 or 17-K-1) has several prehistoric components but was mainly occupied during late prehistoric, protohistoric, and early historic times by peoples who had a Mississippian (including Quapaw phase) artifactual assemblage. It was probably the location of the Quapaw village of Osotouy, where Tonti established the first Arkansas Post (Ford 1961). It was described briefly by the early naturalist Thomas Nuttall (1821).

Palmer was the first to conduct and report on more or less controlled excavations here. Again he was followed and was outdone by C. B. Moore (1908:486−509), who excavated 160 burials and recovered 214 ceramic vessels from this general locality. The Menard site was mapped and tested by Philip Phillips and E. Mott Davis of Harvard University and the Lower Mississippi Survey in 1940−41, tested briefly by Preston Holder for the National Park Service in 1956−57, and trenched more extensively by James A. Ford in 1958. Ford (1961) synthesized the findings of his own and previous investigations. His designations for the mounds (1961:143−44), such as "Mound A" for the large Menard Hill mound, will be used here.

After decades of depredations by grave-robbers and other relic collectors, the site was purchased by the Archaeological Conservancy in 1980, and its name was amended to "Menard-Hodges" in honor of Dr. and Mrs. T. L. Hodges of Bismarck, who had long urged its preservation (Early 1986).

There have been two mysteries about Palmer's 1881 work at Menard: the identity of a small mound in which he found the remains of an aboriginal house and the provenience of a cache of at least twenty-seven ceramic vessels (Holmes 1884:476−77, Figures 150, 151; Ford 1961:161−66, Figures 11, 12) that he found in another location. It appears that both mysteries can be solved, or at least clarified, by careful examination of Palmer's 1881 and 1882 documents and of the site maps (reproduced in chapter 7).

The Small Mound. In the second paragraph of Palmer's letter report to Powell, we encounter the beginnings of an incredible tangle of confusing and erroneous descriptions and measurements by Palmer, and compounded confusion on the part of subsequent commentators. He stated that he found the remains of a house (or "houses") in a small mound at the end of a three hundred-foot addition that was connected to the east side of

Mound A. He went on to remark about this connection again at the end of the second paragraph and in the third paragraph stated that he had found the ceramic cache "near the center of this connection."

The simplest explanation—which I believe to be correct—is that Palmer said "east side" when he should have said "west side" and exaggerated the distance. Palmer seems to have sometimes suffered from directional dyslexia, and frequently was inaccurate in his measurements, which must often have been merely estimates, usually on the side of overestimation; this may be a prime example of both weaknesses.

The map published by Thomas (1894: Figure 137; reproduced here as figure 7.38), based on a now-lost map made by Lewis in 1882, does not show any suggestion of an addition or a small mound on the east of Mound A, and Palmer did not mention an eastern addition during that 1882 return visit. However, the accurate topographic contour map published by Ford (1961: Figures 3, 6; reproduced here as figure 7.39) does show slightly elevated ground between Mound A and Mound E, which is almost 250 feet due east of Mound A. Neither Palmer's "west wing" (actually southwest) nor his "south wing" (actually southeast) extends more than about two hundred feet from Mound A. On the basis of Palmer's "east" and "300 feet in length" statements here, and the situation of Mound E, it would appear at least remotely possible that he was working on this portion of the site during this initial visit.

It is much more likely, though, that Palmer was completely wrong in these 1881 notes about both the distance and direction, and that he was digging in Mound B when he found the house. This was suggested by Ford (1961: 148, 161), although he was apparently quite confused about what Palmer found. The clincher for this interpretation is found in Palmer's notes on his 1882 return visit to Menard with Lewis. After describing the "west" (southwest) wing or appendage as "156 feet long," with other variant but perhaps more accurate measurements, he stated, "It was in the centre of this wing that so many broken yellow flat dishes [actually, open bowls; cf. Ford 1961: 161, Figures 11, 12] were found." This would clearly indicate that the addition or connection that Palmer concentrated on in 1881 had been the southwestern one and that the mound at the end of it, where he found the house remains, was Mound B.

Ford trenched Mound B and found "extensive areas of burned clay [floors] . . . at least two levels of construction were represented in less than 2 feet of depth" (1961: 148). This is in substantial agreement with Palmer's summary of what he found in the mound. Significantly, Ford's negative findings here also match Palmer's observation that "nothing was found" in the way of artifacts in his mound test. Ford jumped to the conclusion that Palmer's ceramic cache had also been found in Mound B, but he remarked, "However, we found no additional fragments of pottery resembling that in Palmer's collection" (1961: 161).

The Ceramic Cache.   In the third paragraph of the 1881 letter, Palmer clearly stated that the ceramic vessel cache was found not in a mound but approximately in the middle of the elevated connection between Mound A and the smaller mound, which must have been Mound B if the interpretation suggested here is correct.

This was contradicted in a massively confused statement by Thomas:

> An opening was made in the larger wing [Palmer's "west wing"]. . . . In an opening previously made on the opposite side of the same wing a thick layer of burnt clay

was encountered and a number of broken pots were found. The small flat-topped mounds [Thomas's map shows them roughly in an east-west line running from southeast of Mound A to southwest of it] . . . are probably house sites. They consisted of a top layer of soil, next a layer of burnt clay, and below this ashes, in which were skeletons and pottery. It was in these house sites that Dr. Palmer made the large find of pottery previous to his connection with the Bureau of Ethnology. (1894:230–31)

Apparently, then, Thomas believed that Palmer's major ceramic cache came not from the "west wing" but from one of the house mounds to the south. His statement that Palmer made the find "previous to his connection with the Bureau" is clearly wrong. We have already seen Powell's letter of June 27, 1881 (reproduced in chapter 3), hiring Palmer as a temporary assistant of the Bureau of Ethnology retroactive to June 1, 1881, and extending to January 31, 1882.

Thomas may never have seen Palmer's November 29, 1881, report to Powell. Quite possibly, the only copies of that letter were retained by Powell and Palmer, the latter copy winding up in the Arkansas archives and in the 1917 publication after Palmer's death. What Thomas undoubtedly did see and use were notes from Palmer's 1882 return visit to Menard (see chapter 7). However, he diminished Palmer's "many broaken potts" from the "west wing" to "a number of broken pots" and changed Palmer's "It was from these [house mounds south of Mound A] that last year so many things were taken by me" to "It was in these house sites that Dr. Palmer made the large find of pottery. . . ." Palmer's "so many things" was probably a reference to the largely plow-damaged vessels, bones, etc., which he described as having come from the field around the mounds, in the latter portion of the November 29, 1881, letter.

Summarizing his own Mound B excavation, Ford confidently concluded, "it is virtually certain that these are the burnt clay layers where Palmer found the cache of bowls" (1961:148). He later stated, with less assurance, that "reading the several sources cited above makes it probable that Palmer found this cache of bowls on top of Mound B. . . ." (1961:161), although he had just quoted Phillips's 1941 manuscript, which referred to Palmer's having found the cache at the center of either the "eastern (or southern) extension" or the "western wing."

Ford may have been misled by Phillips's reference to the "western extension (which we have elected to regard as a separate mound, Mound B)" so that he assumed that the extension (or wing) equaled the mound instead of a ridge leading to it. It may also be relevant that, as noted in a recent biography of Ford (Brown 1978a:26), "It is obvious that Ford was extremely restless at this point in his life. He constantly jumped from one project to another, from one continent to another; and his reports which came out at this time [Menard and Helena] greatly suffered from this lack of attention."

Possibly the wisest comment on this whole situation came from Phillips, who said in his 1941 manuscript (quoted by Ford 1961:160), "Perhaps it is of no great importance just where the stuff was found, though one likes to have a measure of certainty in such matters. The principal thing is that the pots were found in a house site and that there were no burials present." However, it is claimed here that we can have "a measure of certainty" that Palmer found the cache near the center of the connection between Mounds A and B.

Palmer's 1881 Lower Arkansas Valley Documents

AHC Item 10 (1917:432–33)

Arkansas Post, Arkansas Co. Ark.

Landed at the Post late in the afternoon. Staid at a noted hotel.

This place is as old as Philadelphia.[19] It once had a state bank, was the capital of the Province of Louisiana. Some bricks of the government house remains. The town was destroyed by the war and the change of the war. The new town has 30 to 40 inhabitants.

The intrenchments of Confederates in the late war admit river & rains to encroach and carry away the soil until the town may be endangered.

Thanksgiving Day Nov. 24th. I had no turkey. There was no observance of the day. The ground was frozen.

Circus that travels upon a river boat (admission 25 cents).

Gambling tables, Dice Rolet, and guessing for dollars seem to be the main object, so as to pass counterfit money.

There was also a 25 cent side show consisting of an exhibition tent & a dressing tent to accomodate a miserable variety show for which $10 license was paid. Had the whole show exhibited it would have been $100.

The performers were a hard faced lot. The poor crowd of dupes, black & white, by their appearance had better put the money to their own comfort.

For 3 days after my arrival here there was a raw, wet, cold rain, then frost so that the ground was frozen for 3 days, after which it was warm & pleasant.

———————

AHC Item 10 (1917:448)

Arkansas Post, Village on Arkansas River

The first attempt at settlement on the banks of the Arkansas was begun a few miles below the Bayou which communicated with the White River. *An* extraordinary inundation occasioned the removal of the garrison to the borders of the lagoon near Madame Gordons and again disturbed by an overflow, they at length chose the present site of Arkansas. *Post.*

They cultivated peach and other trees.

(Nuttalls' Travells.).[20]

Mound & Grave.

Page 80—

In speaking of the first settlement on the Arkansas River, says, In one of the Tum*uli mounds,* on the bank of the bayou intersected by the falling away of the earth, a pot of this kind still employed by the Chicksaw and other natives for boiling their victuals in, had fallen out of the grave and did not appear to be of very ancient interment.

Page 81—speaking of the mounds the author says, "I suspect that the mounds are merely incidental, arising from the demolition of the circular dwellings in which the deceased had been interred—a custom which was formerly practiced by the Natchez, Cherokees & other natives, Journal of Travells in Ter. of Arkansas 1819 by Thomas Nuttall F.L.S. *1819*

Indians have No Religions.
Vol. 2—Kalm's Travells. says the Indians have no religion.[21]

======

NAA 2400

Palmers Report for November   Mounds of Arkansas
        Arkansaw Post . Arkansaw County Arkansaw
              November 29—1881
Major J. W. Powell
                          Sir
                          Since forwarding my last communication I have visited a section, known as the Menard Mounds, owned by the children of the late Frank Menard Esq . eight miles South East from Arkansaw Post. In a field of 20 acres is situated a mound 40 feet high[22] 965 feet in circumference at base and 300 feet circumference at top, with trees and bushes growing up its tapering sides. I did not open this mound as two cuts had been made into its sides without revealing anything and an eight foot hole dug in the top at which depth was found ashes in which a metalic cross[23] was discovered it was six inches in length of the kind worn upon the neck by Catholicks. As French Traders during the earliest settlements of this section carried on trade with Indians may not this cross have been obtained from them and the soil above afterwards added to give greater height that the mound might afford a more extended view of the river that then run near and of the surrounding country.

From the East side of this mound is connected an addition ten feet high twenty feet across and 300 feet in length, at the end of which is a small circuler mound 15 feet high and 45 feet accross, in which nothing was found.but the evidences of its once having been occupied by houses was verified by charcool ashes and the burnt clay roofing of dwellings As the Arkansaw River once run near the mound it was doubtless occupied during the overflow of that River, so also might have been the connection between it and the larger mound.

Near the center of this connection just under the soil the burnt clay roofing of a house was found then a few inches of ashes and charcool—This house was 15 feet circumference, At one side embeded in this burnt clay debres, was many broaken potts, Their position and the materiel with which they where associated would lead one to the conclusion that the Indians of former days like those of the present time, used the roofs of their hutts to place their pottery upon, as the smallness of their dwellings and the absence

of shelves rendered the frail potts liable to destruction if left on the floor,
The broaken potts hear found differ in ornamentation and form from those
found with the dead thus they are of especial interest.[24] Opposite side of the
house from which the potts was found was several inches of wood ashes,
below which was a hard floor of burnt clay with a smooth surface three
feet accross. This floor must have been made of wet clay smoothed then by
heat burnt hard, The burning down of the house whether by accident or
design, converted the outer clay roofing to a red brick like concistency leaving the impress of the grass and stick supports in it. In the precipitation, the
potts became variously cracked or seperated, four were inside of each other
in the last one was a large peice of the burnt roofing, this material was so
variously mixed among the injured potts that in removing it all kinds became more or less mixed.[25] If these potts had been under the roof instead of
on the top, then they would have been covered more even by the roofing
and been all broaken, and none left upright.

Box No 4 contains all the peices taken out of the above mentioned house
they are packed between layers of hay each kind by itself as much as could
be, could not not place them in paper as there was none to be had. If the
pieces are seperated I think in most instances entire potts can be made.[26]

150   peice of the clay floor mentioned above
151   "   "   "   "   roofing with ashes & charcool attatched as
      mentioned above
152   "   "   "   "   "   found inside of the potts   "
       "   "

These three numbered packages are in box number 3.
In box Number 3 the following numbered packages wil be found, the
paper is brittle that was used so some pieces may get out of the bundles
among the hay if more paper was at hand could have wrapped them better.
137   several packages of stone impliments found in the soil of fied about
      arround the Menard Mounds.
138   Mixed pieces of pottery from field surrounding the Menard Mounds
          From Graves in Field About Menard Mound
The 20 acre field surrounding the Menard Mounds was once covered by
dwellings As you dig in various directions from one foot to two under the
surface you come to burnt roofing of clay, ashes and dirt, then human remains and pottery placed close to the head but no ornament or impliment
was found with them The frequent plowing of the field has broaken up
many of the potts the pieces as far as could have been preseved in the
bundles.
134   Heads of animals one as rattle.[27]
140   several packages under this number of pottery more or less broaken
      and may be a little mixed they where found at the edge of the field previ-
      ous floods having carried away the remains once deposited with them
141   (3) specimens of pottery found with a decayed remains
142   (3)   "   "   "   "   " half grown person decayed
143   pott with crania rest of bones decayed
144   (2) potts one of human forms placed in 4 bundles so they could be
      safer packed crania is in bundle marked 144

145 *(2) potts found with decayed remains*
146 *(4) potts found with the decayed remains of a child*
147 *(3) "   "   "   "   "   "   " " "*
148 *(3) "   "   "   "   "   "   " " half grown person*
149 *(2) crania found with out any article, there is one thing To be said so far during my examination in Arkansaw that if more than one remains is found together nothing is found with them[28] 149 was found together, in same field once six another time three was found together as if laid in a pile and covered over and not a thing with them—It seem that those who are found in their burnt down houses have water and food vessels with them the hands placed each side of the chin and the knees bent up to the chin.[29] May not those found without pottery have met their death by unnattural means*

Respectfully

Edward Palmer. turn over

This field had at various times had many Potts and skeletons plowed up thus giving me greater labour to find those obtained.

"In Order That I May Not Be Idle": Palmer's Investigations in East-Central Arkansas, 1881–82

MARVIN D. JETER AND MARY FARMER

At the beginning of December 1881 Palmer began to explore localities north of the Arkansas River. Again our major sources for sequencing his investigations are monthly reports in the form of letters to Powell. The first of these was written at Indian Bay in southernmost Monroe County, on December 24; the second is undated but must have been written in mid-January 1882.

Once again, there is an occurrence of multiple copies of a document, in this case, three versions of the December 24 report. An edited scribe's copy was included in the papers that went to the Arkansas History Commission; it was split into three entries, which were published in nonchronological order (Palmer 1917:420, 421–22, 433). Here as before, Palmer's original report, now in the National Anthropological Archives, has been transcribed without editing. The January report, on the other hand, was not available to the editors of the 1917 publication. Here the only extant version, Palmer's original, is presented.

In addition to those reports, this phase of Palmer's activity is punctuated by several short notes (more of them dated than usual) about his travels and observations, and especially by several interesting letters from and to Spencer Baird. Palmer's letter of January 10 to Baird is particularly revealing. In it he complained mildly about his unanticipated expenses, inquired about his prospects for additional mound work "in order that I may not be idle," and hinted that he might take employment as a botanical collector again. Baird appears to have acted swiftly to get him some reimbursement and to reassure him about future work.

Maxwell Mounds.   Very early in December, Palmer traveled about fifteen miles northwest of Arkansas Post into the Grand Prairie country of southern Arkansas County and visited a group of small mounds on land owned by John R. Maxwell. Palmer found little and did not record the site's location specifically enough for it to be reidentified.

Maddox Bay or Webster's Camp Mound.   By December 7, Palmer had left his Arkansas Post base and traveled to the White River lowland in southern Monroe County. Here he recorded, but was not permitted to dig into, a mound on Maddox Bay, an old White River cutoff channel. This site is now known as Webster's Camp (3MO3 or 14-L-1). LMS data (Phillips 1970: Figure 445) and the AAS files indicate that it has Baytown and Mississippian components.

Baytown or Indian Bay Mounds.   Next Palmer moved down the valley to examine a site whose name has become one of the culture-historical landmarks of lower Mississippi Valley archeology. The location was near the community of Indian Bay, at the southern tip of Monroe County, near the juncture of Big Creek and the White River, on lands owned by two individuals, one of whom refused permission to excavate. On the other landowner's property, Palmer found several burials and obtained what Hoffman summarized as a moderate-sized collection (1975:18–19). Hoffman also remarked that it was "strange" that Thomas (1894:233) had stated that no explorations were made in Monroe County; this is consistent with Thomas's tendency to ignore or downplay Palmer's 1881 work.

This site is now known as Baytown (3MO1 or 15-L-2) and is the type site (though, as usual, it is not typical) for the Baytown culture. It was mapped by Ford in 1940 and summarized by Phillips, Ford, and Griffin (1951:51). It had at least nine mounds, in a plaza-like arrangement. Mound A, at the south-central edge of the plaza, was the largest (about twenty feet high and more than two hundred feet east-west), but more than half of it had been cut away by floods. Mound B, at the east margin of the plaza, was about ten feet high, about one hundred feet north-south, and had an Anglo-American cemetery on its north end. The site has never been intensively studied, but in addition to the basic Baytown occupation it also has Coles Creek period (probably Plum Bayou culture; cf. Rolingson 1982) and Late Mississippi period components, according to Phillips (1970:916, Figures 446, 447). I have not examined Palmer's collection, but Hoffman noted that its diagnostic materials consisted primarily of Late Mississippian ceramics (1975:19).

Big Cypress Creek or Hall Mound.   Palmer's next site visit was north of Indian Bay, on Big Cypress Creek, where he reported a large mound but found nothing in or near it. This is probably the Hall Mound site (3PH12 or 15-L-3), in western Phillips County (John House, 1986 personal communication). It was described by Phillips et al. as a large rectangular mound (1951:51); on the basis of scanty ceramic collections, it is tentatively assigned to the Baytown period.

East Lake Mounds.   After spending Christmas and recovering from "lumbago" at Indian Bay, Palmer went northwest by stage to Holly Grove in central Monroe County. He stayed here only long enough to make brief and relatively unproductive tests in two of three mounds at nearby East Lake in the White River valley. This site has not been definitely located; two single-mound sites (3MO59 and 3MO60) are recorded in this general vicinity, close together, but Palmer's notes are not detailed enough to tell whether he visited either or both.

Mounds near Clarendon.   Palmer left Holly Grove on December 29 for Clarendon, on the White River in western Monroe County. From there he visited a nearby two-mound site, but one of the mounds had been virtually destroyed, and the other produced nothing in the way of artifacts. No sites at all are now on record in this locality.

The End of the Field Season

The Clarendon exploration was Palmer's last Arkansas field work of this season. January was essentially a total loss due to heavy rains, a freeze, and "the appearance of small pox," forcing his departure at the end of the month. He stayed briefly in Helena but missed any chance he might have had of finding the remarkable Hopewellian burial mounds there, which were not discovered until the 1950s (Ford 1963).

Palmer's East-Central Arkansas Documents for 1881–82

AHC Item 10 (1917:432)

Napoleon Bonapart Menard entltled to thanks of the Bureau of Ethnology.
Left Arkansaw Post for Grand Prairia 15 miles N.W. on a visit to John R Maxwell[30]
As the fires have for years been kept out of the prairia the timber has sensably increased and driven outward and lessoned the arrea of the Grand Prairia.

NAA BAE Letters

SMITHSONIAN INSTITUTION,
            Washington, D.C., Dec. 3, 1881
Dr. Edward Palmer
Arkansas Point

Dear Doctor:
    I am sorry that the circumstances have been unfavorable to your getting more of the mound relics. Dr. Foreman[31] is now unpacking your collections hitherto received, and I am entirely satisfied with the results. Of course I would be willing to see much more, but you have done, I am sure, the best possible under the circumstances.

When you have got through all your funds write me again and I will see what we can do in the way of keeping you there longer. You must use your own best judgment as to the field of exertion. I suppose the further south you are in the Winter the better. Mississippi or even Louisiana might furnish a good show. The two boxes from Pecan Point are here, but are not yet opened.

Yours truly,
Spencer F. Baird.

———————

AHC Item 6 (1917:416)

St. Charles.

Dec. 8th. 81—

The Hotel is kept by one legged confederate soldier. It was used during the war as a United States Headquarters.[32] The building used as a hospital[33] is still standing, but the rest of the town is destroyed. The confederates in cutting their ditches allowed the river & rains to encroach so that the town had to be moved high up from the river.

Darkies with buggies are common.

Saturday *is a great day in day for shopping & getting drunk.* A black man drove me to Indian Bay. He was out collecting a 50 ct. debt from a colored minister of that place. He was free in his denunciations of many ministers.

———————

NAA BAE Letters

SMITHSONIAN INSTITUTION
Washington, D.C., December 17, 1881

Dr. Edward Palmer
Arkansas Post,
Arkansas County,
Arkansas

Dear Doctor:

I enclose a very interesting letter from Mr. Hull,[34] which it may be well for you to take into consideration. The locality is a very celebrated one for game, & it is quite possible it may be one of those undisturbed regions furnishing valuable collections.

I am happy to inform you that, so far, you lead the entire force of mound explorers, nothing received being comparable to what you have actually collected. I hope we may be able to keep you going for a long time.[35]

The boxes shipped from Arkansas Post have not yet come to hand.

Sincerely yours,
Spencer F. Baird

AHC Item 19 (1917:445)

Mounds to watch for game

Big Cypress Creek Ark

*These mounds during the dry part of the year was resorted to by Indians
to watch for game.*

*As the waters overflow the country, the mounds being at the divide be-
tween the overflow and the high lands*

NAA 2400

Report for December

1881

From Indian Bay

Monroe Co. Ark.

*Dec. 26 will be Shipped 3 Boxes of Pottery as mentioned in the the in-
closed Report*

E. Palmer

Indian Bay Monroe County Arkansaw

Palmers Report of Explorations for the Month of December

Major J. W. Powell Smithsonion Institution, Washington

*At the beginning of the month I left Arkansaw Post Arkansaw County,
Arkansaw to visit mounds fifteen miles North West from that place. These
mounds was small a previous party took out of the largest one five skeletons which had nothing deposited with them. Nothing was found in or about
the mounds but camp fire signs. These mounds are situated just inside a belt
of timber in front of which is what is called grand Prarria. Game passing
from the Woods to the Prarria to feed could be watched from these elevations by the hunters. Dec. 7th visited Lawrenceville, Monroe County,
Arkansaw. This place is situated on the edge of Maddox Bay hear is a fine
mound which is used as a grave yard by the setters. A fine bank along the
Bay upon which Indians have long camp the owner of which refused to
have it dug into Near the above mentioned mound is a plowed field belonging to Daniel Thompson Esq in it was found numerous signs of ancient
habitations . This field has been cultivated for several years consequently
what has not been turned out by the plow remains under the soil mostly in
a very broaken condition. Close to the surface in one spot was found the
burnt roofing that was eight inches thick of a house 100 feet in circumference. Nearly embeded in the roof debree was a coconut shaped pot. I am of
the opinion this curious vessel was on top of the house at the time it was
burnt down as it with another broaken pot was in the top of the debre and
not under it*

153   Coconut shaped vessel as mentioned above

154   found with 153—no remains found

155   Part of a dish taken from a house roofing only ashes was under it
156   (3) peices of pottery found 18 inches under ground, with the remains
      of a half grown person.
157   odd pieces of pottery &c

Dec 12 visited Indian Bay, Monroe County, Arkansaw
   at this place is a mound owned by A. Spencer. it is 30 feet above high
water of the Bay and 250 feet long, permission could not be obtained to
open it

   At the edge of Indian Bay Corporation is a large mound now used as a
grave yard by the people at the base of it is a field owned by Dr. Henry
Shipman In it is two small mounds 3 to 4 feet high & 30 feet in circumference. In one two feet under the surface was found a skeleton of a half
grown person. with the three vessels under Number 158. No beads or other
things found.
   If vessels are found with the dead they are placed arround the head.
159   The skeleton found with this vessel was nearly destroyed by plowing
      the field. A piece of the vessel was also carried away by the plow.
160   The broaken pottery under this number was taken from the other
      small mound before mentioned which appears to have had on it a
      two room stick hut with clay roof upon which must have been placed
      the potts—by the distruction of the house by fire, the said potts was
      precipitated and mixed in the debree in a very broaken condition. No
      skeletons or other articles was found under the fallen roofing debree.
      (Present Indians place their crockery on house roof).
161   The broaken pottery under this number was taken from under the
      burnt roofing of a house situated 35 yards from, the above men-
      tioned mound , They must have been in the house at the time it was
      burnt down as they was entirely covered over . If they had been on
      the top of the hut then they would be variously mixed in the burnt
      roofing quite near the surface.
162   Each packages contains the broaken pottery found on the floor of as
      many houses as there are packages each was covered over with the
      burnt roof debree. No skeletons or other articles was found
163   Broaken pottery found under the burnt and fallen clay roofing of two
      hutts. or may be they appear judgeing from the position of the mate-
      rial, to have been attached to each other. They where but 10 feet
from 161 The peices belonging to each house are together as found. The
falling of houses may have mixed them, especially in the case of 161
and 163
164   Wasp Nests[36] taken from the burnt roofing of houses 161 and 163
165   Stones supposed to have been utalized—stone impliments or rocks
      are very scarce along the river bottoms of Arkansaw
166   Piece of the hard burnt floor of 163.
   The people in many section call the burnt roofing mentioned above ,
"brick batts" considering the ancient inhabitants used them in making kills
in which they burnt their pottery , The fragmentary and unshapable

character when taken into consideration, with the impress of grass &
sticks—deside it is burnt clay roofing.
In the field surrounding the mound was found two skeletons without any-
thing deposited with them.

    160-161-162-163 where in no instance found more than one foot below
the surface.

    13 miles north of Indian Bay on what is known as Big Cypress which
goes dry in summer. Hear is located a large mound, As nothing was found
in or about it and taking into consideration its position I am of the opinion
that it was used as a temporary resort in hunting its elevation afforded a
good oppertunity to watch for game as they receed from the water as it
overflow the country, The mound being at the divide between the over-
flowed and the higher lands.

    At permanent water only is to be found the remains of large settlements.

167   *Bark from the Cypress Tree which can be obtained sixty or more feet*
        in length it is very durible . is used in filling up mudholes, it last for
        years with out decay the black mud seem to tan it adding to its
        strength. Why may not the Anciend Inhabitants have used this bark
        for the covering of their dwellings and allso as cloathing Indians of
        the Colorado River used the strips of the Willow and cottonwood
        bark for making their skirts. then why where not the bark of the
        Cypress tree adabted for ancient Indian skirts and shoes. in the same
        manner as the Willow and Cottonwood. bark by the Indians of the
        Colorado River

              Edward Palmer
              Dec 24th 1881

P.S Am indisposed from a severe attack of of Lumbago so that it is with
much difficulty that I can write or do anything .

                 E. P.

AHC Item 5 (1917:422–23)

         Indian Bay   Monro Co.   Ark.

Christmas day at Indian Bay. This is a short crop year. Merchants & land renters complain of non settlements of debts.

Every species of jug & bottle are carried away filled with whisky . Not only were the necessaries of life carried away but also the luxuries.

The wearing apparel bought by the colored people was not adapted to the condition of poor people.

Is not a dry season a blessing if we utilize its dictates .

Two days before Christmas Baley's Family Troop, consisting of Father, Brother, Wife and their 6 children arrived and performed in the school house, to whites, only, at 25c. per. head, if colored were admitted it was only by special permission.

Take the human race as a whole, there is nothing in color, its in the quality of the human composition . In the south & the north so much is wasted on Christmas.[37] The day before Christmas young & old are trying to catch each other with the cry of "Christmas Gift"! It is a day of extravagance, & a means to dissatisfaction. The poor fret because they cannot do as the rich

Dec. 25th. 1881.

A pleasant spring like day with some leaves on Peach & Apple trees, green weeds & grass.

Dec. 26—81—left by stage for Holley Wood.[38] Ark.

———

AHC Item 8 (1917:437)

Holly Grove & Vicinity.   Ark.

Dec. 26th, 1881—Left by stage for Holley-Wood. Found every body celebrating Christmas. I stopped at Widow Smith's Hotel. The influence of her daughters attracts boards & so her house is full.

Next morning started by team to Mrs. Trotter's farm near East Lake 4 miles from Holly Grove & 6 miles from White River. Staid at the house of Shoebly Taylor. The people were kind but of many words. Theirs was a rented place.

Dec. 29—Left for Clarendon, Monroe Co. Ark. by team 10 miles

———

AHC Item 9 (1917:412–13)

Clarendon, Monroe Co. Ark

Dec. 31st. 1881—was the last day for the sale of liquor—A dull county seat with but little business. There is a miserable hotel which charges $2 per. day for transients, per. week $4.00.

Three beds in a room and two in a bed.—very poor board.

A new railroad (The Texas & St. Louis) is being constructed which fills up every every house.

The old road narrow guage[39] is "The Helena and Arkansas Midland Railroad men at the Hotel let out the old year & brought in the new by a noisy drunk.

———

AHC Item 11 (1917:397)

Helena   Ark

Jan. 2—82

   New Year is celebrated at the P. O .

I called on Major Arnot Harris of the Yeoman, and Dr. S. M. Grant and presented letters from Dr. Morgan Cartwright of Indian Bay.

Jan. 3rd. Left by Ferry Boat to Mississippi side & took cars for Jonestown
with letter to Ex. Governor & Senator J. S. Alcorn.[40]
Returned to Helena Ark. from Forest City & left Jan 11th for Mariana
by boat.

———————

NAA BAE Letters

                                                    Helena Ark.
                                                        Jan 10
Dear Prof
    *Yours of Dec 3 and 17 was received this morning from Arkansaw Post. I
was about starting up the San Francis River to morrow morning. the letter
of Mr. J. M. Null is in time and its contents will receive my utmost attention I had herd of the same locality. but Mr. Curtis[41] visited parts of that
locality and obtained many things for the Peabody Museum*
    *am glad you are satisfied with my work I would like to have collected
more but that was imposible It is best that I continue the work now that I
am at it, as many mounds are known to me in the adjoining states to
Arkansaw and can be easily reached . besides less expensive now I am hear.*
    *Hope the work can be extended into Mexico.[42] My funds wil end with
this month.*
    *It is more expensive than you and my self had supposed as so much
private transportation has to be hired and my board never cost less than
one dollar per day and most of the time two dollars which with the other
expenses consumes all that is received for my work, leaving nothing for my
time. Please let me know at your earliest convenience regarding future
work as by letter from Prof Putnam he may be able after a while to send
me out and my Botanical friends desire more Mexican plants In order that
I may not be idle is the reason why your wish regarding my continuance in
the field is early solicited*
    *I will use my best judgement about localities to visit Have you received
the boxes sent from Arkansaw Post and Indian Bay*
                        Yours very truly
                        Edward Palmer
                            Helena
                            Phillips County
                                Arkansaw

Prof. S. F. Baird
    Smithsonion Institution
        Washington City
            D.C.

SMITHSONIAN INSTITUTION
WASHINGTON, D.C., Jan 14 1882
Dear Major:

I enclose a very interesting letter from Dr. Palmer. I have written him that we wish to keep him in our service as long as we possibly can, & for him to go on at present. I think in view of the admirable work he is doing we might pay some of his extra expenses so as to give him more in the way of salary. Please let me hear from you soon on this subject, or else write directly to the Doctor & advise me of any proposition you make to him.[43]

Maj. J.W. Powell
    [Illegible word]

Yours truly,

Spencer F. Baird

AHC Item 12 (1917:435)

Mariana & Other Places in Ark.

Jan 82—
The colored barbers keep separate shops for white & colored customers.
Jan 18th. 82—

Snow & sleet with ground slightly frozen—a very dissagreable day. Mariana has 800 population—a fine post office . This place is 12 or 14 miles up the Languille River, 35 miles from Helena by river & 25 by land.
2 miles S of this place on the Helena road is the Lone Pine Spring. The tree is yet standing. Here the thief Murrell[44] had his counterfeit shop for making money, vestiges of which are said to still remain.

Travel on the R.R. suspended for several days as the only two engines was injured disagreeable waiting—and when started was slow as freight was taken along and delivered by the way side—steam would give out then a stop to get up a new supply

---

NAA 2400

*Explorations in the State of Arkansaw
for the Month January by Edward Palmer
which are respectfully submitted to
Major J. W. Powell, Smithsonion Institution
Washington City D.C.*

On the borders of East Lake four miles from Holley Grove Monroe Co Arkansaw is situated three mounds one is used as a burying ground by the present races. In one was found a solitary decomposed skeleton and in the other only fragments of pottery was found.

These mounds in my opinion was erected in order to get an elevation suited to watch the approach of game to water and to afford a better oppertunity for killing wild fowels upon the water . The low swampey character of the surrounding country render these mounds necessary. Evidences of numerous camp fires was found in the vicinity of the mounds.

These mounds are five miles from White River

Clarendon, Monroe County Arkansaw is 29 miles from Holley Grove.[45]

Near this place is two mounds one was used during the late war as a burying ground in removing the dead the mound was distroyed. The other other contain graves on its surface of the townspeople—Examining the unoccupied portions in which nothin was found but remains of camp fires, it was probably a hunting camp.

Permanent Camp differ from temporary one the former present the roof remains of dwellings that was burnt down—under which Skeletons and pottery & are found. While the latter has no roof remains—and if Skeletons are found in them nothing is found with them .

In the earth composing these mound peices of vessels &c are sometime found broken while camping

168   Walnutts used as food by the Quapaw Indians before their removel from Arkansaw

In consequence of continuous Rains for sixteen days which have so filled the soil with water making travel impossible. Sever frost now prevent the use of spades upon the soil So have suspended work.

Edward Palmer

———————

Smithsonian Institution Archives,
Record Unit 28, Office of the Secretary (Spencer F. Baird),
Incoming Correspondence, 1879–82

[The following is a U.S. Postal Card, bearing one cent postage, postmarked January 23 (1882) at Forrest City]
Forest City, Arkansaw

Jan. 22

Prof. S. F. Baird
Smithsonian Institution
Washington City, D.C.
In consequence of the appearance of small pox in various places in the interior of this State, and the excessive wet condition of the soil caused by sixteen days of continuous rain, now followed by frost, so that I must soon discontinue work and wil return to Washington in a few days.
Edward Palmer

AHC Item 13 (1917:418)

Journey to Washington D.C.
From Arkansaw

Excessive rains drove me from Arkansas.[46] I arrived in Washington Feb. 2— 1882 just in time *to overhaul 4 Boxes of dirty looking pieces of pottery their peculiar figuering was unseen untill they was washed. these was taken from one mound and formerly was on the house top when it was burnt down they fell remained in three rows one inside or laying by the mouth of the other . [Illegible word, possibly "house"] was originally standing—In the fall of the house the pots was much broaken but the burnt clay roofing kept their forms complete. but they had to be taken out in fragments to be cleaned and reconstructed in Washington.*[47]

═══════

NAA BAE Letters

SMITHSONIAN INSTITUTION
WASHINGTON, D.C.,   Feb. 9. 1882

Dear Major:

As an encouragement to Dr. Palmer and to prevent his leaving our service for that of the Museum at Pumpilla[48] , I told him that we could arrange to refund to him actual expenses for short excursions, fees, occasional purchase of articles, & c. He has accordingly presented to me the enclosed memorandum which I would be very glad if you could pay from the appropriation.

Very truly yours,
Spencer F. Baird

Major J. W. Powell:
Ethnological Bureau
Washington

═══════

NAA BAE Letters

[Note Palmer's use of # for the dollar sign.—Ed.]

Freight on 395 lbs from Sevierville Tenn to Knoxville	# 1.50
Team hire New Market Tenn	# 2-25
" " *Carey ville* "	# 2-00
" " *Poplar Creek* "	# 6-00
" " *Niles ferry* "	# 7-00
Team to Little River Ark. and back to Oseola	# 10.00
Team to visit mounds few miles from Oseola Ark	# 4-25

Team to mounds about Arkansaw Post . ark	# 5-00
Team to mound on Grand Praria ark	# 5-00
Team to White River.ark.	# 00-00
" " *Indian Bay*	# 2-50
Team to Lawrence Ville and back to Indian Bay.ark.	# 7-50
Team to Big Cypress ark.	# 3-50
Team to Clarendon "	# 2-50
Team Friers Point Miss .	# 4.00
Journey to Dandridge Tenn from New Market to examine	
private collections	# 9-25
[A page may be missing here.—Ed.]	
Express on box from Depo to Smithsonion	8-50
	Total 113-25

Extra expenses

Hire of Conveyance to Indians of North Carolina from	
Newport Tenn	# 17-50
Purchase of articles from Indians of North Carolina	# 10-00
Passage by Hack to and from Bakersville North Carolina	
to Johnson City Tenn	# 14.25
For the privalege of opening mound at Sevierville	
Tenn	# 10-00
Hire of Transportation to visit mound at Severville	# 5.75

New Work in East Tennessee

Palmer arrived in Washington from Arkansas around February 10, 1882 (McVaugh 1956:345). As soon as weather permitted, he went to the field in eastern Tennessee again, revisiting Niles Ferry in Monroe County on April 5. He soon moved on to Pikeville in Bledsoe County, thence (on or about April 15) to Dayton in Rhea County; to Chattanooga, on the Hamilton-Marion county line (April 17 or later); and (at unknown dates later in April) to Spencer in Van Buren County, Georgetown in Meigs County, and to Charleston and Savannah Farm in Bradley County (McVaugh 1956:87, 331).

The Niles Ferry site has been summarized previously. In his preliminary catalog of mound sites, Thomas stated that a mound near Pikeville had been reported by Palmer and mentioned several other mounds in that vicinity (1891:199); did not mention Rhea County; listed a few mounds in Hamilton County (1891:204–05) without citing Palmer; listed three mound sites in Marion County (1891:208), citing only earlier visitors; listed only a previously reported "burial cave" in Van Buren County (1891:214); listed several sites, including the now-famous Hiwasee Island site (Lewis and Kneberg 1946), in Meigs County (Thomas 1891:209), citing only Emmert and another assistant, John P. Rogan; and listed eleven mound sites in Bradley County (1891:200–01), including "Graves on the Blackburn farm, 7 miles southeast of Cleveland. Dr. Edward Palmer: Mentioned by Cyrus Thomas, Burial Mounds of the Northern Section."

In his final report, Thomas (1894) did not mention any sites in Bledsoe, Hamilton,

Marion, Van Buren, or Bradley counties, and his (1894:404–07) summaries of mounds in Rhea and Meigs counties did not mention Dayton, Georgetown, or Palmer.

Some additional details of this new east Tennessee work, plus some references to Palmer's plans for upcoming work in Tennessee and Arkansas and some other insights, are in a letter (now in the "2400" file at the National Anthropological Archives) he wrote to Baird.

> Pikeville, Bloodso Co. Tenn
> April 11—1882
>
> Dear Prof
>
> One thing I omitted to say to you before leaving Washington, that is if you hear from the gentleman living on the banks of the Miss. River in Arkansaw who has some pottery, you wrote him about it, allso about a colored man living near him who is said to have many things. let me know In case you do not hear from him I can call and see him as I pass up the Miss. River to visit Rheel Foot Lake.
>
> At Niles Ferry found the Cherokee grave yard had all been destroy. Wishing to go beyond in order to open an important mound but could get no conveyance besides was told no workmen could be got at this time—Inclosed will be found a suggestion as to how this mound can be opened
>
> Pike ville is in Sequachee valley the place General Wilder said had so many mounds. They not being mounds used for habitation contain but little.
>
> The continued Rains greatly impede my work. At Pikeville Bloodsoe County Tennessee is living Colonel S. C. Norwood who I am informed has a stone Idol so called, he being absent could not see it A friend of his says it is a god carved stone image. and he think if you would write to him about it you could get it or at least borrow it for reproduction in plaster. It might be wel for you to write him as he is a man of Means and Liberality.
>
> It has occured to me since leaving Washington to suggest to you that in case you approve of my request as to localities I wish left for me to work in as expressed in the communication left with you—there might not be sufficient work left to be done in Arizona to send another person out to do. As I wish to take from the Gila river as far as the Rio Verde which is north of Fort Whipple. Should it be thought advisable I can visit the rest of Arizona before returning. that is that portion between the San francisco Mountains an Fort Youma leaving the Zuna & Moqua part to Cushing or who ever works it up.
>
> April 15 start for Ray County to look after reported Cherokee graves
>
> Should you have a vacancy hope you will remember H. L. Dyer the person I spoke to you about Any communication regarding the matter can be addressed to my brother who lives near him. You will please pardon my mentioning the matter but I do so as his Father and Grand Parent are invalids and wish to have him occupied so as to be near them
>
> Very truly
> Edward Palmer
>
> Prof S. F. Baird
> Smithsonion Institution
>   Washington City
>   D. C.
> P.S. Let me know if you hear definitely about those stone pipes Dr. Jacks has at Helena Arkansaw.

The Arkansas man whom Baird had corresponded with about the pottery does not seem to be identified in later notes or letters, nor is the "colored man" with "many things." The "suggestion" about the Tennessee mound that Palmer said he was enclosing does not seem to be in the "2400" file.

Palmer's blithe opinions about the amount of work (archeological, ethnological, botanical, or combinations of these) remaining to be done in Arizona are rather astounding. Such statements tend to support McVaugh's contentions that he lacked organizing ability and that his main motivation was "little more than a liking for travel and for strange places" (1956:5, 11−12). Another factor in this particular case may have been revealed in the previous paragraph, where he complained about the rainy weather. The same theme, expressed as a desire to "give up this River work" and return to the arid Southwest, would be expressed in Palmer's letters of February 16 and 18, 1883, to Cyrus Thomas (reproduced in the next chapter).

Frank Hamilton Cushing (1857−1899) was a pioneering and rather eccentric ethnographer. He was at that time "a young protege of Baird's" (and of Powell's), who had been living with the Zuni since 1879 (Hinsley 1981:74,190−207).

It is noteworthy that Palmer was still corresponding directly with Baird, rather than with Cyrus Thomas. As will be seen, there are indications that Thomas may have moved to establish some control over Palmer around the beginning of the Smithsonian's new fiscal year (on July 1), but Palmer appears to have continued to report directly to Powell until December. Late in that month, he began corresponding primarily, if not exclusively, with Thomas. The Smithsonian Institution at this time did not always adhere strictly to a hierarchical chain of command or the "going through channels" institutional mentality; e.g., after his transfer to the Bureau of Ethnology in 1882, Cushing continued to report directly to Baird (Hinsley 1981:194).

Palmer's postscript, mentioning Dr. Jacks of Helena, Arkansas, was followed up, though it is not clear when and how. In his September 14, 1883, letter to Thomas (reproduced in chapter 8, below), Palmer noted that Dr. Jacks had died and that two stone pipes, which had been borrowed from him, might not be reclaimed.

Western Tennessee

About May 1, 1882, Palmer went westward in Tennessee, visiting Paris in Henry County and Savannah in Hardin County early in the month. From around mid-May to early June, he worked in the Reelfoot Lake vicinity of Obion County; later in June, he was at Ripley in Lauderdale County (McVaugh 1956:331).

Thomas catalogued three sites near Paris and three more in Hardin County (two near Savannah), without citing Palmer (Thomas 1891:205). Four mound sites were listed in Obion County, and Palmer was cited three times (Thomas 1891:210−11). Only two sites were listed for Lauderdale County (1891:207), one near Ripley, but Palmer was not cited.

Thomas's brief final summary of western Tennessee sites mentioned several mounds in the Reelfoot Lake vicinity and only a small mound site near Ripley (1894:278−79). Palmer was not referred to at all. Robert Mainfort of the Tennessee Department of Conservation has examined Smithsonian records, and reports (1986 personal communication) that most of Palmer's collections were recovered from one of two mounds at site 40OB2 on Grassy Island in Reelfoot Lake. Thomas (1894:279) remarked that one small mound at this site "was thoroughly explored, yielding a rich return . . ." (1894:279). He went on to list a number of artifacts, including a Mississippian kneeling-human "image vessel" (1894: Figure 175), found with seven of the fifteen skeletons encountered in the mound.

Palmer apparently stayed briefly in Memphis between his investigations at Reelfoot Lake and Ripley. On the stationery of the Worsham House, which seems to have been his regular hotel in Memphis, he wrote the following letter:

June 14, 1882

J. C. Pilling Esq
> Dear Sir
>> Your communication of June 10 to hand. designating two hundred dollars to be used for the month of June ths relieves me of imbarresment. and allows me to continue without interuption.

Respectfully
Edward Palmer
Memphis
Tennessee

James C. Pilling had joined Powell's Rocky Mountain Survey in 1875, and became perhaps the major's closest "friend and amanuensis." Powell brought him to the Bureau of Ethnology in 1879, and he soon became chief clerk of the Bureau and of the Geological Survey (Hinsley 1981:164–66).

Southeast Missouri and Northeast Arkansas Visits

From western Tennessee, Palmer went upriver to Charleston, Mississippi County, Missouri, where he spent June 26–30 investigating the local manufacture of spurious "mound pottery" (McVaugh 1956:166, 331). This may have been a consequence of the "mining fever" of pot-hunting that had occurred in 1879 and 1880 (Thomas 1894:183).

At some time in late June or early July, Palmer went downstream to revisit the Osceola–Pecan Point vicinity in northeast Arkansas. He was definitely there on July 4–5 and picked up a donation of ceramic vessels. McVaugh (1956:254), apparently on the basis of correspondence I have not seen, stated that the Mississippi River was so high that Palmer was forced to abandon plans to work in the vicinity, but other factors may also have been involved.

Return to Washington; Work in Indiana

The "letters received" file in the Smithsonian's National Anthropological Archives contains a copy of a rather cryptic "night message" (apparently a telegram) from Palmer at Memphis, dated July 6, 1882, which states in its entirety, "Am coming to Washington then to explain why."

The recipient is not indicated, but one possibility is that it may have been Cyrus Thomas, rather than Baird or Powell. Palmer's previous correspondence and administrative liaisons had been with the latter two. But July 1, 1882, would have marked the start of Thomas's first fiscal year in charge of the Mound Survey.

This message may well represent the first in a series of minor clashes between Palmer and Thomas (cf. Palmer's account, chapter 2, and Palmer's letter of Jan. 10, 1883, to Thomas, chapter 7). Whatever problems Palmer may have had with Thomas, they do not appear to have affected his relationship with Baird, who hired him immediately after he left the Bureau of Ethnology, as a collector of marine specimens for the New Orleans Exposition (McVaugh 1956:88) and on a number of subsequent assignments.

At any rate, Palmer did return to Washington early in July and remained there until August 10. At that time he left for Vincennes, Indiana, arriving there about August 16 (McVaugh 1956:227). He seems to have used Vincennes as a base for work in the surrounding Knox County, adjacent Pike County, and across the Wabash River in Lawrence County, Illinois (1956:226–27). This was Palmer's only Mound Survey work in the Midwest, and it may be significant that Thomas had spent much of his career in this region. However, Thomas did not mention Indiana at all in his final report (1894), and in a brief summary of Lawrence County, Illinois, referred only to an anonymous "Bureau agent" who had found that "natural hillocks" had been "used as burying grounds by the aborigines" (1894:163).

CHAPTER SEVEN

Intensive Investigations
in Arkansas, 1882–83

The new Arkansas field season, which was definitely Palmer's most intensive and productive in this state, started in earnest in October 1882. The Letters Received file contains the following postcard, postmarked October 5 in Vincennes:

> Major J. W. Powell
> Bureau of Ethnology
>   National Museum
>   Washington City
>   D. C.
>   Vincennes Indiana   Oct 5
>   I send by Express to day a box containing Report for September Envoice of things sent in a box a few days since—and one other communication—There is allso a stone impliment from Kenton Ohio
>   Start to day for Osceola, Ark.
>   Respectfully
>   Edward Palmer

However, the file contains another letter, dated October 8, indicating that Palmer was still in Vincennes on that date. The first precisely dated entry made by Palmer in Arkansas on this expedition is that of October 13, when he was leaving Osceola for the B. F. Jackson Mounds at "Fishmouth Highlands" on Little River (but a monthly report copied by another scribe places this at October 18).

Palmer's detailed itinerary for the entire field season is displayed in table 7.1, and mapped in figure 7.1. In summary, he spent the rest of October and early November in northeast Arkansas and was joined by H. J. Lewis in or near Memphis, just in time for Lewis to sketch the mounds at the nearby Bradley's Landing site. On or about November 9, they arrived in Little Rock and went from there to Lewis's home town of Pine Bluff, on November 11, but were hampered by bad weather.

157

Table 7.1.
Palmer's Itinerary for His Second
Arkansas Field Season (October 1882–February 1883)

OCTOBER

5 —Note to Powell from Vincennes, Ind.: "Start to day for Osceola, Ark."

13 (or 18?)—Journey from Osceola to "Fishmouth Heighlands" and B. F. Jackson Mounds on Little River. Then visited Pecan Point and "Mounds on Frenchmans Bayou." Palmer then went by steamboat down the Mississippi and up the White River, investigating sites near Newport, Jacksonport, and Akron.

27 —Arrived (by train?) at Jonesboro and mentioned but did not visit the "Web" Mounds on Bay Ridge Road. Then went south on Crowley's Ridge to Harrisburg and worked at the nearby Stone and Brookfield mounds.

NOVEMBER

1 —Continued south to Cherry Valley, Cross County; visited nearby mounds but could not excavate.

2?—Continued south to Forrest City.

3 —Left Forrest City for Madison. Probably visited sites on Robert Anderson's farm, Major Chairs's property, Captain Crook's farm, and Anderson Lake from this base overlooking the St. Francis Valley.

5?—Possibly on the 5th or 6th, Palmer "lost a day that was wanted at Memphis" at the Forrest City depot.

7?—About this time, Palmer must have met and hired H. J. Lewis in or near Memphis and gone immediately with him to the nearby Bradley site.

9?—Possibly Memphis for Little Rock on the train.

9 —Little Rock

11 —To Pine Bluff?

13 —Pine Bluff entry includes this date as "first frost." It appears that Palmer and Lewis were rained out of field work for more than a week.

20 —Pine Bluff entry includes this date's cotton prices.

21 —Possibly traveled by train to Walnut Lake Station (and mound) and the nearby Choctaw Mound.

22 —Winchester Station, Drew Co.; on to Taylor's, but "three days & nights rain." Then worked at Taylor and Tillar sites for several days.

29 —"Tillers Station" letter to Powell; has been to Taylor and Tillar, notes finds there and states that "half this month has been waste" due to rains.

DECEMBER

2 —Pine Bluff—letter to Powell.

3?—May have gone to or toward Arkansas City, by way of Wynn Mounds and Ben Franklin Mounds.

4 (or 5?)—From Arkansas City to De Soto–Depriest Mound and J. P. Clayton Mound; apparently started back for Arkansas City on the 5th but had to stay overnight in private homes.

6 —"Returned" to Arkansas City from Depriest Mound.

7 —Probably working out of Arkansas City. Could have seen Arkansas City Cemetery Mound. Probably left by steamboat for the lower Arkansas Valley, stopping off at the "old fortification" en route to Menard. Probably was at Menard much of the time between his visit to the fort and Christmas.

25 —Visited Knapp Mounds. Surface collections and drawings, little or no digging.

29 —Pine Bluff. Letter to Thomas, going to one more place on the Arkansas River, then to Arkansas City.

30 —Note about life in Pine Bluff.

JANUARY

1 —Still in Pine Bluff; the fire.

3 —Arrived at Heckatoo on Arkansas River; stayed at Captain Smith's; rained three days and nights. Then visited Smith's Mound, Adams Mound, Sarassa Mounds.

8 —Heckatoo; note to Thomas: a small box will be sent. Could have gone to Garretson's Landing from here. From Garretson's, he went to: Houson Mounds, Snuggs Mound, possibly Waldstein, and Linwood Station.

9 —Probably at Linwood Station (possibly Waldstein), thence by freight train to Arkansas City, arriving early (one A.M.) on the morning of the 10th.

10 —Arkansas City. Apologetic letter to Thomas; Lewis to be "discontinued." Will leave tomorrow to dig at Knapp.

11 —Probably left Arkansas City for Little Rock & Knapp.

15 —Little Rock; passage on steamer for Reed's Landing (near Knapp). May have begun digging at Knapp.

20 —Little Rock; went eight miles southeast to Thibault. May have also visited the "Ancient Indian Cannal" about this time.

27 —*Arkansas Gazette* reports that Palmer was in Little Rock "a few days ago" and had just dug at Knapp.

27 —In Benton; talks about occurrences a week ago, but may be hearsay. From here to Hughes Mound and Chidester Mound.

31 —Benton; letter to Thomas; came here "a few days since"; "Tomorrow start for the Mississippi River" but "herd of a collection . . . at Arkadelphia."

FEBRUARY

2 —Arkadelphia.

4 —Arkadelphia. Cold, sleet, and snow.

5 —Same; visited prairie mound, two miles from town.

6 —Arkadelphia, "so cold & bad—no work could be done."

8 —Arkadelphia, "cold & slippery . . . I could not go any where."

10 —Arkadelphia, heavy rain; visited salt works on Saline Bayou.

14 —Arkadelphia. Letter to Thomas: "I start to morrow for the Mississippi River."

16 —Memphis. Letter to Thomas. Then (apparently), "left Memphis for Bradley's Landing." Hard rain.

17 —Back to Memphis. Sleet, snow, and ice.

18 —Memphis. Letter to Thomas, refers to Bradley's Landing trip. Discusses lower valley sites and Arizona sites.

MARCH

18 —Vicksburg, Miss. Letter to Thomas, mentions Arkadelphia.

On or about November 21, Palmer and Lewis went by train to southeast Arkansas and began some of their most productive work, closing the month with the sensational finds at the Tillar site. Through December and well into January, Palmer (and Lewis, until January 10) traveled back and forth between Arkansas City, the lower Arkansas River valley, Pine Bluff, and Little Rock, with the work including a return visit to the Menard site, visits to the Knapp Mounds, and the first documentation of the Gardner and Thibault sites.

At some time between January 21 and 27, Palmer went southwest from Little Rock to Benton, thence in early February to Arkadelphia. Again plagued by bad weather, he left on February 15 for Memphis.

Palmer's final effort to work at Bradley's Landing was frustrated by the weather, and he abandoned Arkansas for lower Mississippi Valley sites in Mississippi and Louisiana. He was in those latitudes from late February at least until mid- to late March, at Natchez, Troyville (Jonesville, Louisiana), and Greenville, Mississippi (McVaugh 1956:215, 248, 340), as the river rose and flooded. As noted in chapter 2, Lewis had apparently resumed working as a free-lance artist and may have met Palmer again while drawing the flood scenes.

Palmer's Return to Northeast Arkansas: July and October 1882

MARVIN D. JETER AND DAN F. MORSE

Palmer revisited northeast Arkansas on July 4–5, 1882, apparently only making a brief stopover in Osceola and picking up a donation of eight pots at Pecan Point. As noted above, he then went to Washington and did not return until mid-October. At that time he began an intensive and productive whirlwind tour, first going inland to the B. F. Jackson site, then proceeding a short distance down the Mississippi to pick up yet another donation at Pecan Point and one at nearby Frenchman's Bayou.

Next he apparently went down the Mississippi to the mouth of the White River and took a steamboat up that stream all the way to the Newport-Jacksonport vicinity. There

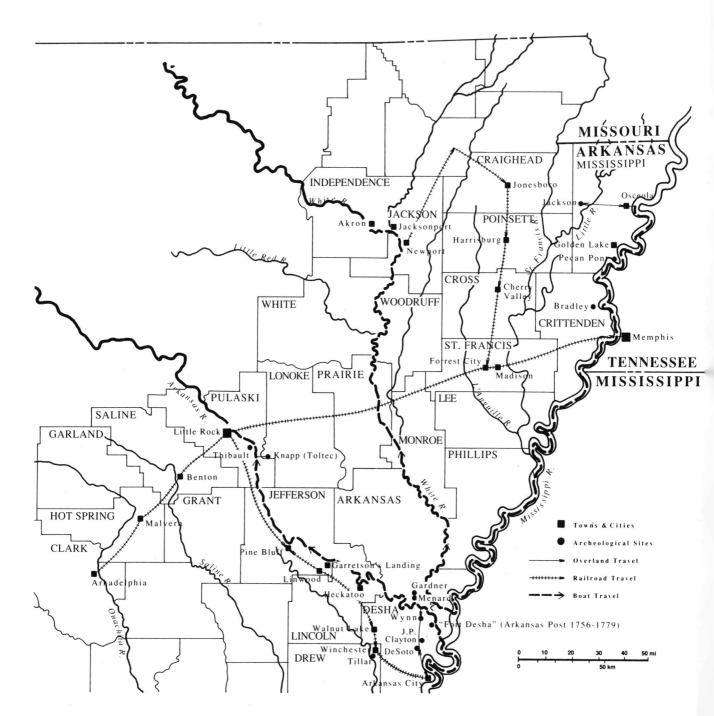

FIGURE 7.1

Map of Palmer's itinerary for the 1882–83 field season in Arkansas.

he investigated several mound sites and again picked up some noteworthy donations. He then went overland, possibly by rail, as connecting lines were in existence, to Jonesboro and began a generally southward tour down Crowley's Ridge, with a visit to small mounds near Harrisburg, where he ended the month.

Although some of the sites, collections, and documentary data are quite significant, there are relatively few entries in Palmer's own hand for this period, and few dated entries. The sequence is based on a scribe's copy of his end-of-the-month report, from the NAA "2400" file. The text of this report is generally in agreement with that of the notes produced by the other scribe and curated in Arkansas, but there are a number of differences in wording. The accounts of Palmer's work at a given site should be read against each other.

The B. F. Jackson Mounds

On either October 13 or 18, Palmer traveled westward from Osceola to a site on a Little River cutoff owned by B. F. Jackson. We have checked land ownership records in Osceola, and on June 15, 1983, we visited the locality indicated by Palmer. This research leaves no doubt that Palmer's B. F. Jackson site was the site now known as Wildy (3MS10 or 10-P-8).

This finding clears up potential confusion with the site presently known as Jackson Mounds (3MS59 or 9-P-3) at the northern outskirts of the community of Dell, some sixteen miles northeast of the Wildy site and twelve miles north-northwest of Osceola. Phillips mapped both Jackson and Wildy as Parkin phase sites (1970: Figure 447) but conceded that both "may be as much Nodena as Parkin" (1970:935). However, Palmer's artifacts from his B. F. Jackson mounds, now curated at the Smithsonian Institution, do not match well with AAS collections from 3MS59, which appears to predate the Nodena and Parkin phases, but closely resemble those from Wildy.

White River Sites

Jacksonport Mound. Palmer reported the demise of a large mound about a mile east of Jacksonport. The Jacksonport Mound site (3JA8) is approximately in this location, on an old meander of the White River, and may represent a remnant of the mound Palmer reported as "all carried away" or another mound at the same site or another site. The AAS files indicate that by 1965 at least half of the mound at 3JA8 had been washed away; the remnant was about fifty feet long, eighteen feet wide, and twelve feet high.

The Akron Mound. Palmer's major find on his first White River exploration was actually a donation of "a fine carved shell" found earlier at the Akron Mound site (3IN3). The cemetery on the mound observed by Palmer still exists at the former settlement location and is known as Akron Cemetery, but the town moved about two miles north to the location presently known as Newark. The shell and other materials from the Akron site are consistent with a Middle to Late Mississippian placement.

Mound Sites near Harrisburg

Palmer's final October explorations were in the vicinity east of Harrisburg, along the eastern margin of Crowley's Ridge. A site number (3PO168) has been designated for his

Stone Mound location about three miles east of Harrisburg, but no mounds are presently known there. His nearby Brookfield Mound, which yielded no artifacts, has not been identified, and no number has yet been assigned.

Palmer's collection from the Stone Mound includes a single Parkin Punctated sherd, which is somewhat surprising—and intriguing. The nearest known Parkin phase (Late Mississippian) village is on the St. Francis River near Marked Tree, more than twenty kilometers (about fifteen miles) to the east. On the intervening braided stream terrace, surveys have located fairly abundant Early and Middle Mississippian sites. Numerous sites, now all obliterated, were once known in the Harrisburg vicinity, and many are assignable to the Middle Mississippian Cherry Valley phase (Morse and Morse 1983: 241–46). Recent surveys near Harrisburg, however, have produced scattered and sparse Late Mississippian remains, mostly Nodena points and end scrapers, but only a very few sherds. Hence, Late Mississippian extractive (mostly hunting and quarry) sites do exist in this region, which was otherwise sparsely occupied after A.D. 1400.

Palmer's Documents for July and October 1882

AHC Item 14 (1917:400–01)

July 4
Osceola Miss Co Ark

Was hear July 4–1882 it was very hot in the day—night wind changed and was very cold, overcoats cumfortable.

Coloured people had a festival Ice cream and cake at night—during the day they had a Barbaque a few miles out of town.

White people a few of them ceased work or partially so many did as usual

Being no Saloons there was sobriety—

A few whites had a picknick in the country.

The Colored people have a society known as Knights of wise men, they paraded at night with music and regalia—swords of wood silvered over each one with lantern, they occasionally at the order of an officer represented in their evolutions that of a ball room

Why all this.

———————

AHC Item 3 (1917:410)

Pecan Point Ark

For a week before the 4th of July—1882 at Pecan Point was 102 1/2 mid-day—night 95 and fell so suddenly during the night of the 4 that by 5 A M on the morning of July 5 the Thermometer registered but 64 A very un-usual condition for the time of year and locality

Overcoats in demand the sudden cold was severely felt by the early risers.

Dr. J. M. Lindsley of this place presented 8 fine Potts.[1]

AHC Item 15 (1917:433)

Journey to Little River
Ark—Oct 13–1882. to Fishmouth[2]
   From Oceola to Little River most of the journey was through dence
woods the water rose last winter 18 feet covering the woods leaving the
water sediment marks on the trees and the Blazed ones by the ax made by
the men in their boats as they sailed along the tree tops so as to marke their
return road
   neither bird or animal seen on the road—Fishmouth Heighlands old river
cut-off.
Cotton though topped is 6 feet high.
Mr. Jacksons mad bees.

AHC Item 2 (1917:433–34)

Mounds & House Sites on
farm of B. F. Jackson 16 miles
North West from Osceola Ark.[3]
   The first mound visited was 4 ft. high, 40 ft. long & 30 ft. wide & of
oval form . Three graves of white people were on the summit but the owner
gave permission to examine between the graves. The first hole dug was 2½
ft. below surface in nice black soil, then 10 inches of burnt clay, 6 inches of
charcoal & ashes, associated with which was a skeleton & potts. In the
2nd. examination the same result was obtained as the first with the skeleton
and pottery . 4 ft. below the former skeleton a hardburnt floor was struck
covered with 2 ft. of ashes with 2 specimens of pottery but no skeleton .
The 2nd. mound visited was 7 ft. high, & 25 ft. across. Graves covered its
surface so no examination was made.

House Sites
   30 yards from the last named mound is a level spot with burnt brick like
stuff protruding more or less from the surface soil . This extended about
[200?] ft. square. A house & out buildings covered a part of it . On removing the brick like substance for 6 inches to 2 ft. two skeletons were found a
few ft. apart (Grown) & one of a child. The former had 5 pots each, the
child one & 2 toy vessels . Ashes were associated with the skeletons .
Several House sites with broken pottery were found .The spot was once
larger but the overflow from the Little River CutOff, which runs by it, has
carried away part of it .
In the 3rd. hole dug—after passing through the top soil, then burnt clay—
charcoal &ashes same thickness as first hole dug—In the ashes was a
broken pot but no remains .
The human remains were found facing some to one quarter others to another, face downward or on the back .

AHC Item 27 (1917:417)

Jackson Mound, Mississippi Co. Ark.
House sights.

Close to the above *mound* after digging *through the burnt clay and ashes.*
Then at four feet a hard burnt floor (or fire place) somewhat round was found this was covered with about three inches of ashes and in which was found two entire pots.

Following in the same level a broaken pot was found without human remains but with burnt clay and ashes as the preceeding

---

AHC Item 2 (not in 1917)

Fishmouth Highlands,   Ark.
Mounds & House sites . On Farm of B. F. Jackson, 16 miles
N. of West from Osceola, Miss. Co. Ark.

House Sites.		House Sites.	
(1) Mussel Shells	71200	(3) Crania fragments	71183
"	71167	"	71149
"	71166	"	71201
		"	71182
		"	71184
(2) Amimal Bones	71205	(4) Charred Fungus	71169
"	71199		
"	71168		
"	71171	(5) Paint =	71,170
"	71202		
"	71203		
"	71204		
(6) Pottery	71,151	Mound Pottery	
"	71,155	71195	71432
"	71 156	71194	71233
"	71 157	71233	71198
"	71158	71190	71154
"	71159	71207	71156(V.)
"	71160	71152	71165
"	71161	71176	71192
"	71162	71191	71153
"	71163	71193	71179
"	71166	71197 = Mud floor-ing.	
"	71172		
"	71173		

"	71177
"	71179
"	71180
"	71185
"	71186
"	71187
"	71188
"	71189

Mud Daubers
Nest =   71186
Pottery   =71206
[See figure 7.2]

———

AHC Item 2 (cf. 1917:401)

Near Osceola, Miss. Co. Ark.
B. F. Jackson entitled to thanks of Bureau of Ethnology .
P.O. address = Louise P.O. Miss. Co. Ark.[4]
2 faces of pottery[5] from a gentleman in Osceola.

———

AHC Item 3 (1917:409)

Pecan Point, Miss. Co. Ark.
Mrs. Mc. Gavock is entitled to thanks of Bureau of Ethnology.
Oct. 1882—

At one place $3\frac{1}{2}$ ft. under the surface was found a layer of hard wood ashes $1\frac{1}{2}$ ft. thick & nearby was a skeleton & 2 pieces of pottery. In other localities the soil is generally $1\frac{1}{2}$ to 2 ft. over the remains, in the above it is bet. 3 & 4 ft. over. The excess in this locality has been added at various times by the overflow of the Mississippi River near by since the burials were made.—

———

AHC Item 27 (1917:427)

Mounds on Frenchman's Bayou 6 miles
W. of Golden Lake P.O. on Mississippi
River Mississippi Co. Arkansas[6]
These house sites consists of several elevations of circular form & composed of sandy loam . The highest is 8 ft. & covered with graves. Most of the mounds are in ploughed fields cultivated for years & are above the overflow. The human remains, pottery & etc . once these must have been near the surface, the plow having cut to pieces everything there originally .

FIGURE 7.2

a.

Pottery vessels in the Palmer Collection from the B. F. Jackson Mounds, Mississippi County, Arkansas:

a. *Barton Incised jar with "late" attributes such as incising well below the neck and vestigial, non-functional "handle" appliques on the neck (Smithsonian National Museum of Natural History specimen number 71162).*

b. *Large Barton Incised sherd from a jar with incisions on the lower body (cf. the late Mississippian* var. Kent *of Phillips 1970:4b; 71172).*

c. *Parkin Punctated jar with vestigial "handle" appliques (71158).*

d. *Nodena Red and White wide-mouthed bottle (71161).*

e. *Old Town Red jar with suspension holes (71155).*

f. *Mississippi Plain bowl with scalloped rim (71160).*

g. *Mississippi Plain jar (71156).*

(Photo Nos. 88-12965, -12978, -12968, -12953, -12974, -12970, and -12958, respectively, Department of Anthropology, Smithsonian Institution.)

b.

c.

d.

e.

f.

g.

There is an abundance of pieces of brick like substance with ashes, animal bones, & mussel shells.

Nothing was found in place as originally.

A house is standing on one of the mounds. In the garden was dug up a stone bead and a piece of pottery

Presented by J. W. Uzzell .

—————

AHC Item 27 (not in 1917)

Golden Lake Post Office
Frenchman's Bayou Ark.
J. W. Uzzell presented one stone Bead & piece of pottery .

AHC Item 24 (1917:392)

Prohibition Tows Arkans
Steamboats & Express Co evade the law
   The Steamer Josie Harry mail boat to White River had on board numer-
ous jugs of whiskey and Brandy ordered from Memphis for parties in the
prohibition towns
   The Common Deck hands often at the end of the month owe at the bar
of the Steamer more than the pay due them.

AHC Item 27 (1917:427–28)

Stephens' Mounds ,(6)miles
South of Newport,Jackson Co.
Ark.
   On the farm of G. R. Stephens 6 miles South of Newport is a
mound, 5 ft. high, &15 ft. across, & circular in form . A few inches under
the soil, in the centre, 2 skeletons were found. In plowing over it the skull
of one was nearly carried away. They lay face down & each in a different
direction & quite opposite. 2 wheel like tools and a bone tool covered with
copper stain were found with them. The copper may have been taken away
by the plow. Two pieces were found. One had 3 pieces of bone stained with
copper—
The other skull had pipe & pieces of pots—
There was some little charcoal & ashes but no brick stuff .
Pipe = 71217—
Hairpins 71227
Grooved Discs 71,222
412–13–14–15–

AHC Item 27 (1917:420–21)

Mounds at Akron, Independence
Ark.
9 miles N. W. of Jacksonport on Big bottom[7] of White River is a large
mound 7 ft. high, & 300 ft. across, of circular form. It is covered with
graves of the townspeople as it is on the outskirts. In digging the graves
many things have been taken, From one grave a fine carved shell [fig. 7.3]
and a number of shell beads were found and presented to the National
Museum by M. A. Mull of Jacksonport. Jackson Co. Ark . A figure of clay

FIGURE 7.3

Engraved shell in the Palmer Collection from the Akron Mound, Independence County, Arkansas. (SI-NMNH specimen number 71229; Photo No. 88-12979, Department of Anthropology, Smithsonian Institution.)

was taken out at the same time with the shells. It was sold to Dodd, Brown & Co. cor. 5th & St. Charles st. St. Louis Mo.
Large Shell = 71226
Beads.   71228–29
  There is another mound near the above. It is 4 ft. high & 50 ft. across. One foot from surface found 6 inches of burnt clay brick stuff, then 5 inches of ashes & charcoal. A few important[8] things were found—Turned over the whole mound. The base is of clay & sand. (Nos. 71219–20–21 .)

AHC Item 22 (1917:396)

Harrisburg Poinsec Co

Ark—1882

Hotel 150 per day food badly cooked & badly served the beds wretched drinking water with insects in it.
No shoe mender in the place
150 Inhabitants
Poor brick court house jail inside—but unfinished
There is a Doctors Shop Printing Office—Post office all in court house owing to its unfinished condition prisoners are sent to other jails

Harrisburg
Saloons

Saloons are voted out of town . But drunken men are seen.
Kansas eggs may be around filled with Whiskey and sealed with white wax and sold 10 cents each or one dollar per dozen. A grocery has an inner room and a Saturday crowd is especially noticible—from other days.

———

AHC Item 22 (1917:397)

("Stone") Mound on farm of T. G. Stone[9]
3 miles East of Harrisburg, Poinsett Co. Ark.

3 miles E. of Harrisburg, Poinsett Co. Ark on the farm of T. G. Stone is a mound 15 ft high, 15 ft across at top & 200 ft. at base . After digging off the top soil of 18inches, (2) skeletons were found 3 ft.apart, with face down, one to the W. & the other South. Nothing but pots were found with them . A large Oak tree grew in the centre about 3 ft. in diameter, the roots of which had broken the pottery No ashes, bones, charcoal, burnt clay, bones of food animals or birds were found. the first (2) ft. was black loam—then clay with gravel[10]
Specimens of Pottery from Mound—
71208–71209–71210–71211–71212–71213–71214–
71215–
Mussel Shells = 71231–71230—
420

———

AHC Item 22 (1917:397)

Brookfield Mound, 3 miles E. of Harrisburg
Poinsett County Arkansas .

¼ mile East from the "Stone" mound, & in the thick woods belonging to J. C. Brookfield[11] is a mound 10 ft. high, 15 ft. across with small bushes growing on the summit. A hole was dug from the summit to the base without finding the least trace of anything indicating that man had occupied it . First a few inches of soil, then a mixture of clay & gravel.

———

AHC Item 22 (1917:396)

Harrisburg, Poinsett Co. Ark.

J. H. Hall and S. G. Stone are entitled to the thanks of the Bureau of Ethnology.

E. T. Walker presents 3 ears of corn said to have originated from corn found in a mound[12] on the San Francis River . No—419—This rare & new corn

———

NAA 2400

Report of Dr. Edward Palmer
for month of October, 1882

On October 18th I started in a mule team from Osceola Mississippi County Arkansas for B. F. Jacksons Fishmouths Highlands situated on that part of Little River cut off by the earthquake of 1811 and 1812 and which is now but a Slough. The river is some distance from it. This locality is sixteen miles by township lines, and north of west from Osceola, Mississippi County, Arkansas.

Jacksons Mounds

The first mound I visited, was oval in form, four feet high, forty in length and thirty feet wide. Its sumit is occupied by the graves of three white people. Two and a half feet below the surface, I found ten inches of burnt clay. six inches of charcoal and ashes, also two skeletons with pots lying on each side of the heads. In digging close to the above, through the burnt clay and ashes to a depth of four and a half feet, we struck a hard burnt floor. It was covered with ashes and two entire pots were found. A broken pot was also found, with burnt clay and ashes— as the preceding one. No remains were found with either.

The second mound was circular in in form. Seven feet high, and twenty five across. Its surface was covered with graves so that no examination could be made of it. ———

Thirty yards from the last named mound is a level spot covered with a brick like substance, which could be seen more or less above the soil. Underneath this were found the skeletons of two grown persons and of one child. With each of the large skeletons, were found five pots—with that of the child, one pot.—and two toy vessels. Several pieces of broken pots were found, all being from six inches to two feet under ground.

Mounds on Frenchmans Bayou

Six miles west of Golden Lake Post Office on the Mississippi River is the farm of J. W. Uzzell from whose door yard many things have been dug up. Number 400—A bead, and a piece of pottery were all that were saved. A short distance from this house, along the bank of the bayou, there are several slight elevations, more or less circular in form. These have heretofore been considered artificial, but examination proved them to be natural, and formed by the water. The plow has destroyed the remains once deposited there, with the pots. Kitchen refuse, and an abundance of ashes, and brick like substance was found.

Here 'tis but lightly covered, so during an overflow would be easily destroyed. On the other hand, the land lying along the water courses, is soon overflowed, and the sediment then thrown up, forms a thick covering of earth for the dead as at Pecan Point. It is four feet deep.

Newport. Jackson Co. Arkansas
The mounds once existing here have all been removed to give place for sawmills railroads &c.

Jacksonport. Jackson County. Arkansas

One and a half miles north of this place, on the border of Mr. Kindmans farm, the road passes the farm, and takes a sharp curve. At this point, there is a narrow strip of land, back of which is a slough. Here had been an old Indian camp, for peering out of the soil we found a quantity of brick like material.

Here were three elevations, The central one being three feet high, and fifteen feet across, and circular in form. Its situation is in the center of the Curve.

On the side, a few feet apart, was a mound, one and a half foot high. and ten feet across. From six to ten inches of brick like substance was found, some showing the impressions of cane, as though they had been placed close together, and mud laid over them. Other patches had soft mud thrown between small pools[13] for as many as three impressions were seen. Some muddaubers nest were also found.

At the bottom of one mound, was found a hard burnt clay floor perfectly smooth (See 409) In the other was found a broken pot. (See 410) This place was called by some—Old Brick Fort.

One mile east of Jacksonport on the bank of White River, there stood at one time a large mound, but during the last years overflow, it, with a foot or more of soil, for a considerable distance around was all carried away, and with it, skeletons, pottery, & fragments of which, with arrow points, nut crackers of stone (See 411) and much of the burnt like roofing is scattered about. I was told by a gentleman, who passed over the spot while it was covered with water, that he saw many things that had been buried and were washed out.

Stevens Mound.
Six miles south of Newport, on the farm of G. R. Stevens. there is a mound

five feet high, and fifteen feet across. Circular in form. In the center were found two skeletons. In plowing over the mound, parts of the skulls were carried away. They were found face down, as the teeth and jaws were discovered in opposite directions. One female skeleton was found. and with it. two wheel like tools, and a bone tool covered with copper stain. (See 412) The copper must have been taken out by the plow, as none was found. Two pots were also found. (See 413) There were two male skeletons, one with a pipe. (See 414) and the other with pots. (See 415)

Akron Mounds.

At Akron, big bottom of White River, Independence County, Arkansas, nine miles north west of Jacksonport, there is a large mound, seven feet high and three hundred feet across. It is circular in form and covered with graves. In digging a grave at its base. a fine carved shell and a number of circular circular beads were found. Mr. M. A. Mull of Jacksonsport, the owner of the shell, and beads. presents the first (See 416) and a sample of the beads (See 416) to the National Museum.

A so called. Idol. was found at the same time, and it is now in the possession of Dodd, Brown and Co., corner of 5th Avenue and St. Charles street, St. Louis, Missouri. Near the above mound, stands the Union Church of this section, and on the opposite side from the former mound, stands another smaller one, four feet high, and fifty feet across. One foot from the surface, was found six inches of burnt brick like substance, then below this was five inches of charcoal and ashes. Between these mounds, and a slough (formed from Black River) is a narrow strip of land, which was a famous camping place for Indians. In the last mentioned mound, only a few unimportant articles were found. (See 418)

Jonesboro. Craighead County. Oct. 27—

Twelve miles east of this place, on the Bay Ridge road, are the celebrated Web Mounds.[14] As I was informed by a trustworthy gentleman, that both the mounds were covered with graves and that the road was nearly impassible, I concluded not to visit them.

No. 419 Corn from Mounds, on San Francis River.

Three ears of this corn is sent and donated to the National Museum by E. T. Walker of Harrisburg. Poinset County. Arkansas. John Spannor of Bay Village, Cross County, while on the San Francis River, found some corn growing on Indian mounds. It is of a reddish color, and leaves the ear (in color) as if slightly parched. He gave some to Dr. A. R. Joiner, and E. T. Walker of Harrisburg. Poinset County. Dr. Joiner was absent, but the latter gentleman presents to the National Museum—three, out of the five ears, which were in his possession. It is said to grow freely, and needs but little care. I am informed, that the mound on which this corn was found growing, had been well dug over by relic hunters, who finding a pot of the corn, spilt it in the soil, causing it to take root and grow as found. In color and form of grain it resembles the Peruvian corn, found with mummies in Peru.

Its curiously colored grain, is distinctive from any other corn now grown in this section or in the United States.

Stones Mound.

Three miles east of Harrisburg. Poinset County Arkansas . on the farm of S. G. Stone, there is a mound fifteen feet high and fifteen feet across at the top, and two hundred feet at its base. At eighteen from the top, and three feet apart, were found two skeletons; their faces downward, one to the west, the other toward the South. Nothing was found with them but pots, which are sent under (No 420) A large oak tree grew in the center, and its roots had broken a considerable amount of pottery. Neither ashes, charcoal, burnt clay roofing, bones of food, animals, or birds were found.

Brookfield Mound.

One quarter mile from Stones mound in the same direction, we find a mound owned by J. C. Brookfield. It is ten feet in height, and fifteen feet across. Small bushes are now growing on it. There was nothing found in it, nor was there the least sign of its ever having been occupied. These two mounds are located on rising ground, above a slough which contains water a part of the year. They command the approaches from several ravines, from which the enemy might emerge. They also afforded an opportunity for hunting game, as its situation lies from high land to water.

All the mounds with one or two exceptions had been dug over previous to my visit, by A. L. Lewis[15] of St-Paul, Minnesota. This was a great disappointment to me, as I had hoped to find this lonely spot untouched. The following gentlemen have rendered me assistance in giving information as to where mounds could be found, and also permission to open any that might be found on their premises.

B. F. Jackson, Louise, Post Office, Mississippi County, Arkansas.

G. R. Stephens, J. W. Stayton, Joe N. Stayton, E. L. Watson. all of Jacksonport, Jackson County, Arkansas.

J. H. Hall, S. G. Stone. both of Harrisburg, Poinset County, Arkansas.

The following gentleman made donations to the National Museum. See 416 & 417. M. A. Mull presented a fine carved shell and some beads.

E. T. Walker, of Harrisburg, Poinset County, Arkansas, presents to the National Museum, three ears of corn. ["See. 419." is inserted in the margin here.] This rare and new corn originated from Indian Mounds on the St. Francis River. Arkansas.

Catalogue of contents of box 3

No 408.   Bead, and piece of pottery, found two feet below the surface, in the garden of J. W. Uzzell. Frenchmans Bayou, Arkansas ; Mississippi County.

No 409	Pieces of burnt hearth of fire-place.
No 400[16]	A broken up pot. These two numbers are from mounds one and a half miles north of Jacksonport. Jackson County. Arkansas,. and near Mr Kindmans farm.
No 411	Arrow points, and stone implements found on the banks of White River, one mile east of Jacksonport, Jackson County, Arkansas.—found after the overflow of White River, last spring.
No 412	A tin box containing articles found with the skeleton of a female, taken from Mr. G. R. Stephens mound. six miles south of Newport Arkansas.
No 413	Pottery found with (412)
414 & 415	Specimens found with male skeleton, in Mr G. R. Stephens mound, as mentioned under number (412)
416 & 417	Carved shell, and some beads, presented to the National Museum, by M. A. Mull. Jacksonport, Jackson County. Arkansas. They were taken out of a mound, while digging a grave on it, at Akron, Independence County, Arkansas.
No. 418	Odd things, taken from a small mound at Akron, Independence County, Arkansas.
No. 419	Corn presented to the National Museum by E. T. Walker, of Harrisburg, Poinset County, Arkansas. It is derived from seed taken out of a mound on the St. Francis River, Arkansas.
No 420	Pottery taken, with two skeletons, from a mound on the farm of T. G. Stone, three miles east of Harrisburg, Poinset County Arkansas.

"They Are Getting Ready to Waste It": Palmer's Visits to Cherry Valley and the St. Francis Valley

MARVIN D. JETER AND DAN F. MORSE

At the beginning of November 1882 Palmer moved farther southward along Crowley's Ridge to the new community of Cherry Valley. His comment, "A fine timber country but they are getting ready to waste it," is also applicable to the archeological sites he was about to visit. First, he made a brief trip to a nearby mound site which is now known to have been highly significant—and has been largely "wasted" by relic collectors. Due to several circumstances, he did not work there but did produce a hasty sketch map.

Next Palmer went south to Forrest City, where his first Arkansas season had ended. From there, or from the nearby hamlet of Madison overlooking the St. Francis River floodplain, he explored several sites with mounds and house mounds. Even then, road construction and related encroachments of civilization were impacting and destroying portions of these sites.

The segment of the St. Francis Valley picked by Palmer was just downstream from the Parkin phase territory where his late colleague Edwin Curtis had worked so successfully in 1879 (Morse and Morse 1983:19), and on the northern border of the protohistoric Kent phase (1983:297–98, Figure 12.1), which has equally spectacular sites, ceramics, and other artifacts, especially downstream near the river's mouth (House 1987).

Palmer was again largely frustrated by circumstances, in this case the repeated use of mounds as places of refuge for cattle during flood seasons. Compared to the hauls made by later explorers (especially C. B. Moore 1910), not to mention those of the indefatigable grave robbers of northeast Arkansas, his collections from this valley seem paltry indeed.

Once again there are relatively few documents and almost nothing in the way of substantive archeological comments in Palmer's own handwriting. Instead there is another "dialogue" between two of his scribes' versions of his notes. The nature of his lost original monthly report, which actually covered only the first week or so of November, can only be approximated through a comparison of these two secondary versions.

In addition to copying or rewriting Palmer's (edited) words, the scribes also drew their own versions of his rather crude sketches. In one of the latter, showing Chairs's Mound, Palmer appears to have invented his own kind of abstract art: a combination of a plan view with the four cardinal directions indicated and a profile view showing strata. The sketches and the references to them were deleted from the 1917 Arkansas publication.

The scribe's documents that found their way, scattered haphazardly and mixed with a few of Palmer's own notes, into the 1917 publication seem to have been written well after Palmer's return to Washington, as they contain some of the five-digit Smithsonian numbers used by the National Museum. A complete and previously unpublished monthly report by another scribe furnishes the sequence of site visits and concludes this section.

Visit to the Cherry Valley Mounds

Palmer only made a day trip to this remarkable site. His Taylor and Leptrot mounds (now designated together as the Cherry Valley mound group, 3CS40 or 11-M-1) were the last remaining Cherry Valley phase mounds when we visited the locality in June 1983, and they were in the process of being destroyed by relic hunters using power equipment.

Earlier, when pot hunting was threatening the site, salvage excavations at three of these mounds were conducted by the Gilcrease Institute of Tulsa (Perino 1967). Nearly five hundred burials and about three hundred ceramic vessels were recovered, along with structural remains and radiocarbon samples. The Cherry Valley phase is now regarded as a major early Middle Period Mississippian manifestation, dating around A.D. 1050 to 1150 (Phillips 1970:929–30; Morse and Morse 1983:241–46).

Thomas did not list this site in his catalog (1891:17) and did not mention Cross County at all in his 1894 final report. Palmer's previously unpublished crude sketch, copied by a scribe, of this mound group as it was in 1882 is thus a contribution to the literature, albeit a minor one.

Explorations in the St. Francis Valley

Robert Anderson Farm. Here Palmer noted and sketched a group of house remains that were being destroyed by a road and briefly tested two small mounds located nearby. Thomas cataloged the site (1891:24) and described it (1894:228–29), including a highly stylized version of Palmer's sketch (Thomas 1894: Figure 136). The site has not been reidentified, and Palmer's data are insufficient for a cultural assignment, although the "houses" with abundant burnt daub were probably Mississippian.

Chairs's Property. Here a very similar situation was recorded. Again, what were apparently houses were damaged by the road. A larger nearby mound was tested briefly, with no cultural materials found. The site was cataloged and briefly described by Thomas (1891:24; 1894:227–28). It may be the Crow Creek site (3SF31 or 12-N-14), of uncertain Mississippian phase affiliation.

Crook's Mound. Palmer conducted a very limited test here and found nothing diagnostic. Thomas listed and summarized the site (1891:24; 1894:228), which has not been located.

Anderson Lake Mounds and Houses. On the farm of John Anderson, Palmer recorded three mounds but apparently only briefly tested one of them at most. He also noted the presence of yet more "house sites" affected by the road and (in the monthly report) the existence of a "fine carved stone pipe" owned by a local farmer.

Thomas listed and summarized the site (1891:24; 1894:228). Palmer's "Lake Anderson or Mud Lake" must be the cutoff channel of the St. Francis River northeast of Forrest City, extending from north-central St. Francis County into southeastern Cross County. There are several known sites in this locality, but none closely matches Palmer's description.

Palmer's Cherry Valley and St. Francis Valley Documents

AHC Item 16 (1917:435)

Cherry Valley Cross Co Ark

Nov 1–1882   *Thre Months Old*
    A new place built on the bottom lands on the Crawleys ridge branch St Louis Iron mountain R. Road
Three new stores going up
one frame and one log dwelling finished
A well is dug
Hotel commenced
There is a frame boarding house in which is the post office.
Blacksmith shop under boards
A saw mill under upright boards and an upright board shanty
A fine timber country but they are getting ready to waste it[17]
Cotton bales—Cotton seed and Staves await shipment.
    Each man expects a fortune in a hurry and he praises the rail Road
    Land owner gave for Depo lot 200 by 1,500 feet deep
    Lots (Front) 50 feet by 100 back sell for 20 dollars
One Acre blocks back part sold for 50 dollars.

AHC Item 16 (1917:439)

Forest City Ark.   Ark.
I arrived late, & the hotels being full had to take a room at a colored
restaurant
Helena & Iron Mountains R.R.

———————

AHC Item 16 (1917:439–40)

Forest City Ark
   *No Saloon—Drug stores have a hole in which the money and bottle is
placed the money go the bottle is filled returned and no one seen.*
   Seeds of the China tree used to cure botts in horses
   *A Captain Cook would not allow his mounds disturbed because his
negroes would not rent his land for fear of hants as they express*
*The place has 900 inhabitants and no bakery, bread is brought from
Memphis or Helena*
*Turnips one cent each—Apples and Irish potatoes 1 dollar per bushel,
Sweet potatoes 50 cents bushel. Beef 10 to 15 cents pound Chickens small
25 cents each (no bank)*

———————

AHC Item 17 (1917:434)

   Left Forest City for Madison San Francis Co Ark
   Nov 3–1882 by two mule team
*An Exconfederate Soldier for driver—he called homemade Tobacco Arkan-
saw scrip he told his experience as a prisoner at Camp Butler Springfield
Ohio*[18] *and Erie Penn—Apple and Peach trees in bloom*
   Neglected grave yard of U. S. Troops at Madison.

———————

AHC Item 27 (1917:415)

[This uncaptioned entry in Palmer's handwriting refers to the "House Sites
on farm of Robert Anderson"; see the following entry and the monthly
report at the end of this section.]
   *There is now to be seen the space of fifty feet square covered with brick
like substance part is in a cotton field all but 10 feet of the balence has been
a wagon road for many years thus the brick roofing and whatever was
deposited under it has been destroyed as deep ruts are made through it. The
remaining 10 feet was at a projecting point into the river and presented the
appearance as shown in the diagram*

AHC Item 27 (1917:415)

House Sites on farm of Robert
Anderson 12 m. N. E. of Forest City, Sanfrancis
Co. Ark On San Francis River

The remains appear to be house—outlines. From Anderson's farm 2 miles S.W. was the old Burnt Mill,[19] and 3 miles N. the old Military Ferry that crossed the San Francisco River. At this place on the immediate bank is a projecting point which I am told was at one time much larger but from time to time it has caved in, until now there is not much more than about 10 ft. projecting into the river. I was informed that human remains, much pottery & many stone implements were washed out by the disintegrations of the point by water & lost the settlers putting no value on them

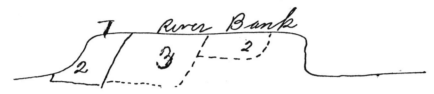

1 = San Francis River
2 = parts of 2 squares the rest carried away—
3 = a complete square—Its outer edges with those of partial squares were slightly elevated above the surface all of which was form of brick like substance with grass impressions—Both the edges & centre of the squares & halves were as firm as a floor made so probably by the tramping of animals who sought this high spot during the overflows. The outer edges must always have been higher than the middle or they would have been even with the centre. There was no soil over it, the cattle loosing it & the rains carrying it away—
No. 3 had a space of 8 ft. its edges raised from 1 to 2 inches, sloping toward the centre. This square was floored with 8 inches of burnt clay, then 8 inches of ashes & charcoal—then black loam. No further examination could *not* be made as the public road runs by the edge of it and the people feared to have the point disturbed as it would be easier acted upon by the water . There seems to be about 2 foot rise here.
No 4 = public road .
No 5 = a clear space between the square—one of the half squares & the river. This is naturally a high point—
71433 = burnt clay from square No (3) .
Stone Implements from ploughed field near = 71050–71434–71435–71436–

AHC Item 27 (1917:415-16)

Two Mounds on Anderson
Estate ¼ mile from former place.
12 m. N.E. of Forest City Ark .

(1)
¼ mile back from former place is a mound 3 ft. high & 45 ft. across—
This mound is bare of vegetation or trees, but large trees surround it. During every high rise of the San Francis River Cattle have been kept upon this
mound until it is stamped solid. Permission was given to dig a small hole in
the centre. The 1st. foot & a half consisted of a mixture of clay(burnt)
ashes, & soil. The balance was sand . It is near the bank of a slough.
(2) The second mound is ½ mile in a direct line from the above and on
bank of the same slough. It is 5 ft. high, & 50 ft. across.The cattle kept
upon it during the overflows have made it quite hard—no brick like substance was found—
First 3 ft. was black loam—then yellow clay—The owner did not wish
these mounds disturbed at the outer edges as he kept his cattle there upon .
The water would penetrate & carry the earth away .
Large trees & thick cane surround the mound.

———————

AHC Item 16 (1917:441)

House Sites, called Old Brick
Fort or House on the property of Major Chairs known
as the Blackwell Patric farm
4 miles S. E. from Forest City .
SanfFrancis Co. Ark.,
and 150 ft. from Crow Creek.

   This is called by some people the Old Brick Fort or House from the
quantity of brick like material found more or less exposed .
   There are (3) of these House sites. A public road runs by the only perfect
one & cuts through the other two as the following diagram indicates.

(1) This square was not formed with
regular edges but with irregular
edges like the outer one . Found 8 inches of roughly
burnt clay in this square. then 6 inches of ashes &
the balance black loam .

This spot is about 2 ft. higher than the surrounding country. It is 30 ft. long & 10 ft. wide. I am told that in making the road 5 ft. was cut away . Nothing found .

(1) The fire that the clay must have been fierce and the clay at some distance above the fire judging from the irregular way it is scattered around the edges. This irregular square presents a very uneven appearance as the burnt clay projects above the soil to some degree .

The roadmakers dug it up somewhat

(2). A large poplar tree stands here 3 ft.through . & 100 ft high .

(3) represents a fine poplar tree of same proportions as (2)

(4) Some years ago a large oak tree stood on this spot and was blown down. I was informed by Captain W. J. Crooks that he passed at the time & saw the bones of a skeleton & some broken pottery adhering to the roots of the tree. H. B. Batte also passed and took out a fine pipe from the roots .These things are lost.

5−5 are 2 small patches of burnt clay with very irregular edges, the public road cut through them & is fast wearing them away.These 3 house sites are about 90 ft. apart.

Major Chairs lives at Columbia, Tenn. His agent A. C. Hickey gave me permission to examine the mounds .

———————

AHC Item 16 (1917:441)

Chairs' Mound—on property of Major
Chairs. 4 m. S.E. from Forest City—
San Francis Co. Ark.

On the same estate as the house sites but 200 yards from Crow Creek. It is 10 ft. high 36 ft. across—Small truck grown over it . The back water of San Francis River comes near to this mound.

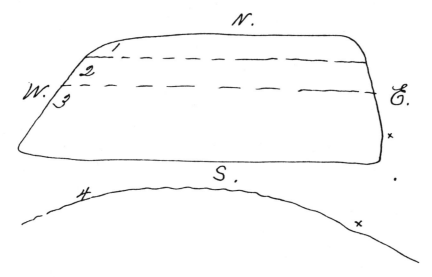

1 = 6 to 10 inches of loam—
2 = 1 foot of yellow clay.
3 = the base white clay—
no evidence of occupation.
+ + indicate the spots where larg oak trees stand
4 = public highway.

―――――

AHC Item 16 (1917:440)

Crook Mound—
10 miles S. East of Forest City,
San Francis Co. Ark.

This mound is situated on the farm of Captain W. J. Crook, 10 miles S. E. from Forest City. and 60 ft. from Tuni Creek.

It has been cultivated for over 15 years.& besides during the overflows cattle are kept there for months. Their constant tramping has so mixed up the soil, that but little of the soil as it originally was remains . I found (3) small spots, however of original deposit with 4 to 12 inches of loam & 3 inches of burnt clay—then ashes variable in thickness .

The base was of clay—It is oblong in form 15 feet high 408 ft. long. and 150 ft. wide . It has been very deeply ploughed. A skeleton or two with a few pots has been taken out.

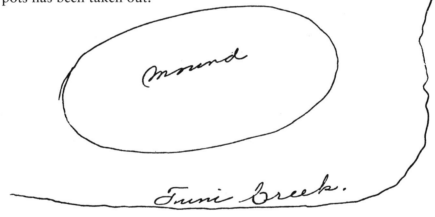

Extensive Examination could not be made as the owner feared that water would effect the mound and make it an unsafe place for their cattle
This place is at the foot of Crawleys Ridge .

―――――

AHC Item 16 (1917:441)

Mounds on Lake Anderson.
10 miles N.E. from Forest City,
Ark .

Lake Anderson or Mud Lake is 6 or 7 miles long & about 200 yards wide and ¾ miles to the San Francis River .

Here are some mounds on the farm of John Anderson on the bank of the Lake .

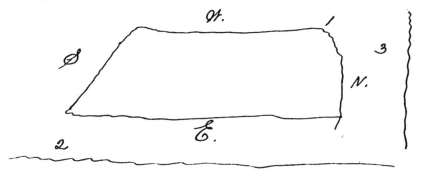

(1) Here stands a Red Oak tree 3½ ft. in diameter . This mound is 12 ft. high, 30 ft.across at the top and 55 ft. at the base . No burnt clay or evidence of its being utilized were seen.

(2) Is a Public Road .

(3) A deep ravine extending from the mound to the Lake forming a fine place to shelter canoes. At first water may have been the ravine but it is now much filled up—The earth may have been taken from here to make the mound.

300 yards from 1st. mound is another on the Bank of the Lake. It is 5 ft. high, 45 ft. wide and circular in form . Cattle tramping over it have rendered it very hard & thoroughly mixed. the materials composing it,It consists of Clay, loom, ashes, & burnt Brick like material .

Still farther to the south is another 75 yards from the last mentioned mound. It is round in form, 5 ft. high, & 55 ft. across. Its composition is like that of the former , and is equally mixed and as hard tramped .

There is a depression in the Lake Bank in front of the mound & so a good view of the lake is had .

These mounds are in a bottom covered by timber of large size .

AHC Item 16 (1917:442)

House Sites, Anderson Lake .
San Francis Co Ark.
10 miles N. E. of Forest City Ark.

¼ mile from the last mentioned mound & close to the bank of the lake are several patches of brick like material finely ground. For years the public road has passed over them so that whatever was originally beneath this burnt clay has been destroyed by vehicles which have worn deep ruts in the ground.

These house sites are only 1½ feet above the general surface .

NAA 2400

["Monthly" Report]
Mounds On the farms of J. M. Taylor
and W. Leptrot.
Cherry Valley Cross Co. Arkansas.
I visited this section in order to explore a group of mounds located on two
adjoining farms near by. I found it a new place containing only four. and
those unfinished buildings. After much solicitation, I gained the consent of
a farmer to take me to the mounds. It was getting late in the day, on which
we reached the dwellings occupied by the owners, and finding that one
farm had that day been sold to a party who lived some distance off, making
it impossible for his consent to be gained, we proceeded to make inquiries
about the remaining one, and this we found had been opened and examined by Mr. A. L. Lewis.[20] I should like to have stayed, if only for a few
hours, but there being no public house, and much sickness in the private
families. I had no place to stay, besides the team which brought me, had to
return immediately. I however managed to take a hasty sketch as I stood in
the waggon. I then proceeded to Cherry Valley.

Location of the two mounds.
No 1 . . . Spring at the edge of Crawleys Ridge.
No 2 . . . Outline of mounds, that were covered with weeds and
            underbrush.

No 3 . . . Outline showing the position of the other mounds, which are
situated in a rich section, at the base of Crawleys Ridge, three
miles north east of Cherry Valley.

These three mounds are 210 feet apart, 25 feet high, 20 feet across at the
top 200 feet across at the base.

Ruins of Houses on Robert Andersons Farm,
on the bank of The Saint River. twelve
miles North East of Forest City, Saint Francis
County Arkansas.

Two miles South West, was the old burnt mill, and three miles north the old
Military Ferry across the Saint Francis River. At this place on the immediate bank of the river, is a space of fifty feet square, which is covered with a
brick-like substance. part of it lies in a cotton field, and the remainder,
(with the exception of ten feet) has been a waggon road for many years,
thus destroying the brick, and whatever else had been there deposited. The
remaining ten feet were at a point which projected into the river, and
presents this appearance.

No 1—A square space of eight feet. Its edges raised from one to two inches,
and sloping towards the center. This space was covered to the depth of
eight inches with this brick like substance. Under this we find eight inches
of ashes, and charcoal, then black loam.

No 2—Parts of two squares, the remaining portion having caved in. A
gentleman informed me, that when he settled here, (thirty years ago) this
point extended out one hundred and fifty feet further, but at every rise of
the river, large slices caved in exposing to view human remains. pottery,
pipes, and stone implements. The settlers attaching no value to these articles, took no pains to preserve them. Consequently all have been lost. No
excavation was allowed by the owner, as it would materially injure the
road. Judging from the brick matter found, it would appear that the outlines seen were those of houses.

Mound.

One fourth of a mile back from the above place, there is a mound three feet
high, and forty five feet across. Large trees surround it, but neither tree or
vegetation is found on it. During every high rise of the river, the cattle are
placed here for protection, and the tramping of the animals have so packed
the ground, that is has become perfectly solid. One foot and a half of the

top consists of brick stuff and ashes, mixed with the soil. The remainder of the mound consists of sand.

No examination was allowed. This mound is near the bank of a slough.

Half a mile, in a direct line from this mound, and on the same slough, there is another one, five feet high, and fifty feet across. The cattle are kept upon it during an overflow, and have so trampled it, that the soil has become as hard as a floor. There is no brick substance found in its composition, which consists of three feet of black loam and clay. The owner, keeping these mounds for the safety of his cattle, did not wish them to be disturbed, there being no other place of refuge during an overflow. Tall cane and large timber surrounds the mounds.

House Ruins, on the property of Major
Chairs of Columbia Tennessee

I obtained permission from the agent of Major Chairs, (Mr A C Hickey) to make any examination I might desire.
This place is known as the Blackwell Patric, Farm. Four miles south east from Forest City, Saint Francis County, Arkansas, and one hundred and fifty feet from Crow Creek; there is what is called by many, The old brick house, or fort. so called from the quantity of brick like substance found here, near the bank of Crow Creek, and which originally appeared to have had this shape.

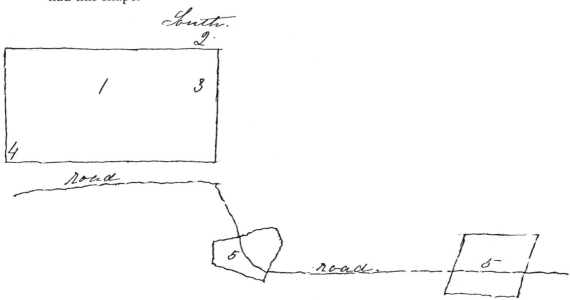

The square outline No 1. was filled with eight inches of brick, ashes and black loam. It is but two feet higher than the surrounding surface, and was thirty feet in length, and ten feet wide. In cutting the road through it. I am told that five feet were taken off it.—Nothing was revealed on examination.
No 2.   Large poplar tree, three feet through, and one hundred feet high.
No 3.   Poplar tree. Similar to the other.

No 4   Some years ago, a large oak tree stood on this spot, but was blown down. Captain W. J. Crook, informed me that he passed the place at the time, and saw broken pots, and the bones of skeletons adhearing to the roots.

H. B. Batie also passed and took from the roots a fine pipe. None of these things have been preserved.

No 5.   Two patches of brick substance, which were at one time much larger. The many years travelling over, has worn these patches away. These three, are about ninety feet apart.

Chairs Mound.

Mound on the same estate as the above, two hundred yards from Crow Creek. The back water from the St Francis River comes near to this mound.

Ten feet high

N

W

Loam. 6 to 10 inches.

Yellow clay / 1 foot
White clay. / the balance

E

Small brush growing over the mound. 32 feet across.

S

White oak. 2½ feet through.

road

Large white oak 2½ feet through.

Crook Mound.

Ten miles south east from Forest City and twenty yards from Tunic[21] Creek, on the farm of Captain W. J. Crook, there is a mound that has been cultivated over for fifteen years, and during an overflow is used as a refuge for cattle. as they are kept on here for months the constant tramping has so mixed the upper portions together, that but little distinction is to be made. As it was covered with cotton, I could only dig between the rows. There seemed to be from four to twelve inches of loam. three inches of burnt brick, then a variable thickness of ashes, and lastly clay. These measurements were taken where the tramping had not mixed the soil. The mound was oblong in form, had been deeply plowed, and a skeleton or two, with a few pieces of pottery taken out.

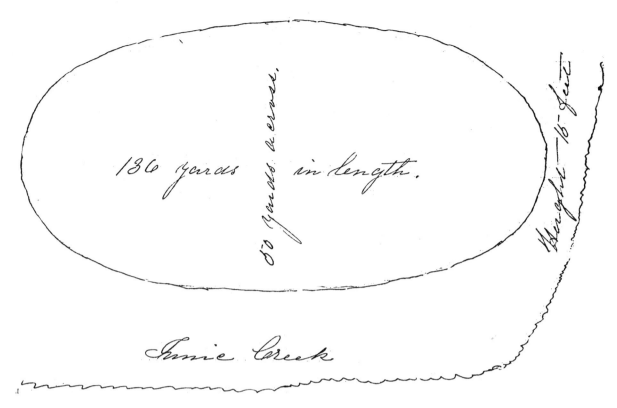

136 yards in length.

80 yards across.

Height — 16 feet

Innie Creek

Mounds on Lake Anderson.

Ten miles, North East, from Forest City, we find Lake Anderson, or Mud Lake. It is from six to seven miles in length, and about two hundred yards in width, and three quarters of a mile from St. Francis River, which river probably ran where the lake now is. Here on land belonging to John Anderson, are some mounds. The following mound was originally higher, but has probably been reduced in height by the trampling of cattle, which were placed there durring the overflow.

Up

12 feet high.

80 feet across on top.
55 "   "   "   " at base.

S

N

No brick like substance found, or any evidences of Indian life. The mound is composed of clay loam as far as seen.

Covered with weeds. and grass.

E

Road.

Three hundred yards south of the above mentioned mound, and on the bank of the Lake, there is another one, circular in form, five feet high, and forty five feet across. This has also been used as a shelter for the cattle, durring an overflow, and the constant trampling, has so thoroughly mixed the materials of its composition, (which consists of clay. loam, ashes, and a burnt brick like substance). that it has become perfectly hard.

Still further South, about seventy five miles[22] from the last named mound, there is still another. This is also circular in form. There is a depression in the Lake bank, just in front of this mound, so that a good view of the Lake can be had. This soil has also become thoroughly mixed and hardened, by the trampling of the cattle. it is five feet high, and fifty five feet across. These mounds are in a level bottom, and covered with dense timber of the finest sort.

Brick like Substance.

One fourth of a mile from the last mentioned mound, close to the bank of the lake, the road passes over a spot which is thickly covered by fine particles of brick like substance. Whatever was originally beneath this, has long since been destroyed by passing vehicles, which have worn deep ruts in the road. A cotton fields adjoins, in which there is a partly destroyed mound, belonging to Hirum Hueston, who plowed up here a fine carved stone pipe. It is of importance and should be obtained so that a copy might be made. The owner is an ignorant man, and has no idea whatever of Science. If you wish to obtain it, I would advise you to ask Judge Henry Hulbert of Forest City, (who has great influence over the man) to borrow it for you. If he succeeds, you might suggest that he pack it in a box and send to the National Museum by express, expenses to be paid there. Judge Hulbert may be able to prevail upon the man to sell it.

A. C. Hickey of Madison, St Francis County, Arkansas, has a pipe made of clay and on it is the face of an alligator. He was absent at the time of my visit, but I am informed that should you desire to borrow it, the gentleman, who is an intelligent man) will no doubt let you have it, so that a cast might be made. Should you write, ask for its locality. I was informed it was from the St. Francis River.

AHC Item 16 (1917:440)

Forest City Depo
Wishing to go to memphis by the memphis and Little Rock Rail Road at 6 A.M. Was on hand with my trunk as the train arrived—the checker refused to check the trunk because it was not at Depo twenty minutes before the train arrived so it could be entered on book for the train
The Ticket agent said to him check it as there was time but he refused— so I lost a day that was wanted at Memphis

"A View of Mound": Palmer and Lewis at the Bradley Site, 1882

MARVIN D. JETER

Dates of Arrival at Memphis and Work at Bradley

By a process of bracketing, we can conclude that Palmer arrived at Memphis about November 6 or 7, 1882. He had gone from Forrest City to Madison on the third and had explored four different sites or site clusters from that base, which probably would have taken at least two days. Then he had "lost a day" (perhaps the fifth or sixth) at the Forrest City Depot. On the late end of the bracket, he arrived in Little Rock from Memphis on the ninth.

This barely allows time for the considerable work that was done, probably with a paid crew probing for burials accompanied by artifacts, at the Bradley site opposite and just upstream from Memphis. At least two days, most likely the seventh and eighth, must have been spent at Bradley, and perhaps the sixth was, too.

Beginning of Association with Lewis

For the first time, Palmer was accompanied by H. J. Lewis, who produced three pencil drawings showing views of the Bradley mounds—and marking a decided change for the better in this department of Palmer's investigations. Extant copies of Palmer's notes, however, matter-of-factly refer to these drawings as "Plates" A, B, and C (See figures 7.4, 7.5, and 7.6), without any reference to Lewis.

The surviving documents do not offer a clue as to the circumstances under which Palmer and Lewis met. An educated guess would be that Lewis was doing some free-lance sketching on a Mississippi riverboat, on the Memphis waterfront, or even at Bradley's Landing, as he had already done in the Pine Bluff vicinity, and that a chance meeting led to their two-month association.

The Bradley Site

Morse and Morse (1983:285–86) have called Bradley the "most spectacular" of a cluster of Nodena phase sites near Wapanocca Lake. Three Arkansas site numbers (3CT7, 3CT9, and 3CT43; the LMS number is 11-P-2) have been given to an "almost continuous" scatter of debris along a two kilometer stretch of Bradley Ridge, "a prominent relict natural levee of the Mississippi River."

As previously noted, Bradley may have been the capital of Pacaha, the most powerful "province" (chiefdom) encountered by the De Soto *entrada*. Although the Morses had proposed Pecan Point for this distinction (1983:311–12, Figure 13.2), Hudson suggested that Pacaha was somewhere between Wapanocca Lake and Pecan Point (1985:4), and the Morses now believe Bradley to have been at least as likely as Pecan Point (1987 personal communication).

Palmer's Work at Bradley

Our only source that actually describes Palmer's work at Bradley consists of six pages of scribe's notes in the Arkansas History Commission's "Item 27" files. These notes briefly describe Lewis's drawings, but these remarks were edited out of the 1917 publication. They also include lists of "Thomas numbers" and "Smithsonian numbers" (also edited out in 1917), indicating that they were written in Washington. The Arkansas files also include one partial list of Smithsonian numbers, on the reverse side of another entry in the "Item 19" file. From the National Anthropological Archives' "2400" file, we have only a list, in Palmer's handwriting, of a separate sequence of "Thomas numbers" for Bradley specimens purchased by Palmer.

Palmer's remarks about Lewis's drawings do not completely agree with the drawings themselves. It appears that at least four mounds are depicted. I visited site 3CT7 in May 1986 with David Dye of Memphis State University; all but a trace of one mound had been destroyed at that site, which we then believed to be the most likely candidate for the site visited by Palmer and Lewis. Dan Morse (1989 personal communication) suggests instead that it may have been site 3CT43 (which has itself been massively damaged in recent decades), or some combination of two sites that are now regarded as separate, or possibly even a site that is now lost. The Mississippi River has been active in this vicinity, and it appears that the Bradley's Landing–Oldham Post Office base of Palmer's operations may have been obliterated by the river and/or levee construction. More intensive work with old maps and land ownership records may resolve the situation. But at present, due to the changed landscape and the inadequacies and contradications in the notes and drawing captions, it is not possible to identify Palmer's site.

Palmer did not dig in the mounds, he said, due to their already having been extensively ransacked and the farmer's not having picked the cotton crop on them. This is not shown in the drawings, but in some later drawings Palmer explicitly stated that Lewis had omitted the vegetation to show mounds more clearly. Instead he says, "I turned my attention to the house sites found all over the field."

The list of "Thomas numbers" includes seventy-three specimens of pottery from the house sites; there are sixty such Smithsonian numbers. Thomas catalogued the site (1891:17), noting "Relics of various kinds found," but did not mention Palmer. In his final report he summarized the site (1894:226–27), stating that "about seventy whole vessels and numerous fragments were obtained," and included a Holmes engraving derived from Lewis's "Plate C" (1894: Figure 135). He noted that "unfortunately the explorer's report on these interesting works is very brief" and did not mention Palmer in this site summary. However, much later in the report (1894:663), he did cite and quote Palmer on his typical findings in low house mounds, referring back to the Bradley site summary.

Palmer's artifacts from Bradley have not been intensively analyzed in the light of modern archeological knowledge. Hoffman examined these collections briefly and noted that they consisted primarily of various Mississippi Plain vessels, with Parkin Punctated being the most common decorated type, and single specimens of Walls Engraved and Carson Red on Buff, plus elbow pipes, stone discoidals, a spatulate celt and other celts, a "spade" (or hoe?), and abrading stones, plus some skeletal material (1975:10–11).

As in the cases of Pecan Point and Menard, Moore followed Palmer with more intensive excavations and correspondingly more spectacular results—in this case, 181 burials and 258 ceramic vessels (1911:427–46). He stated that there was "abundant evidence of aboriginal intercourse with the whites" (1911:435), but, as noted by the Morses, he provided few details and no further discussion (1983:286).

Palmer's 1882 Bradley Site Documents

AHC Item 27 (1917:402)

Bradley's Landing, Oldhams P. O.
Chittenden Co. Arkansas.

Boat hotel—a railroad hand waiting for a boat spent $25 amoung loafers in 3 hours while dressed in the poorest clothing. He praised the James Boys as heroes. He was from Mississippi.

———————

AHC Item 27 (1917:403–04)

Mounds, House sites & etc.
    Bradleys Field 1 mile from
        Bradley's Landing or Oldham
            P. O. Chittenden Co. Ark.

These mounds, House sites & etc. are owned by Mrs Bradley & are situated in a field 1 mile from the landing—

Plate A. [fig. 7.4]

Is a view of mound looking west on Wappanocka Creek.
Mound 1—is 7 ft. high, 60 ft. long and 40 ft. wide with a flat top.

Plate B. [fig. 7.5]

View of same mound[23] looking East or directly opposite from (Plate A) & showing the timber on made land since the Mississippi River ran past the mound. There is no overflow of this field now.

Plate C—[fig. 7.6]

This is view of Mound is looking N.E.—the old Bayou bed in the background—it also represents the field in which the house sites are found from which the specimens were taken (see numbers on accompaning (page 5)—Mound no. (2) on this plate is 30 ft. high, 200 ft. long, & 150 ft. wide. Mound No(3) is 30 ft. high, 100 ft. wide & 130 ft. long. Mound No(4) is same as No(1) & covered over with graves—[24] The upper soil of the mound is sandy—the base seems to be clay.

The field containing these mounds comprises 25 acres which have been cultivated for 30 or 40 years. A creek runs back of the field called Wappanocka or Wappanoca. It empties into the Mississippi River 1 mile from Bradley's Landing. It runs N. W. to S. E. and is 7 miles long. The field is not now overflowed.

The land outside the field shows that a river once ran by there & then there may have been overflows as on examination, the spot not disturbed by cultivation & the plow shows a deposit stratified as if deposited by water. Where no human remains are found the same stratified soil continues of sand or clay with vegetable remains

The Mississippi River is ¼ mile directly opposite. This seems to have been made since the river ran by the field in which are the mounds. Many of the trees on this land are 5 ft. in diameter, & 80 ft. high. The human

Plate A

not view

View of Mound on Byou - looking west - 1

View of Mounds looking East

Plate B

FIGURE 7.6

"Plate C—A View of the Bradly Mounds looking North East . . ." by H. J. Lewis. (National Anthropological Archives, Smithsonian Institution.)

FIGURE 7.4

"Plate A—View of [Bradley] Mound on Byou—looking west . . ." by H. J. Lewis, early November 1882, Crittenden County, Arkansas. This is the first drawing made by Lewis for this project. The captions on this and the other Lewis "Plates" are by Edward Palmer. (National Anthropological Archives, Smithsonian Institution.)

FIGURE 7.5

"Plate B—View of [Bradley] Mounds looking East" by H. J. Lewis (National Anthropological Archives, Smithsonian Institution.)

remains & etc. found in this field are found varying in depth from 3 to 5 ft. The mounds occupy the highest spot, so the further you go from the mounds the deeper are the things found. This would be the case by overflow, the greatest deposits in the low places. The soil is of a sandy nature in the higher & greasy clay in the low parts.

The mound had been so much dug up by relic hunters that I feared not much good could be done, besides the renter of the land would not grant permission as the cotton was not yet gathered,[25] so I turned my attention to the house sites found all over the field.

In the same field as the mound are many house sites, Out of these house sites many things have been taken from time to time. Examining the undisturbed portions clearly proved that 3 to 5 ft. was the depth the house sites are found.

They were without any regularity, some are near together, while others are far apart. The human remains are found without any preference to facing any one quarter of the compass. Some were face up, others down or on the side, & but few bones could be saved. Some skeletons had one pot, others had more, with them together associated with other articles. After the top soil was removed—was burnt clay which was sometime a foot thick either crumbling with impressions of grass & sticks or hard with reed impressions. Then more or less ashes associated with some 6 inches of burnt grass with which were the human remains—

Pottery thus found is numbered with Prof. Thoma's numbers as—
811—12—13—14—15—16—17—18—19—20—21—22—
823—24—25—26—27—28—29—30—31—32—33—34—
835—36—37—38—39—40—41—42—43—44—45—46—
847—48—49—50—51—52—53—54—55—56—57—58
859—60—61—62—63—64—65—66—67—68—69—70.
871—72—73—74—75—76—77—79—80—81—82—83—84—

Pipe = 878—   beads = 1463—
Mortar =1458   Mortar 885—

Smithsonian Numbers.—

Stamp = 1459   burnt clay   (reed impressions) = 896—
                        & 897—.

Burnt clay with stamped impressions = 71058
      "   reed   "   = 71097
Charred Straw Matting (Thoma's number = 553)

Smithsonian Numbers.

White Paint 71132—39—41
Mussel Shells 71095—
Human Lower Jaw 71147
Bone tools 71142—43—44—45—46
Stone Implements = 71096—71123—24—25—26—27—28—
                71129—31—33—34—35—36—37—40—80—
                71100
Pottery 71068—76101[26]—22—71062—71094—59—65—52—54—88—
      71037—77—78—53—71—69—92—91—61—63—66—53—56—90—89

71075–76–78–54–67–73–59–93–61–64–51–55–57–85–86–
71082–80–81–72–74–
71116–15–11–48–4–88–14–19–12–23–21–13–10–8–5–20–
Stone Implements—Thomas' numbers.
1456–54–53–47–62–46–61–60–55–64–45–
1457–51–48–50–51–
900–898–89–
Mussel Shells 1464.
Human Bones
872–91–90–94–93–95
Bone Tools.
886–87–88–89–

───────────

AHC Item 19 [reverse of another entry] (not in 1917)

71080—Earthen Vessel & pieces.   Indian [illegible]
  to   Site-moun[d?]
71083   Brady's La[missing]
                                 opp. Memphi[missing]

71083 Earthen Toy Vessel
  &
71084
71085
  to Earthen Vessels (broken)
71093
71093 Earthen Vessel(broken) handle
71094   "   "   fragments
71095 Knives marked with notches
71096 Pieces of Spear Heads & 2 arrow Heads.
71097 Baked clay with moulded impressions
71098 Rubbing Stones
71099 Charred Grass Matting
71100 Rubbing Stone with Grooves, lava
71101 [missing at bottom of page]

───────────

NAA 2400

Ark
Specimens purchased at oldham or Bradleys landing (Crittenden Co) ark
From House sights below the surface surrounding mounds
List of Prof Thomas numbers
3580
3581

3582
3583
3584
3585
3586
3587
3588
3589
3590
3591
3592
3593
3594
3595
3596 Stone hoe donated by Cap Charles Morris[27] *but from the same locality as the above.*

Travel to Little Rock and Pine Bluff, November 1882: Rain Delays and Observations

MARVIN D. JETER

Palmer traveled by train from Memphis to Little Rock on or about November 9, 1882. Judging from the racist remarks Palmer attributed to a fellow traveler, Lewis must have been in a separate car. It appears that they, or at least Palmer, stayed in Little Rock until the eleventh, when he caught another train to Pine Bluff, again overhearing racist sentiments.

From Palmer's November 29 letter to Powell, we know that "half this month" was a "waste" due to rain; this must be the explanation for the fact that Palmer was still in Pine Bluff on the twentieth and that no work had been done. The next dated entry notes his arrival at Winchester Station on the twenty-second, but he must have spent the twenty-first traveling from Pine Bluff to Walnut Lake Station and working near there.

This section merely presents Palmer's notes on his observations during this interval between archeological explorations. In addition to remarks about race relations, Palmer recorded some economic data about cotton farming and processing (this is in line with his long-standing interest in uses of plants), plus a note about black superstitions and a few other brief observations.

Palmer's Little Rock and Pine Bluff Documents, November 1882

AHC Item 30 (1917:428–29)

Memphis for Little Rock
On the Cars was (A. Philips) a rough specimen of the old planter he said

he dispised the negro because he said he was not now a profitable and
dependent work man, he blamed the Republicans for it all. He said the race
is decreseing and as soon as the old negroes are gone—The new race must
move or be killed. The two races cannot live together. A shower of oaths a
large whiskey bottle and all round him a filthy floor with tobacco juice—
He said he was a Democrat of the straight kind , he rejoiced at the defeat of
the Republicans. The discussion changed when the subject of the Demo-
crats fathering the liquor queston was mentioned. Two gentlemen of the
state said they had all along voted with democrats but now they could not
support such immorality
this silenced the man of filthy habits.

AHC Item 16 (1917:429)

Little Rock,   Ark.

1882—Nov.
Passed 2 school houses for white & colored both alike, children well fed &
clothed.
Pyracanthus in bloom Nov. 9th, 1882.[28]
Visited U.S. Armory's building, large & in good repair . The air of comfortable independence pervades it. The building looks as if newly repaired .
Nov. 11—1882 While passing the cars as they came in from Pine Bluffs, a
gentleman said—"The cars are crowded, that's like the darkies, they are
always on the move; he is good for nothing;- he never will have anything;
he is only fit for a slave!"

AHC Item 21 (1917:413–14)

Pine Bluff Arkansas.

Henry J. Lewis[29] is entitled to the thanks of the Bureau of Ethnology and
also J. W. Bocage, J. M. Taylor, & G. W. Davis.
One fine pipe donated by E. W. Martin
6 stone implements & 5 specimens of pottery (good) donated by J. M. Tay-
lor. (sent 2 photographs May 17th. 1883).[30]
One fine Stone Spade donated by Major G. W. Davis.
Pine Bluff has 28000 negroes and 8000 whites. Passengers were discussing
that point as to what might be expected.
Nov. 13th. 82—the first frost,
Cotton seed at oil mill will pay renter $8.00 per ton.-but planters $10
Formerly only sheep and cows ate the the seed.
The lints gets into the throats of hogs & kills them.
Cotton Seed & meal sell at $15 to $20 per. ton cake sent to Europe. The
hulls are used for fuel & ashes for lye.

Lint is taken from the seed by a fine gin. 25 lbs. of lint in a ton of seed & this sells at 5 cents per. lb.

100 lbs. of cotton seed generally yields 30 lbs. of lint cotton.

In 1882 Nov. 20th. the highest price at New Orleans was 11½ cts , the lowest 8½ cts. per. lb.

1 bale to the acre if properly cultivated. It takes a ⅓ of its value to pick it.

Rent for Land.

½ when team & food are furnished for the same they pay for ginning.

Cotton

80 lbs. of lint-cotton per. acre & pay for ginning.

$6 to $8 in money per. acre & if goods are furnished—a mortgage is taken on the crop—15cts. a bale for weigher—A certificate is given, the owner takes this & a sample and sells.

The cotton factor arrainge to supply the merchants money at 8% per. annum. in 2½% accepted. drafts on Merchant. 2½% for advancing money at end of 3 mos. it is compound interest. River insurance, fire insurance, & repairs to bale—then you pay 2½% commission for sales & storage.

The merchant to meet these expenses must double on his goods.

1863–64 cotton was $1. per. lb.

1865 5 cts per. lb.

1866 35 cts "

Land Rent $15 an acre.

Negroes Graves.

The spades used to dig graves are left 10 days on the grave[31] after it is filled up. They believe snakes can be enfused into the limbs & stomach of each other by conjurers by giving them cooked reptiles broken up fine & mixed with their food.[32]

Poor Hotel—no single rooms—

$2–per. day.

"I Commenced to Find Pottery, Remains, & Etc.": Palmer's Investigations in Southeast Arkansas, November 1882

MARVIN D. JETER

By about November 21, the rains had relented enough to permit field work. Palmer and Lewis boarded the L.R., M.R.&T. Railway and headed southeastward from Pine Bluff. During the next week or so, they excavated and sketched at four sites in northwestern Desha County and adjacent northeastern Drew County. The last two of these sites are particularly important in this region's archeology. A summary follows.

Mound at Walnut Lake Station

The major result here was Lewis's excellent drawing of the little passenger train chugging into the station (fig. 7.7). Palmer's shaft to the mound's base found nothing but sandy loam. Thomas only referred to this site in passing, as a "conical mound at Walnut Creek station" (1891:17; 1894:237).

This mound has been completely obliterated, apparently many years ago. The community known in Palmer's day as Walnut Lake is now known as Pickens. On December 20, 1982, just over one hundred years after Palmer's visit, I visited the location with Mr. R. A. Pickens, who had lived there more than sixty years at that time. He had no recollection of a mound but did indicate the former location of the railroad water tank shown at the left in Lewis's drawing. Two of the concrete supports for the tank were still present. AAS site number 3DE92 was assigned to this historic and prehistoric site location.

Choctaw Mound

This mound almost certainly had no relation to the Choctaw Indians, taking its name instead from Choctaw Bayou, which was probably itself named during the removal of the Choctaws from Mississippi through the Arkansas Valley to Oklahoma in the 1830s (DeRosier 1970:144–45).

Palmer found only a few potsherds in his test excavation here. The site was mentioned only in passing in the preliminary report (Thomas 1891:18) and not at all in the final report (1894). It has not been definitely located, but the vicinity was visited by myself and Mr. Pickens, who inquired locally and reported that local collectors had dug into the mound remnant.

Again the major result was a Lewis drawing (fig. 7.8). It shows a cabin being built, with some of the logs apparently taken from trees growing on the mound. AAS site number 3DE93 has been assigned to this site, which should have both a prehistoric and a historic component.

The Taylor Mounds

Palmer and Lewis next moved south a short distance by rail to Winchester, in the northeast corner of Drew County. After getting lost in the woods and losing three days to rain, they must have put in several days at one of the most important and intriguing sites in southeast Arkansas, the Taylor Mounds site (3DR2). Palmer seems to have conducted rather limited excavations, or at least met with limited success in finding whole artifacts, due to previous intensive pot hunting.

Again Lewis produced a remarkable set of drawings. The first (figure 7.9), is indeed, as Palmer stated, in the imaginative "bird's eye view" style that was popular at that time, e.g., for drawings of cities. Several of the other drawings can be abutted to produce a panoramic vista.

Thomas summarized the Taylor Mounds briefly (1891:18; 1894:239–40), without citing Palmer. He did publish a Holmes engraving, probably derived from a Lewis drawing which was lost in the process (1894: Figure 149).

I have visited this site on several occasions and have also examined artifacts from the site at the Arkansas Archeological Survey's UAM station and in private collections (but only a few of Palmer's artifacts at the Smithsonian). The site appears to have been intensively occupied during the Baytown period; by far the most common decorated potsherds are of the Mulberry Creek Cord Marked type. There are also some evidences of a very late Marksville period occupation and of a Late (possibly protohistoric) Mississippi period component. The time of construction of the major mounds is unknown, as no controlled excavations have been made.

The numerous low mounds, none of which are discernible today due to many decades of farming, were probably house sites as Palmer suggested. Such mounds have generally been associated with Mississippian groups. Although some Mississippian artifacts have been found at this site, they are quite sparse, especially by comparison with the abundant earlier materials. Palmer's collections from this site have not been studied intensively but certainly should be as a prelude to any new investigations.

Hoffman summarized Palmer's Taylor artifacts as mainly sherds representing the Marksville, Baytown, and Coles Creek periods, but did note the presence of a Mississippi Plain vessel, shell-tempered elbow pipes, and a large sandstone effigy pipe representing a kneeling human figure (1975:12–13). More recently, a local collector obtained a fragment of a kneeling-figure pipe from atop Palmer's Mound 2 here; I borrowed it and sent it to the Smithsonian Institution, where physico-chemical tests identified it as a variant of bauxite called "Missouri fire clay" (Bruce Smith, 1983 personal communication), rather than the Arkansas bauxite that had been expected.

During the spring of 1988, I visited the site several times, specifically in search of evidence of Mississippian artifacts in the former house mound locations, but none were found. Artifacts were generally very sparse there, although the earlier materials were still very abundant between the mounds.

The Tillar Mound

Late in the month, perhaps around November 27 or 28, Palmer went to a nearby mound on the property of J. T. Tillar, which was being farmed by his host, W. B. Dumas. Here he made one of the most significant finds of his entire Arkansas project, a mass burial of at least fifty-eight individuals, accompanied by at least twenty-three ceramic vessels, two pipes, and other artifacts.

The Tillar site (3DR1), and the "Tillar phase" of which it was a part, have been intensively investigated in recent years by myself (Jeter 1981, 1982b, 1986a), and I located the remnants of Palmer's site on April 9, 1983, during a survey with the assistance of Arkansas Archeological Society members. This and related sites appear to represent the remains of Protohistoric (late 1400s to late 1600s) Mississippian peoples, quite possibly "Tunicans" such as the Tunica themselves or the apparently related Koroa.

Analysis of Palmer's collection has identified a ceramic assemblage overwhelmingly dominated by late varieties of shell-tempered types, including Mississippi Plain, Winterville Incised, Barton Incised, and Leland Incised (Jeter 1981). Several of Palmer's vessels and other artifacts from this site are illustrated below (figs. 7.19–7.21).

It may be recalled that Palmer expressed disappointment to his biographer William Safford (1926:481), feeling that his efforts for the Mound Survey had not been adequately recognized. He contrasted Thomas's indifference to the attitude of botanists, who had named new species in his honor. In the type-variety system of ceramic classification, the type is more or less the equivalent of a genus, and the variety is analogous to a specific name. In an earlier report on a nearby and related protohistoric site (Jeter, Kelley, and Kelley 1979:260), it was noted that there was no variety name for Winterville Incised bottles decorated with interlocking S-shaped designs (the "guilloche"), and one of Palmer's vessels from the Tillar site was illustrated as a comparative example (1979: Figure 6b). That vessel (fig. 7.19a) and similar bottles (e.g., 1979: Figures 6a, 6c) are hereby designated as Winterville Incised, *var. Palmer*, in honor of the discoverer of the Tillar phase.

Palmer's Southeast Arkansas Documents for November 1882

AHC Item 21 (1917:427)

Mound near Walnut Lake Station.
Desha Co. Ark.

The mound is situated on the banks of Walnut Lake near Walnut Lake Station, on the Little Rock, Mississippi & Texas R. R .and commands a fine view of the lake. The mound is owned by Mrs. Moses. P. Embree, who gave me permission to examine it. Nothing was found however. It is 8 ft. high, 15 ft. across at the top & 40 ft. at base. I dug a shaft to the base. It was entirely of sandy loam.

Walnut Lake is 6 miles long & and of an averge width of 75 yards. No sign of occupation was found.

Explanation of Plate [fig. 7.7] showing Walnut Lake with Railroad Cars crossing the bridge.

FIGURE 7.7

"Plate D—Showing Mound at Walnut Lake Station . . ." by H. J. Lewis, late November 1882, Desha County, Arkansas. (National Anthropological Archives, Smithsonian Institution.)

Desha Co. *Ark.*

Choctaw Mound. at the junction of Wells & Choctaw Bayou's with Walnut Lake and 4 or 5 miles S of E. from Walnut Station on the Little Rock, Mississippi & Texas R.R.

It is situated on a fine rich bottom of loam & clay & commands a fine view of the surrounding country . I did not ascertain who was the owner— It would make a grand signal station. It is 10½ ft. high, 40 ft. through at the base gradually tapering to 4 ft. at the top.

1 foot of loam was removed & the mound was solid to the bottom, of solid clay with here & there fragments of pottery but no ashes or charcoal, no burnt brick like substance or any remains of settlements.

From Choctaw Bayou to Felix Smiths' plantation at Heckatoo is said to be a dry communication that was used by the ancient inhabitants and also from Wells Bayou was a dry communication to Star City, county seat of Lincoln Co. Ark.[33] It is a hilly country

Choctaw Mound.
Plate E. [fig. 7.8]

1 = Wells Bayou
2 = Choctaw Bayou
3 = Walnut Lake the entrance to the two Bayou's.
   View of Choctaw Mound looking S.W. & showing the conjunction of Choctaw & Well's Bayou's with Walnut Lake.

AHC Item 27 (1917:394)

Winchester Station, Drew Co. Ark.

W. B. Dumas entitled to thanks of Bureau of Ethnology .

Nov. 22–1882—

75 cents on 100 lbs. of lint cotton is taken for ginning cotton (a bale)— formerly it was $1.00. In some places the seed is taken for the ginning.

AHC Item 20 (1917:437–38)

Hollywood Plantation. Ark.
Taylor Mounds.

Nov. 22nd. 1882. Leaving Winchester Station for Dr. J. M. Taylor's 4 miles—got lost by not being rightly directed & went 10 miles out of our way. After miles of wandering, it being dark & hearing chopping, followed the sound & came upon 2 men chopping poles. Went to their cabin to hire one & team to take us

Plate E a View of Choctaw Mound - looking, South west - Showing the conjunction of Choctaw and Wells Byou with Walnut Lake -

FIGURE 7.8

"Plate E a View of Choctaw Mound—looking South west . . ." by H. J. Lewis, late November 1882, Desha County, Arkansas. (National Anthropological Archives, Smithsonian Institution.)

> *To the Taylors Mounds*
> *Darkies excited over sculls would not touch them. One took two sticks to take one up one would not sleep with my colored man because he handled bones. He said he feared the dry bones would shake about him at night.*
> *Three days & nights rain*
> *W. B. Dumas kindly entertained us.*

———————

AHC Item 20 (1917:438–39)

Hollywood Plantation
     Mounds. on the farm of Dr.
J. M. Taylor, 4 miles West from Winchester
Station, Drew County Ark,. on the L. R.
Mississippi & Texas R. R.

I found this celebrated group of mounds in a field of 63 acres. known as the "Mound Field".

This field is bounded by Bartholomew Bayou and a line of what is supposed to be artificially made ponds, running E. & W. Some of these hold water most of the year.

It is from these very probably that the earth was taken to build the mounds. They are largely filled up now. Before the War the ponds had large trees growing about them. These were cut down, the ponds drained and cultivated. For several years they have been neglected and trees are growing up. These intersect Bartholomew Bayou.

Bayou Bartholomew is said to be 500 miles long & 60 ft. wide in channel & 200 ft. from bank to bank. There is often an 18 ft. rise of water but it never overflows its banks[34] which are on an average 24 ft. high, It runs N & S.

The lower part of this mound field is made up from the overflow of the Arkansas River,. when it runs over Ambro Bayou below Pine Bluff. There is now a levee there so no overflow comes from this source.[35]

The top soil is black sandy loam & the bottom is sandy loam of light yellow clay.

The upper part of the field is stiff black loam & subsoil is a stiff waxy clay of a reddish to black soil.

Plate A. [fig. 7.9]

Is a birds eye view of Taylor group of Mounds looking West. Examining the subsoil about the mounds brought to light numerous pieces of pottery, mussel shells, bones & stone implements that had been turned up by the plow. This field has been cultivated for years. There are many house sites to be found in this field. All that I found had mostly been previously disturbed,. For years various ones have dug & ploughed up skeletons, pottery & etc. At 2 ft. deep I found an abundance of ashes in which were the following.

Turtle Shell = 71249—Pipe = 71235
Mussel Shells 71250
Pots.   71245
Pottery Frag-
ments.   71251
Stone Implements ploughed out—71246—44
                             71223—43
                             71242—40
                             71338[36]—41
                             71247

Plate (B)

[Lewis's "Plate B" from this series has not been found. It probably was used as the source for an engraving by W. H. Holmes that was published in the final report on the Mound Survey (Thomas 1894: Figure 149) and is reproduced here as figure 7.10. The line of trees curving into the distance from the right margin marks the bayou bank, and the cluster of trees on the left marks a pond location, as indicated in Palmer's comment which follows.]

Plate A— a Birds Eye View of Taylor Mound looking west —

FIGURE 7.9

"Plate A—a Birds Eye View of Taylor Mound looking west" by H. J. Lewis, late November 1882, Drew County, Arkansas. (National Anthropological Archives, Smithsonian Institution.)

Is view of mounds looking E. with Bayou Bartholomew to the right & ponds on the left.

    Plate C. [fig. 7.11][37]

View of mounds looking South West with Bayou in background .
Specimens borrowed of J. M. Taylor of Pine Bluff, Arkansas. are from this place .
(To be entered here the Borrowed pottery from J. M. Taylor.
[The rest of this page is blank.]

    Plate E. [fig. 7.12][38]

Is a view of mound looking due W. showing the connections of the Bayou & ponds . Bayou to the left and ponds to the right. This plate connects with D at 1—1 so marked on margin of plates .

    Plate D . [fig. 7.13]

Is a view of ponds looking North West. with the large mound to the left and showing the openings between the ponds .

    Plate F. [fig. 7.14]

a continuation of the pond view looking due North, with the common woods in the back ground.
Plates D & F. connect at 2—2 marked above timber line .
    The openings between the ponds vary in width from 30 to 100 ft. You

FIGURE 7.10

Engraving by W. H. Holmes, probably derived from H. J. Lewis's (missing) "Plate B" sketch of the Taylor Mounds, looking east. (From Thomas 1894: Figure 149, courtesy of Smithsonian Institution.)

pass from these outlets to cleared land & back of which are natural woods .
Mound No (1) on the plates is 30 ft. high of sandy loam mixed with clay.
Mound (2) is 14 ft. high & 100 ft. wide at base & 30 ft.through at top . It is of sandy loam at top & clay at base.
Mound (3) Is 9 ft. high, 18 ft. through at top & 30 ft. at base-& of same composition as No (2).
Mound (4) together with and the rest of the unmarked mounds average 5 ft. high & 15 ft. through and are of same composition as (2) & (3) Nothing was found in these mounds . The action of the plow & rains in uncovering mounds, and the repeated examinations of various ones with spades has left nothing to be found . many fine things have been taken out of the house sites found between the mounds in this field .

   This mound field is 15 ft. above the water channel of Bayou Bartholomew—No overflow—

Plate A.

Represents a drain running through length of the field. This to carry off the surface waters.

———————

AHC Item 20 (1917:438)

Dr. J. M. Taylor entitled to thanks of Bureau of Ethnology.

———————

FIGURE 7.11

*"Plate C. View of [Taylor] Mounds looking Southwest . . ." by H. J. Lewis. The
right portion of this drawing can be joined to the left portion of "Plate E" (fig. 7.12),
to extend the panoramic view. (National Anthropological Archives, Smithsonian
Institution.)*

AHC Item 27 (1917:394–95)

Filler[39] Mound, Drew Co. Ark.
2½ miles S.W. from Winchester Station

The Filler Mound is situated on the farm of J. T. Filler 2½ miles S.W.
from Winchester Station, on the Little Rock, Mississippi River, & Texas R.
R. Drew. Co. Ark .

The mound is 450 ft. from the bed of Bartholomew Bayou. It is 2 miles
by section lines from the mounds on Hollywood plantation. Mr. W. B.
Dumas who having this farm rented kindly gave me permission to dig into
the mound. It is 9 ft. high, 18 ft. across at top and 45 ft. across base.

As the iron probe indicated there was something below. I commenced on
one side so as to dig over the entire mound. At one foot below the surface I
commenced to find pottery, remains, & etc.

This deposit of bodies deepened to 2 ft. toward the centre. They were
without any definite order of of deposit or did they face in any one
direction.[40]

The bones of one body often lay across another or under, Sometimes the
vertebrae of one were found pressed between the upper & lower jaw of
another . Two or three heads were very near together. It was a very difficult
task to extricate the bones, pottery & etc. owing to the irregular manner of
intermixture with the soil. 25 skulls were so decayed that they could not be
saved. A number of sound bones were saved which may be useful to study .

4 pots were taken near one head, 2 near another with a pipe . also several
mussel shells were found—2 were near the heads. Two turtle shells were

Plate E. View of Mounds looking due west, Showing the Connections of the Byou and Ponds – Byou to left and Ponds to the right –

FIGURE 7.12

"Plate E. View of [Taylor] Mounds looking due west . . ." by H. J. Lewis. The left portion of this drawing can be connected to the right portion of Lewis's "Plate C" (fig. 7.11), and its right portion can be connected to the left portion of "Plate D" (fig. 7.13) to produce part of the panoramic view. (National Anthropological Archives, Smithsonian Institution.)

Plate D. View of Ponds looking North west – with large Mound to the left – Showing the opening between the Mounds –

FIGURE 7.13

"Plate D. View of Ponds looking North west" by H. J. Lewis. The left portion of this drawing can be connected to the right portion of Lewis's "Plate E" (fig. 7.12), and its right portion can be connected to the left portion of "Plate F" (fig. 7.14) to complete the panorama. (National Anthropological Archives, Smithsonian Institution.)

Plate F a continuation of Ponds—View looking due North . . . by H. J. Lewis. The left portion of this drawing can be connected with the right portion of "Plate D" (fig. 7.13) to complete the panorama. (National Anthropological Archives, Smithsonian Institution.)

FIGURE 7.14

inside of Cook Pot. The soil in which the deposit was found was vegetable loam & sand. Sandy loam was at base of mound .

        Plate A.

Represents Filler Mound before it was dug into .[41]

        Plate B. [fig. 7.15]

Represents as near as can be how the mound looked in uncovering it .

Some of the skulls were in fragments so were many of the small bones . It rained during the examination & the specimens had to be gotten out as quickly as possible & placed to dry .

The drawing gives a fair idea of the irregular way in which things were mixed up .

[This is clearly a reference to Lewis's "Plate C," reproduced here as figure 7.16. Lewis's "Plate B" and this drawing were copied by W. H. Holmes as engravings intended for publication in Thomas's final report but were not published. Holmes's versions are reproduced for the first time here, as figures 7.17 and 7.18.]

Bayou Bartholomew is on the right of picture[42] & does not overflow its bank.

Along Bartholomew Bayou the soil is sandy & the subsoil a yellow clay—No burnt brick like substance or ashes were found in or about the mound.

FIGURE 7.15

"Plate B. a Face and Section View of Tillers Mound" by H. J. Lewis, late November 1882, Drew County, Arkansas. (National Anthropological Archives, Smithsonian Institution.)

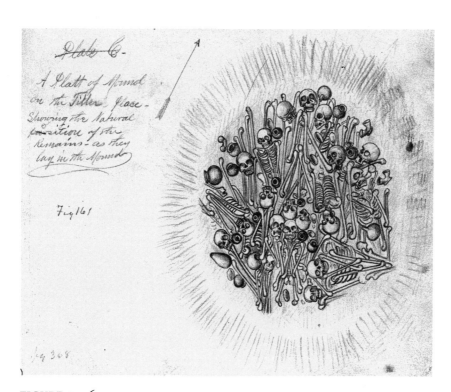

FIGURE 7.16

"Plate C" [Plan view of the skeletons at the Tillar site] by H. J. Lewis. (National Anthropological Archives, Smithsonian Institution.)

FIGURE 7.17

Profile view of the Tillar Mound, by W. H. Holmes, after Lewis's "Plate B" (fig. 7.15).
(National Anthropological Archives, Smithsonian Institution.)

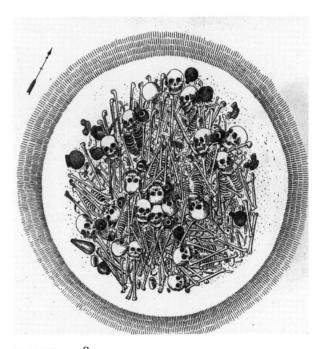

FIGURE 7.18

"The Tiller Mound, Drew Co. Ark." [Plan view] by W. H.
Holmes, after Lewis's "Plate C" (fig. 7.16). (National
Anthropological Archives, Smithsonian Institution.)

Pottery Numbers .

[Selected vessels from Palmer's Tillar collection are illustrated in figure 7.19.]

71319	71269	71260	71316	71252
71261	71258	71271	71264	71266
71257	71268	71267	71273	71276
71263	71270	71318	71317	
71256	71272	71266	71259	

Skulls—

71308	71302	71304	71287	71291
71306	71305	71314	71289	71299
		71286		
71313	71315	71290	71295	
71283	71284	71296	71307	
71285	71285	71301	71312	
71292	71293	71294	71281	
71298	71300	71282	71309	
	71303	71297	(many old bones from different skeletons.)	

Stone Spade. 71274 [This artifact, made of Mill Creek chert from southern Illinois, is illustrated in figure 7.20.]

Pipes 71255–54. [These pipes are illustrated in figure 7.21.]

Mussel Shells 71278–79–80

Animal bones 71277

Turtle Shells 71275

NAA BAE Letters

[This letter was written on a merchant's letterhead. The lettering is partly missing, but the last line of the heading read, "DRY GOODS, GROCERIES, WINES, LIQUORS, CIGARS AND TOBACCO." Palmer scratched out the next line, which read, "Walnut Lake, Ark."]

Tillers Station, Arkansaw
Nov. 29, 1882

Major J. W. Powell

Dear Sir

In consequence of sickness and excessive rains wil have to defer the report for November[43] for a few days so that drawings &c can be sent with it by Express as by mail from hear would injure them .

To day send four boxes of Specimens Box, A, and B. are pottery &c all from Tiller Mound—Except a few packages that are marked Taylor Mound.

A subsequent letter will fully explain these mounds and their relation to the specimens. Could not seperate and mark the specimens as they had to be taken out of the Mound during a rain shower and packed at once

Boxes C and D. Are entirely bones from the Tiller mound—This had not been disturbed and yielded some fine sculls, and pottery some was a little broaken and by an accident some of the broaken tops of the water vessels was mixed with the peices of other dishes—but they can be applied to the propper vessels during their process of mending

It has rained for three days and nights without intermission—One half of this month has been a waste owing to heavy rains Start for another mound to day[44]

> *very truly*
>> *Edward Palmer*
>> *Pinebluff*
>> *Arkansaw*

NAA BAE Letters

> NUNN HOUSE   ANDREW NUNN, MANAGER
> Pine Bluff, Ark., *Dec. 2, 1882*

Major J. W. Powell
> *Dear Sir*
>> *To day is forwarded by Express a box of specimens marked box. E . Arkansaw, Palmer and to your address—The specimens unmarked are from the Taylor mound wil be refurred to in Report for November. They are borrowed for the use of the National Museum from. J. M. Taylor of Pine Bluff They are different from any thing you have from Arkansaw I promised they should be returned to him with out charges In order to borrow them promised you would send him a photograph[45] of the things sent. A pipe which is marked is in the same box is borrowed from E. W. Martin of Pine Bluff. It should be returned in the same box with the things of Mr. Taylor as the two gentlemen are in business together.*

In the same box is a fine stone spade borrowed from Major G. W. Davis of Pine Bluff it is marked it is to be returned without charges to him at Pine Bluff it is a fine specimen.

Wil forward Report for November to morrow
>> *Yours very truly*
>> *Edward Palmer.*

"A Novel Procession": Palmer's 1882 Investigations in Eastern Desha County

MARVIN D. JETER

Early in December 1882 Palmer and Lewis concluded their stay in Pine Bluff and again ventured into the archeological void that was southeast Arkansas. This time they visited a series of sites in eastern Desha County, using Arkansas City as a base. Little in the way of

FIGURE 7.19

Pottery vessels in the Palmer Collection from the Tillar site, Drew County, Arkansas:

a. *Winterville Incised,* var. Palmer *bottle (SI-NMNH specimen number 71258).*

b. *Winterville/Wallace Incised jar with "Tillar mode" punctations around neck (71270).*

c. *Barton Incised jar with handles (71267).*

d. *Barton Incised jar with flaring lip (71269).*

e. *Bell Plain "helmet bowl" (71271).*

f. *"Tillar Engraved" (informal type) bottle (71257).*

g. *Mississippi Plain triple horizontal compound bowls (71273).*

h. *untyped shell-tempered jar with horizontal encircling incisions and "tick" marks.*

i. *Mississippi Plain "neckless bottle" (71256). Compare Vessel i to the vessel in the southwest margin of Lewis's "Plate C" (fig. 7.16).*

(Vessels a–b and d–h are, respectively, Photo Nos. 82-2489, -2502, -2497, -2484, -2486, -2479, and -2495, Department of Anthropology, Smithsonian Institution; Vessels c and i are, respectively, Arkansas Archeological Survey Negative No. 782454 and 782434, courtesy of Department of Anthropology, Smithsonian Institution.)

a.

b.

c.

d.

e.

f.

g.

h.

i.

FIGURE 7.20

Mill Creek chert hoe (71274) in the Palmer Collection from the Tillar site. This artifact would have been about a foot long before it was broken. Its rounded working end is highly polished from digging, or possibly weeding agricultural fields, in silty loam soils. The stone raw material was obtained from well-known Mississippian quarries in southern Illinois. (Photo No. 82-2482, Department of Anthropology, Smithsonian Institution.)

excavation was accomplished, at least partly due to ongoing usage of the mounds in this flood-prone landscape, but Lewis did produce a significant series of drawings.

Aside from those drawings, there is no documentation whatever in the NAA "2400" file for this episode. (Clearly, the information did reach the Smithsonian, though, as it is summarized by Thomas 1894:237–39.) However, the Arkansas History Commission has documents in both Palmer's and a scribe's handwriting that are just complementary enough to provide glimpses of the sites visited and, fortuitously, the probable sequence for this poorly dated series.

All four of the entries that are solely by Palmer himself were written at two different times. The first part of each entry is a summary of a site investigation, written in black ink. The second part in each case is an explanation, written in pencil, of Lewis's drawings of the mounds in question. Although these entries do not give the dates of site visits, they are on numbered pages, and the sequence makes geographic and logistical sense.

The earliest entry, by this criterion, is that for the Wynn Mounds, on Palmer's page 80 (this is a floating sequence; there are no entries from other regions with page numbers near these). These mounds are in northeast Desha County, near the Arkansas River, and could easily have been the first visited after a short boat trip downriver from Pine Bluff. The next, on page 81, is the Franklin Mound near Arkansas City. Later evidence suggests that Palmer and Lewis stayed in Arkansas City briefly before making their next foray.

FIGURE 7.21

Pipes in the Palmer Collection from the Tillar site (left: 71254; right: 71255). Both are of the "elbow" form, and are shell-tempered. Compare the base of the specimen on the left with the pipes in Lewis's "Plate C" drawing (fig. 7.16). (Photo No. 82-2481, Department of Anthropology, Smithsonian Institution.)

The next entry, on page 82, deals with the J. P. Clayton Mound, on a recently abandoned railroad route north of Arkansas City. Palmer's remarks on Lewis's drawings of this mound link it to the nearby De Soto or De Priest Mound. Pages 83 and 84, which presumably summarized the latter mound, are missing, but other entries in a scribe's hand and Palmer's provide some information on it. Particularly useful is the remark that Palmer had returned from De Priest's Mound to Arkansas City on December 6. The last of Palmer's numbered entries, on page 85, tells of his visit to the Arkansas City Cemetery Mound.

Three scribe's entries close out this episode. The first two are brief notes, and the last summarizes the Old Fortification on the Arkansas River. As previously suggested, Palmer probably visited this historic site on his way back to the Menard site.

The Wynn Mounds

Palmer's short note indicates only a minimal examination of the "Wyenn" Mounds. Thomas added, "As this [the largest mound] is used as a graveyard it could not be explored nor was permission granted to examine the others which are small and of the usual conical form" (1894:239).

This site is on modern records as Wynn (3DE7 or 17-L-4) and was briefly visited by myself and a local amateur, Lamar "Curly" Birch, in the spring of 1988. Phillips et al. summarized it as having a "large rectangular platform mound and small conical mound" and assigned it to their "D–C" time range, which is now known as the Coles Creek period (1951:54). Phillips tentatively assigned Wynn to his Toltec phase of that period (1970:916, Figure 446). Collections from the site are still inadequate, however. Its relationships vis-a-vis "real" Coles Creek culture of the Lower Mississippi Valley and the contemporary "Plum Bayou culture" recently defined by Rolingson (1982:87–93) for Toltec and related sites remain to be elucidated.

The Ben Franklin Mounds

Again Palmer seems to have made only a cursory examination, perhaps frustrated again by cattle. This site was not mentioned in Thomas's final report (1894), though it probably is included in the "groups of mounds not far from Arkansas City, by a swamp. Reported by Dr. Palmer" listed in his catalog (1891:17). It has not been definitely located.

The J. P. Clayton Mound

This was a large mound, located beside a railroad right-of-way that had recently been abandoned. It had long been used as a cemetery when Palmer arrived, and he could not dig in it.

The descriptions of this site's location by both Palmer and Thomas are massively confused. In a remarkable phrase, Palmer said it was "twelve miles due East and West from Arkansas City," and added that it was on Cypress Creek as well as the railroad line. It could not have been east of Arkansas City, as that would put it in Mississippi. Cypress Creek is north of Arkansas City, not west.

Thomas did not mention a Clayton site in his Desha County summaries (1891:17–18; 1894:237–39) but referred to four Clayton mounds in his Jefferson County sections (1891:19; 1894:242), giving a legal description for a location "16 miles southeast of Pine Bluff" on the property of Powell Clayton. That location is nearly fifty airline miles from Arkansas City, and Palmer's extant notes describe only single mounds at each Clayton site. It is clear that Thomas conflated Palmer's two "Clayton Mound" sites and combined them into one.

Clues to the J. P. Clayton Mound's location are furnished by Palmer's captions for the Lewis drawings of the site (figs 7.25 and 7.26). In the caption for "Plate A" he wrote that it was "2½ Miles North East of What is Called the De Soto Mound" and that the old state levee was between Cypress Creek and the mound. It is now clear that Palmer's "De Soto or Depriest Mound" is the site now called the Cook Mound. Land-ownership records checks and other local investigations reveal that J. P. Clayton did own land at the right distance and direction from the Cook Mound at the time of Palmer's visit and that there was at least one mound on this property. It is quite possible that the J. P. Clayton Mound was destroyed during massive levee construction after the 1927 flood or even incorporated into the levee. No site number has been assigned.

The De Soto–De Priest–Cook Mound

This large mound was also close to Cypress Creek. Palmer apparently did not dig here because H. Y. De Priest was living and farming on its top. Here again Palmer and Thomas are in disagreement, and the evidence is all on Palmer's side. Thomas stated that the De Soto Mound was in Jefferson County, "13 miles southeast of Pine Bluff and 2½ miles northwest of the Clayton mound" (1891:19; 1894:243), but this is totally inconsistent with Palmer's statements about the proximity of Arkansas City, Cypress Creek, and the Mississippi River.

Furthermore, the 1878 and 1882 Colton maps (but no other contemporary map consulted) show a De Soto community about eleven airline miles north-northwest of Arkansas City and just west of Cypress Creek. By section lines, which is the way Palmer often measured distances, this community could be reached from Arkansas City by going about ten miles due north, then three miles due west, which would yield Palmer's total of thirteen miles. Obviously Thomas had thought Palmer's two Clayton mound sites were the same Jefferson County site, and that this nearby De Soto Mound was also in that county. Clearly he did not study the notes or readily available maps closely.

The De Soto community is shown on the Colton maps in the northeast quarter of Section 1, Township 11 S, Range 2 W. Partially in the southwest quarter of the same section is the large Cook Mound (3DE5 or 17-K-5), which is almost certainly Palmer's "De Soto or Depriest Mound." Land-ownership records show that H. Y. De Priest owned property in this immediate vicinity at the time of Palmer's visit.

The Cook Mound abuts the west side of the modern Mississippi River levee and has not been subjected to intensive excavations. Small collections from eroded spots have been obtained over the years by both the AAS and LMS. Phillips et al. assigned it to their "D–B" time range (1951:54), i.e., the Coles Creek to Middle Mississippi periods in present terminology. Phillips assigned Cook to both his Toltec (Coles Creek period) and his "particularly tentative" Bellaire (Mississippi period) phases, noting inadequate collections in both instances (1970:916–17, 944, Figures 446, 447). The Toltec Mounds and related sites have been reclassified under the "Plum Bayou culture" concept by Rolingson (1982:87–93); it is not clear whether the Coles Creek period component at Cook is closer to this or to Lower Valley Coles Creek culture. The Bellaire phase is culturally within the Plaquemine tradition (Jeter 1982a:105–06).

None of the collections obtained from this site so far include indications of occupation into the Late Mississippi period, let alone into Protohistoric times. So, even if De Soto's men did visit this locality (cf. Hudson 1985:8–9, Figure 1), it is unlikely that this site was being utilized by Native Americans to any significant extent by that time.

Lewis's drawing of this mound has not been found. It was redrawn by W. H. Holmes and published in the final report (Thomas 1894: Plate IX). That version is reproduced below as figure 7.29; note the De Priest cabin and orchard, as described in Palmer's notes. Thomas's locational error has been compounded in the Smithsonian's otherwise praiseworthy 1985 paperback reprint of his 1894 final report. The redrawn engraving was selected as the cover illustration and was identified on the back of the new title page as "The De Soto Mound, Jefferson County, Arkansas." This has also been corrected in a review (Jeter 1986b:249).

The Arkansas City Cemetery Mound

Here again, Palmer was prevented from digging by the mound's modern use. The Arkansas City Cemetery Mound (3DE15) is still undisturbed, except for recent burials. Its cultural and chronological placements are undetermined.

Lewis's drawing of this mound has not been found but undoubtedly served as the model for Holmes's engraving published by Thomas (1894: Figure 147), which is reproduced below as figure 7.30.

The Old Fortification

On the way back from this expedition, Palmer and Lewis made a brief stop at a historic site that he referred to as an "Old Fortification." As mentioned previously, Arkansas Post was first established by De Tonti in 1686, probably at the Menard site, and was abandoned by 1699. That location was reoccupied by Law's Colony from 1721 to 1749, after which it was moved upstream to Ecores Rouges, the location of the present Arkansas Post National Memorial. But in 1756 it was moved downstream to a location in Desha County because the Ecores Rouges site was too inconvenient for Mississippi River convoys. It remained at this Desha County location until 1779, when it was moved back to Ecores Rouges due to decreased river traffic and intensifying floods (Arnold 1983).

Palmer's Old Fortification apparently was the remnant of the 1756–79 occupation in Desha County. Thomas mentioned it in passing as an "Ancient Fort on the Turner Place, near the Arkansas River" (1891:18). In the final report, he included most of the information given here by Palmer and also stated that it was "square, measuring 150 yards from side to side" and that a "graded or covered pathway" extended 250 yards from the west side toward the former bank of the river (1894:237–39).

The extant notes do not refer to a Lewis drawing of this site, but Thomas published an engraving by Holmes (Thomas 1894: Figure 148), probably derived from a Lewis "bird's eye" sketch. Thomas's caption for this illustration (fig. 7.31) provides an object lesson about the dangers of careless punctuation and proofreading. It said, "Old French Fort Desha, Arkansas." The omissions of a comma and a word (it should have said "Old French Fort, Desha County, Arkansas") have resulted in the misnomer "Fort Desha" that is commonly used. In fact, the Desha family did not arrive in this region until the nineteenth century (Morris Arnold and S. D. Dickinson, 1986 personal communications).

McClurkan visited a location believed to be the last remnant of "Fort Desha" (although he incorrectly gave occupation dates of ca. 1735–50; 1971a, 1971b). He gave it the number 3DE23 and suggested that it probably had been virtually obliterated by flood erosion.

Palmer's 1882 Eastern Desha County Documents

AHC Item 21 (1917:418–19)

Desha Co

Wyenn Mounds or as this locality is known by the name of Mound Lake which is 25 miles from mouth of old Arkansaw River and 16 miles from the present mouth of that river

This group of mounds is situated on the bank of a Lake. The largest mound is 15 feet high and 50 feet through and 130 feet long

Its appendage is three feet high 140 feet long and 60 feet wide of a sandy soil

No brick like substance found a numerous settlement did not reside hear judgeing from the few fragments of potts stone impliments &c found. The

*large mound is covered with cane and trees in it is deposited the remains of
the dead of this settlement for 30 years*

*The house of Mr. Wyenn is on a small mound and fruit trees are planted
on another*

*This place is not disturbed by overflow and has been cultivated for many
years*

*Plate A [fig. 7.22] view of the Wyenn Mound looking North West.
Plate B [fig. 7.23] Front view of the Wyenn Mound looking due north.
showing the mound group*

———————

AHC Item 21 (1917:419)

Desha Co

Franklin Mound
*Near the junction of Opossum fork and Cypress break .which is six miles
North West of arkansaw city Desha. Co. Ark. is three mounds on the farm
of Benjaman Franklin[46] About 200 yards from Cypress break to first
mound on which is erected a cattle shed—Fifteen yards to center one and
30 yards to outer or third one. Average height seven feet average length
14 yards on top.31 yards at base—Width on top 11 yards*

*Dense cane with scattering trees surround these mounds.—during the over-
flow from the streams these mounds sumits are above water and cattle resort there to. all the top soil is tramped off leaving the yellow clay as
compact as can be made*

nothing to indicate life found[47]
*This view [fig. 7.24] of the Ben Franklin Mound looking north showing
Cypress Brake in the background with opossum fork on the left.*

———————

AHC Item 21 (1917:419)

Clayton Mound at the 9 mile post[48]
*Twelve miles due East and West from Arkansaw City Desha county Ark.
Is situated a very fine mound on property of J. P. Clayton.[49] It is nearly hid
by large cane bushes & trees. one oak is three feet through and two others
are three feet six inches*

*For many years this spot has been used as a burying ground It is due E.
& W. on Cypress Creek*
It has an appendage which enables an easy assent

*No brick like substance was found on the surface—This appendage is 65
feet long and 60 feet accross—and seven feet high*

FIGURE 7.22

"*Plate A   A View of the Wyenns Mound on Mound Lake . . .*" *by H. J. Lewis, early December 1882, Desha County, Arkansas. (National Anthropological Archives, Smithsonian Institution.)*

FIGURE 7.23

"*Plate B   Front View of the Wyenn Mounds . . .*" *by H. J. Lewis. (National Anthropological Archives, Smithsonian Institution.)*

A View of the Ben Franklin Mounds looking North showing Cypress brake in the background with Oposum fork on the Left—

FIGURE 7.24

"A View of the Ben Franklin Mounds looking North . . ." by H. J. Lewis, early December 1882, Desha County, Arkansas. (National Anthropological Archives, Smithsonian Institution.)

> *The mound is 30 feet high 125 feet long and 65 feet wide—of sandy soil*
> > *It stand in a dence thicket of cane It is*
> *2½ miles North East from the Desoto mound*
> *Plate A [fig. 7.25] show Cypress Creek on the right and showing the old state Levee between the creek & mound.*
> > *Plate B. [fig. 7.26] near view of showing the opposite end of Plate A and is without the cane represented.*

[The "2400" file also includes an engraving by Holmes, obviously derived from Lewis's "Plate B," which was intended for Thomas's final report but was not published. It is reproduced here as figure 7.27. Note the editorial comment, "Too steep—lengthen slopes" at the top. In addition, the "2400" file contains a preliminary sketch by Lewis of the west side of the J. P. Clayton Mound, which is reproduced here as figure 7.28. It was not re-

H.J. Lewis
View of Mound 2½ Miles North East of What is called the DeSoto Mound -. Showing Cypress Creek on the Right -
Showing the old State Levee between - the creek & Mound -
Plate A

FIGURE 7.25

"Plate A—View of [J. P. Clayton] Mound 2½ Miles North East of what is called the De Soto Mound . . ." by H. J. Lewis early December 1882, Desha County, Arkansas. (National Anthropological Archives, Smithsonian Institution.)

ferred to by Palmer in the present entry but was captioned in his handwriting. Note also the editorial question, "Jefferson Co.?"]

AHC Item 18 (1917:443)

De Soto or Depriest Mound. 13 miles
N. W. of Arkansas City, Desha Co.
Ark.

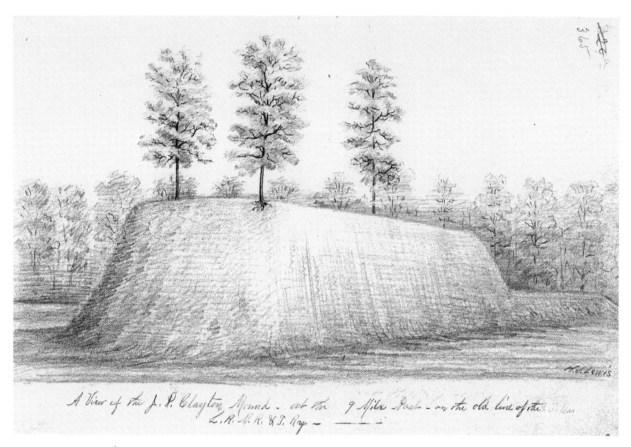

FIGURE 7.26

"Plate B—A View of the J. P. Clayton Mound at the 9 Mile Post on the old line of the L.R.M.R.&T. Ry" by H. J. Lewis. (National Anthropological Archives, Smithsonian Institution.)

This mound is generally known as the De Soto mound, it being supposed by some that De Soto camped here during one winter.

H. Y. Depriest now owns it[50] & has his house on the attachment or slope from the mound.

It is close to the bank of Cyprus Creek, which empties into the Mississippi River 8 miles from the mound.[51] This stream is 30 to 40 yards wide & 20 ft. deep.

Five miles in a direct line is the Mississippi River.[52] Back of the mound is a large pond from which the earth was taken to build this mound. It is of a black & sticky nature.[53] Fruit trees are planted on the top & corn &etc. have been cultivated there. No brick like was found on it—A few pieces of pottery were turned up by the plow. The mound is 60 ft. high on the backside but sloping toward the addition upon which the house stands. This attachment was probably to enable an easy ascent to the mound. The mound is 110 ft. across, 144 ft. long & has ½ acre on top.[54]

FIGURE 7.27

The J. P. Clayton Mound, by W. H. Holmes, after Lewis's "Plate B" (fig. 7.26).
Note the editorial comment, "Too Steep—lengthen slopes" at the top. (National
Anthropological Archives, Smithsonian Institution.)

The accompaning view is of the so called "De Soto" mound on Cyprus
Creek looking S. W. with Cyprus on the North.

[Lewis's drawing of this mound has not been found. Holmes's engraving,
derived from it, was published by Thomas (1894: Plate IX) and on the
cover of the Smithsonian 1985 reprint of Thomas's final report. It is reproduced here as figure 7.29.]

—————————

AHC Item 17 (1917:443–44)
Depriest Mounds 13 miles N.W. of
Arkansas City.
Returned from Depriests' Mound to Arkansas City Dec. 6—82—
There *was the necessity of stopping on the journey I staid with a poor but*
very accomodating white man
    The Colored driver of the two mule wagon and my colored artist stoped

FIGURE 7.28

*Preliminary sketch of "A View of West side [of J. P. Clayton Mound] showing Small
Mound in the rear . . ." by H. J. Lewis. Note the editorial question, "Jefferson Co.?"
at the top right. (National Anthropological Archives, Smithsonian Institution.)*

with a friend of the driver the bil of the two was three times as much as
mine.

Alarm of fire brought out a crowd a new store on fire two stories high no
fire department—with buckets soon put out the fire

Side walks so staked in place that rise as water rise they remain and the
people walk on the water.[55]

Dec 1882 was like may much of the time

———————

AHC Item 17 (1917:444)

Arkansas City   Ark.

1882
Noted for saloons and a hard crowd. There is a fine oil mill.[56]
Feb 27–82 water rose 18 inches above the city Hotel floor. & on the level 5
or 6 ft.

FIGURE 7.29

"The De Soto Mound, Jefferson [sic; actually Desha] County, Arkansas" by W. H. Holmes, after a (missing) drawing by H. J. Lewis. This site is now known as the Cook Mound. Note the DePriest cabin and orchard atop the mound, as described in Palmer's notes. (From Thomas 1894: Plate IX, courtesy of Smithsonian Institution.)

Wooden court house, & jail & a wooden town.
At the hotel cockroaches march over the table, the wall & floor, no water or fire in rooms, a filthy place—$2 per. day—An obliging land but does not know his business.
Dec. 6—82—Transit of Venus-a clear & warm day, at Sundown clouded and at night a fearful wind. At 7 next morning clear & cold.—Staid all night in an open house.—very uncomfortable.
The day of the Dec. 6th. was unusually bright with a peculiar blue sky. Roads fearfully muddy—

AHC Item 21 (1917:442–43)

Desha Co. Ark
Mound at Arkansaw City Desha Co Arkansaw. Little less than one mile north of Arkansaw City is a mound situated on a level bottom that overflows by the Mississippi River. which is one mile back of Cypress swamp that is contiguous to mound and from which the prehistoric people may have obtained their water—supply . This mound during last years

overflow which was of unusual height was five feet above water. Since the settlement of the country this mound has been used as a burying ground its surface is thickly studdied over with graves. In digging which bones— pottery—and brick like substance is turned out. giving evidences as to its having been inhabited previous to the advent of the Whites. It was probably nearly square originally

Should any one depart this life at Arkansaw City during an overflow the remains is taken to this mound in a boat followed by the inhabitants in various kinds of water crafts. a novel procession

Alianthus trees[57] *have taken freely to the mound an oak or two of natural growth remains on its surface*

The Mound is 108 feet long—72 wide and 12 feet high.
There is about 35 feet of a slope at East end which was produced by the breaking down of the mound surface.

This view of the mound shows Cypress Bayou in the Background allso the graves on the top and right hand end

[Again, Lewis's original drawing has not been found, but Holmes's derived engraving was published by Thomas (1894: Figure 147) and is reproduced here as figure 7.30.]

FIGURE 7.30

"Mound near Arkansas City, Desha County, Arkansas" (the Arkansas City Cemetery Mound) by W. H. Holmes, after a (missing) drawing by H. J. Lewis. (From Thomas 1894: Figure 147, courtesy of Smithsonian Institution.)

AHC Item 27 (1917:417)

4 miles from Lunar Landing, Ark.[58]
Major W. B. Street lives on the River about 4 miles above Luna Landing.

AHC Item 17 (1917:444)

Arkansas City.   Ark.
Col. B. F. Grace, James Murphy & J. D. Coates are entitled to the thanks of
the Bureau of Ethnology.

AHC Item 27 (1917:401)

Remains of Old Fortification on
Arkansas River. Desha Co. Ark.
On what is known as the Turner Place & now owned by the widow of
Thomas Bizzell are the outlines of an old fortification.
400 yards from the old part of the Arkansas River there is ¾ of an acre
within its boundry. It is 4 ft. high. It has been a garden for years. There is a
path from it to where the Arkansas River formerly ran. This path is 35 ft.
wide at the part & 15 ft. at the lower part. There appears to have been 50
yards of new land made from this path to the now River Mr. Oliver Bizzell
who lives near informed me that 35 years ago these trees that now grow on
the new made land were then but small sapplings, while some of them,
now, are 3 ft. through.

This fort was made very probably to protect a French trading post. As
Mr. Oliver Bizzell says, numerous thimbles, pipes, broken dishes, parts of
revolvers, gun, & pieces of silver coin have been found, as if the centre had
been used for gun sight . The remains of an old Forge were uncovered a
short time ago and Chinese & other coins were found with broken articles
of Indian origin. A chinese coin and part of a pistol (stone) were presented
to that gentlemen, who also says that stone bullets moulds have been
found.[59] The specimens mentioned have been forwarded under the Number 422.

Not far from the Fort is a ridge that appears to have had houses of European origin upon it.

At one corner of the fort is a hole 16 ft. deep, supposed to have been a
magazine.
At this De Soto, is said to have encamped or may have built it as some say.
Part of a stone pistol found here No 798—the chinese coin.

[Once again, a Lewis drawing was probably made (although the notes do
not refer to it) but has not been found. A derived Holmes engraving was
published by Thomas (1894: Figure 148) and is reproduced here as figure
7.31.]

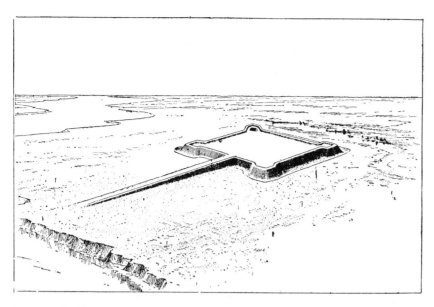

FIGURE 7.31

"Old French Fort Desha [sic], Arkansas" by W. H. Holmes, after a (missing) drawing by H. J. Lewis. This site actually must have been the remnant of the temporary (1756–79) location of Arkansas Post in Desha County. (From Thomas 1894: Figure 148, courtesy of Smithsonian Institution.)

"Mounds So Beautifully Situated":
The 1882 Return Visit to the Menard Locality

MARVIN D. JETER

As previously discussed, Palmer must have returned to the Menard site, this time with Lewis, for at least several days after leaving Desha County. They may have stayed in the Menard locality for a week or two, as they also visited the nearby Gardener site and are not known to have worked anywhere else until Christmas Day at the Knapp Mounds.

Again there are no relevant documents in the "2400" file except for Lewis's and Holmes's drawings, and there are none in Palmer's own hand except for his captions and other markings on Lewis's drawings. For site descriptions and summaries of field work, we have only a scribe's documents from the Arkansas History Commission. These include two somewhat redundant entries for the work at Menard, one for Gardner and one for the mounds between the two major sites. They are undated or, worse, wrongly dated ("1883" appears near the beginning of two of them, apparently indicating the year of the scribe's rewrite rather than of the site visit).

Significant portions of these entries consist of comments on Lewis's drawings. As usual, such passages were heavily edited by deletions and rewritings in the 1917 publication, sometimes with absurd results.

The Return Visit to Menard

This time Palmer made three "cuts" into the side of Mound A, finding "basket-loaded" soils from several sources (a common kind of mound-fill situation) but nothing remarkable in the way of artifacts. He also made an excavation into the north side of Mound B, noting three distinct strata representing a burned house. A similar finding was made in Ford's "Trench (Cut) 10" in this mound (1961:148, 161). The major efforts (or at least, results), though, seem to have involved drawing and mapping the site.

The Gardener (Wallace) Mounds

Palmer and Lewis next moved "east" (actually northeast) along the southeastern margin of Little Prairie (an outlier of the Grand Prairie; cf. Ford 1961:140, Figure 1) almost a mile, to a site Palmer called the Gardener Mounds.

This is clearly the site now known as Wallace (3AR25 or 17-K-3). Modern quadrangle maps indicate a Gardener cemetery adjacent to it. This is also Palmer's spelling on his captions for the Lewis drawings. Either the scribe's "correction" to "Gardner" was right and the U.S. Geological Survey is wrong, or Palmer spelled a name correctly for a change.

Palmer noted that the site had already been farmed for years and that the surface was "covered with pieces." His test pits in the large mound were unproductive artifactually, but he did at least provide minimal documentation for its size and composition. This is fortunate, for it seems to have been obliterated by the time of C. B. Moore's 1908 visit.

Palmer gave up too soon here. Moore visited the "Wallace field" as part of his Menard explorations and noted the common occurrence of "mortuary tributes" with burials, although he did not really differentiate one site from the other (1908:486–93). Wallace and other protohistoric to early historic aboriginal sites in this vicinity have been vigorously looted by relic hunters for many years. The Wallace site was at one time regarded as the probable site of Osotouy and the first Arkansas Post (Phillips et al. 1951:414–18), until Ford's reassessment (1961).

Palmer's 1882 Menard and Gardener Site Documents

AHC Item 24 (1917:431–32)

Menard Mound. or Hill
owned by Napoleon Menard 7 miles
West by land of Arkansas Post,
Arkansas River, Arkansas Co. Ark.
(423–24–25)

1883.[60]
Menard Mound or as it is commonly called, Menard Hill is ¼ mile in a direct line from the Arkansas River to Poynters Post Office and Ferry. & 7 miles West,[61] by land, of Arkansas Post. It is situated on the farm of Napoleon Menard and is one of the best known mounds in the state.

A View of the North side showing the Manard Bayou in the back ground —

FIGURE 7.32

"[Plate] 1   A View of the North side [of Menard Mound A] . . ." by H. J. Lewis, mid-December 1882, Arkansas County, Arkansas. (National Anthropological Archives, Smithsonian Institution.)

Plate I . [fig. 7.32]

Is a birds eye view[62] of the north side showing Menard Bayou in the background. This mound is 70 ft. high,[63] 150 ft. wide at the base & 45 ft across at the top. I think it was originally circular. Sheep & individuals climbing up its sides for several years have made the sides very irregular, besides the digging into its sides to see what could be found accelerated its present ragged condition . I examined 3 cuts made 10 ft. into its side and found mixed composition of sandy loam, black vegetable earth, and clay. This may be owing to the earth having been taken from several places and thrown without order on the mound.

[There is also in the "2400" file an engraving by Holmes, derived from Lewis's "Plate I," which was intended for publication in Thomas's final report but was not used. It is published here for the first time, as figure 7.33. Note the editorial comment "Too Steep altogether" in the lower margin. *Frank Leslie's Illustrated Newspaper* had no such qualms, however. The redrawn version of this drawing that appeared in that paper pushed vertical exaggeration well beyond the point of absurdity; it is reproduced here as figure 7.34. See chapter 9 for further discussion.]

FIGURE 7.33

Menard Mound A, by W. H. Holmes, after Lewis's "Plate 1" (fig. 7.32). An editorial comment "Too steep altogether" appeared at the bottom (but compare figure 7.34). (National Anthropological Archives, Smithsonian Institution.)

Plate 2—[fig 7.35][64]
A front view of the mound looking North, the main woods being in the background. This view shows the (2) wings of the mound; the larger or the west wing is 20 ft. high.& 156 ft. long & 27 ft. wide at the narrowest part, the widest part is 60 ft. The south on lowest wing is 7 ft. high & 175 ft. long & 60 ft. wide.

These wings are of Sandy soil with yellow clay subsoil—
Some few pots were taken out last year.

Plate 3. [fig 7.37]
Is a view of the north side of the mound showing the section view of west.[65]

Wing No (1). is composed of 6 inches of sandy loam,
Wing No (2)—6 inches of burnt clay—
    "   No (3) 3   "   of matting &corn.Not much of the matting or corn

M.ANARD MOUND

FIGURE 7.34

"Manard Mound" (Menard Mound A), from Frank Leslie's Illustrated Newspaper,
May 26, 1883.

FIGURE 7.35

"[Plate] 2 A Front View of the Menard Mound—looking North . . ." by H. J. Lewis.
Mound B is on the left, and Mound A is in the center. Note the editorial "X" above
Mound A. (National Anthropological Archives, Smithsonian Institution.)

could be saved so badly burnt were they; On the same side of the wing but
nearer the mound were found many broken pots under a thick layer of
burnt clay, last year. On the opposite side of this northern mound was to be
found not even burnt brick stuff. 30 acres are included in the space around
the mound in which are many house sites from which many pieces of pottery have been taken, numbered 426—

Plate 4.

[This Lewis drawing has not been found. It must have been the model for
Holmes's engraved plan view map of the Menard site, which was published
by Thomas (1894: Figure 137), and is reproduced here as figure 7.38. An
accurate topographic contour map was made by Philip Phillips and E. Mott
Davis in 1941 and was published by Ford (1961: Figures 3 and 6). A simplified version of that map is reproduced here as figure 7.39.]

Is the ground plan of the mound and the house sites seem as a cluster of
small mounds, the highest not more than 2 ft. with flat tops and all consist
of soil, burnt clay & ashes with which skeletons, pottery & etc. were
found. It was from these, that last year so many things were taken by me.
The line running through the small mounds indicate a fence. Near by is the

FIGURE 7.36

Photograph of Menard Mounds by Philip Phillips, Lower Mississippi Survey, Peabody Museum, Harvard University, 1941. Mound B is on the left, and Mound A is on the right. Compare Lewis's "Plate 2" (fig. 7.35). (Courtesy of Lower Mississippi Survey.)

Menard Bayou or (the old bed of White River) across which is a road leading to Poynters Post Office on the Arkansas River.

Specimens from the Mounds.

(71437–38–39)

Thomas Numbers—Surface finds—

727–29–12–18–

Though forwarded as from Menard Mound they are entered as from Arkansas Post as the two are near together.

_____

AHC Item 4 (1917:447)

Menard Mound, 7 miles west of
Arkansas Post, Ark.

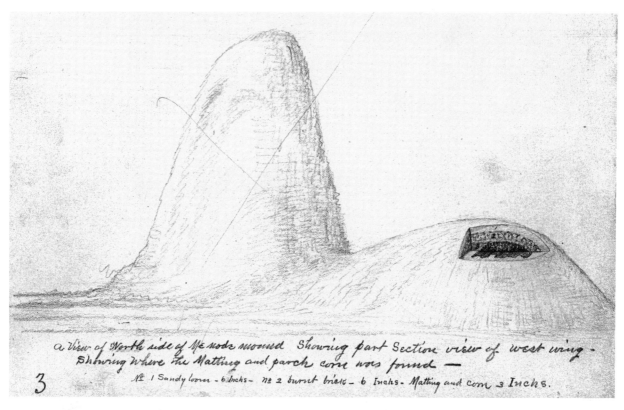

FIGURE 7.37

"[Plate] 3—A View of North side of [Menard's] mound [Mound A] Showing part Section view of west wing [Mound B]" by H. J. Lewis. Note the numbered (1-2-3) strata, and Palmer's legend: "No. 1 Sandy loom – 6 Inchs— No. 2 burnt brick [daub] – 6 Inchs– [No. 3] Matting and corn 3 Inchs." (National Anthropological Archives, Smithsonian Institution.)

1883—[66]

The large mound seen in the picture[67] is 70 ft. high, 150 ft. wide at base & 45 ft. wide at top.—It was originally circular, but sheep, cattle & individuals climbing up its sides accelerated the present rugged sides. Its. composition is a mixture of sandy loam, black vegetable earth, & clay irregularly intermixed, which may be owing to the material being collected from several parts.

This mound, as 2 wings or appendages, the larger or west wing is 20 ft. high 156 ft. long, 27 ft. wide at narrowest part, & 60 ft. at widest part. It was in the centre of this wing that so many broken yellow flat dishes were found. This visit yielded charred corn, matting, & etc. which have been forwarded under 423–24–25 (See plate showing section.[68]

No 1 = 6 inches of soil, No 2 = 6 in. burnt clay, No 3 = 3 in. matting & corn, these were found on the north side of wing which is covered with brick like substance, while the opposite side of this wing has none.

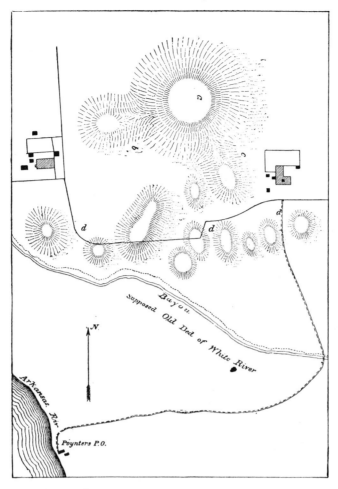

FIGURE 7.38

"Plan of Menard mounds" by W. H. Holmes, after a
(missing) map by H. J. Lewis. (From Thomas 1894:
Figure 137, courtesy of Smithsonian Institution.)

The south or lowest wing is 7 ft. high, 175 ft. long & 60 ft. wide. These
wings are of sandy soil with yellow clay subsoil

———

AHC Item 24 (1917:432)

Menard, Mound   Arkansas Co.
Ark.

Napoleon Bonaparte Menard entitled to thanks of the Bureau of Ethnology.

———

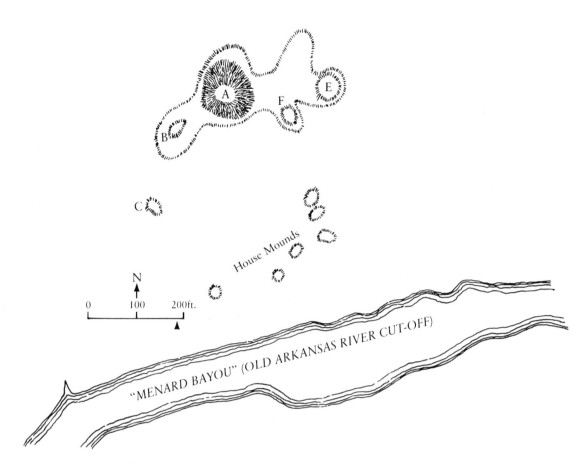

FIGURE 7.39

A modern map of the Menard site. (After Ford 1961: Figures 3 and 6.)

AHC Item 24 (1917:402)

Gardner Mound.
On the farm of William Gardner.
1 mile E. of Menard Mound.[69]
Arkansas Co. Ark.

One mile east of the Menard Mound & near the bank of the Menard Bayou is the farm of William Gardner. Here is a mound that has been cultivated for years. It has sloping sides. The plow has turned up the soil and the rain has beaten it down, leaving what ever was beneath near the surface and easily to be disturbed. The surface is covered with pieces.

The mound is 10 ft. high, 115 ft. long and 75 ft. through. I sank several holes in the mound. Found only sandy loom & no brick like substance.

Specimens from Surface
(Thomas' Numbers—714–13–16–17–15)

[This scribe's document does not refer to Lewis's drawing of the Gardner mound, but it is plainly captioned as such in Palmer's handwriting and is reproduced here as figure 7.40. Below the mound drawing is a plan view map, an innovation that Lewis repeated at several other sites. Despite Palmer's lack of notable finds here, the *Frank Leslie's* artist again added a more sensational touch to his revision of Lewis's drawing by enlarging the diggers and giving them a large pot to exult over. The *Leslie's* version is reproduced here as figure 7.41.]

———————

AHC Item 24 (Not in 1917)

Cluster of Mounds. (in the Woods
between the Gardner & Menard
Mounds,   Arkansas Co. Ark.
    Surrounding the Gardner mounds are extensive woods, mostly of Red Oak. A strip of prairie separates the Knapp[70] Mound from the Gardner Mound.
    The following diagram [fig. 7.42][71] explains the position of the mounds so beautifully situated in the woods.
(1) = Menard Bayou or what is supposed to be the old bed of the White River[72] that once ran by here and emptied into the Arkansas River nearby.
(2) = cluster of small mounds in thick woods. Some few immediately on the surface yielded burnt clay and some ashes—others nothing. They varied from 1½ to 4 ft. high (flat top) and from . 4 to 10 ft. across. & were composed of light soil.
(3) = are the woods extending from mounds round the prairie to—(4)
(4) = the road leading bet. the Gardner & Menard Mounds.
(5) = field
(6) = prairie.

"This Celebrated Group": Palmer and Lewis at the Knapp (Toltec) Mounds, 1882–83

MARVIN D. JETER AND MARTHA ANN ROLINGSON

On Christmas Day 1882, Palmer and Lewis arrived at the Knapp Mounds site, on an old Arkansas River meander belt southeast of Little Rock. They worked there, making surface collections and drawings, until about December 28; on the twenty-ninth, Palmer wrote to Thomas from Pine Bluff. During the first days of 1883, Palmer and Lewis worked at several other sites along the lower Arkansas River, finally arriving at Arkansas City again. There Palmer received communications from Thomas ordering him to dismiss Lewis, return to the Knapp Mounds, and conduct excavations there.

FIGURE 7.40

"A View of the Gardener Mound looking due South" by H. J. Lewis, mid-December 1882, Arkansas County, Arkansas. This site is now known as the Wallace site. The plan view map on the bottom half of this drawing appears to have been a preliminary version of the one reproduced below as figure 7.42. (National Anthropological Archives, Smithsonian Institution.)

FIGURE 7.41

"Searching a Mound" from Frank Leslie's
Illustrated Newspaper, *May 26, 1883. Compare
Lewis's "Gardener Mound" drawing (fig. 7.40).*

Palmer may not have returned to Knapp until January 15, when a note states that he took a steamer to a nearby landing. Even so, he probably got in at least four or five days of digging (with a hired crew, according to an *Arkansas Gazette* article of January 27, 1883); another note states that he went from Little Rock to another nearby (Thibault) site on January 20. During January, he excavated in five of the Knapp mounds (Rolingson 1982:2, 71–72, 84–85).

Palmer's "Knapp Mounds" site is now known as the Toltec Mounds site (3LN42 or 14-H-1). It has been a National Register of Historic Places site since 1973, an Arkansas State Park since 1975, the location of a research station of the Arkansas Archeological Survey directed by Rolingson since 1978, and a National Historic Landmark since 1979.

The Misnomer—and Palmer

"Toltec" is a misnomer (Rolingson 1982:1), based on a variant of the mound-builder theory, which was believed by Gilbert Knapp (1827–1900) and his wife Mary Eliza Feild Officer Knapp (1825–1905). Mrs. Knapp had previously been married to William P. Officer (1810–1851), who had owned this property.

It is interesting to speculate as to how the Knapps came to believe in the Toltec theory and whether Palmer himself had any hand in this. As noted previously, he had by this time expressed his notions about relatively civilized, mound-building "Toltecs" and rela-

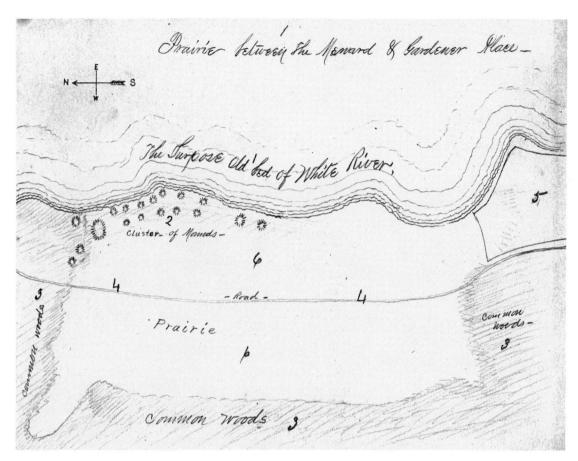

FIGURE 7.42

"Prairie between the Menard & Gardener Place" by H. J. Lewis. Palmer's "Surpose Old bed of White River" is actually an old Arkansas River meander loop. (National Anthropological Archives, Smithsonian Institution.)

tively savage "Aztecs" in several publications, especially in "Remarks Concerning Two Divisions of Indians" (Palmer 1877b).

Certainly such ideas had been in circulation at least since their espousal by Benjamin Smith Barton in 1787 (Willey and Sabloff 1974:31) and the Rev. Thaddeus M. Harris of Massachusetts in the early nineteenth century (Thomas 1887:82–83; 1894:598), but the name "Toltec" does not appear to have been applied to this site until after Palmer's visit. In particular, it is of interest that in letters of April 8, 1876, to Dr. William H. Barry of Hot Springs, Arkansas, and April 11, 1876, to Secretary Joseph Henry of the Smithsonian Institution Mrs. Knapp did not mention Toltecs, although she did refer to mounds in "the city of Mexico" in both letters. Also, Palmer stated explicitly that the site's name was Knapp, derived from the farmer of the surrounding fields.

The first published mention of "Toltec" in connection with this site appears to have occurred in the *Arkansas Gazette* on March 28, 1888. An article (page 5, column 1) announced the development of the planned "new town of Toltec" on a railroad that was nearing completion. Gilbert Knapp and E. F. Officer were reported to be the proprietors of the townsite (which never developed). Shortly afterward, the Goodspeed (1889:19–20) history stated that Mr. Knapp was convinced that the mounds were made by the Toltec race and that he had named the new railroad station "Toltec" in their honor. The first person to call widespread archeological attention to the "Toltec Mounds" was C. B. Moore (1908:557), who noted that they were " . . . described as the Knapp Mounds in the [Thomas 1894] Twelfth Annual Report . . . as doubtless they were called at the time of the publication of the Report."

The key, but probably unanswerable, question is precisely when and how the Knapps became convinced that the Toltecs had built the mounds. It is quite possible that Palmer, who came here as an official representative of the Smithsonian and a widely traveled archeologist, had a major part in the convincing or in reinforcing such beliefs if the Knapps already held them.

Later Work at Knapp

Palmer's inaccurate measurements of the mounds here during these 1882–83 visits were unacceptable to Thomas, who ordered him to return and try again. He did this in early July, 1884—the last work he did for the Mound Survey. Once again, his results were unsatisfactory (he seems to have reported "slope heights" rather than vertical heights). The job was eventually done right by Holmes, who visited the site in August 1890 on his way to investigate the novaculite quarries near Hot Springs (Rolingson 1982:74).

After Palmer's visits and the return visit by Holmes, scientific investigations at this site languished for many decades. Although Thomas had called it "the most interesting group in the state, and, in fact, one of the most important in the United States" (1894:243), Moore dismissed it in two short paragraphs, remarking, "The mounds were visited by us, but investigation was not deemed advisable, as there seemed to be no history of the discovery of artifacts in the vicinity" (1908:557).

The first controlled excavations at Toltec in the twentieth century took place in the summer of 1966, in a nine-day training dig for the University of Arkansas Museum and the Arkansas Archeological Society, directed by Charles R. McGimsey III (Davis 1966; Phillips 1970:916; Anderson 1977b; Rolingson 1982:2, 72; Miller 1982:30). Since 1976 the Arkansas Archeological Survey has conducted an ongoing research program here, including 2½-week Society/Survey "summer digs" in 1979, 1988, and 1989. The preliminary findings through the 1979 field season have been summarized by various researchers in a volume edited by Rolingson (1982). More recently, Rolingson has worked with an astronomer on a comparative study of mound alignments and spatial arrangements at Toltec and other sites in the Mississippi Valley (Sherrod and Rolingson 1987).

Chronology and Cultural Affiliation

Although this site has a Mississippian appearance with its mound-and-plaza arrangement, it has been apparent for some time that the major occupation occurred during the Coles Creek period (Phillips 1970:916–17; Belmont 1982:64). Recent investigations indicate that "the major occupation is a continuous and developmental one spanning the late Baytown and early Coles Creek periods, . . . roughly A.D. 500 to 900" (Rolingson 1982:7; this span includes the middle Coles Creek period in some terminologies, e.g.,

Belmont 1982a:70). Later occupations appear to have been superficial.

The differences between Toltec (and related sites) and "classic" Lower Valley Coles Creek sites, in terms of ceramic decorations, lithic assemblages, and other aspects, are significant enough to warrant the definition of a new concept, that of Plum Bayou culture (Rolingson 1982:87–93). Sites assignable to this culture have been found up the Arkansas Valley beyond Conway (Hemmings and House 1985), north to the Little Red River valley in Van Buren and Cleburne counties, and southeast along Bayous Bartholomew and Macon nearly to the Louisiana state line. Some sites in the Yazoo Basin of northwest Mississippi may also be affiliated (Belmont 1982a:70).

Documents

Unfortunately, we do not have original notes in Palmer's handwriting for either of these separate visits, although the December 29 letter alludes briefly to the earlier work. There are no monthly reports or other directly related documents in the "2400" file. We have only a scribe's notes from the Arkansas History Commission's files. These notes contain only one two-word insertion in Palmer's handwriting and combine references to the drawings made in December and the excavations done in January.

In fact, these two episodes of field work are so inextricably bound together in these notes that a departure from this volume's attempts at a strict chronological sequence is warranted. The mid-January work at Knapp will also be included in this section, rather than after the early January work on other sites.

Another departure from the usual practices will be made here. Lewis's drawings, and others derived from them, are of particular interest in understanding the appearance of this site a century ago and provide insights into the editorial decisions that went into the production of Thomas's 1894 final report. Extended comments on some of these drawings will be inserted, in editorial brackets, at appropriate places in the scribe's text. Finally, the plan view maps of the site produced by Lewis and Holmes are of especial interest and will be discussed at length at the conclusion of this section.

Documents for Palmer's 1882–83 Work at the Knapp Site

AHC Item 21 (1917:426)

Knapp Mound, 17 miles below
Little Rock Ark.

Dec. 25–82—Visited the Knapp mound. It was situated midway in a field. A colored woman invited me to dine with her in her cabin. My coat pocket yielded an apple and some pecan nuts. There is a great waste of powder at Christmas in
this section
Except 203 all were surface finds.

———————

Knapp Mounds or Mound
Lake, 17 miles S. E. of Little
Rock, Pulaski Co. Ark.[73]

This mound derives its name from a field by its banks owned by Mr. Gilbert Knapp,[74] in which field is one of the finest group of mounds in Arkansas. This lake is 3 miles long & about ¼ mile wide and more resembles an arm of a river than a lake[75]

The field in which is situated this celebrated group of Mound contains 90 acres and has been cultivated for 30 years or more. It is connected with the lake by an embankment 1 mile long , 5 ft. high, 5 ft. across at top & 8 ft. at the base. It starts at the Lake, circles around the field and connects again at the lake .

In 1844 during the period of the greatest overflow ever known in this section, these mounds were above the water and many families with their household effects & live stock came here for safety.

Plate I . .

[This Lewis drawing is reproduced here as figure 7.43. It has been published and discussed by Rolingson (1982:74, Figure 43). In addition to the large Mound A, it shows Mound R on the left, and at the extreme right, adjacent to the base of Mound A, a low rise (now designated as Mound Q) with a log building atop it.]

Mound Lake in the background, west—

This largest mound[76] of the group is 100 ft. high, 204 ft. long at base 165 ft. wide. It measures 60 by 70 ft. on the top and is nearly square. It has natural bushes & trees covering it—Some elms are 18 inches through. The owner gave permission to have a shaft dug on the vacant summit. After going down 10 ft, it became so hard that it was abandoned. It was 8 ft. square. At first were 2 ft. of vegetable mould, in which were mixed some animal bones & pieces of pots. Then for 8 ft. was sandy loam which became so hard that at 10 ft. solid clay was struck & I could go no further . A tunnel had been made some time since by a relic hunter in the back of the mound & the same hard conditions of sandy soil were met.

I myself dug a tunnel in the side midway between the top & the base but found the same hard sandy loam. The top and sides were examined without finding even brick like substance.

Plate II .

[This Lewis drawing has not been found, nor has any redrawing by Holmes or others.]

Is a view of the second largest of the mounds looking N.E. and showing the Leevee[77] in the background along the edge of the main woods .

This mound[78] is 75 ft. high, 85 ft. wide on top & 110 ft. long. At the base it 180 ft. long & 155 ft. at the west end, but at the East end it is 175 ft. wide. It presents a prominent squarish front.

A shaft 10 ft. deep was sunk & 8 ft. wide in the summit. At first was 2 ft.

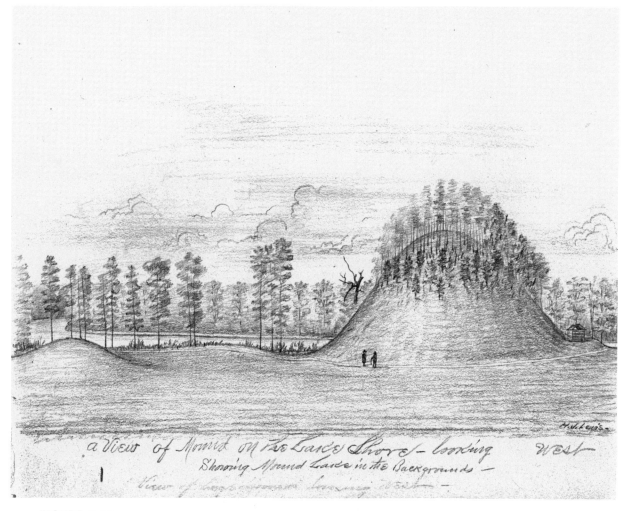

FIGURE 7.43

*"[Plate] 1—A View of Mound [A at Knapp] on the Lake Shore . . ." by H. J. Lewis,
late December 1882, now in Lonoke County, Arkansas, but then in Pulaski County.
(National Anthropological Archives, Smithsonian Institution.)*

of black sticky clay. In the centre of this cut were found 2 fine crystals[79] No.
71345—
At this depth were found a few pieces of pottery, but no ashes or burnt clay.
At 2 ft. the soil changed to a yellow greasy clay which continued for 8 ft.
when it became too hard to work. There were no indications of a change,
& nothing showing human occupation was found in this formation.

The exterior of the mound presented the same yellow clay & extended to
the base. The top has been cultivated as a garden for years.

Fifty feet from the mound is a pond of water 15 ft. across, & 260 ft.
long[80] and is grown over with trees & bushes. This pond may have been
made by taking earth to build the mound.

View of Mounds 3-4-&5- looking South west- Showing Levee in the back grounds. Show its connections with the Lake- on the Right of Picture- South of the large mound - on the Lake Shore -

FIGURE 7.44

"[Plate] 3—View of Mounds 3-4-&5- [at Knapp] looking South west" by H. J. Lewis. (National Anthropological Archives, Smithsonian Institution.)

Plate 4 shows this pond correctly. An Elm tree 18 inches in diameter stands on one side of the mound.

Plate 3—
[This Lewis drawing is reproduced here as figure 7.44. It has also been published by Rolingson (1982: Figure 44). Despite Palmer's "looking S.W." statement, it appears to be a view looking south from the vicinity of Mound A, showing Mound C on the left, Mound D on the right, and Mound E in the middle distance (Rolingson 1982:74).]
Is a view of Mounds 3, 4, & 5 looking S.W. & showing levees in the background. & its connections with the Lake on the right of the picture S of Large mound on the lake shore .

The largest of this group[81] & the 3rd. in size in the Knapp field is a mound 12 ft. high, 48 ft. wide, 57 ft. long on top & nearly square. At the base it is 108 ft. long, & 90 ft. wide. A cut 11 ft. deep & 5 ft. square was made in the centre of this mound. For from 4 ft. it was sandy soil with vegetable mould, & intermixed here & there with a piece of pottery &

animal bones. In the centre at 4 ft., deep, a broken pot was found at 5 ft. a yellowish sandy soil with a little clay took its place for 7 ft. when it became so wet & without any ashes & etc, that I abandoned it.

The second largest mound[82] to be seen on (plate 3) is the 4th. in size of the group.

It is 5 ft. high, 102 ft. long and 78 ft. wide. A cut 4 ft. square & 4 ft. deep yielded a mixture of sandy soil with a good admixture of vegetable matter. In this were irregularly mixed pieces of pottery & animal bones.

Upon this mound seems to have been two kinds of house sites. For instance 4 places were seen which have burnt clay & 5 places with ashes & human bones only. For years this mound has been ploughed over & having sloping sides the rain has washed off the soil & bares from time to time the articles deposited. Examination showed that at 1½ ft. below the surface is found what the plow has left undisturbed. The plow has mixed up things in this mound.

Protruding out of the soil but a very little as if turned out of one of these house sites, with burnt clay, was a stone tool somewhat a hide dressers iron tool & with it were fragments of human bones.

From another of these house sites where burnt clay had been turned out by the plow & at the same time partially exposed were 3 broken pots & some human bones.

In the second division of House sites without burnt clay, the plow had much mixed the soil with ashes, & human remains & pottery fragments.

From one of these spots a small medal[83] (71346), human remains, & fragments of pottery were taken—the soil was sandy—

The smallest mound[84] seen on (Plate 3) with the 2 smallest ones[85] in (plate 4) and small mound like[86] at the side of the largest mound (Plate 1) average about 4 ft. high, about 100 ft. long & 78 ft. wide.

Holes 4 ft. deep were dug in them from the centre. Their composition was a light sandy soil with an admixture of vegetable mould with here & there pieces of pottery, animal bones, Mussel shells, and stone implements.

[The following Lewis drawing ("Plate 4") has been published by Rolingson (1982: Figure 42) and is reproduced here as figure 7.45. Note the editorial dotted lines reducing the heights of the two largest mounds and the note, "Substitute Holmes sketch."

A preliminary sketch, apparently made by Holmes in Washington before he visited this site in 1890, showing these mounds with reduced heights, is in the "2400" file. However, nothing like it was published in Thomas's final report. It was published by Rolingson (1982: Figure 45) and is also reproduced here, as figure 7.46. Note the fishing boat added to emphasize Mound Pond.

Another version by Holmes was published in the final report (Thomas 1894: Plate IX) and again by Rolingson (1982: Figure 41). It follows Lewis's original very closely and is reproduced here as figure 7.47. Quite possibly, Holmes agreed with Lewis's version after seeing the mounds himself.

A comic ending to this sequence is provided by the version produced by

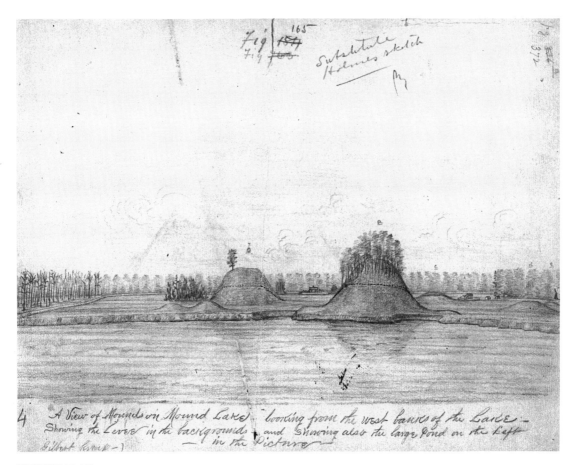

FIGURE 7.45

"[Plate] 4—A View of [Knapp] Mounds on Mound Lake—looking from the west banks of the Lake . . ." by H. J. Lewis. Note the editorial dashed lines cutting down the heights of Mounds A and B, and the note "Substitute Holmes sketch" at the top. Compare figures 7.46 through 7.48. (National Anthropological Archives, Smithsonian Institution.)

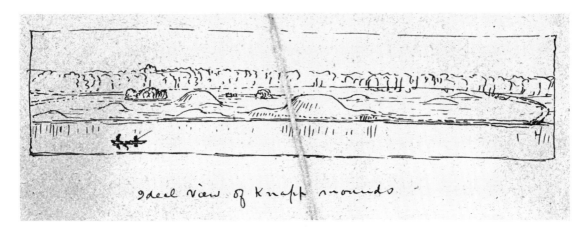

FIGURE 7.46

"Ideal View of Knapp Mounds" by W. H. Holmes. Compare the editorial dashed lines in figure 7.45. (National Anthropological Archives, Smithsonian Institution.)

FIGURE 7.47

"The Knapp Mounds, Pulaski County, Arkansas" by W. H. Holmes. Note the close resemblance to the original version of Lewis's "Plate 4" (fig. 7.45). (From Thomas 1894: Plate IX, courtesy of Smithsonian Institution.)

FIGURE 7.48

"Knapp Mounds" from Frank Leslie's Illustrated Newspaper, *May 26, 1883. Compare figures 7.45 through 7.47, and note the mule wagon in the miraculously dried-out lake bed.*

Frank Leslie's engraver in 1833 (previously published by Rolingson 1982: Figure 47), reproduced here as figure 7.48. It focuses more closely on the large Mounds A and B. In the foreground, Mound Pond has been dried out, and a mule wagon placed in it.]

Plate 4.

Is a view of mounds looking from the West bank of the Lake & showing the levee in the background an the large pond[87] on the left in the picture. The trees are left from off the bank of the Lake, so that the caves[88] may be clearly seen, on each side of the largest mound. May not the earth have been obtained here to build the mound, while at the same time these caves afforded anchorage for canoes.

Plan of Mound Lake.

These specimens though not all actually dug out of mounds, were found on top & were turned to view by the plow from the interior of the mound.
71345–[52?]–33–43–54–35–44–49–34–36
71445–41–49–44–50–48–43–51–47–42–46
71253–
Mussel shells 71,356
Animal bones—71341–42
Chrystal Chips 71352
From 3 large mound 71338
   " 2 " " 71340 to 71345
   " 1 " " 71339—

Plate 5. [fig. 7.49]

This plate is a diagram of the mound field or mound lake ,as it is variously called. The mounds and ponds are entirely surrounded by the lake & ancient Levee.

Maps of the Knapp Site

MARVIN D. JETER AND MARTHA ANN ROLINGSON

The Lewis "Plate 5" drawing (fig. 7.49), made in December 1882, is the earliest plan view map of the Knapp or Toltec Mounds site. It was suggested by Rolingson (1982:73, Figure 40) to have been drawn "about 1890, perhaps by William H. Holmes," but that is incorrect. It is different in a number of ways from the version published in Thomas's final report (1894: Plate X), which almost certainly was drawn by Holmes.

In 1982 Rolingson had not seen the plan view maps of other sites produced by Lewis and Palmer, published for the first time here. These maps are stylistically identical to "Plate 5" with regard to details such as depiction of mounds and bodies of water, handwriting of printed and written legends and labels (except for the letters labeling the mounds, which may have been added by Holmes or Thomas), and the north arrow device. Although Palmer left the Mound Survey in 1884, "Plate 5" bears the number "5" in Palmer's handwriting (cf. similar numbers on other Lewis drawings and maps), and is in agreement with Palmer's text. Also, in three places the embankment is labeled "levee," a

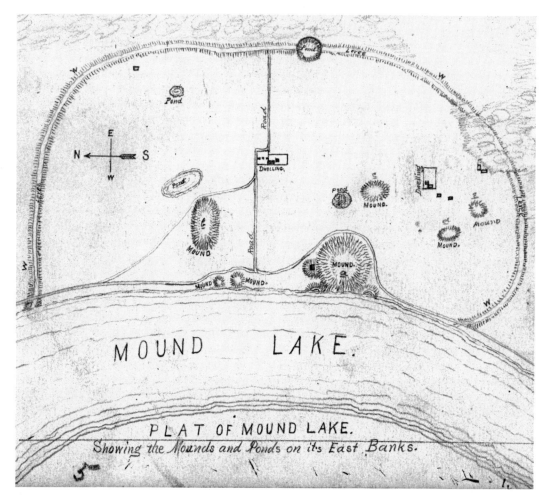

FIGURE 7.49

"Plat of Mound Lake Showing the [Knapp] Mounds and Ponds on its East Banks"
by H. J. Lewis. This is the first map of this site; compare figures 7.50 and 7.51.
(National Anthropological Archives, Smithsonian Institution.)

term used by Palmer; Thomas called it a "wall" (1894:243). This drawing shows
Mounds F and P as adjacent but separate, in agreement with the Lewis/Palmer "Plate 4"
(fig. 7.45) and is generally in agreement with that drawing (i.e., both show the inlets or
"caves" described by Palmer as indentations in the lake bank on either side of Mound A).
A minor exception is the log building which was shown atop Mound Q in the Lewis/
Palmer "Plate I" (fig. 7.43); it was apparently depicted by a black square in "Plate 5" but
was not shown in "Plate 4."

For comparative purposes, Holmes's plan view map, published in Thomas's final report (1894: Plate X) and more recently by Rolingson (1982: Figure 2), is reproduced here
as figure 7.50. Rolingson attributed this map to Palmer's 1882 visit (1982: 2, 73), but, as
previously noted, almost all of the figures for Thomas's final report were done by Holmes.
This one appears to be stylistically very similar to other plan view maps in that volume,

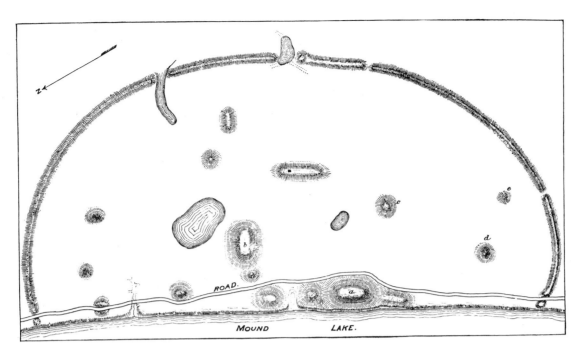

FIGURE 7.50

"Plat of the Knapp Mounds, Pulaski County, Arkansas" by W. H. Holmes. (From Thomas 1894: Plate X, courtesy of Smithsonian Institution.)

including at least one, a map of the Carson Mounds in Mississippi, that was explicitly credited to Holmes (Thomas 1894:253, Plate XI).

It is of some interest to compare the Lewis/Palmer and Holmes/Thomas versions to an accurate modern topographic map (Rolingson 1982: Frontispiece), reproduced here as figure 7.51. Both of the old maps have obvious strong and weak points. Holmes's north arrow is almost in agreement with magnetic north, whereas the Lewis/Palmer arrow is about 40° east of magnetic north. (Palmer may have had a bad compass; his directions are frequently well off the mark.) Holmes's embankment, though, is a schematic half-oval, whereas Lewis's version more accurately depicts some relatively straight segments.

Lewis's Mound A is more nearly circular than the contour map indicates but perhaps closer to its true shape than Holmes's elongated version. Lewis's map more correctly depicts what is now called Mound Q, adjacent to the north side of Mound A, but Holmes's includes what is now called Mound R, extending south of Mound A, whereas Lewis omitted it completely.

Both depict Mound B as more elongated than the modern map does. Holmes indicated a small mound immediately west of Mound B, but Lewis did not, and no such mound or mound remnant has been found. Rolingson (1982:72) commented that the rendering of Mound P on the lake bank, in the version we now attribute to Lewis, "makes more sense than the Mound P location adjacent to Mound B shown on the Thomas map" since the modern contour map (fig. 7.51) shows Mound F as a small elongated ridge that could include Mound F at the south end and Mound P at the north

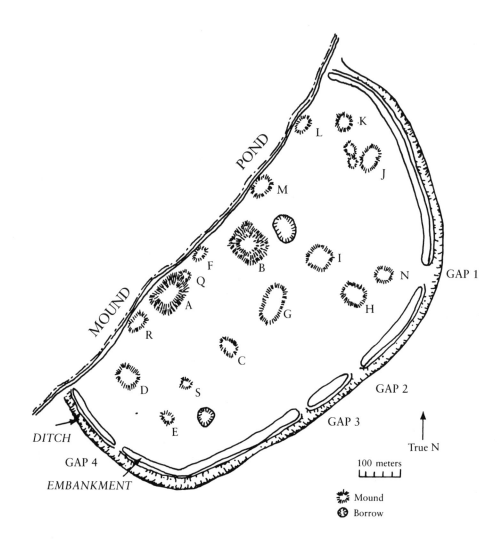

FIGURE 7.51

Modern map of the Toltec (Knapp) Mounds site. (After Sherrod and Rolingson 1987: Figure 3.)

end. None of the recent AAS excavations have been in either of the potential Mound P locations.

Using Mounds A and B, the lake shore, and the embankment as relatively standardized reference loci, some rough comparisons of placements of other features can be made. Both Lewis and Holmes depicted Mound C to the southwest of its actual location. Lewis's Mound D is closer to the correct location, and both are off to the southwest on Mound E. Both indicated Mound F on the lake bank north of Mound A, but Lewis showed an adjacent but distinct mound (P), whereas Holmes inexplicably showed that mound close to Mound B. Holmes showed an elongated mound with a house on it just east of the actual Mound G location; Lewis showed no corresponding mound at all but did indicate a "dwelling" with outbuildings in that vicinity.

Holmes, but not Lewis, indicated mounds near the lake bank in the northern part of the site; these are now called Mounds L and M. Several other mounds were shown by Holmes, but not Lewis. They have since been leveled by agriculture, but their former presence has been suggested by controlled surface collections (Laurin 1981; Rolingson 1982: 5−7, Figure 4) and other techniques (Kaczor and Weymouth 1981) to be tested by excavations (e.g., Miller 1982: 30−36).

"Assorting the Relics": From Which Site?

MARVIN D. JETER

At least since 1962, Arkansas archeologists have been aware of the existence of a remarkable drawing (shown here as figure 7.52) of Palmer and Lewis "Assorting the Relics of Knapp Mound's," which accompanied an article in the May 26, 1883, issue of *Frank Leslie's Illustrated Newspaper*. But, as discussed in chapter 9, there are a number of exaggerations and inaccuracies in that article and some of the other drawings. It is quite likely that the "relics" in question here, if they represent any real collection at all, were *not* actually from the Knapp/Toltec Mounds.

Rolingson (1982:74, 83−84) has briefly discussed Palmer's collection from the Thibault site near Little Rock. Palmer visited that site in late January 1883, shortly after his return to Knapp, and the collections from the two sites became mixed at the Smithsonian. She suggested that the artifacts shown in the *Leslie's* picture were actually "those from the Thibault site, and very unrealistically portrayed" (1982:74). Palmer had obtained whole vessels and crania, both of which are shown in the picture, from Mr. Thibault, but not from the Knapp Mounds.

Yet there are also problems with this alternative suggestion, beyond the lack of resemblances between the illustrated vessels and those from Thibault noted by Rolingson. One difficulty is that by the time Palmer obtained the Thibault collection, Lewis was no longer officially associated with him on this project, and had not been for some ten days. It has already been suggested that despite the Thomas-ordered "discontinuance" of Lewis, Palmer may have worked informally with Lewis at sites in Louisiana and/or Mississippi, as late as March 1883. Lewis lived in Pine Bluff, relatively close to Little Rock and the Thibault site, and was already involved in selling his free-lance drawings to Eastern periodicals. It is not at all beyond the realm of possibility that after his dismissal he got together with Palmer in Little Rock for a sort of grand-finale illustrated summary of their Arkansas work. But this is conjecture, and the fact of his dissociation from Palmer's project cast some doubt on the "Thibault" alternative.

More doubt arises from consideration of a more viable alternative. Palmer and Lewis obtained numerous ceramic vessels and crania from the Tillar site in late November 1882. As noted in chapter 9, these finds were sensational enough to gain the notice of newspapers in both Pine Bluff and Little Rock. More to the point here, there are some definite resemblances between some of the Tillar vessels and some of those depicted in the *Leslie's* engraving.

FIGURE 7.52

Palmer and Lewis "Assorting the Relics of Knapp Mound's" (sic), from Frank Leslie's
Illustrated Newspaper, *May 26, 1883. See the text for comparisons of vessels
caricatured here with those from the Tillar site (see figure 7.19).*

Admittedly, the *Leslie's* vessels are sensationalized caricatures, as are the depictions of
mounds in that article. However, even the ridiculous exaggeration of Menard Mound A
(fig. 7.34) was clearly derived from Lewis's original (fig. 7.32). The *Leslie's* engraver enlarged the sizes of typical Arkansas mortuary vessels, though the designs were somewhat
simplified and (inaccurately) stylized. The shapes were generally distorted: one vessel
(center foreground in figure 7.52) looks more like a Mediterranean amphora than an
Arkansas form; another (the one nearest Lewis) looks like nothing so much as the first
Arkansas Razorback "hog hat".

But, there are nevertheless some resemblances to vessels, or vessel attributes, in the
Tillar assemblage. One is the presence of two long-necked bottles (the "hog hat" vessel
and the one on the extreme right, behind Palmer in figure 7.52); there are two such
vessels in the Tillar collection, but none from Thibault. Another is the presence of handles
on four of the *Leslie's* "vessels"; one of the Tillar jars (fig. 7.19c) has handles, but none of
the Thibault vessels do. Two of the *Leslie's* jars have four handles, as does the Tillar

specimen. Four of the *Leslie's* vessels (three of them with handles) have stylized decorations resembling the Barton Incised type; there are two Barton vessels (including the one with four handles) in the Tillar collection, but none from Thibault. One of the *Leslie's* vessels (below Lewis's hand) has a very definite "Mississippian jar" form, which is represented in the Tillar assemblage, but not in the Thibault collection. Finally, the shape of the huge plain vessel shown behind Lewis's hand closely resembles that of the unusual Mississippi Plain "neckless bottle" from Tillar (fig. 7.19i; cf. also Lewis's illustration of the vessel in the ground, in figure 7.16, lower left).

In summary, Lewis was definitely with Palmer when the Tillar artifacts were obtained, and the Tillar vessels or vessel attributes have several definite resemblances to the *Leslie's* caricatures. If the *Leslie's* "Relics of Knapp Mound's" represent artifacts from any single actual Arkansas site, the most likely candidate is Tillar.

"Many Mound Pictures Could Be Made": New Year's Planning at Pine Bluff

MARVIN D. JETER

After about four days of work at the Knapp Mounds, Palmer returned to Pine Bluff on or before December 29 to close out the month's business and plan for the remainder of the field season. He stayed in Pine Bluff over the New Year's holiday and apparently did not do any field work until he left on January 3.

The only documents we have from this five-day period are a December 29 letter to Thomas in Palmer's own hand and a scribe's one-page copy of notes for December 30 and January 1–2. The letter summarizes the contents of separate packages and proposes a scheme of work in the upcoming months, possibly retaining Lewis to make "many mound pictures." Although the notes condemn the "idlers" he observed in Pine Bluff, "a bankrupt city," Palmer seems to have been doing a bit of idling himself over this holiday.

Palmer's Pine Bluff Documents, Late 1882–Early 1883

NAA BAE Letters

Pine Bluff Ark. Dec 29[89]

Prof Cyrus Thomas
    Dear Sir
            To day forward by Express a package addressed to you at the National Museum.—It contain numerous mound drawings & notes
    I have allso sent by express a package containing a few stone things from the plowed field surrounding the Knapp Mounds And some water Lilley seeds used as food by Indians
    In the Express package is a letter for you—In which I state that when the Miss-River rise the Government wil have plenty boats idle if one could

be got to go up the Sanfrancis River[90] many mound pictures could be made provided you desire me to continue the man that makes the drawings. Many specimens may have escaped those that have previously visited the mounds along that River. If it would not warrant having a Government boat.I could visit the more important mounds by regular Steam boats that run along that river

If you desire this work done while I am at it wil try and hold on and finish it I would make the following proposition should you desire the mounds along the Sanfrancis and the unvisited mounds on each side of the Mississ River as far as New Orleans visited, and take the man to make drawings, I wil try and accomplish it—Should you not desire me to take the sketcher then I wil do the work alone—In either events—it would be best as soon as one place more on the Arkansaw is visited and a group at Cotton plant[91] which has to be reached part by water and part by Rail Road by the same road can visit Helena and by team can get to Old Town[92] the important place the Mississippi boat could not land me at as the water was so shallow. then the mounds along the Sanfrancis river as after the overflow set in not much can be done excep immediately about the mounds. By this time the Mississ River will have risen sufficient for boats to land any whare then can go down visiting on each side towards New Orleans.

Please inform me at once as to your views upon this proposition.   You had better write to me at Arkansaw City Desha Co, Ark.
Very Respectfully
Edward Palmer

———————

AHC Item 21 (1917:413)

Pine Bluff. Ark.
Dec. 30–1882—Since the Saturday before Christmas all has been holiday, through the finest of weather, and thousands of bales of cotton remain unpicked.

Yet on this day the town is full of idlers, acting as though the world owed them a living work or play—a dancing bear show.
Jan 1–83. Fire broke out in one of the best brick blocks. It is a bankrupt city—the fire department unorganized—no head—
Demoralization & destruction of property Street scene next morning.

"Not Even Ashes or a Scrap of Pottery": Investigations in the Lower Arkansas Valley, January 1883

MARVIN D. JETER AND MARY FARMER

On January 3, 1883, Palmer and Lewis traveled downstream from Pine Bluff to the Heckatoo community on the Arkansas River in northeastern Lincoln County. They worked from that base until the eighth, then moved back upstream to Garretson's Landing, just across the Jefferson County line, and operated from there for two more days before setting out for Arkansas City on January 10. All of the sites visited from both bases were south of the Arkansas River.

This expedition was quite unproductive in terms of artifacts. Several of the mounds Palmer tested did not yield any traces of occupation. In other cases, he was frustrated again by use of mounds as cemeteries or by an unpicked cotton crop. Lewis produced at least five and possibly six drawings during this period; five have survived, including one that is probably the last he made for Palmer.

Even though Heckatoo is named for a Quapaw leader (who was also known as Heckaton; Baird 1980), this general locality seems to have been a relatively low density zone for the kinds of late sites, with abundant burial goods, that the Mound Survey emphasized. Site distribution maps indicate a cluster of Quapaw phase sites downstream in the Menard vicinity and another upstream near Little Rock, but few in this stretch of the valley (Moore 1908: 480; Hoffman 1986: Figure 3.1). Palmer's "Sarassa Mounds" were probably Quapaw phase house sites but had already been heavily affected by plowing and were in cotton at the time of his visit. Moore's (1908: 524) Douglas site, a short distance southeast of Heckatoo, was simply missed by Palmer.

Almost all of the surviving written documents were produced by scribe; the sequence is derived from a few dated documents and the alphabetical order of plate letters assigned by Palmer to Lewis's drawings. Brief summaries of the sites visited—and an attempt to solve a riddle—follow.

Sites Visited from Heckatoo

Smith's Mound.   Palmer tested a mound owned by his host, Captain Smith, and found nothing. There is no Lewis drawing and no reference to one. This mound has not been located.

Adams Mound.   This mound was near Smith's and also yielded nothing. Lewis made a sketch (marked "A"). The site has not been located.

Sarassa Mounds.   As noted above, this group of house mounds had been plowed over for years, resulting in a dense surface scatter, but Palmer was not allowed to dig. Both Lewis's plan view map (marked "B") and a remark by Palmer that the mounds were "arranged around a space of 5 acres of ground" would seem to suggest that the settlement pattern may have involved houses around an open central plaza. But Palmer also called the map an "outline drawing," and it may be that Lewis only drew the mounds around the perimeter of a densely settled site, which seems more likely.

Thomas mentioned this site only as a "group of small mounds near Heckatoo" and did not use the "Sarassa" name (1891:20; 1894:241–42). Hoffman, in his inventory of Arkansas materials at the Smithsonian, noted that the Heckatoo site had yielded celts and discoidal ("chunkee") stones (1975:16). These are consistent with a Late Mississippi period or protohistoric placement in these latitudes. The site has not been definitively located.

The Stoneville Enigma. Hoffman also remarked that the other of the two Lincoln County catalog lots was from "a mound near Stoneville. . . . The site looks ceramically like a classic Quapaw phase site and someone should pore over old U.S.G.S. maps for Stoneville" (1975:16).

I also noticed the mysterious "Stoneville, Lincoln Co., Ark." artifacts at the Smithsonian in 1980 and 1983 and agreed that they looked like Quapaw phase (and/or other Late Mississippian) materials, but I was baffled after working in this region five years and never encountering any record or recollection of such a community in Lincoln County. But, in a serendipitous scanning of McVaugh's (1956:123–352) long geographical index of places visited by Palmer, the name "Stoneville, Mississippi" suddenly jumped out (1956:325). Palmer had visited the Avondale Mounds in that vicinity (near Greenville, in the southern Yazoo Basin; cf. also Thomas 1891:126; 1894:259) during or after the March 15–19, 1883 period (1956:340), and had gone from there to Memphis on March 27 (1956:251). It is also noteworthy that, after his dismissal from Palmer's project, H. J. Lewis had sold a drawing of the March 23 flood scene at Greenville to *Frank Leslie's* (see Chapter 2), and that Holmes's illustration of the Avondale mounds (Thomas 1894: Figure 161) looks suspiciously very much like Lewis's style (including two men placed beside the mounds, almost a Lewis trademark).

Further inquiry among modern Mississippians (John Connaway, 1985 personal communication) revealed that Avondale is the site now known as the Leland Mounds. It has a long history of post-Palmer exploration (Moore 1908:594; Brown 1926:81–82; Philips et al. 1951:57; Phillips 1970:455–57).

There still remains the enigma of the true provenience of the "Stoneville, Lincoln County, Ark." materials at the Smithsonian. It may be relevant that Palmer said in his Sarassa Mounds notes, "During the following plowing whatever is found is to be sent to the National Museum." The Stoneville artifacts have a significantly higher National Museum number series (82476–82480) than Palmer's other collections from this season. The Leland site is southeast of the Quapaw phase distribution but does have a component of the somewhat similar Hushpuckena-Oliver phase (Phillips 1970:941–42, Figure 447). More intensive research and analyses might solve this riddle, but for now all that can be said is that these artifacts are probably from Sarassa or Leland—or both.

Sites Visited from Garretson's Landing

Snuggs Mound. Palmer examined an old pot hole and made a test of his own, finding nothing. Lewis made a drawing (marked "C"). This is almost certainly the Long Lake site (3JE34), recorded in 1961 as having a small conical mound, about thirty feet in diameter but only about four feet high. The only artifacts found at that time were a few small arrow points, which suggest a relatively late prehistoric component, probably Coles Creek period or later.

Houson Mounds. Both of these mounds were in use as cemeteries, and apparently no artifacts were observed. Lewis made a drawing (with no letter designation). The Blankinship site (3JE20) was probably the same site; when recorded in 1961, it had one small mound, about thirty feet in diameter and five feet high, but no artifacts were recorded. An attempt to locate it in 1969 was unsuccessful. The locality has been intensively farmed, and it may have been destroyed.

Waldestein Mounds. Palmer's very brief note merely stated that there were graves on these mounds and that no signs of occupation were seen. There is no reference to a Lewis drawing in this note, but there is an otherwise unaccounted-for Lewis drawing (marked with the letter "F") that probably represents these mounds—and his last official drawing for Palmer. The scribe's note does state that the "Waldestein" mounds were "1½ miles N of Linwood Station on the R. R. to Arkansas City." Linwood was the nearest station to Garretson's Landing at that time, and Palmer's January 10 note (see the next section) said that he had arrived at Arkansas City "from Garretson's Landing . . . by freight train," so all of the circumstantial evidence fits.

The most likely candidate for identification as this site is the Cherry Hill mound and cemetery site (3JE63). Due to the presence of the cemetery, it has not been excavated, and the prehistoric affiliation is unknown.

Palmer's January 1883 Lower Arkansas Valley Documents

AHC Item 23 (1917:390)

Heckatoo, Lincoln Co, Ark

Jan 3. 83—arrived at Heckatoo.
    Captain Felix R.R. Smith entertained me—It rained 3 days & nights making it wet & miserable.

———————

AHC Item 23 (1917:391)

Smith's Mound, Heckatoo, Lincoln
County Ark.
    On the farm of Felix R.R. Smith in S. W. quarter section 17—Rainge 7 S. 5 W.[93]
It is 7 ft. high; 30 ft. wide & 38 ft. long. Stump of a tree 2½ ft. in. diameter stands on the top . A cut 5 ft. deep and 3½ ft. square was made—Sandy loam 6 inches, & the rest was stiff clay with no evidence of occupation— Not even ashes or a scrap of pottery—
    Around is very rich soil, but low, & covered with fine timber. A Cyprus swamp is near.

Heckatoo, Lincoln Co. Ark.

Cap. Felix R. R. Smith entitled to thanks of Bureau of Ethnology

AHC Item 23 (1917:392)

Adam's Mound. 2 miles W. of S. from
Heckatoo, Lincoln Co. Ark.

This mound is near the Smith mound on land belonging to Major J. D.
Adams. It is in N.W. quarter section, 20 West side near the N. W. corner
Rainge 7 S. 5 W. and is 60 ft. W. of a cyprus Bayou.[94]

This mound [fig 7.53] is 20 ft. high, 60 ft. wide, & 90 ft. long. Trees 2 ft.
through are growing on its summit. Its summit was covered by deer, &
other wild animal tracks. Its. outward appearance is that of a mass of yellowish waxy clay. A cut was made 6 ft. deep & running 6 ft. back. Nothing
but stiff clay was found, not even a bone or piece of pot. On the top a cut
was made downward with the same result.

The land around is low & during heavy rains is more or less under water.
The soil is very rich & covered with cane and large trees.

AHC Item 23 (1917:391)

Sarassa Mounds near Heckatoo,
Lincoln Co. Arkansas .

The outline drawing of this group of mounds marked (B) [fig. 7.54]
shows them correctly. They are of sandy loam, and have been cultivated for
years, They are thickly scattered over with brick stuff , pieces of pottery &
stone implements—The materials left under the soil appear to be only 18
inches under—according to the limited examination I could make. The cultivation of the land confirmed this also. As the mound was covered over
with cotton not gathered, the owner did not wish it disturbed, besides, the
earth was very moist.
During the following plowing whatever is found is to be sent to the National Museum. These mounds are arrainged around a space of 5 acres of
ground and are from 3 ½ to 4 ft. high & 25 to 30 ft. in diameter . The
mounds vary in distance apart from 10 to 150 ft. At the lower part of the
plot is a slough covered with weeds and water & from this earth may have

adams Mound — (a) — looking due South —

FIGURE 7.53

"Adams Mound—([Plate] A)—looking due South" by H. J. Lewis, early January 1883, Lincoln County, Arkansas. (National Anthropological Archives, Smithsonian Institution.)

been taken to make the mounds. Specimens found on surface are numbered. Pottery = 71416—
Stone Implements=71413–14–15–17–18–19–21—

AHC Item 23 (1917:391)

Sarassa P.O. Mounds, Lincoln Co, Ark.
near Heckatoo.

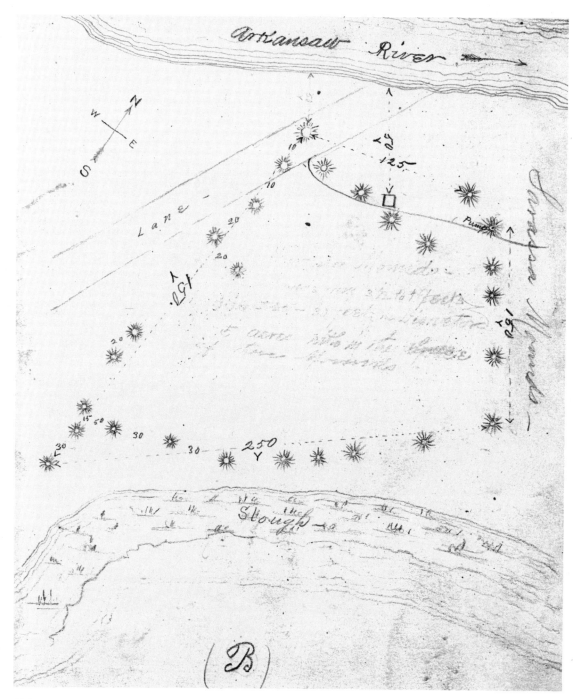

FIGURE 7.54

"[Plate] (B)—Sarassa Mounds," plan view map by H. J. Lewis, early January 1883, Lincoln County, Arkansas. (National Anthropological Archives, Smithsonian Institution.)

The soil is sandy, & much roofing is found. Long Lake–
These mounds are strewn over with pottery , having been cut up by the
plow, & was originally only 18 inches under the ground. Covered by a fine
growth *of weeds* above of which *fragments were collected.* For 3 days the
rain made this *it difficult to work.*

NAA BAE Letters

[Postcard from Palmer to Thomas]
> *Heckatoo Lincoln Co*
> *Arkansaw Jan 8*
> > *Sir*
> > > *A small box of specimens wil be forwarded to your address*
> *from this place in a day or two*
> > > > *Respectfully*
> > > > *Edward Palmer*

AHC Item 21 (1917:436)

Garrettson's Landing, Ark. R. Ark.

Mr. Garrettson informed me that his mother who lived here, from her
childhood, while the Choctaws[95] Indians were here, often spoke of their
burying their dead by laying them upon the mounds, & covering them over.

AHC Item 21 (1917:436)

Garrettson's Landing, Jefferson Co,
Ark.
Major H. P. Spellman[96] entitled to the thanks of the Bureau of Ethnology .

AHC Item 21 (1917:436–37)

Snugg's Mound, 1¼ miles S. from
Garrettsons' Landing on Arkansas
River. Jefferson Co. Ark.
(owned by children of late Mr. Snuggs)
This mound [fig. 7.55] is situated on the estate of Mr. Snuggs.[97] It is 10 ft.
high, 35 ft. long & 25 ft. wide. I made a cut 5 ft. deep & 4 ft. square in the

FIGURE 7.55

"[Plate] (C)—View of Snuggs Mound looking Due South" with *"Diogram of Snuggs Byou"* plan view map by H. J. Lewis, early January 1883, Lincoln County, Arkansas. (National Anthropological Archives, Smithsonian Institution.)

side, & found nothing but clear sandy soil—Previous to my visit, a large hole had been cut from the top to the bottom but nothing but sand was found—No sign of ashes or even of pottery was seen. 75 ft. from this mound is Long Lake across which are dense woods.

———————

AHC Item 21 (1917:436)

> Houson Mounds. 2 miles N.E. of
>   Garrettsons Landing on the Arkansas
> River, Jefferson Co. Ark.

2 miles N.E. from Garrettsons Landing are 2 mounds on the Houson farm.[98] They are close to the road leading from Garrettsons' Landing to Linwood R. R. station on the R.R. leading to Arkansas City .

The mound marked (A.) [fig. 7.56] is 25 ft. high, 44 ft. vide, & 55 ft. long. It is flat on top & covered with graves. No pieces of pottery, bones or burnt clay seem to have been turned up in digging the graves. Its exterior showed a sandy soil. It is 45 ft. from Cyprus Bayou which is back of it.

Mound (B) is 350 yards in a line from (A) & 400 ft. from Cyprus Bayou.

It is 30 ft. high, 50 ft. wide & 60 ft. long—Graves are on its top—No examination was allowed—It is of sandy soil—The land around is a rich bottom—The accompaning plate shows Cyprus Bayou associated with the mounds.

———————

AHC Item 27 (1917:402)

> Waldestein[99] Mounds 1½ miles N. of
> Linwood Station on the R.R. to
> Arkansas City.

These mounds [fig. 7.57] are in the thick woods. Graves are on the tops, They are composed of sandy soil, but no outward signs of occupation were seen.

These mounds are built on the bank of Long Lake.

They average 15 ft. high, 38 ft. wide, and 45 ft. long.

———————

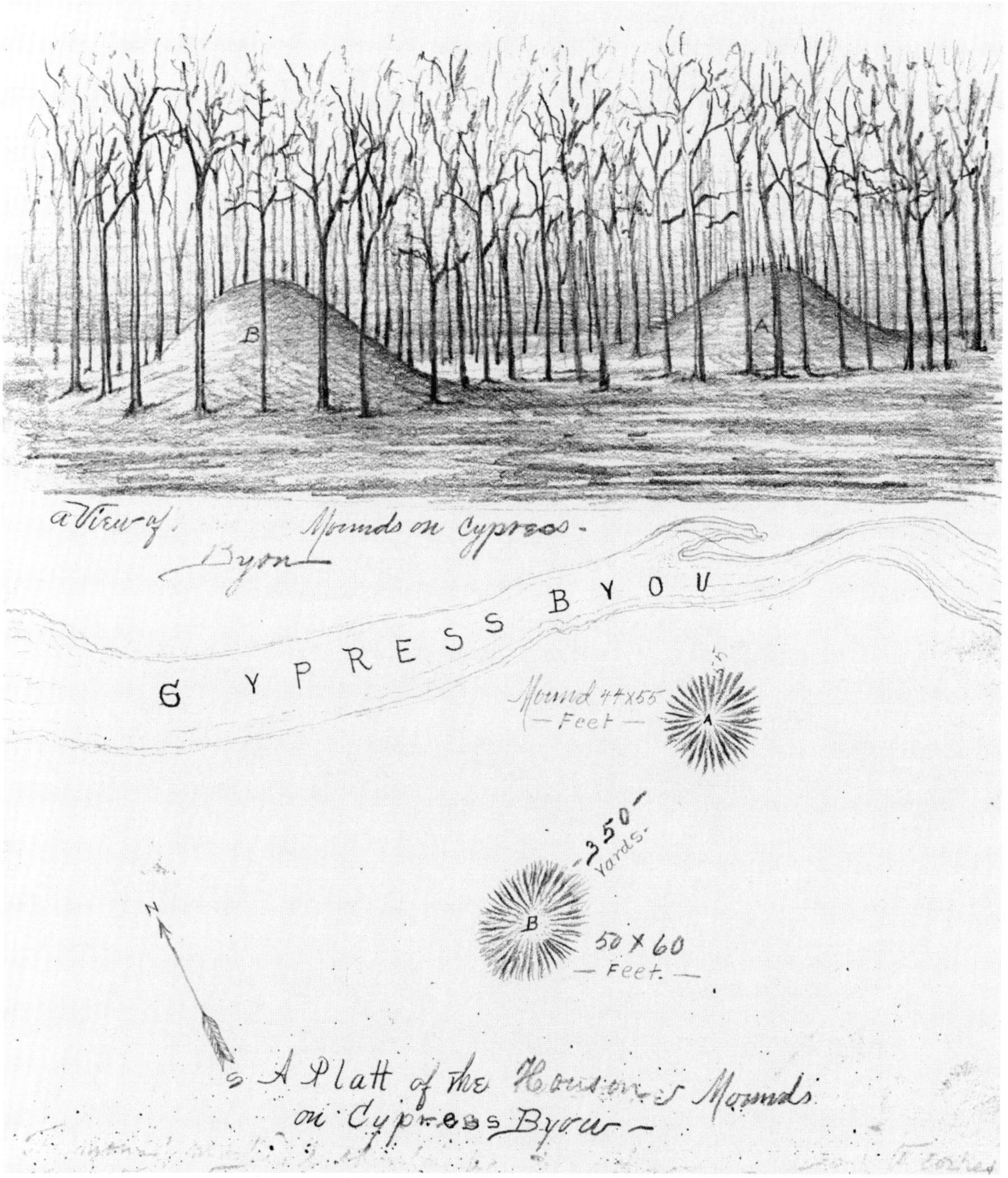
a View of Mounds on Cypress Byou
CYPRESS BYOU
Mound 44 x 55 Feet
350 Yards
50 x 60 Feet.
A Platt of the Houson Mounds on Cypress Byou
A
B
N
S

FIGURE 7.56

"A View of [Houson] Mounds on Cypress Byou" with "A Platt of the Houson Mounds on Cypress Byou" by H. J. Lewis, early January 1883, Lincoln County, Arkansas. (National Anthropological Archives, Smithsonian Institution.)

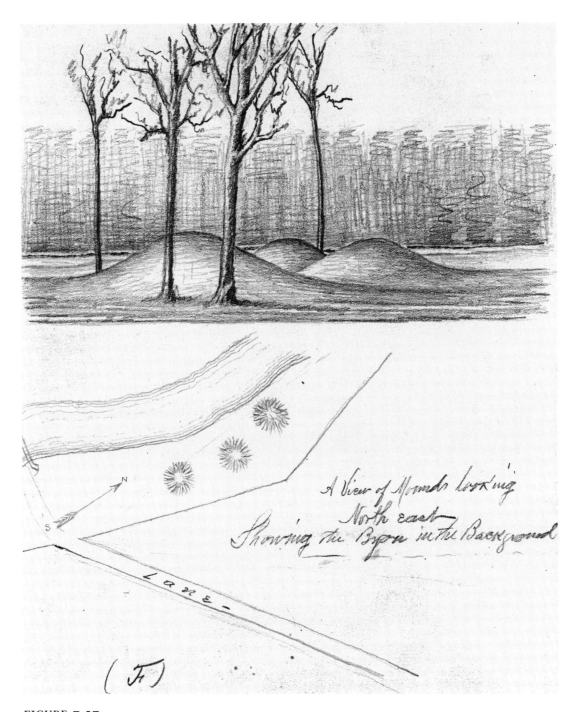

FIGURE 7.57

"[Plate] F—A View of [Waldstein?] Mounds looking North east . . ." (with plan view map) by H. J. Lewis, early January 1883, Lincoln County, Arkansas. This is apparently the last drawing made by Lewis while working with Palmer on this project. (National Anthropological Archives, Smithsonian Institution.)

"Discontinueing My Man":
Trouble in Arkansaw City

MARVIN D. JETER

At one o'clock in the morning, after a rough day of traveling, Palmer and Lewis straggled into Arkansas City again, only to find Palmer's hotel full (Lewis's situation is not recorded). Waiting for Palmer were several letters and a telegram from Thomas. These have not been found but must have been rather sternly worded. Palmer's reply makes it clear that Thomas had ordered him to dismiss Lewis and had chided him for discrepancies and for not digging enough in general. In particular, Thomas must have told him in no uncertain terms to return to the Knapp Mounds for intensive excavations.

Palmer's January 10, 1883,
Arkansas City Documents

AHC Item 17 (1917:444)

Arkansas City.   Arkansas
from Garrettsons Landing Miss. River[100]

1883
Jan 10. at 1.a.m. arrived at Arkansas City by freight train, City hotel was full so had to sit in a chair by the fire. Had walked or rode all day in the mud & it was very cold, all the way from Garrettsons Landing on Miss. River.

———————

NAA BAE Letters

Arkansaw City Jan 10

Prof Thomas
Please find inclosed a news paper article relating to the old Fort & Indian town of Natchez[101]
When I wrote to you last at Pine Bluff expected to go that day but the boat delayed me a day longer so sent to Arkansaw city for my mail, but the Post Master failed to send me your letters relating to discontinueing my man nor did I get your Telegraph untill my arrivel at this place to day I pay him off to morrow, My object in having him was to try and show clearly the mounds and their surroundings
As I shall be alone wil do my best with diagrams &c following out as close as possible your wishes expressed in your letter of Jan 6th. I was sorry that at the time of my visiting Knapp Mounds they could not be opened then for the reasons I stated, the time that would have to be wasted in waiting for hands could be used in visiting another place not far off—I thought of saveing time and the hardship of staying at the only place while

doing the work, the house being very cold which does not agree with my
Rheumatism—when Mr Knapp goes to his farm he takes Survants and
stops at his own house closeing it up when he leaves it for Little Rock—
Judgeing from your letter you would rather the mounds be opened by me
so as I can go back to the mounds to open them without much trouble start
for that purpose to morrow—wil follow out your wish to the letter as ex-
pressed in your letter of the 6th of January
Arround each drawing[102] sent was wrapped the notes pertaining to them in
a general way many of them was occupied as I thought therein stated by
grave yards orchards or buildings. The mounds I have in view to open in
future are unoccupied as far as I am aware of. Whatever is wanted to make
my notes and work satisfactory can I hope be added on my return—wil try
and have no discrepences in future
It is quite cold, some Ice and rather hard frosts for this section
   very truly
    Edward Palmer

"What A Farce of Justice!": Investigations Near Little Rock, January 1883

MARVIN D. JETER

Palmer probably returned to Little Rock by the eleventh or twelfth and set about hiring a crew to excavate at the Knapp Mounds. On Monday, January 15, he took a steamboat to Reed's Landing near the site. During the trip he made a poignant observation about a racial incident.

Palmer seems to have worked at the Knapp Mounds until the nineteenth; those excavations have been summarized above. He returned to Little Rock by the twentieth. From there he made two more forays, one to an important protohistoric site and the other to a spurious "Indian Canal."

The Thibault Site

On January 20 Palmer went eight miles southeast of Little Rock to the home of J. K. Thibault, who had been assiduously digging into a protohistoric site on his property and accumulating a remarkable collection of ceramic vessels and other artifacts. Due to bad weather, Palmer did not visit the site himself but did accept some donations of artifacts. Upon his return to Arkansas in September, he borrowed a number of specimens from Thibault and his relatives (see Palmer's letter of September 14, 1883 to Thomas, in chapter 8).

Rolingson (1982:83–84) has published a brief discussion of the Thibault collection, which was mixed at the Smithsonian with Palmer's materials from the Knapp site. Although, as noted above, I doubt that the *Leslie's* drawing depicts Thibault artifacts, I do believe that the actual artifacts in the Smithsonian collections may well be from the Thibault site, as Rolingson indicates.

Thomas summarized the Thibault site briefly (1891:24; 1894:245), citing Palmer in his catalog entry and noting in the final report that some of the specimens had been "represented in Mr. Holmes's papers." The principal example of this was in "Ancient Pottery of the Mississippi Valley" (Holmes 1886b:382, 410–11, 415, Figures 373, 424, 434).

This site has not been definitely located; there is a cluster of Quapaw phase and related sites in this vicinity, all heavily damaged by agriculture and construction, including the Little Rock Airport. The site number 3PU1 has nevertheless been assigned to Palmer's Thibault collection.

The "Ancient Indian Canal"

Palmer also went about ten miles east-northeast of Little Rock to visit an alleged Indian canal near the Galloway community. It is, however, a natural stream course. Palmer may have been predisposed to find canals after actually observing them in the arid Southwest; he was also influenced by the false analogy of Southwestern Pueblos when he interpreted Mississippi Valley house ruins. Here Palmer tried his own hand at sketching, in Lewis's absence (figs. 7.58, 7.59). This site was not mentioned by Thomas (1891, 1894).

Documents

This period is represented only by five entries in a scribe's handwriting. All are on file at the Arkansas History Commission.

Palmer's Little Rock Vicinity Documents, January 1883

AHC Item 24 (1917:428)

Little Rock,   Ark.

Jan. 15—1883 took passage on the steamer, Woodson for Reed's Landing.[103]
A colored lady school teacher, a very promising person, bought a cabin ticket & was refused by a white woman to stay in the cabin by the assumption of the woman supposing she was the wife of an officer. She complained to the clerk who ordered her out to the room of the colored chambermaid. She talked of prosecuting. The captain who came in said the law allowed him to assign passengers to any part of the boat that he chosed.
    What a farce of justice! A known lie, a prejudice against reason.
Jan. 20—1883—In the early morning lightening & thunder with heavy sleet & very cold. Travelled 8 miles S.E. of Little Rock to J. R. Thirbault[104] who has a fine private collection of mound. specimens . His wife an educated woman shares his joys, a woman whose father allways instructed her to observe natural objects. .

_____
_____

Thibault Mounds. 8 miles E of S of
Little Rock, Pulaski, Co, Ark.

1883—

These mounds are situated on the farm of J. K. Thibault Esq. 8 miles S.E. of Little Rock. Ark, . Then are small averaging $1\frac{1}{2}$ ft, high above surface & 18 ft. in diameter . These mounds have so little slope that the plow and rains have not materially worked off the surface.

The owner had practically examined the most of them carefully and as soon as the weather permitted said he would finish them . A foot of soil being removed you strike burnt clay, then ashes & with these, human remains, pottery & etc . This gentleman presented through me to the National Museum several specimens of Crania. and pottery under Smithsonian numbers— Mr. Thibault has been asked to lend several of his finest specimens to the Nat. Museum. those taken from his mounds.
Pottery (Donated) = 71322–24–26–21–20–23–28–27–29–25–30–
71332–31–

Crania (Donated) = 71347–48–49–50

—————————

Thibault Mounds, near Little
Rock, Pulaski Co. Ark.

1883

The Arkansas River is now 1 mile distant from the mounds. Judging from the surroundings the river once ran by this ridge upon which are the mounds, the spot being inhabited. These mounds might be called house graves. the huts seem to have been erected 5 or 6 ft. apart over the mounds. As the soil remains, as it was originally, the plow has not materially disturbed whatever is under the soil & in the house remains.
My visit to this gentleman J. K. Thibault was during a heavy storm & seeing that it would put him to great inconvenience I returned to Little Rock. His house was undergoing repairs. A fine collection—He is giving all his duplicates[105] to the National Museum & will lend his choice specimens that drawings & cast may be made from them .
This gentleman presented me with several specimens for the Nat. Museum which are sent in packages marked X. His collection cannot cannot be purchased, or obtained by exchange. He has some rare painted specimens of pottery[106] & some with curious inlaid ornamentations.[107]
He has a happy househould, the wife and children taking an interest in his mound examinations.
He has also some curiously shaped specimens of pottery[108] & some pipes, slate beads the finest ever seen by me . A curious paddle shaped implement made of slate.[109] I have pointed out to the owner several choice articles which will be desirable to borrow.

A sister Mrs. Helen E. Hobbs, and a brother-in-law F. T. Gibson have both some choice specimens which Mr. Thibault will borrow from them and send with his specimens should you so desire .

———————

AHC Item 16 (1917:429)

        Little Rock.   Arkansas .
Thanks of the Bureau of Ethnology are due to the following—
J. K. Thirbault—
F. T. Gibson
Gilbert Knapp .
J. K. Thirbault donated 14 fine specimens of pottery .

———————

AHC Item 27 (1917:429)

        Ancient Indian Canal .
          Pulaski Co. Ark.
     (11 miles N.E. of Little Rock Ark.).
    This water course has the appearance of being artificially cut—It is somewhat irregular in form and is said to be nearly as it was when the country came into the possession of the whites.
    It connects Mills Bayou[110] with Galloway Lake. Mills Bayou empties into the old Arkansas River, & thus the ancient inhabitants had a continuous water communication .
        Plate A . [fig. 7.58]
    Is a birds eye view of the ancient canal and its connections .
        Plate B . [fig. 7.59]
    Is from a distance .

"The Character of the Pottery Changes": Explorations in South-Central Arkansas, Early 1883

MARVIN D. JETER AND ANN M. EARLY

Palmer's next dated entry describes the town of Benton, about twenty-five miles southwest of Little Rock, as of January 27, 1883; he may have arrived there a day or so before. From this base, he visited two sites in the Saline River valley, the Chidester "House Sites" and the Hughes Mounds. There is not a clue in the extant documents as to the order in which they were visited, but Thomas consistently mentioned Chidester first (1891:24; 1894:245–46).

Galloway Lake

Mills Byou.

Plate. a Birds Eye View of an ancient cannal and it's connections —

FIGURE 7.58

*"Plate A. Bird's Eye View of an ancient cannal and its connections" by Edward
Palmer, late January 1883, Pulaski County, Arkansas. (National Anthropological
Archives, Smithsonian Institution.)*

Palmer was preparing to leave Benton for the Mississippi Valley on January 31 but
apparently, while closing a letter to Thomas, "herd of a collection in possession of a
gentleman at arkadelphia" and changed his plans instantly. He seems to have arrived in
Arkadelphia, about forty-five miles southwest of Benton, on or before February 2. He
managed to visit several nearby sites and obtain some donated artifacts, but his activities
were hampered by bad weather. After almost two weeks, he gave up, writing Thomas on
February 14, "Start to morrow for the Mississippi River."

The sequence of his site visits in this locality is derived primarily from an undated set
of notes in the "2400" file in his handwriting, on very large (about 10 inches x 18 inches)
sheets of paper bearing page numbers 50, 51, 52, 54, 55, 56, and 57. This document was

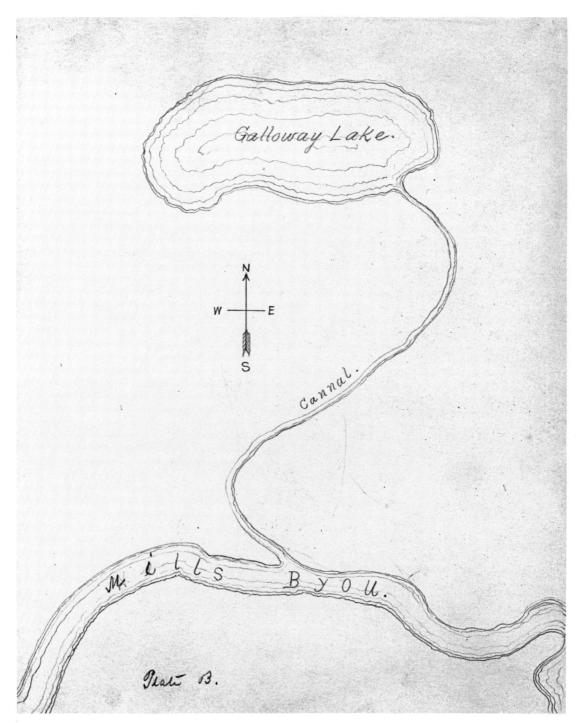

FIGURE 7.59

*"Plate B." [Plan view map of Galloway Lake, the "cannal," and "Mills Byou"] by
Edward Palmer. (National Anthropological Archives, Smithsonian Institution.)*

written in Washington, for it includes "Smithsonian" specimen numbers. It places his visit to the Saline Bayou (Bayou Sel) salt works relatively late in the sequence (it is on page 55), which is supported by a scribe's entry in the Arkansas archives stating that he visited that site on February 10.

Caddoan Archeology

In this initial foray, Palmer satisfied his own impression that "below Little Rock . . . the character of the pottery changes, becoming more ornamental." Although he did not realize it, he had in effect begun the scientific investigation of Caddoan archeology. Caddoan pottery is now well known for its often remarkable quality and elaborate decorations (Bohannon 1973; Schambach and Miller 1984; Early 1988), and the Benton vicinity is at the northeastern margin of its distribution. The overall Caddoan culture area includes southwest Arkansas, southeast Oklahoma, northeast Texas, and northwest Louisiana.

Palmer's visits to Saline and Clark counties at this time and his return visits in September followed by work in the intervening Hot Spring County in October 1883 were nevertheless disappointing to him. They would have been more so if he had known how many mound sites he had failed to discover in this region. Whether because of poor weather or poor informants, he was not aware of several significant mound sites in the heart of this region. It is incongruous that he recorded the location of the Triggs mound, for instance, when the much larger Barkman (3CL7) and Fisher (3HS22) mounds lay just a few miles away. Palmer's information is historically interesting and in a few instances gives us some details of known sites in these vicinities but does not add significantly to archeological knowledge in this part of Arkansas.

In the middle and upper Ouachita River basin, mound building appears to have begun during the development of the Caddoan tradition between A.D. 1000 and 1200, as the valleys of the Ouachita, Caddo, Little Missouri, and Terre Noire Creek became relatively thickly populated. The distribution of Caddoan components currently on record indicates that the densest population appears to have been near the junction of the Caddo and Ouachita rivers just north of Arkadelphia (Early 1982), but there seems to have been some shifting of sociopolitical centers in the region through time.

Sites in the Benton Vicinity

Chidester. Palmer said that this site was southwest of Benton, but Thomas placed it southeast of that community (1891:24; 1894:245). Since Palmer also said it was "near the banks of the Saline River," he must have been right about the direction. There are no known sites that fit either location, although prehistoric Caddoan sites are numerous in this portion of the Saline River valley. The site had been damaged by flooding when Palmer visited it, and it may have been washed away since then. His description suggests that the site may have been a group of low mounds capping burned structures, constituting a settlement possibly associated with the nearby Hughes Mound, which was probably nearby.

The single vessel recovered (fig. 7.60), a bowl, has the distinction of being the first Caddoan artifact recovered by the Mound Survey from a Caddoan site (some of Palmer's Thibault pots are probably Caddoan trade vessels). It is classed as Hempstead Engraved, *var. Hempstead* (Miller n.d.), a type/variety more commonly found in the Ouachita and Little Missouri drainages to the west. This pottery type is earlier than the ceramics recovered to date from the Hughes Mound, and, if the two sites are related, the Chidester location must have been connected to a very early component at Hughes.

Hughes Mound. This large mound (3SA11) is a local landmark. Although local diggers had found burials and artifacts here, Palmer dug fairly extensively and found nothing in the way of artifacts. He did encounter burnt daub and/or house floors in several instances, though. He also hired a photographer, with unknown results, and had a drawing made by someone (see figure 7.61).

Surface collections from the site and brief test excavations by members of the Arkansas Archeological Society all indicate that it belongs at least in part to the late prehistoric to protohistoric Caddoan occupation of the Saline River valley, but no contact period artifacts have yet been traced to the site. It may have been the protohistoric sociopolitical center of Caddoan settlement on this northeast frontier of the Caddoan area. Some artifacts from here are in the Lemley collection at the Gilcrease Institute in Tulsa.

Sites in the Arkadelphia Vicinity

Cash Mounds. Palmer was told that "some fine specimens" had come from this site eight miles northwest of Arkadelphia but found nothing himself. Low "house mounds" such as those apparently present here were fairly numerous in the Arkadelphia vicinity before modern farming obliterated most of them. This site has not been located.

Triggs Mound Sites. Palmer visited three mound sites on the Triggs property, but the last one was given the name "Russell Farm Mound." The first was a two-mound site four miles northwest of Arkadelphia but apparently not on a river; he tested both mounds and found no artifacts. The second was a larger mound, three miles northwest of town, on the Caddo River. Here he dug three test pits in the main mound and six "holes" in its "wings," finding only a bare trace of occupation in the latter loci.

The Triggs holdings were fairly extensive, and Palmer's descriptions are too vague to be of much help in reidentifying these sites. There is a Triggs site (3CL26) on the south bank of the Caddo River, but it is about four miles due north of Arkadelphia. The lower Caddo River valley, near its confluence with the Ouachita, is lined with archeological sites belonging to the Archaic through the Mississippi culture periods. In the immediate vicinity of the Triggs site is the Barkman site (3CL7), a pyramidal mound center, and a number of cemeteries and sites with low conical mounds. Additional Caddoan components are recorded nearby along the Ouachita River (Early 1982). There is not enough information on the Barkman site to determine its place within the Caddoan tradition, but it could have been the local center with which some of the sites on the Triggs lands were associated.

Russell Farm Mound. This site was on land that had recently been acquired by Mr. Triggs, again on the Caddo River but about four miles northwest of Arkadelphia. Here a low mound had been nearly destroyed by flooding the previous year. Palmer came back with ten vessels and other artifacts, but it is not clear whether they were excavated by him or given to him by Triggs or others who had salvaged them after the flood.

Several of these vessels are illustrated in figure 7.62. This is one of Palmer's better

Caddoan collections and could be a "grave lot" from an early Mid-Ouachita phase burial, perhaps dating to the A.D. 1300s. Types/varieties represented include variants of Military Road Incised, Moore Noded, Hempstead Engraved, *var. Fulton* (Miller n.d.), and an engraved design related to Crockett Curvilinear Incised (Bohannon 1973:44).

Once again, the site has not been reidentified. It may have been destroyed by the river.

Bayou Sel.   At this heavily utilized salt works near Arkadelphia, Palmer observed several partly destroyed mounds and obtained a few specimens, including "a very fine Pott," which is illustrated below (fig. 7.63). This is a shell-tempered engraved vessel somewhat resembling the late Caddoan types Avery Engraved and Foster Trailed-Incised in shape and design.

Saline Bayou drains the east side of the Ouachita alluvial bottomland in the vicinity of Arkadelphia, and numerous prehistoric sites of several different cultural periods are located along it. Near Arkadelphia the principal sites are Caddoan occupations, and the most substantial is Bayou Sel (3CS27), which is a multiple component site used primarily as a salt-producing location. The site was tested in 1939 by Philip Phillips of Harvard University, and again in 1968 by Frank Schambach and James A. Scholtz of the Arkansas Archeological Survey. The portion tested has at least seven stratified occupations, ranging from the earliest to latest Caddoan phases in the Ouachita Valley, and apparently including a historic Quapaw component as well as at least one Anglo-American occupation. The vessel collected by Palmer may have come from this site itself or from another in the immediate vicinity.

Bayou Sel is now on the National Register of Historic Places and is protected for future study. It represents an interesting phenomenon, the intensive salt collecting activities begun in this region by Mississippi period Caddoan peoples. Salt processing appears to be linked to dietary change, to regional trade patterns, and to the manufacture of shell-tempered ceramics.

O'Baugh's Mill Mound.   At this location on the Ouachita River a mile southeast of Arkadelphia, Palmer investigated another flood-eroded mound. He obtained one nearly whole vessel and a few other artifacts. The illustrated specimen (fig. 7.64) is a shell-tempered jar, a late variety of the type Military Road Incised, and suggests a late Caddoan (Mid-Ouachita phase) association. There is no site currently on record in this vicinity; perhaps the remainder was carried off by subsequent flooding.

Scott and Fuller Mounds.   Palmer also borrowed specimens from two Arkadelphia residents during this visit, for plaster casts to be made. Three vessels were borrowed from C. C. Scott and were said to have come from a mound ten miles west of Arkadelphia. They include a classic late Caddoan Foster Trailed-Incised jar, a Foster-like ridge-pinched jar, and an engraved bowl (fig. 7.65). From George Fuller, Palmer borrowed an engraved bottle (fig. 7.66) said to have come from "a large mound on the bank of the Little Missouri River," which flows eastward into the Ouachita about twenty-five miles below Arkadelphia.

Neither of these sites has been reidentified. The Calloway mound site (3CL156) is in the general vicinity of the Scott finds, but not enough is known about it to assign a period of occupation.

Palmer's Early 1883 Documents for South-Central Arkansas

AHC Item 25 (1917:405–06)

Benton, Saline Co. Ark.

Mending street holes with broken pots from pottery factory .
It contains 700 or 800 people.—
The Indian finds are very badly exaggerated, The roads are very bad—A reported buried city.[111]
Jan. 27—83—a wet day—at night heavy rains, with thunder & lightening. The same thing ocoured 1 week ago, very warm, the sun came out a few minutes. *Bees & moths came out*—
Idle men are common—Many good houses idle—Good careful farmers wanted—
Instead of making compost heaps of leaves & weeds for their farms & gardens, prepare their fences, buildings, & put their tools in order for commig spring & get their wood ready, they idle away the mild winter, & the spring finds them with all their work at once on their hands.

———

AHC Item 25 (1917:407–08)

House Sites on Farm of J. T. Chidester
3 miles S.W. of Benton, Saline Co . Arkansas.

These are situated on the farm near the banks of Saline River . For the space of 10 acres it was 4 ft. higher until last year than the surrounding surface—The excessive overflow of the river uncovered this spot very irregularly revealing house sites. The 10 acre spot, now, presents a very uneven appearance, the water having left here and there evidence of occupation & exposed more or less various patches of brick like substance, ashes, charcoal on slight elevations of black earth,. the brick stuff being carried away—In 2 instances parts of skeletons were found in the black earth. Under one of the brick patches was found nearly a complete bowl [fig. 7.60] & 2 slate pendant near by—Near one of the black piles of ashes were found some human bones, pieces of pottery & a stone flesher. Near another pile of ashes was found a stone implement. Several stone implement more or less associated with these house sites. Many things were washed out during the overflow & carried away—
Pottery = 71420—
Slate Pendants 71440—
Stone Implements = 71428–26–32–22–23–31–27–29
71425–24–30—

———

FIGURE 7.60

Hempstead Engraved ceramic vessel (SI-NMNH specimen number 71420) in the Palmer Collection from the Chidester site, Saline County, Arkansas. This is apparently the first Caddoan vessel obtained from a true Caddoan site in Arkansas by a "scientific" investigator. (Photo No. 88-12952, Department of Anthropology, Smithsonian Institution.)

AHC Item 25 (1917:406)

Benton Saline Co. Ark.

J. T. Chidester entitled to thanks of Bureau of Ethnology .

―――――――

AHC Item 25 (1917:406–07)

Hughes's Mound . 3 miles S.W. of
Benton, Saline Co. Arkansas.

On the farm of Geo. Hughes is situated a fine mound 100 yards from the Saline River . From appearance this river once ran within 50 feet of this mound. The land around has been cultivated for years. Some years since, a farm house & its out-building stood encircling this mound. It became necessary to dig post holes & level several small mounds when skeletons, pottery, stone implements & etc. were found under ashes & brick like substance.

This mound is S.W. to N.E. and has 2 parts an elevated somewhat circular part & an elongation or a long mound attached to its base. The highest part is 80 ft. long & long part is 110 ft. long. The N.E. part of long mound is 54 ft. across but at near the junction of the elevated part it is 70 ft. across. At the top of the highest part of the mound it is 34 ft. across, The total width including the slope base & attachments is 124 ft.

Height of the mound proper is 25 ft.

The lean to, at its highest part which is next to the mound proper is 12 ft. the lower or N.E. part is but 10 ft. high. Various parties, it is said, have dug into the mound & found various things which the soil does not indicate.

In the centre of the mound proper a hole 4 ft. square & 10 ft. deep was dug when it became hard & without the least indication of an deposit. It was simply sandy loam . The prober touched nothing below this.

Examining the appendage with a long iron rod, 6 places were struck that were proved by spade examination to be about 3 inches deep of brick like stuff, then 4 inches of ashes & charcoal . After this nothing but sandy loam was found.

The brick deposit was about 2 ft. below surface—

By spade examination of 4 places the same results were reached but not topped with burnt clay .

At the depth of 5 ft. was sandy loam with nothing below . I am of the opinion—that if anything was ever deposited in this mound it has been taken out. I saw no signs of human remains

The earth was frozen hard, which made the examination more difficult. Near the N.E. end. of this mound is the river, a good view of which can be had from the top of the mound. The surrounding level bottom land are also seen for a distance (long)

A photograph[112] of this mound was taken from the S.W. end. Wind & storm prevented any other. From appearance one is inclined to the opinion that this mound was first a long low mound. & that the tall part was an after addition;—that the centre half of the long part had two feet added to it, because, at that depth charcoal, ashes & brick stuff were found. The other half of the long part of this mound was two feet lower indicates this as the original height. Two feet below surface, ashes, & burnt clay were found .

The land is all covered about this time by the high rise of the Saline River . After taking the photograph, I had a pencil drawing made from it & from notes , because the photographer could not owing to bad light take in the entire mound at the time of my visit .

[The drawing was apparently used as the source for an engraving by Holmes, that was published in the final report (Thomas 1894: Figure 151) and is reproduced here as figure 7.61. It shows a winter scene, with trees bare and footprints in the snow.]

FIGURE 7.61

Engraving of the Hughes Mound, Saline County, Arkansas, by W. H. Holmes, after a drawing by an unknown artist, or possibly after a photograph. (From Thomas 1894: Figure 151, courtesy of Smithsonian Institution.)

NAA BAE Letters

Letters had better be addressed to me at Memphis Tenn from which place I can have them forwarded at any time

Benton. Saline Co. Ark. Jan 31 1883

Prof Cyrus Thomas

       Dear Sir

           Came to this place a few days since to look up a sunken city reported to be hear which was not the case . See that part of January Report[113] to day forwarded under heding of Chidesters House Graves—A few specimens was obtained which are sent in a box by Expressed they are numbered and by those numbers refurred to in that part of the report relating to Chidesters house graves

    I would especially call your attention to that part of January report relating to the Thibault Mound collection should you desire to borrow any articles from him I would do so now for as soon as he commence to plow and put in his crop he wil have but little time to attend to packing it up.

    He has had no experience in packing up Any thing of the kind it may be advisable to give him a hint or two about packing.

    A small box is forwarded by Express containing negative and prints of

*the Hughes Mound which wil be refurred to in January Report which is
included in the box with the negative*

*In the top of the box of specimens sent by Express is a package of pencil
drawings of mounds each of which is lettered and the notes relating to
these in January Report are correspondingly lettered.*

*To morrow start for the Mississippi River to visit the places which in
your previous letters you requested me to examine*

*Just as I was about leaving for the Mississippi River, herd of a collection
in possession of a gentleman at Arkadelphia there is mounds at or near that
place so visit these before going to the Mississippi River*

*To night there is every appearance of a great storm coming hope it wil
not interfear with my plans—it is now very wintery cold & unpleasant
Yours very truly*

Edward Palmer.

AHC Item 26 (1917:405)

Arkadelphia, Clark Co. Ark.

Feb. 2—1883—
Arkadelphia has 1600 inhabitants, no saloons, 2 years since there were 352
majority against saloons. Last year election only (Oct 3—1882) 19 against
saloons—
A place not benefited by R.R.
Some Chills & fevers seen even at this time—Picturesque rolling gravelly
hills—Some small flowers in bloom in the warm bottoms .
Feb 4—1883—Cold weather, sleet & snow. Stalagmites covered the ground
irregularly patches variously tinted with the mud.
Feb. 5—Snow & sleet covered the ground, bad travelling, but went 2 miles
out into the wood to mound that was natural.
Feb. 6th. 83—So cold & bad—no work could be done .

AHC Item 27 (1917:390)

Feb. 6—83—
Blind man keeps a book & new's store, walks about, makes long journeys,
can tell the right from the left turn in roads, by lying down, can distinguish
the different kinds of money (coin), He is also an inventor of a fire screen.
Feb 8th. 82 [114]—was so cold & slippery, that I could not go any where,
nearly froze in the open & bad hotel .
Feb 10—82—Heavy rain, & at night thunder & lightening .
A second blind man of the place invented the glass slide for the cracker
boxes.
Visited the old Indian Salt Works near by, on Saline Bayou.

Another very wet night (Feb 10–82) which was a great dissapointment, & much loss of time, which those at a distance[115] may not be disposed to recognize as a fact or reason for not more being done in winter, This state is not a very sunny part of the south—a small repetition of last February. The salt works are 1 mile from the banks of the Ouchita River and 2 miles S. E. of Arkadelphia, but along the banks of the Saline Bayou. They are wells, which are salt as also is Saline Bayou.

———————

AHC Item 27 (1917:404)

Mounds near Arkadelphia, Clark Co. Ark
Natural mounds & sometimes used by Indians.[116]

———————

AHC Item 24 (1917:394)

Mounds on Farm of Woodly Triggs,
4 miles N.W. of Arkadelphia Clark Co, Ark.

———————

AHC Item 24 (1917:394)

Mounds 3 miles North of Arkadelphia,
Clark Co. Ark .

Mounds are owned by W. A. Triggs.

———————

AHC Item 24 (1917:404)

Mound Russel Farm 4 miles N. W.
from Arkadelphia, Clark Co. Ark.

This farm is owned by W. A. Triggs.

Pottery 214—Stone implements under that number were surface finds.

———————

AHC Item 24 (1917:394)

Mounds 6 miles South of Arkadelphia
Clark Co. Ark.

These mounds are in the woods.

AHC Item 24 (1917:393)

Arkadelphia, Clark Co. Ark.
(Salt Wells—Near—)

Pottery borrowed from C. C. Scott of Archadelphia & also from George
Fuller of the same place.

The numbers that were loaned by the above are 790–91–92–93–

Feb. 1883—Since visiting that part of the Arkansas below Little Rock it has
seemed to me that the character of the pottery changes, becoming more
ornamental.[117] I therefore visited Arkadelphia to see if the same conditions
extended that way. By the few specimens obtained am satisfied that it does.
Near Arkadelphia was the centre of a large settlement of Indians, when the
whites first settled there. The Whites resorted here for the purpose of making salt from Saline Bayou which is 2 miles S. E. of Arkadelphia & 1 mile
from Ouchita or Washita River . The Indians were soon disposed of their
home for the white intruder wanting salt, The whites having suitable tools
to dig the salt had much the advantage of the Indian with his crude implements. The whites had iron vessels to boil down the water while the Indians
only had pails of unglazed earthen ware.

During the late war the confederates made salt here and nearly obliterated
all traces of the Indian occupation. A few parts of mounds or what was
formerly mounds occupied by Indians, remain as these fragments would
indicate. Fragments were round.

AHC Item 24 (1917:404)

Mounds, Saline Bayou 2 miles S.E.
of Arkadelphia, Clark Co. Ark.

Nos. 210–11–12–13–

NAA 2400

Clark Co. Ark.
        Natural elevations that have sometimes been utalized by the
early inhabitants
        For many miles arround and between Benton and Arkadelphia Clark Co.

Ark on the hill lands are numerous elevations having the appearance of Indian Mounds. they are of sandy soil—with gravelly subsoil examined a number their formation is natural—several parties have told me of things found in them but I never found even a fragment of pottery in or about them.

on the Farm of L. Bunk Cash, 8 miles N . W. from Arkadelphia and one mile from Dagray Creek is three elevation that have been cultivated over for years they are close together of ovel form about 5 feet high—18 wide and 30 feet long of sandy soil

The owner informed me some fine specimens of pottery was taken out of these mounds with skeletons at the time of the Centennial the pottery was sent to Philadelphia with other Arkensaw specimens this statement was verified by others. I found not a trace of anything

The hill land section is mostly of pines and these water formed mounds are very numerous the spac between seem to be thus made by water the mounds being what was left undisturbed

Mounds   Clark Co   Ark

On the Farm of Woodey Triggs 4 miles north of West from Arkadelphia Clark Co Ark is two mounds of red clay one was 5 feet high 20 accross and 30 feet long of an irregular circular form—The other is 1 1/2 feet high 10 feet accross and 15 feet long this one had been plowed over for years ashes and a few small pieces of pottery found on the surface a hole dug to its base showed nothing but red clay

In the larger one a hole was dug from the top to base but yellow clay only found

Near by is a large hole from which the earth may have been taken to make these mounds

Trigg Mound   ,Clark Co   Ark.

Three miles from Arkadelphia north on the banks of the Cado river is the farm of W. A. Triggs hear is a mound represented by the accompanying outline.

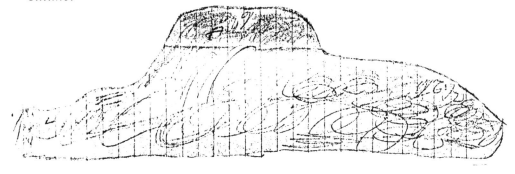

Total length 160 feet. Height of main part of mound 9 feet—one wing is 6½ the other 4 feet high—The main part is 39 feet accross the wings 30 feet. Immediately back of the mound is holes from which the earth was taken to make this mound. It is 600 feet from the Cado River—Trees are growing all over it some are two or more feet through—dug three hole down from the summit five feet deep it was pure loom not a trace of oc-

cupation besides in making a rode that passes by the mound—a slice of its side was taken of nothing but loom shows.

in The two wings dug six holes and two feet under the surface slight traces of ashes & burnt clay was met, below it was loom.

Clark Co   Ark
Russel Farm Mound.

Now owned by W. A. Triggs 4 miles North West from Arkadelphia Clark Co. Ark.

 near the bank of Caddo Creek—this stream overflows its banks last year and nearly carried away the mound—and from the appearance of the fragments of the mound left it was about five feet high—30 feet long and 25 feet accross—A large hole near by is whare the earth was taken to make it—is of sandy soil burnt clay and ashes are seen in two places in what is left of the mound—Several specimens of pottery was found either with their tops projecting out of the ground or laying down as released from the soil—Several stone impliments was found near intermixed with the dirt removed from the mound by the water. fragments of human bones was with them—

[Examples of the pottery from this mound are illustrated in figure 7.62.]

Pottery numbers   71311–71369–71365
        71364–71368 71361
        71359–71357 71371
        71373
clay Stem   71372
Stone impliments 71384–71388
        71381–71380
        71382 71372
        71386

Clark Co Ark
Saline Bayou 2 Miles South East

of Arkadelphia , Clark Co Ark—

 This Bayou was found in possession of the Indians making salt there and the whites drove them away for many years the early white setlers hear made Salt—and during the late war the Confederate Government made salt hear for the Army

 Hear are numerous salt Wells and remains of the evaporators on this spot is to be seen parts of several mounds—a road cut through one

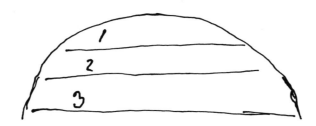

FIGURE 7.62   *a.*

Ceramic vessels in the Palmer Collection from the Russell Farm Mound site on the Triggs property near Arkadelphia, Clark County, Arkansas:

a, b, c. *Military Road Incised jars (71364, 71365, and 71368).*

d. *untyped engraved bottle (71361) with design resembling Crockett Curvilinear Incised (cf. Bohannon 1963:44).*

e. *Hempstead Engraved bowl (71369), resembling* var. Fulton *(Miller n.d.).*

f. *large sherd from a Moore Noded bowl (71373).*

These vessels appear to represent a good early Mid-Ouachita phase assemblage (perhaps a "grave lot"), dating around the A.D. 1300s. (Respectively: Photo Nos. 88-12981, -12966, -12982, -12954, -12967, and -12969, Department of Anthropology, Smithsonian Institution.)

b.

c.

d.

e.

f.

FIGURE 7.63

A finely engraved bowl (71362) in the Palmer Collection, from the Saline Bayou site near Arkadelphia in Clark County, Arkansas. Its shape and design resemble those of vessels of the late prehistoric to early historic type Avery Engraved (cf. Schambach and Miller 1984:119–20, Figure 11–38a). (Photo No. 88-12957, Department of Anthropology, Smithsonian Institution.)

> *1–2 feet loom*
> *2–4 inches burnt clay*
> *3–5 inches of ashes*

In No. 3 layer was found part of a skeleton with a very fine Pott. Number 71362—
[This vessel is illustrated in figure 7.63.]

In two other places in this fragment of a mound was the same stratification of loom burnt clay and ashes found but nothing in—the composition of the mound between the stratified parts was full of animal bones mussel shells & pieces of pottery number 71375—

In locating an evaporating vat a mound was nearly destroyed—in what was left was part of pot & scull. 71371

In Another Mound nearly obliterate the center presented this form

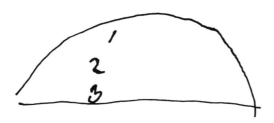

1–2 feet black soil
2–5 inches burnt clay
3–8 inches ashes resting on a hard clay floor
1½ inches thick and five feet diameter number 711358
The many years this spot has been occupied by whites has obliterated
nearly everything of the Indian occupation

Mound at oboughs Mill ,Clark Co, Ark

Nearly one mile S. E. of Arkadelphia Clark Co, Ark. on the bank of the
Washita River is J. H. Oboughs Mill by which is to be seen a fragment of a
mound the flood rise of last year carried away the balence several skeletons
Potts &c was washed out by the water
*   In the remaining part a Pott some mussel shells, &c was found –it was*
very black soil
Smithsonion numbers   71384 disk pottery
Fragments of potts 71374
*   Pott 71367*
[This vessel is illustrated in figure 7.64.]
*   Stone impliments 71378*
Mussel Shells 71390–71389

Clark Co Ark

*   Pottery borrowed from C. C. Scott of Arkadelphia Clark Co Ark they*
was taken from a mound 3 feet high 10 miles West of Arkadelphia num-
bered 71363
*   71366*
*   71370*
[These vessels are illustrated in figure 7.65.]
*   One specimen of Pottery borrowed from George Fuller of Arkadelphia*
taken from a large mound on the bank of the Little Missouri River . 71360
[This vessel is illustrated in figure 7.66.]

―――――――――

NAA BAE Letters

Arkadelphia. Ark Feb 14 1883
Prof Cyrus Thomas
*   Dear Sir*
*   Have not herd from you for some time the incle-*
ment weather has prevented me from being certain as to a safe place to

FIGURE 7.64

Military Road Incised jar (71367) Palmer Collection, from the O'Baugh's Mill site near Arkadelphia, Clark County, Arkansas. This is a late prehistoric or protohistoric variety of this type. (Photo No. 88-12955, Department of Anthropology, Smithsonian Institution.)

> *have my accumulated mail forwarded to but to morrow hope to receive it then wil write fully—Cannot do any more hear now owing to the excessive rains & floods*
> *Start to morrow for the Mississippi River to work down it to the places you have previously written to me about.*
>
> *I send to day two boxes by express addressed to Major Powell*
> *These specimens wil all be refurred again to in report for this month.*
> *   The following Specimens found at the old Indian Salt works 2 miles South East of Arkadelphia Clarke County Arkansaw*
> *210 Broaken pot found in a mound with a decayed skeleton.*
> [This ends the first page; the rest of this letter is missing.]

FIGURE 7.65

a.

Ceramic vessels in the Palmer Collection from the C. C. Scott Mound site near Arkadelphia, Clark County, Arkansas:

a. *Foster Trailed-Incised jar (71363) with punctated rim (a very late protohistoric or early historic "Caddo V" trait; cf. var. Shaw of Schambach and Miller 1984: 121).*

b. *untyped ridge-pinched jar (71366) with a design resembling that of Foster Trailed-Incised vessels.*

c *and* d. *side and basal views of an untyped engraved carinated bowl (71370) with a design resembling those on late prehistoric to late protohistoric Hudson Engraved and Maddox Engraved vessels.*

(Respectively: Photo Nos. 88-12962, -12960, -12973, and -12971, Department of Anthropology, Smithsonian Institution.)

b.

5 CM.
2 IN.

c.

d.

FIGURE 7.66

*Untyped incised and engraved bottle (71360) in the Palmer Collection from the
George Fuller Mound site on the Little Missouri River south of Arkadelphia, Arkansas. No type or chronological placement has been established for such vessels,
but several have been found on Caddoan sites in Arkansas. (Photo No. 88-12964,
Department of Anthropology, Smithsonian Institution.)*

"Soil Like A Morter Heap":
Another Attempt at Bradley;
End of the Second Arkansas Season

MARVIN D. JETER

By February 16, 1883, Palmer had arrived again at Memphis, hoping to revisit the Bradley site, which had been covered by cotton when he left it in early November. Despite bad weather, he made the attempt but could do nothing due to flooding and cold weather. He did write Thomas two interesting letters, before and after the Bradley attempt, discussing various possibilities, including the extension of the Mound Survey to Arizona.

Another letter, written from Vicksburg a month later, alludes to his plans to revisit the Arkadelphia locality and discusses several highly significant sites in Louisiana and Mississippi that he had visited or planned to visit.

Palmer seems not to have returned to Washington after leaving the flooded Mississippi Valley this year but to have worked at sites near Memphis, all over Alabama, and once again in eastern Tennessee; his whereabouts and activities are poorly documented and dated for this period (McVaugh 1956:135, 251, 331). Furthermore, between June 24, when he was in St. Louis, and his arrival back in Arkansas in mid-September, "nothing is known of his movements" (1956:141). The broken thread will be picked up again in chapter 8.

Palmer's Mississippi Valley Documents,
February–March 1883

NAA BAE Letters

[The following letter, on the stationery of the Worsham House in Memphis, is reproduced in figure 7.67.]

Feb 16, 1883

Prof Thomas
            Rains & Snow have rendered it impossible to do any more work in this section now
    And the rivers are all ready to overflow their banks and great fears are entertained by many that the country along the rivers for miles wil be inundated.
    Came to this place to take the Cars for New Orleans to do the work you wrote me about there. After which wil return up the river to examine the other mound you wrote about the water must go down before it can be done if the bottoms are not overflowed the excessive local rains have made the soil like a morter heap. After finishing at New Orleans, there is ten important places that I am desirous to examine as they occupy very prominent positions and likely to yield valuable results , Then I desire to return to Washington and give up this River work .

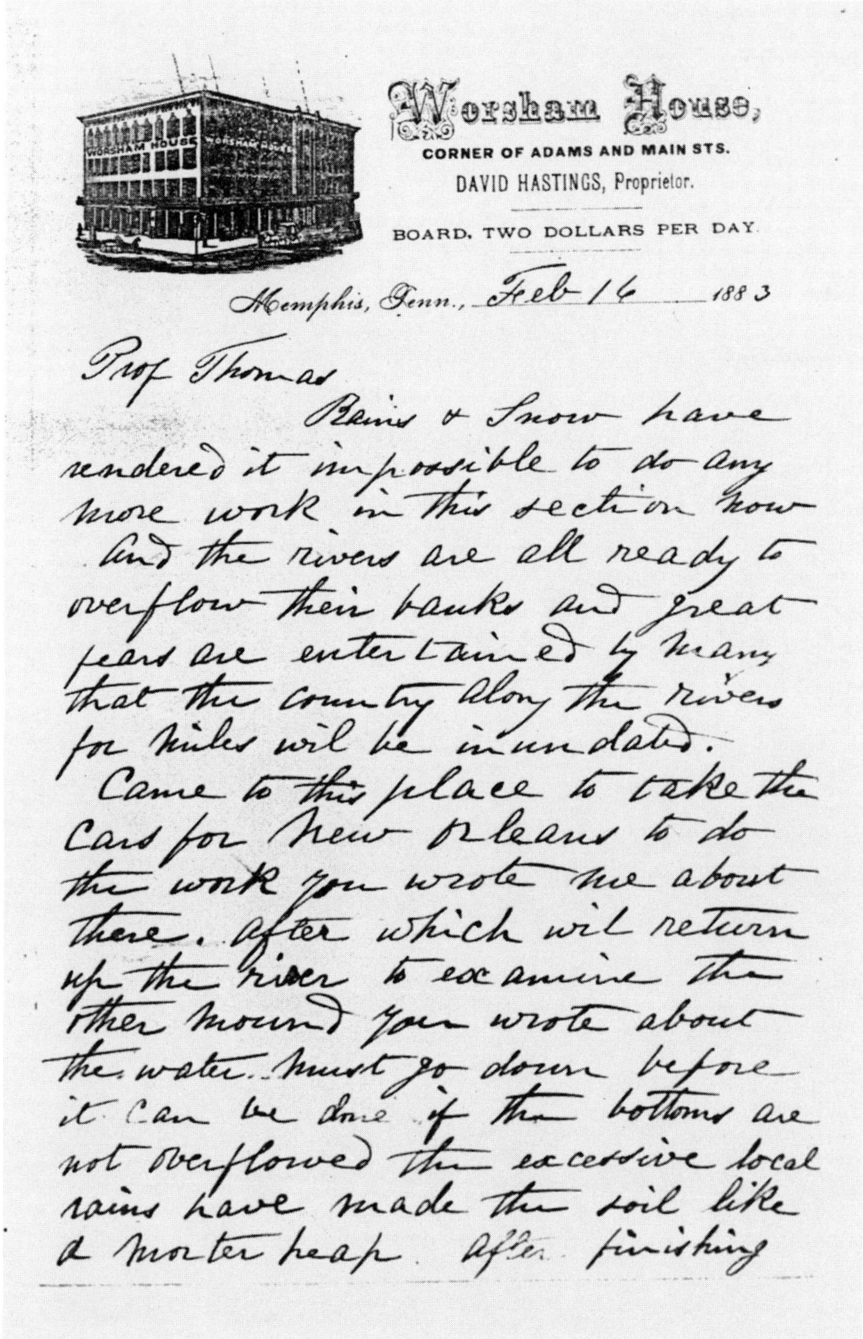

Worsham House,
CORNER OF ADAMS AND MAIN STS.
DAVID HASTINGS, Proprietor.
BOARD, TWO DOLLARS PER DAY.

Memphis, Tenn., Feb 16 1883

Prof Thomas

Rains & Snow have rendered it impossible to do any more work in this section now And the rivers are all ready to overflow their banks and great fears are entertained by many that the country along the rivers for miles wil be inundated.

Came to this place to take the Cars for New Orleans to do the work you wrote me about there. After which wil return up the river to examine the other mound you wrote about the water must go down before it Can be done if the bottoms are not overflowed the excessive local rains have made the soil like a morter heap. After finishing

FIGURE 7.67

First page of Palmer's February 16, 1883 letter to Thomas. (Arkansas Archeological Survey Negative No. 832002, courtesy of National Anthropological Archives, Smithsonian Institution.)

Please inform me if you have received the boxes that I have informed you
of sendind
  Address me at New Orleans , La.[118]
      Yours very truly
          Edward . Palmer .
P.S. The inclement weather has prevented me from doing as much as de-
sired up to the present time
          E. P.

––––––––––

AHC Item 27 (1917:417–18)

          Bradley's Landing
Feb.16– 1883—left. Memphis for Bradley's Landing. The river had overflowed the bank so that the hotel could not be reached. There being no
other place to stay I went back to the steamer. It rained very hard, a sheet
of water all round the landing. I could not hire a boat or owner, it being
dark *next morning Ice every where In the afternoon heavy snowstorm*
which covered the ground and it was exceedingly cold for this section

––––––––––

AHC Item 27 (not in 1917)

          Memphis for Bradleys Landing, Ark.
              Chittenden Co.
1883—
Left Memphis by steamer for Bradley's Landing. to finish some began there.
   The cotton has now been gathered from around the mounds . I landed in
a rain shower. The place contains a few very small dwellings, 1 store, & a
boarding house. The river had overflowed its banks so that the water cut off
access to the only place to [virtually illegible; appears to be "stop" and
"board" written over], the boarding house, and seeing the water had extended to the mounds returned to the steamer & to Mamphis. At night a
fierce storm of sleet & snow prevailed extending into the next day .

––––––––––

NAA BAE Letters

[This letter is also on the Worsham House letterhead.]
              Feb. 18, 1883
Prof. Thomas
Dear Sir
   Yours of the 11th was received on my return from Bradley's Landing,
which place was so inundated with water from the Mississippi River that

nothing could be done. Besides, a fiesce snow storm prevailed, the water cutting off the only place of shelter, a hotel, so had to return to this place. As I wrote you the other day, it is not possible of doing anything now along the Mississippi River. In answer to your letter, wil say that I agree with you in going to Louisiana and to the mounds near Natchez. To one in Adams Co., Mississippi which by an old history is said to be 175 feet high,[119] *also to three or four along the Mississippi River of unusual importance, which it seems important—as I know whare they are and have now by experience assertained much more about them than a stranger would know—have concluded as you have that it is best that I attend to these important mounds before leaving for Arizona. The other day in my letter, asked you to write me at New Orleans. At that time, was told I could reach the mounds you wrote about near Natchez best by takeing a boat at New Orleans. Today, have assertained by a person acquainted with that section to go to Natchez direct by Rail Road from Memphis is best, then by private conveyance to the mounds. It is thought that section is not overflowed yet, and as it is now become cold, the Mississippi may soon run down so that I can yet finish the few desired mounds along that river before leaving. You had better write me at Natchez instead of New Orleans. Be assured that the work above spoken of wil be done as soon after the first of March as practicable. Should it be desirable in consequence of any unknown cause to me that I should go sooner to Arizona, write me to that efect at Natchez.*

I am of the opinion it would be best for me to come to Washington before going to Arizona. The cost is not very great, and the numerous details to be added to the reports of work done in Arkansaw can far better be added when we can go over the report together, having the specimens at hand.[120] *As accidents occur in traveling, it would be best that the entire work be reviewed and made satisfactory before going to Arizona.*

The important places to visit in Arizona: Between Prescott and the Colorado River is ruins of mounds at Peacock Springs.[121]

In Chino Valley and along the Verde River is numerous ruins, also mounds, besides two kinds of stone piles, one long, the other round.[122]

In southern Arizona, along the Salt and the Gila River is numerous mounds & ruins.[123]

At Hayden's Ferry is numerous mounds. A friend of mine living near that place has written me about the wonderful ruins and mounds of that section, and Dr. C. C. Parry wrote me about the same place as worth a careful examination for the hidden treasures believed to be hidden there.

These are the most important places I now remember in Arizona. The Indians living in the above sections can also be visited, as they have many things the Museum desires.

> *Yours truly,*
> *Edward Palmer*

———————

Vicksburg   March 19
   Prof Cyrus Thomas
                Dear Sir
                  *Since writeing my previous letter . I have nearly gone
the rounds to carry out the program outlined in a previous letter to you
came to vicksburg in order to reach an important place by rail but water is
over the country for 40 miles so had to abandon the trip start to morrow
for Greenville Miss then to Friers Point*[124] *to visit a mound a few miles
from that place if the water wil admit it there have recently been three feet
of water over that section—have one place to finish above Memphis this
wil take me to the end of March*
   But there is two places near Arkadelphia[125] *which if visited now wil take
me into April before finishing I fear thay are under water now so wil not go
there now.*
   I send to day a box by Express
*215—Fragments of pottery &c from the field around the so called Saltzer-
town Mound*
*216 These two bundles under this number had better be kept tied up they
are burnt cane found a foot thick 30 foot from base of the large mound at
Troyville at the junction of Tensas—Witchita and little river and extending
some distance into the mound*[126]*—Have drawing showing this*
*217 Mixed pieces of pottery from Troyville from surface of nearly de-
stroyed mounds.*
   *There is one package marked in my name. please ask Dr. Foreman to
take care of it. Have drawings of all mounds visited which wil bring with
me Yours truly*
                  Edward Palmer

CHAPTER EIGHT

Mopping Up,
September–November 1883
and July 1884

During the first or second week of September 1883, Palmer returned to Arkansas from parts unknown. Apparently, his first visit this time was not on Mound Survey business but to try the baths at Hot Springs as a cure for his rheumatism. However, he found "fever and ague" raging there and left to resume work.

Palmer's final season in Arkansas gives the impression of having been something of a mopping-up operation. He took care of various items of unfinished business, such as visiting some mounds he had missed near Arkadelphia and picking up donated and loaned specimens from Mr. Thibault and his relatives. He extended his work around some previously visited bases, such as Arkadelphia and Newport, with some emphasis on the western fringes of his overall Arkansas coverage area. He also did some filling-in along the western margin of the White River valley and on both sides of the Arkansas Valley, in east-central Arkansas, and finally along the Mississippi River again, apparently leaving Arkansas in early November. A final, and unsuccessful, mop-up was his return visit to the Knapp Mounds on July 1 to try to obtain satisfactory measurements of the large mounds, after which he returned to natural history collecting in Florida.

Palmer did visit several very interesting sites during this last season and made some significant collections, but the season was not as productive in terms of artifacts as it might have been, given the experience he now had. It appears that he and Cyrus Thomas shared the decision-making about which sites and localities to visit. On October 1 Palmer wrote Thomas about "other parties" being in the field and said he thought it best to avoid worked-out places. This may well have fit in with Thomas's general strategy of trying to obtain a good sample of the range of variation within any given class of mounds. By now, Baird's original emphasis on artifact collections had been superseded by the Powell-Thomas orientation on definitively solving the mound builder problem. Thomas apparently wrote Palmer about where to go at least once during this season, in a letter that Palmer received on October 27.

It is difficult to trace Palmer's sequence of locality and site visits during much of this season, due to undated entries and other problems. An approximation of his itinerary can be made, though; it is summarized in table 8.1, and mapped in figure 8.1.

Table 8.1.
Palmer's Itinerary for His Final Arkansas Field Season
(September–November 1883 and July 1884)

SEPTEMBER

?—Went to Hot Springs early in September.

12—Borrowed collections from Mr. Thibault and relatives in and near Little Rock.

14—At Little Rock; wrote letter to Thomas.

16—At Bryant Station, Saline County.

17—Took train from Bryant Station to Arkadelphia.

19—At Arkadelphia; wrote note about butchers. No further dated entries until October 1.

During late September, must have worked at Carpenter Mounds near Arkadelphia and at various mound sites near Okolona, southwest of Arkadelphia.

OCTOBER

1—At Malvern Junction; wrote letters to Thomas.

2—Left Malvern for Judsonia. Must have visited "Choctaw burying ground."

5—Left Judsonia for West Point.

6—Worked at mounds near West Point.

No further dated entries until October 27. May have worked at sites in White, Woodruff, Prairie, Lonoke, and Jefferson counties during this period.

27—Left Indian Bayou for Lonoke; received letter, rode wagon to catch midnight train.

28—By train to Newport, thence to Batesville, thence to Jamestown.

31—Left Jamestown for Little Rock.

NOVEMBER

1—At Little Rock; letter to Thomas; starting for Helena, intending to proceed down the Mississippi River. May have worked in Poinsett and Crittenden counties, northeast Arkansas, then gone downvalley to Helena and out of the state.

DECEMBER

4—In Washington, D.C., briefly.

JANUARY TO MAY, 1884

Worked in Alabama, Georgia, and South Carolina.

MAY

26—Arrived in Washington from South Carolina. The length of his stay is unknown.

JUNE

30—Arrived in Little Rock.

JULY

1—Revisited the Knapp Mounds and remeasured the large mounds.

13—At Cedar Keys, Florida; about to leave for Key West.

Return to Arkansas, September 1883

MARVIN D. JETER

As previously noted, Palmer's whereabouts and activities are unaccounted for between June 24, 1883, when he was in St. Louis, and mid-September, when he turned up in Arkansas again. According to McVaugh (1956:141), he stated in St. Louis that he was planning to start for Mexico "in a day or two," but the nature of that mission (if it occurred at all) remains mysterious.

The only items of evidence for his return to Arkansas are the two documents transcribed below. The first is a letter of September 14 to Thomas, written by Palmer in Little Rock, stating that he had already visited Hot Springs but had left due to a minor epidemic there. He had then visited mounds, apparently those near Arkadelphia that were referred to in his letter of March 19, 1883. He also stated that on September 12 he had borrowed a number of mound specimens from Mr. Thibault and his relatives in the Little

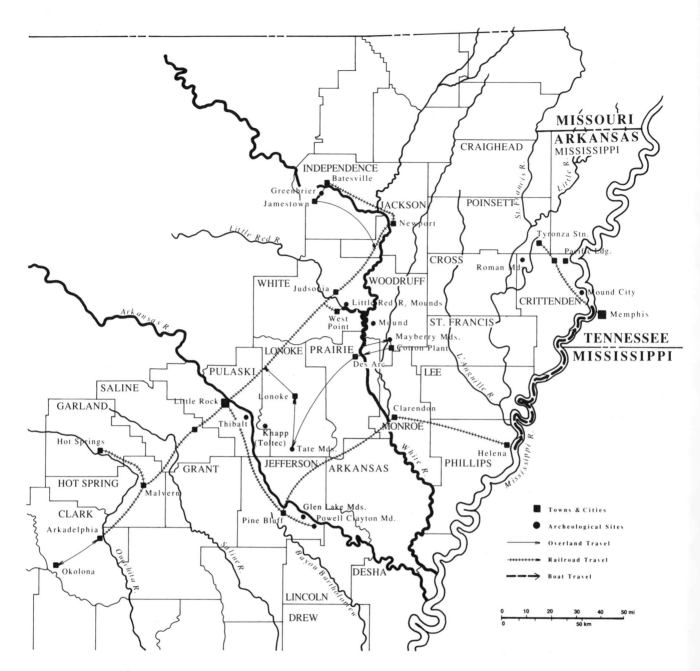

FIGURE 8.1

Map of Palmer's itinerary for the late 1883 field season and the mid-1884 revisit to the Knapp Mounds.

Rock vicinity. The second item, also in Palmer's own hand, must have been written much later in Washington, for it is a list of Smithsonian specimen numbers for the Thibault artifacts (his specimen numbers for this season are in the 87000 series, whereas those at the end of the previous season were in the 71000 series).

Documents for Palmer's Return to Arkansas, September 1883

NAA BAE Letters

> Little Rock Ark Sep 14
> Prof Cyrus Thomas
> Dear Sir
> On reaching this State found that Fever & Ague was very bad in Hot Springs. So visited Major Davis who went with me to visit two mounds[1] the overflow of last Winter prevented us from then visiting it is several years since the Major saw them—as you wil see by the accompanying accounts we found them dug out.
>
> The Major has a fine field of jute 8 to 10 feet high—he is letting it seed so that if the Miss-River Desha Co[2] is successful with the fiber of their large jute crop the Major wil have a good criterion to follow and plant largely next year for the fiber the plant is cut while in bloom—in gooing to seed the fiber becomes brittle. I suggested to the Major to sell the stems to the paper makers after he has gathered the seeds. The Major had in his orchard the finest fruit I have seen in Arkansaw. His corn is good and his cotton crop though not like last year wil be as good as his neighbours it has been very dry in Arkansaw lately The Major & Mrs. Davis are suffering from chills. Mr Beatie of Carbondale arrived at Major Davises the night before I left there.
>
> By a late Helena Arkansaw paper I see that Dr. Jacks of that place is dead it was from him those two carved pipes in stone was borrowed which you have though in Dr. Jacks care they belonged to D. M. Beams near Cotton Plant[3] Woodrough Co. Ark. I gave you this address so as to write him when last in Washington if you have not herd from him now that Dr. Jacks is dead you may not be called on for them.
>
> Visited Little Rock Pulaski Co. so as to go to Mr. Thibaults the gentleman who has the fine collection of mound specimens and promised some time since to lend them to the National Museum seeing his brother who informed me they had not been sent because they was afraid they could not pack them properly so I went out there on the 12 for that purpose, and was allowed to select what ever in my judgement was of advantage to the Museum. The specimens borrowed are sent in boxes No 1 and 2—Those donated are sent in box no 3—
>
> I would suggest that in unpacking the boxes—the suggestions embodied in the Catalogue herein inclosed be carried out—then there wil be no mistake I think.

For fear you might be absent and the boxes opened, wrote a note to Dr. Foreman to urge they be not opened untill the Catalogue from you be received so as to prevent confusion with the borrowed and donated specimens. Box no 4 sent contained borrowed specimens from F. T. Gibson and Mrs. Helen Hobbs of Little Rock relatives of J. K. Thibault to whom these things can be returned and he wil deliver them to the owners.

  E. Palmer

NAA 2400

      Pulaski Co. Arkensaw
List of specimens borrowed from
 F. T. Gibson   ⎫ *Little Rock*
 Mrs. Helen Hobbs ⎬ *Arkansaw*
 J. K. Thibault   ⎭

 These specimens where obtained from the Farm of J. K. Thibault 8 miles South East of Little Rock Pulaska Co Ark
 The mounds of this locality where reported to you last year when the Mr. Thibault Donated a number of specimens. Since he has donated the following with Smithsonion Numbers . Last Donation
87742
  3
  4
  5
  6
  7
  8
  9
87750
  1
87683 Borrowed from F. T. Gibson
87684
  5
  6
   Borrowed of Mrs. Helen Hobbs
87689
87690
  1
  2
  3
  4
87687
  8

Borrowed of J. K. Thibault

87695	87713	8771
6	4	2
7	5	3
8	6	4
9	7	5
87700	8	6
87701	9	7
2	87720	8
3	1	9
4	2	87740
5	3	1
6	4	88445
7	5	6
8	6	
9	7	
87710	8	
1	9	
2	87730	

"I Slept in a Corn Crib": Palmer's Return Visit to South-Central Arkansas, September 1883

Marvin D. Jeter and Ann M. Early

On September 16, 1883, Palmer returned to south-central Arkansas by train. His first stop was at Bryant Station near Benton in Saline County, apparently wishing to visit mounds near there, but he could not hire a wagon and continued to Arkadelphia.

From there he visited the Carpenter Mounds site and dug fairly extensively there, but the work was unproductive in terms of artifacts. Next he traveled to the small town of Okolona, about thirty kilometers (or twenty miles) southwest of Arkadelphia, and visited several small sites in that vicinity, with virtually no luck at all. This was the southwesternmost locality visited by Palmer in Arkansas.

He then took the train northeast from Arkadelphia to Malvern in Hot Spring County. He visited two more sites near there but was refused permission to dig.

Altogether, this was a rather frustrating expedition, especially given the actual archeological richness of this region, as noted in our comments on his first venture into Caddoan archeology.

Carpenter Mounds

Here Palmer referred to "a group of mounds." He made a crude sketch of the largest mound and tested it with three fairly large trenches, recording the stratigraphic sequence of deposits in general terms. He seems to have encountered a burned house in the first trench, nothing obvious in the second, and burials on a house floor in the third. He also tested two nearby small mounds, finding probable house floors but only potsherds and no burials.

Cyrus Thomas did not mention this site in either his 1891 catalog or his 1894 final report. From Palmer's description, this would appear to be the Moore site (3CL56), although it is closer to Arkadelphia than Palmer's estimate of six miles. This site has been heavily damaged by relic collectors, but when previously visited it consisted of a pyramidal mound, two low conical mounds, and cemetery areas. Artifacts indicate that it belongs to the Mid-Ouachita phase, and it may have an additional, even later Caddoan component. Burned floors of the type described by Palmer are datable by the archeomagnetic method, and a sample taken from a structure in the upper levels of the large mound yielded a date of A.D. 1400 ± 20 (Wolfman 1982: Table 11-1).

Sites near Okolona

Okolona Mound.   Here Palmer was denied permission to test a mound that the owner offered to dig at Palmer's expense. The site was not mentioned by Thomas. No site is now on record here, and the mound may have been a natural feature.

Mound on Island.   Palmer was told of a mound on an island at the Antoine–Little Missouri river junction, which had been "all dug out" by unsuccessful treasure hunters. Thomas (1891:17) summarized Palmer's description but did not mention this or any of the other Okolona sites in his final report.

Hays Mound.   Palmer visited this mound but judged it to have been virtually ruined by previous diggers. He only made a brief test and found a few sherds in an ash bed. He also reported the destruction of "numerous house sights" with burials here, due to flooding and plowing. Thomas (1891:16) gave a fairly detailed summary of Palmer's findings.

The Hays site (3CL6) is indeed a well-known mound and cemetery site that has been extensively "potted" by collectors. The mound was land-leveled in 1971, but before it was completely destroyed it was tested by the Arkansas Archeological Survey, with emergency funding by the National Park Service (Weber 1973). Portions of the early stages of mound construction were identified as low earthworks supporting buildings that were radiocarbon dated to about A.D. 1050–1250. Corn and a variety of nuts and seeds were recovered, along with animal bones and shells.

Logan Mounds.   Palmer made very rough sketches of three mounds here. He tested only the largest and hit a burned house floor with only potsherds found in the exposed portion. This may be the Hardin site (3CL279), but, if so, Palmer significantly underestimated the large mound's size. No controlled excavation has been done here.

Sites near Malvern

Here the owners of the Gibson and Clem mounds had their own plans, and Palmer did not dig. Thomas merely listed these sites in his catalog (1891:18), and did not mention Hot Spring County at all in his final report. These sites have not been located.

Palmer returned to Malvern and wrote Thomas an interesting letter about the intensive competition, amounting to a bidding war, that was already building among out-of-state connoisseurs of Arkansas artifacts.

Documents

The documentary situation begins to become rich and strange here. We have notes in

Palmer's own hand for all of the sites in this section—in fact, for some of them, we have two sets of his notes. His final versions, done in Washington as evidenced by the Smithsonian numbers, are used here, with endnotes identifying significant variations in his field versions. There are also a couple of instances of similar entries by a scribe; in these brief cases, both versions are presented. There is another complicating factor. Although Palmer's final version of the Arkadelphia-Okolona site visits appears to be in chronological order, the Malvern sites are included in the final version of another document that is definitely not in order. The individual site entries have been reordered here.

Palmer's South-Central Arkansas Documents, September 1883

AHC Item 28 (1917:394)

Bryant Station, Saline Co. Ark.
Sept. 16–1883—Visited Bryant Station.
No team could be had to go into the country, all having gone to camp meeting[4] in the boarding house.
Had to get the station keeper to go with me to the Saw Mill & get me a chance to stop until next days train for Arkadelphia.

———————

AHC Item 27 (1917:405)

Arkadelphia, Clark Co. Ark.
The following are entitled to the thanks of the Bureau of Ethnology .
W. A. Trigg
C. C. Scott
George Fuller.
L. E. Gibney .
Sept. 19—1883—The butchers ring a bell, a mornful toned bell, when they kill meat, to bring up the mourners for the writchet stuff called beef .

———————

AHC Item 27 (1917:416)

Carpenters Mounds 6 miles South
of Arkadelphia, Clark Co.
1883—
6 miles south of Arkadelphia is what is known as Carpenters' Field & 200 yards from the Ouachita River is a group of mounds. These mounds are located amidst dense woods & cane. Trees cover the greater portion of the mounds. The 2 largest trees are oak measuring 3 & 4 ft. in diameter & 125 ft. high . A Slough runs back of the mounds & empties into the Ouachita

River 200 yards off . Did not remeasure the mounds as Mr. Gibney had accurately done that before. At 10 ft. from west end of the mound made first trench 12 ft. long & 8 ft. wide.—found 2 ft. of soil—then 8 inches to 2 ft. of burnt clay with impressions of grass & sticks which is sent under a. Among the irregularly arrainged mass was found a mud-daubers nest sent marked with letter B. Third layer was ashes varying from—[The page ends here, and the next page of this scribe's entry has not been found. The 1917 publication also indicated this. Palmer's original version (below) is complete.]

———————

AHC Item 27 (1917:416)

> *On opening the Carpenters Mound—there was only one chance for food or lodgeing*
> *A Colored wooman provided food for me at her Cabin and I slept in a corn crib*
> *walked to and frofrom the mound some distance*

———————

AHC Item 27 (1917:404–05)

Carpenters Mound 6 miles S. of
1883—
  Arkadelphia, Ark.
Took food a colored woman cooked & I slept in a corn crib.
Walked to & from the mounds—it was cheaper—

———————

NAA 2400

> *Carpenter Mounds*
> *Clarke County . Arkensaw*
> *Six miles South from Arkadelphia Clarke County is what is known as Carpenter field. Two hundred yards from the ouchita River is this group of mounds located amid dence woods and cane . Trees cover the greater portion of the mounds.*
> *The two largest trees are oaks measureing respectively three and four feet diameter . and about 125 feet high*
> *A Slough runs back of the mounds then empties into the ouchita river 200 yards off.*
> *The largest mound is 125 feet long and Presents this outline.*

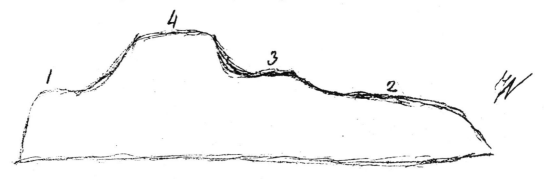

Point 1 is five feet high Point 2 is 6½ feet high Point 3 is 8 feet high while No 4 is 12 feet high .

Near no 2 of the Diagram was made the first trench 12 feet long and 8 feet wide through two feet of soil.then burnt clay varying from 8 inches to two feet with impressions of grass and sticks which was sent under Letter (A) Among this very irregular arranged mass was found a mud daubers nest sent under letter (B)

Third layer of this cut was ashes varying from 1 to 2 feet in which a few peices of Animal bones some mussel shells was found more or less calcined[5]

They are sent under letter (C) in different packages but need resorting there was also found two round peices of charcool as if from posts , they where three inches in diameter .

Fourth layer in this trench was burnt clay as if a floor varying from from one to one and half feet thick covering a space from five to six feet each way specimens of which are sent under letter D .

Second trench dug was midway between no 2 and 3 of the diagram it was 18 feet long 8 deep and 6 feet wide of yellow clay only .

Third trench dug was at no 3 of the diagram 10 feet long and 9 wide after removing two feet of soil came to a pott laying on its side close by was the head of a child then another pot on its side then a toy vessel these are sent under letter (F.) The skeleton could not be saved . In an opposite direction but on the same level floor was found another skeleton much decayed of a grown person with which only a much broaken pott was found which is forwarded under letter (E) These skeletons lay north to South upon what appear to have been the floor of a hutt five or six feet in width two feet thick apparently circular . some ashes was on the floor with some burnt musselshells.

Two other holes was dug in the sumit of the mound at no 4 but only yellow clay found with fragments of pottery intermixed which are sent under letter (J)

As there have been but little rain during the summer , it is allmost impossible to dig to the base of this solid yellow clay mound as a pick was useless . The shape of the mound would indicate that it was made at different periods.

Package sent marked letter (G) was found 6 inches under the surface while digging first trench at West end

Near the large mound is two small ones about three feet high and 33 feet diameter. removing the top soil came to red clay upon which was found ashes and charcool with musselshells with a few fragments of pottery but no skeletons .

Package letter (H) found on the bank of the Ouchita River at arkadelphia .

———————

NAA 2400

List of Specimens Carpenter Mounds[6]
Clarke County Ark
87753 *Smithsonion Numbers*
4
5
6
7
8
9
87760
1
2
3
4
5
6
7
8
9

───────────────

NAA 2400

Okolona Mound Clarke Co

Okolona Clarke Co. Arkensaw

Near the center of this place is a mound in a very conspicuous place . it is circular in form of about 12 feet high . 25 feet diameter on top and 50 at base—of a mixture of red clay, sand, and small gravel stones.[7] on the sumit stand a solitary oak near three feet through.

Formerly low places existed near the mound which held water most of the year these are now nearly filled up. No permanent water nearer than Little Mo River five miles off. A large hole had been previously dug into the top and a tunnell into one side of the mound. The present owner would not allow me to toutch the mound.

But he was willing to take the mound down at my expense provided he could do it as it suited him . and all the specimens found therein I should pay him for, in addition to paying his price for takeing down the mound, of course these conditions where rejected.[8]

Mound on Island

Clarke. Co. Ark . on an Island, formed by the Antoine River being cut accross by the Little Mo River

This Island is three miles South West of Okolona Clarke Co Ark on which is a mound 5 feet high and 25 feet diameter—It is made entirely of sand . It had previously been dug out hoping to find treasure . A rumour

says[9] that years ago a man was killed for his money which his murderers hid on this Island—Thus the mound has been dug out to find it—but it was a failure
Dence woods cover the Island.

Hays Mound

Clarke Co Arkensaw

    Five miles South East of Okolona Clarke Co Ark. is the farm of John Hays on which is a mound 15 feet high and 54 feet in diameter flat on top . composed of sandy loom . It is covered with small trees—The soil to make it was taken from its base back of it

    It is one half of a mile from Blue Lake and one mile from the Little Mo River. This mound had been previously so dug into that it was not considered profitable to dig into it more except in an undisturbed portion two feet below the surface where was found a house sight here was ashes and a few peices of pottery sent under no 21. The sumit of this mound was for many years occupied by a house .

    A slightly raised ridge contiguous to the mound was uncovered by water two years ago when numerous house sights was exposed with pottery skeletons &c, The plow has since oblitterated all traces of them .

Logan Mound

Clark County Ark

    Three miles South of Okolona Clark Co Ark. is the farm of the late John Logan hear is a strip of woods rendered irregular by numerous natural elevations more or less circular these are very common over this section of Ark. Upon one spot was three of these natural elevations in line with only a narrow space in between . These had been artificially added to. leaving a part as it was originally which now forms a lean to from the artifical portion to the adjoining mound except to that of the last mound no 3 when the slope is outside. They have once been covered with large trees only a few are now standing the largest about three feet through

    Mound No 1 is 15 feet high and 48 feet Diameter flat on top. two large shafts had been previously dug into the sumit and a tunnel run into the end next to the adjoining mound showing the composition to be of yellow clay. In an undesturbed portion of the sumit I dug a square hole of 8 feet each way at two feet debth came to a quantity of ashes[10] in which was some fragments of pottery sent under no 20 . thes where laying upon a smooth surface as if a floor of red clay so coloured by heat about 3 inches thick. immediately under it was yellow clay

    at five feet the mound became so hard that the pick made no impression upon it it appeared to have been put up wet. it having a grainless look , but compact & shiney.

Specimens
87794
87795
from this
mound—below
the summit

Letter.A. outline of lean to or what seem to be of natural origin when the artificial portion was added when the natural elevation was probably of half moon shape reaching to the narrow divisions between it and is neighbour No 2.

Mound no 2 is about five feet high and 48 feet each way . The lean to is 3 feet high and 33 feet each way same shape as the apparent appendage or natural portion of mound 1 letter A.

Two large trees on its sumit which was not allowed to remove these filled the mound with roots this in connection with the hard earth or yellow clay prevented an extensive examination

outline of mound no 2

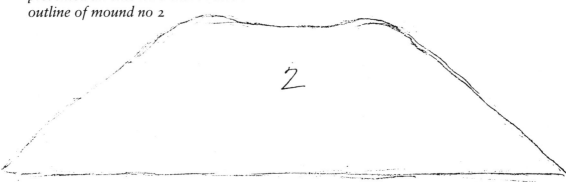

outline of no 3 with lean to of the same size of no 2

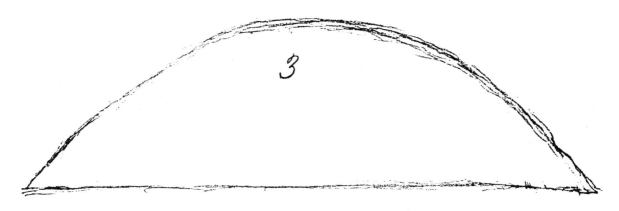

no fragments of anything found found on the surface of the mounds or the surroundings[11] *which indicate there was no permanent settlement hear— during rainey times water stand in holes there is no natural water in this locality.*

———

NAA 2400

Gibson Mounds
Hot Springs County Arkensaw
Six miles South West of Malvern Hot Springs County Ark. on the

*Ouchita River is a group of mounds belonging to J. C.[12] Gibson Esq. Who
wil not allow outsiders to molest them because he had arranged with J. K.
Thibault to open them conjointly as soon as they could get time to do so.
The National Museum to have the duplicates and to have the uneiks to
make casts of.[13]*

Clem Mounds
Hot Springs County Arkensaw

*Three miles South West of Malvern Hot Springs County. Ark is the farm
of the Rev. J. T. Clem on the ouchita River, hear is 5 mounds flat on top.
The River overflows and cover the land round the mounds. The soil is
black waxey bottom*

*The owner was not willing to allow me to open the mounds unless I paid
not only the expenses for that purpose but paid him for everything taken
out From his remarks he expected to be the Judge of what the things was
worth. I had before seen some things he had taken out of these mounds
and sold for a large price to private parties—besides I found that Salley &
McCray had sold to the Smithsonion a number of specimens which they
allso had taken out of these mounds. so did not think it advisable to com-
ply with the gentlemans excessive demands.*

——————

NAA 2400

List of specimens[14] from
Cem Mounds
Hot Springs Co Ark presented by S. G. Steele
Smithsonion Numbers

8780 2
*   3*
*   4*

——————

AHC Item 24 (1917:418)

Malvern, Hot Springs Co.
Ark.

1883—
(3) stone implements donated to the National Museum by T. G. Steele for
which he is entitled to the thanks of the Bureau of Ethnology.

——————

Malvern Junction[15]
Oct 1

Prof Cyrus Thomas
            Dear Sir
                        I sent to the address of Major Powell one week since a
box of Specimens.
            Mr. Valentine[16] of Richmond is instituting every effort to
get work done in this state he is writing to every one he thinks wil help
him, asking them if it wil be convenient for them to open mounds for him
and on what terms. If not to recommend some one competent. L. E. Gibney
of Arkadelphia handed me two letters from Valentine to read which ex-
plains his plans and gave names of those who are helping him.

    At the Rail Road Stations, notices are posted stating that the highest cash
price wil be paid for any Indian antiquities . The figures of a pipe Spear &
Stone axe head the poster—There are other parties in the field after mounds.
In consequence of which think it best to visit the localities likely to yield
good results—avoiding the places worked out by others

    If you could inform me how long it is contemplated for me to be in the
field then I could work back through the best field. If it's contemplated for
me to go to Mexico this Winter. Should I not go there, would you wish me
during the winter to work back by New Orleans to look round the lakes
then along the cost of Alabama to Mobile the rivers that empty into that
harbour may have mounds. The North Carolina Coast may have shell &
other mounds.

    Hot Springs did not suit me so much Malaria there an unusual thing—
Am trying a new treatment for Rheumatism. Have written to McChesney
for vouchers to sign for September pay if he has signed ones then send
check to me at this place
    Very truly

            Edward Palmer .   Malvern Junction
                        Hot Springs County,   Ark.

"Scarcely Discribable": Palmer's Return to East-Central Arkansas, Late 1883

MARVIN D. JETER, DAN F. MORSE, AND MARY FARMER

On October 2, 1883, Palmer caught a train from Malvern to Judsonia, a small town
about fifty miles northeast of Little Rock. Then as now, and probably prehistorically, a
major route of travel ran along this southwest-northeast diagonal across the state.

    A scribe's note states that Palmer left Judsonia for nearby West Point on October 5,
but there are no more dated entries until October 27. The sequence of his site visits during and after that period is rendered problematical by the fact that his lengthy final

summary of site visits is clearly out of order. It consists of eighteen pages of legal-sized paper, numbered consecutively from page fourteen through page thirty-one (as before, this is a floating sequence). It begins with the Gibson and Clem mounds near Malvern in Hot Spring County, discusses a dozen other sites, then ends with the "Choctaw Burying Ground" at Judsonia—the place he traveled to directly from Malvern.

Worse, the sequence between the Malvern and Judsonia sites makes little sense logistically, as may be seen in the following summary:

Gibson and Clem mounds near Malvern
Greenbrier "house sights" near Batesville
Clayton and Glen Lake mounds near Pine Bluff
Tate Mounds in southern Lonoke County
Pitman and Hill Bayou mounds near Des Arc
Tyronza Mounds in eastern Poinsett County
Goach Mounds near Helena
Little Red River and Mayberry mounds in Woodruff County
Little Red River and Arnold's Crossing mounds near West Point and Judsonia
"Choctaw Burying Ground" at Judsonia

Fortunately, several clues in these and other documents permit a reordering that appears more plausible. Palmer's field specimen numbers 22 through 27 were assigned to finds from the Little Red River mounds near West Point. The only other field numbers given are 100 through 106, for the Tate Mounds. A scribe's note states that Palmer went from Indian Bayou toward Lonoke on October 27 but changed his plans, caught a train to Newport, and went to Batesville and nearby Jamestown from there. Another scribe's note says he left Jamestown for Little Rock on the thirty-first, and on the next day, November 1, he wrote Thomas that he was about to go to Helena.

In short, it appears that most of the sequence in Palmer's final document is reversed. It seems that sites, or more commonly clusters of sites, were written into this document in a rather haphazard order by Palmer in Washington. The most likely actual order of site visits and trips is:

Gibson and Clem mounds near Malvern
"Choctaw Burying Ground" near Judsonia
Little Red River and Arnold's Crossing mounds near West Point and Judsonia
Little Red River and Mayberry mounds in Woodruff County
Pitman and Hill Bayou mounds near Des Arc
Tate (Indian Bayou) Mounds in southern Lonoke County
Greenbrier "house sights" near Batesville
Trip from Batesville-Jamestown to Little Rock
Clayton and Glen Lake mounds near Pine Bluff

From Pine Bluff, Palmer could have easily made railroad connections to Helena or Tyronza.

Judsonia–West Point Locality

"Choctaw Burial Ground." Palmer simply reported the recent destruction of a so-called

Choctaw burial ground. Thomas cataloged the site (1891:24) but did not mention it or any others in White County in his final report. The site has not been reidentified, but some general possibilities are discussed in an endnote to Palmer's entry.

Mounds on Little Red River.   Palmer excavated in four small "house mounds" near West Point, finding three vessels, potsherds, and a few other items. The site was mentioned in passing by Thomas (1891:25). Hoffman stated that Mississippi Plain sherds, an arrow point, and daub were present in the Smithsonian collection (1975:24). No landowner's name was given by Palmer, and the site has not been reidentified.

Arnold's Crossing.   Here Palmer again reported the recent destruction of "house sights" by flooding and plowing. Thomas listed the site (1891:24), but it has not been located.

Woodruff County Sites

Little Red River Mound.   Here Palmer tested another low "house mound" and found only burned structural remains. Thomas cataloged the site (1891:25) but did not mention Woodruff County in his final report. Moore tested a low mound in this vicinity, finding only a few human bones and fragments of a bowl (1910:348). The site has not been located.

Mayberry Mounds.   In the Cache Valley near Cotton Plant, Palmer reported two mounds but could not dig there. His report was cited by Thomas (1891:25), who followed Palmer in placing it "3 miles east" of Cotton Plant, but the Cache River is west of that town. This site (3WO27) was actually about four miles west-northwest of the town but has been completely leveled. It was summarized briefly by House (1975b:159). It seems to have been occupied mainly during the Coles Creek period and affiliated with the Plum Bayou culture, with some evidence of earlier and later components.

Sites near Des Arc

Pitman Mounds.   Palmer reported that two low mounds had been "plowed out" here and that little evidence remained. Thomas (1891:23) cited Palmer's summary but did not mention any Prairie County sites in the final report. This site has not been definitely reidentified.

Hill Bayou Mounds.   Here there were two somewhat larger mounds. Palmer examined one that had been massively pitted but did not find any evidence of habitation, and the owner refused permission to open the other. Again Thomas listed the site (1891:23), but it has not been reidentified.

The Tate Mounds

On Indian Bayou, in southern Lonoke County, Palmer made some of his most important finds of this field season. He described three mounds: one fairly large, one medium-sized, and one small and plowed down. He first dug the medium-sized mound thoroughly, finding fifty-four extended burials "without order as to the points of the compass," plus numerous potsherds and other artifacts. He did a fair job of describing the stratigraphic situation in general terms and made some other useful observations. He also tested the large mound extensively by tunneling into its sides and digging four large holes in its summit, finding only burned house floors and a few potsherds.

Thomas cited Palmer's summary in his catalog (1891:20) but, strangely, did not mention this site in his final report. Hoffman stated that Palmer's collection consisted primarily of plain grog-tempered pottery, with a few plain shell-tempered sherds (1975:17).

This site is now known variously as the Coy, Indian Bayou, or DuPree Mounds (3LN20). It has been heavily damaged by intensive agriculture, and only the large mound has been visible for several decades. It has also been heavily impacted by relic collectors for many years. Collections curated by the Survey indicate that the principal occupation was affiliated with the Plum Bayou culture of the Coles Creek period. It was in all likelihood a secondary center affiliated with the Knapp Mounds site, which is only about twenty kilometers (or twelve miles) to the northwest (Rolingson 1982:92). Recent investigations at this site are summarized in endnotes to Palmer's remarks.

Greenbrier House Sites near Batesville

Palmer next traveled by train to Batesville and visited another important site in that vicinity at the mouth of Greenbrier Creek. It appears that he merely surface-collected a number of plowed-down house mounds and did not excavate. His collections have not been examined for this research. Thomas cited Palmer and summarized his description (1891:19) but did not mention the site in his final report's section on this county (1894:224–25). In fact, he stated that the "only works reported in this county" were those at Akron, although he had listed others in the 1891 catalog.

The Greenbrier site (3IN1) is the type site for the Late Mississippian Greenbrier phase (Morse and Morse 1983:298–300, Figure 12.1). The Morses suggested that the village sites of this phase may have been missed by De Soto's reconnaissance party, which encountered only temporary encampments of hunters. However, Hudson (1985:6) has hypothesized that the Greenbrier phase is the "Coligua" of the De Soto accounts, and the Morses agree that this is plausible. (See also Dickinson 1986; Akridge 1986.)

Sites near Pine Bluff

Clayton Mound.   Palmer visited a medium-sized mound on the land of Powell Clayton, who had been governor of Arkansas during Reconstruction. The mound had been dug into, and Palmer merely examined the craters, finding no evidence of occupation.

Thomas referred to four mounds on the Powell Clayton property (1891:19; 1894:242–43). It is apparent, though, that Thomas not only confused this site with the J. P. Clayton Mound in Desha County, which Palmer visited in early December, 1882, but also combined them. In his Jefferson County mound description (1894:243), Thomas gave the much larger measurements that Palmer gave for the Desha County mound, not mentioning a Clayton Mound at all in his Desha County sections (1891:17–18; 1894:237–39). This site has not been definitely relocated.

Glen Lake Mounds.   Nearer to Pine Bluff, Palmer visited two mounds on an old Arkansas River cutoff. One had been mutilated by relic hunters but showed no evidence of habitation, and he could not reach the other, across the lake. Thomas cataloged the site (1891:19), but did not mention it in his final report.

The mutilated mound has not been reidentified. The mound that Palmer could not reach here is apparently at the site now known as Cottondale (3JE18). When recorded in 1961, it was described as a medium-sized village with a mound sixty feet in diameter and six feet high. Artifacts found there included Nodena points, small corner-notched arrow points, small scrapers, and large quantities of shell-tempered pottery; all of this suggests a Mississippian occupation, probably mainly of the protohistoric Quapaw phase. As might be expected, it has been heavily damaged by relic collectors.

Palmer's East-Central Arkansas Documents, October and Early November 1883

AHC Item 28 (1917:417)

Malvern for Judsonia Ark.
Oct. 2–1883 left . at 11 ½ Malvern for Judsonia—arrived at 2:30—wet night—walked with heavy baggage to town—a deception—Inquired of mail man about hotel, if one was near by, "O, Yes, I keep one!" he said, so followed him. Next day I found one near the depot.
Oct 5 left by horse car for West Port 4 miles fare 50 cents.

———————

NAA 2400

Choctaw Burying Ground[17]
White Co Ark
   At Judsonia White Co Ark. is the so called Choctaw crossing of Little Red River hear was the so called Choctaw burying ground. A late overflow of the river carried it away. Those who visited the spot during the receeding of the water assert that the remains where only two feet under ground many choice specimens with skeletons where carried away by the flood, others found claiments among the people. The plow has since finished the distruction
   This place was originally called Prospect Bluff.

———————

AHC Item 28 (1917:396)

Mounds, West Point, White Co. Ark.
on Little Red River
Oct. 6–1883 agreed with some black men for $1.00 per. day to open mounds, At night one came & said they did not like to handle dead bones that it was[18] money enough for that kind of work . I told them I would handle the bones, as it was necessary to have them, I told him $1.25 per. day would be paid. He said he was going to church that night & would let me know early the next morning, this he did not do. Picked up a black man

& boy & finished the work. West point was once a famous river centre but now nearly deserted. R. Roads the cause—It is nicely situated amoung oaks in a dry bluff land on Little Red River—

———————

NAA 2400

Mounds Little Red River[19]

White County Ark
Three miles N. E. of West Point on the north side of the Little Red River
White County Ark . In dence woods is 4 mounds. The soil of a black sandy Loom. The river overflows, covering the mounds which are a short distance appart near the bank of the River which afford fine fish and the woods in past days was stocked with game.

neither about or on top of the mounds was seen a fragment of any thing indicating the spot had ever been occupied.

The first mound opened was 4 feet high and 50 feet diameter

uncovered the mound from center outward the first foot & half was of black sandy loom Then in the center an inch of burnt clay which thinned towards the outer edge of the mound a specimen of which is sent under no 25. only one piece of pottery found, Under the burnt clay was five inches of a mixture of ashes & earth in which was found a broken pot sent under no 24 . Below this mixture was found two feet of burnt clay a sample of which is sent no 23 among the clay was found a broken pott sent under no 22 no animal or human bones found

Mound No. 2 is 3 ½ feet high 40 feet Diameter—First dug through 1 ½ feet of black loom, then one foot of ashes & earth in which a broaken pot was found it was sent number 26—immediately below was found one foot of burnt clay sent under no 27 nothing found below this

Mounds 3 & 4, each 3 feet high and about 40 feet diameter first found a foot of black loom then in the center was 4 inches of ashes in which was a few peices of pottery and two mussel shells—In the center of the mound for the space of 5 to 6 feet of it's diameter was burnt clay to the base with nothing else.

———————

NAA 2400

List of specimens[20] *West Point*
White Co Ark north side
Little Red River
   Smithsonion Numbers
87796
      7
      8
      9
87800
      1

House sights Arnolds crossing[21]

White County Ark

   House sights at arnolds crossing 3 ½ miles from West Point White County Ark whare is arnolds crossing of Little Red River on the old McDaniels farm hear is the old house sights that was washed out by a flood some years ago. A large space was covered by these house sights which was a short distance appart and easily told by a circular patch of black earth left more or less intack by the water, the earth from between was carried away . Many human remains was uncovered, with pottery and a great variety of impliments—The plow since has obliterated all traces of these house sights .

Mounds Little Red River[22]

Woodrough County Ark

Five miles below the mouth of Little Red River whare it empties into white River, east side near Nigger Hill . on that stream in dence woods & cane is a mound commanding a view of a bend of the River and the low back country which overflows but not the mound . it is in Woodrough . Co. ark. The mound is three feet high and 45 feet diameter of black sandy Loom Six inches below the surface came upon burnt clay which was full of impressions of reeds & poles under this was 6 inches to a foot of ashes and large Charcool—only one small peice of pottery found . did not save it or the burnt clay as a box just sent contained the same. Nothing else found in the mound

Mayberry Mounds

Woodrough County Ark

Near Cash River 3 miles East of Cotton Plant Woodrough Co. Ark. is the Mayberry farm on which is two mounds occupied by a house and orchard so no examination was allowed .

Pitman Mounds

Prairie County ark

Two miles S. E. of Desark in a bend of White River close to Round Lake Prairie County ark. hear is the Pitman Farm on which is two mounds originally am told was 4 feet high & 20 in diameter—they have been cultivated over for years

Skeletons and Pottery have been plowed out—but little of the mounds remain .

Hill Bayou Mounds

Prairie County Ark

Six miles N. E. of Desarc. Prairie County Ark. is Hill Bayou near the edge of which is two mounds in sight of each other about 8 feet high and 50 feet diameter . Previous to my visit one mound had a large pit dug into it extending to its base and takeing out the greater part of the mound . The work done, show only redish sand, close examination fail to detect the slightest particle of any thing that pertain to Indian habitation . The other mound the owner refused to have examined.

It had been cultivated over and in searching over its outer surface a fine stone impliment was found .Just underneath.

This section overflows up to one third of the mounds surface

They are rather sharp on top, a dence forest of large trees surrounds the mounds.

88130 This fine stone impliment from this mound.[23]

━━━━━━━

AHC Item 27 (1917:417)

Dasaic[24] Arkansas .

1883—

Leaving Desaic, I remarked to the hack driver—"What a neat comfortable house & what beautiful flower gardens!" Yes said he—"That's our county clerk, how that wife's family have sprung from nothing since the war!. They made up their minds to do something & they have succeeded remarkably well.

Lady at hotel married a soldier who was from the East.

━━━━━━━

AHC Item 27 (1917:411)

Indian Bayou   Ark.

1883

The quarters occupied by me at Indian Bayou are scarcely discribable— Slept in a lean-to with part of the end out. The host said he was not prepared to entertain strangers—Poor methods & poor ways .

━━━━━━━

AHC Item 27 (1917:411)

A. J. Tait[25] Mounds, Indian Bayou,
22 miles S. of Lonoke, Lonoke Co. Ark.

1883—

Tate Mounds

Lonoke County   Ark

Twenty two miles South of Lonoke Lonoke Co Ark. is Indian Bayou on the bank of which is the farm of A. J. Tate hear is four mounds At 150 feet from the Bayou is a mound 10 feet high upon which the owner has his house.

Three hundred feet from Indian Bayou is a mound 8 feet high and fifty feet diameter. For several years it has been cultivated over is circular in form and flat on top.

The owner freely gave permission to open it commenced work at the outer edge turning the earth which is a sandy loom behind me, when at the debths of from 1½ to 2 feet, skeletons was met and found all over the mound laying without any order not overlaying each other but in full length. The cause of the difference in debths is owing to the unevenness of the mound base upon which the skeletons was laid . Some parts was several inches higher than others, thus—some skeletons would be nearer the surface than others, The rains would allso wash off some of the fresh stirred soil bringing hidden things nearer the surface . Skeletons to the number of 54 was found they was laid without order as to the points of the compass At one place two heads came together from opposite directions at another three. At the middle of a skeleton or near the shoulders would be found the head of another, they was laid in every which way over the mound . Many of the remains being near the surface was crushed flat and the rains entering freely the light soil soon decayed the bones so that to take them out was futile. only one skull and that in peices could be saved. The bottom of the mound was firm with an un evenness that would be caused by much tramping on a very wet surface. probably caused when the bodies was laid thereon.

Five roundish piles of ashes as if fire places was found the bodies laying close to, but no signs of heat could be detected on the bones. nor any marks of violence.

In the soil covering the remains was found numerous peices of pottery sent under number 104 , a broaken pot no 105 Crania 103

Pipe 101. Stone knife 100. Arrow points 102—106 a pecular stone impliment which was previously taken out of this mound and by the owner given to R. B. Carllee of Duvalls Bluff Ark.[26] who presents it to the National Museum.

All the remains must have been covered up at the same time for one after another they where met with only the difference caused by the uneven base and the plowing.

Midway diagnally from the above and the largest mound of the group is a small mound so reduced by cultivation that little of it is to be seen. numerous fragments of pottery cover its surface.

The largest mound is 750 feet from the Bayou, is 13 feet high and 69 feet

diameter 169 feet long is circular with flat top.[27] *Tunnelled into its sides*
and dug four large holes into its sumit nothing but loom found except near
the surface was found a few fragments of pottery . And about a foot below
the surface was found at three different places a hard level. fire place upon
which was ashes. heat had redened these wel defined spots which was
about an inch thick and two feet diameter[28]

Though the country is now above overflow, When the river run as no
doubt it did whare now is only Indian Bayou it might then have overflowed
the land about the mounds.

———————

NAA 2400

List of specimens[29] *from Indian*
Bayou Mound Lonoke ,Co. Ark
        Smithsonion Numbers

88126
    7
    8
    9
88131
88102
    3
    4
    5

———————

AHC Item 27 (1917:421)

Indian Bayou, Lonoke Co. Ark.

1883—
R. B. Carlee of Devalls Bluff Arkansas presents a fine stone implements obtained at Indian Bayou. She is entitled to thanks of the Bureau of Ethnology.

———————

AHC Item 27 (1917:411)

Indian Bayou Ark.

1883—
Left Indian Bayou latter part of Oct. 27/83 for Lonoke, Lonoke Co. Ark.
22 miles by a two horse wagon with a cotton cover.—a very rain, raw day—
At post Office at Lonoke Received letter odering me back to Indian Bayou
by end of November.[30]
As my wagon was going over to the Iron Mt. R. R. went with him to

flagstation 22 miles only for midnight trains. Conductor kindly sat up with me to flag train at 11 ½. At 2 A.M. reached Newport. Went to bed. Hotel kept by colored men—very good fare & lodging—Town was lately burnt out. All appears new & now commencing to build brick houses.—
a hard name—gamblers—Saloons
Started on Sunday for Batesville Jefferson[31] Co Ark.

———————

NAA 2400

House sights
Independence County Arkensaw

At the mouth of Greenbrier creek whare it empties into White river and three miles S. W. of Batesville Independence[32] Co Ark . on the Stone Farm is a space[33] covered with numerous house sights. they where once more discearnable by years of cultivation they are nearly obliterated. now they are thickly strewn over with fragments of burnt clay, flint chips. peices of artificially broaken stones and much fragmentary pottery .[34] S. B. Fesmore[35] while plowing in this field last year cut a pot in two he informs me it was full of parched corn of the kind known as squaw corn which was sent to the Smithsonion Institution .[36]

———————

NAA 2400

List of specimens[37] collected from
house sights GreenBrier creek
Independence County, ark
Smithsonion Numbers

88132
3
4
5
6

———————

AHC Item 28 (1917:411)

Batesville, Jefferson Co. Ark.
1883—
A neat place full of business, situated amoung the hills
Left by Jamestown 7 miles S.W.

———————

AHC Item 28 (1917:402)

Jamestown, Jefferson Co.   Ark.
1883
There is here situated what has been called an Indian Mound. It is however
a natural one, very irregular & large for an artificial. It is in a hilly country,
not wanting artificial elevations .
Travelling in heavy rains, brought on neuralgia which gave me much pain
& no sleep—face much swollen
Oct. 31–1883. Left for Little Rock.

————————

NAA BAE Letters

Little Rock, Ark. Nov 1

Prof Thomas
    Dear Sir
        Came hear to day. Found little about Batesville & New Port,
Independence Co[38] *ark a party had been there. Start to day for Helena*[39] *in*
order to get transportation to a place 14 miles from there away from Rail
Road and River. finishing this wil go down the River to Vicksburg to take
train for Delhi La.[40] *Rains & overflow prevented me from visiting the*
mounds near this place last Winter—Can return to Vicksburg and take
train homeward by way of Jackson Miss & Taladega Alabama at the for-
mer place is a State collection[41] *at the latter place mounds & grave yard*
said to be Creek Indians[42] *that I desire to examine.*
            Yours truly
            Edward Palmer

————————

NAA 2400

Clayton Mounds[43]
Jefferson County Arkensaw

15 miles S. E. of Pine Bluff down the Arkansaw River in a bend is a mound
on the plantation of Powel Clayton[44] *near the River bank it is 10 feet high*
60 feet diameter flat on top . Three large holes had been dug into its sumit
to its base its composition is clear sand. examined the disturbed and un-
disturbed parts but not a fragment was found not even ashes. A fine view is
had of the River Bend from this mound and the surroundings which is now
dence woods. A good location for game in former days.

Glen Lake Mounds
Jefferson County   Ark
Nine miles S. E. of Pine Bluff on the farm of Major C. Brackenridge is Glen

Lake.[45] *near its banks and on each side is a mound. one could not be reached. The other had been previously so mutulated that nothing of its previous size and appearance could be told it is of clear sand. The part standing had been dug to the base . A fine view of the Lake and surroundings could once be had from this mound.*

A house now stand on part of its base and cotton surrounds it not a fragment of any thing was to be found in the field surrounding it

"Nearly Distroyed": Palmer's Last Work in Northeast Arkansas, Late 1883

MARVIN D. JETER AND DAN F. MORSE

The reconstruction of Palmer's early November 1883 itinerary at the close of this last real field season in Arkansas is uncertain, because none of the documents are dated and none contain field specimen numbers. It is assumed here that instead of traveling directly from Little Rock to Helena, as Palmer said he planned to do in his letter of November 1, he first visited the mounds near Pine Bluff. Then he could have proceeded from Pine Bluff to Helena, changing trains at Clarendon. From Helena he could have visited a site, then gone upriver to Memphis, caught a train to Tyronza Station, and worked his way back toward Memphis, then proceeding down the Mississippi Valley and out of the state.

The first bit of evidence for this is that, of the sites included here, only the Goach Mound near Helena and the Tyronza Station site are included in Palmer's eighteen-page final version of a document covering his late September and October work in south-central and east-central Arkansas. The other northeast Arkansas sites are covered in a separate three-page document and are here presumed to be later visits than Helena and Tyronza.

In the three-page document Mound City is discussed first, then Gilmore Mounds, and then Roman Mounds; but this order is assumed here to be backwards, like that of the eighteen page document. In his Tyronza notes, Palmer referred to artifacts from that site that were said to be in the possession of Capt. Charles Morris of Pacific Landing in Crittenden County. This suggests that after Helena Palmer next visited Tyronza Station then worked his way back to Memphis. Pacific Landing was near the railroad route between Tyronza Station and Memphis, and there is a note from "Pacific Place," acknowledging a donation from Captain Morris and stating that Palmer had seen his "mound collection."

Goach Mound

Palmer said in his November 1 letter that he was planning to visit a site fourteen miles from Helena, but there is no indication of such a site visit. That site may have been Old Town, which is about the right distance from Helena and which Palmer had mentioned in his December 29, 1882, letter to Thomas, but was apparently visited by another "Bureau assistant" (see note 92, chapter 7) rather than Palmer. Instead, his notes state that he visited the Goach Mound, six miles from Helena, but found a modern cemetery on it.

This site has not been reidentified. Once again, Palmer missed the Hopewellian burial mounds on the southern outskirts of Helena, which went undetected for many decades (Ford 1963).

Tyronza Station

Palmer stated that there were once forty-two mounds here but that most of them had been destroyed or nearly destroyed by railroad construction (presumably, they were both cut through and used for fill dirt) and by plowing. Most of them were apparently low house mounds. Palmer reported some finds made during railroad work and also tested several mounds himself, sometimes finding burned daub and/or artifacts, with a few faunal remains, but no burials.

Interestingly, on each full page of Palmer's final version of his Tyronza work, someone wrote "no good" faintly in the margin. The major Mound Survey exploration at Tyronza was by Col. P. W. Norris, in early 1884; Thomas probably sent him there to follow up on Palmer's work. Thomas only mentioned this site briefly in his preliminary catalog (1891: 23), but he gave it a relatively detailed summary in the final report (1894: 203–07, Figures 112–16), with a table listing the attributes of seventeen mounds, a plan view map, stratigraphic sections of mounds, and an illustration of clay casts of corncobs. It would appear that these mounds were by no means totally destroyed and that Palmer was outdone by Norris here, at least.

Tyronza Station (3PO34 and 3PO35 or 11-O-13) was shown as a Parkin phase site by Phillips (1970: Figure 447), but it is probably beyond that phase's limits. According to Phyllis Morse (1981:49, Figure 19), "the last definite Parkin phase site located along the Tyronza is the Barton Ranch site," which is more than twenty kilometers (over ten miles) from Tyronza Station. The various Tyronza collections at the Smithsonian have not been examined during this research; Hoffman (1975:20–21) noted that there was a large amount of material from this county and that there might be a thesis project in it.

Sites between Tyronza and Memphis

Roman Mounds.   Here, at a location in the northwest corner of Crittenden County and only six miles from Tyronza Station, Palmer reported fifty mounds, topping even the Tyronza count. He stated, however, that they were found over a distance of about four miles. So it appears that house mounds along the Tyronza River were involved, probably constituting a number of different sites. Palmer was only permitted to dig small test pits, which were generally unproductive, although structural remains were found in two cases. This site was not mentioned by Thomas in either his 1891 or 1894 reports, and Palmer's data are too vague to permit assigning site numbers to his operations here.

Gilmore Mounds.   Here, also in northwest Crittenden County, two mounds had been cut through by the railroad, and three others had previously been "potted." Thomas cataloged this site (1891:17) but did not mention it in his final report. No modern site number has been assigned here, and the remaining mounds may have been destroyed by more recent construction and farming.

Mound City.   Palmer could not dig in the large mound here and merely observed that a road cut through small mounds had exposed structural remains, burials, and broken pottery. Again, the site was only cataloged by Thomas (1891:17).

Mound City (3CT4, 5, and 6) should not be confused with Mound Place (3CT1), a generally later site in the same county, or with another Mound City site (17-M-6) in Mississippi. It is one of the few really early mound sites noted by Palmer and the Mound Survey in Arkansas. It has a possible Tchula period (before about 100 B.C.) component (Morse and Morse 1983:145, Figure 7.1) and also "could be a major Marksville site [c. 100 B.C.–A.D. 400], complete with mounds" (1983:172, Figure 8.1). There are also Baytown and Middle period Mississippian components present. The site has been heavily damaged in the 1980s by being used as a source of fill dirt for construction.

Palmer's Northeast Arkansas Documents, Late 1883

NAA 2400

Goach Mound
Philips County   Ark
Six miles South of Helena ark on the farm of James Goach is a mound which is covered with a modern Grave Yard.

———————

NAA 2400

Tyronza Mounds
Poinset County Ark
At Tyronza Station on the Memphis Kansas City and Springfield Rail Road in Poinset County Arkansa on land owned by Mrs. Martha Starker and O. Thorn Esq a group of 42 mounds that once was hear, but few remain, the Rail Road run through them they averaged from 2 to 8 feet high .

The largest remaining is 30 by 50 and the smallest is but 15 feet in diameter they where all circular in form.

The largest is covered by a house the next in size by a modern grave yard. Three others used to keep stock on during the overflow. these the owner did not want disturbed. many of the small mounds had been plowed over for years Nothin but burnt clay and fragments of pottery found in these, now scarcely noticible

In one mound nearly distroyed by the Rail Road a broaken pot and some fragments of human bones but no burnt clay found. though plenty of ashes. Was informed several skeletons was distroyed by the Rail Road hands. with which there was pottery &c but no burnt clay—Though plenty of ashes near which the skeletons was found as if left in house sights. not in mounds but near them . In a nearly distroyed small mound . imbeded in burnt clay about a foot thick was a pipe—part of a very thick pot. and a lump of burnt clay with a grove in it. In another nearly distroyed small mound was *found below one foot or so of burnt clay and about 6 inches of ashes part of a burnt clay floor or hearth upon which was found a conical shaped lump of burnt clay—In taking away the balence of the mound two others of these lumps of burnt clay was found which lay near in fragments. The Rail Road hands found several like this one two of which are in the collection of Captain Charles Morris of Pacific Landing Crittenden Co Ark*

In a peice of ground that never had been disturbed but on which stand large trees and cane is seen some small mounds all more or less covered by burnt clay in examining these some had only a few peices of pottery among the burnt clay or in the ashes below

Two of these mounds had been twice occupied, As after going through the ashes of the first house. a thin layer of earth was met then ashes on a hard burnt floor or fire place burnt black having grass impressions in its mixture as if grass was put therein to give solidity. no burnt clay of the roofing kind was met

Two of the mounds had a foot of burnt clay on them. Had scarcely penetrated three inches below the surface when commenced to turn up broaken pottery which was found throught these two mounds so thoroughly mixed in the the burnt clay as if they where associated with the clay when it was precipitated and formed this mound mass.[46]

The outer surface of these mounds was very irregular, burnt clay could scarcely be made into a rougher mass,. Had these mounds been plowed over the pottery in them being near the surface it would have all been carried over the surface or mixed with the soil in fragments as is the case of the mounds before mentioned that have for years been cultivated over. The soil is black sandy . Not a trace of Human bones found in any of the mounds covered by burnt clay in this locality . A few fragments of animal bones and mussel shells was found in the ashes.

There is no natural permanent water supply nearer than one and a quarter miles. This locality is between dead timber Lake and Tyronza River which is a natural stream and was in existence at the time the country was anciently inhabited

It was to far to carry water from this stream—The ancient people may have lived hear only during the time water from rains or overflow from Miss River filled the low place with water .

Dead timber Lake was made by the Earthquake of 1812 therefore could not have been used for its water by the ancient people that inhabited the house sights or mounds of this section

From same locality Mrs. Martha Starker donated one water vessel and two stone knives.

———

NAA 2400

List of specimens[47] *numbered from Tyronza . Poinset Co Ark*

Prof Thomas numbers

3546	*3568*
3547	*3569*
3548	*3570*
3549	*3571*
3550	*3572*
3551	*3573*
3552	*3574*
3553	*3575*
3554	
3555	
3556	
3557	
3558	*Mrs. Martha Starker from*
3559	*the above locality donated*
3560	*specimens under following numbers*
3561	*3577*
3562	*" 8*
3563	*" 9*
3564	
3565	
3566	
3567	

AHC Item 27 (1917:412)

Tyronza Station, Poinsett Co. Ark.

1883—   on Memphis, Kansas City & Springfield R.R.
Mrs. Martha Starker presents 2 spear heads and a piece of a fine water
vessel for which she is entitled to the thanks of the Bureau of Ethnology .
These were ploughed from a mound.

AHC Item 27 (1917:411)

Roman Mounds, Highland Lake
Chittenden Co. Ark.

1883
At the N. W. corner is the farm of John W. Roman—Blackfish P. O.—It is
6 miles S. W. of Tyronza Station on Memphis, Kansas City, & Springfield
R. R.[48]
The owner commenced with little but is now building a good house. There
is plenty arround and a good orchard .—a pleasant man & wife—good
food—clean though poor & without education they show the qualities to

rise in station & wealth. He is a man of true economy—
There are several mounds in the woods in a very isolated place.

———————

NAA 2400

Roman Mounds
Crittenden County Arkensaw
These mounds are on the border of Highland Lake Crittenden Co in the
North West corner of the county on the farm of John W. Roman 6 miles
South West of Tyronza Station on the Memphis Kansas City and Springfield
Rail Road . Hear is 50 mounds varying from 3 feet to 10 high and 20 to
100 feet diameter . They are about 30 to 100 yards appart and found in the
space of about four miles .

The owner possessing many head of Stock did not wish to have the
mounds cut through . but admitted small holes to be dug in the center . As
the country overflows he feared the water would easily penetrate and dis-
troy his mounds they are composed exclusively of black sandy loom . The
examination allowed revealed nothing indicating they had been inhabited .
Except in the two nearest Highland Lake. These are commonly called
cinder Heaps. They are about 4 feet high composed entirely of burnt clay. a
foot or more in thickness—some as light as cinder having the appearance
of Lava[49] *that in the interior was the heaviest*

The examination of these two

Burnt clay pils gave the impression they where once small rounded
toped buildings . . There was numerous impressions of poles sticks & cane
in the mixture with no indication of fire on the outside mass but under-
neath was a thick layer of ashes.[50] *The owner gave permission to open as he*
was going to cart one on top of the other to rais it entirely above overflow
for the safety of his stock . None of the other mounds had any burnt clay in
them .

A dence forest of Timber & cane surrounds the mounds[51]

———————

NAA 2400

John W. Roman.[52] *Highland Lake Ark—*
Blackfish Post Office , Crittenden County Ark , has a fine stone with mor-
tar on each side—he has promised to send it addressed to major J. W.
Powell have told him a letter of acknowledgement woulde sent him

———————

AHC Item 27 (1917:412)

Mounds, Gilmore Station . Chittenden
Co. Ark. 28 miles N.W. of Memphis Tenn.

House sites

1883—
28 miles from Memphis Tenn. on the Kansas City, Springfield & Memphis
R.R. is Gilmore Station. In making the R.R. two small mounds were cut
through. Three others remained but they had been dug into.

The house and gardens of Mrs. Gilmore is on natural high ground &
from which house sights have been ploughed out.
This thrifty farm & cattle ranch was made so by its late owner, who commenced with nothing, by economy & push, he died though young with
plenty.

———————

NAA 2400

Gilmore Mounds
Crittenden   County   Arkansaw
Gilmore Station 28 Miles West of Memphis on the Memphis
Kansas City and Springfield Rail Road . In making this road two mounds
was cut away . Three other mounds remain but had been opened .

The house and garden of Mrs Gilmore are on a naturally formed peice of
ground—from which several house sights have been plowed out

———————

AHC Item 27 (1917:412)

Pacific Place, Chittenden Co.
Ark.

1883.
Captain Charles Morris presents of very fine stone spade for which he is
entitled to the thanks of the Bureau of Ethnology.
Saw his mound collection—He has a very fine farm but a very poor cotton
crop this year—pleasant, old fashioned hospitality. He wants to sell to give
his children advantages of society & & the school.

———————

NAA 2400

Arkensaw
Mound City . Crittenden Co. Ark
*Eight miles up the Miss. River from Memphis is the landing for Mound
City. And one mile from it is. the mounds. The owner was absent was*

informed he would not allow of the large mound being disturbed. As this
section overflows which cause this mound to be the resort for live stock .

Some small mounds near the large one had been cut through in making a
road . leaving fragments of human & animal bones much broaken pottery
and burnt clay scattered about.

Judgeing from the appearance of the country the Mississippa River once
run near the mounds

AHC Item 27 (1917:427)

Scanlon's Landing 12 miles below Memphis, Chittenden Co. Ark.[53]

"Hope They Wil Be Satisfactory": Palmer's Knapp Mounds Measurements, July 1884

MARVIN D. JETER

Palmer's last official act for the Mound Survey in Arkansas was less than impressive. Apparently at Thomas's request, he returned to Little Rock on June 30, 1884, possibly from Washington, where he had arrived in late May (McVaugh 1956:245, 345). He went to the Knapp Mounds on July 1, and proceeded to remeasure the two largest mounds.

We have three versions of the results, and they are rather inconsistent. The first version is in Palmer's own handwriting, accompanied by his rough sketches of the two mounds' outlines. The second version, also in the National Anthropological Archives (but not presented here), is a fairly close scribe's copy of Palmer's original, but it has a few additional measurements and has one of Palmer's sketches attached to it by gummed labels. The third, at the Arkansas History Commission, is by another scribe but has a line at the bottom added by Palmer: "The above are my own measurements."

Yet something went awry in transcription. Neither of Palmer's two most important measurements for the "tall conical" Mound A was matched in the Arkansas scribe's version, which added several other measurements. And, of twelve measurements given in Palmer's original for the "Second Large (square) mound," there are discrepancies in four of the Arkansas scribe's versions.

Palmer stated that his measurements were "according to your plan," presumably referring to Thomas, but they are poorly organized and virtually useless, because he dealt with slope heights without recording slope angles. They were made along sides and slopes denoted by compass readings, such as southwest and northeast; however, it is apparent from his "north arrow" on Lewis's plan view map of this site (fig. 7.49), and from other evidence, that his compass was very inaccurate. At any rate, Thomas was not satisfied with Palmer's results and instead used measurements obtained by Holmes in 1890 (Thomas 1894:244; Rolingson 1982:1, 74).

After finishing this work at the Knapp Mounds, Palmer went again to the Salsertown site near Natchez to make some more measurements. Then he bade the Mound Survey farewell and returned to natural history collecting for Baird. He probably did this with a feeling of relief; as noted by both of his botanical biographers, he found the Mound Survey much more difficult than his principal lines of field work. At any rate, he headed for Florida and a busy period of collecting marine specimens from the Gulf and Caribbean for the upcoming World's Industrial and Cotton Centennial Exposition (December 1884 through June 1885) at New Orleans. His "finely prepared" specimens were well received and took some "65 large shipping cases" to send them to Baird's burgeoning National Museum (McVaugh 1956:88). Palmer's last letter to Thomas, concluding "Leave to morrow by Steamer for Key West," is transcribed at the end of this chapter.

Palmer's July 1884 Documents

AHC Item 29 (1917:426–27)

Knapp Mounds.

July 1–1884—
  Visited the Knapp Mounds on the west side of the Arkansas River[54] and measured the mounds .
I was very kindly entertained by a colored family named Sparks. Color line departs when hunger demands something to eat. They were in position to give it and did not want to charge, but that would not do so paid to my own satisfaction.
  Mr. Knapp had given me a letter to Mr. Sparks.
  There is a way too, that will please, if the intention is at hand .
  Crops are backward because of the late wet spring—
Cotton blooms rare.

——————

NAA 2400

Knapp Mounds
Measured according to your plan
  The tall conical mound of the Knapp Group —
  Circumference at base 743 feet
  Slope height South East side 106 feet
  Slope height S.W. side 108 feet
    See Diagram [fig. 8.2] of this mound the actual base marked 2 to this the measurement was made .
  The mound was built upon a slight rise a road having been cut near the base of the mound some of the earth was removed -thus the mound look as though it stood upon a flat basis is artificially made no 1 represent it
  on the S. E. this base project 47 feet
  on the S. W. " " " 57 " five inches , if this natural base of the mound is to be taken into its measurements then its height wil be very fictitious . its true base is at (2) The N. W. and N. E. slope measurements would not be of use as the base there is changed—the average of the two

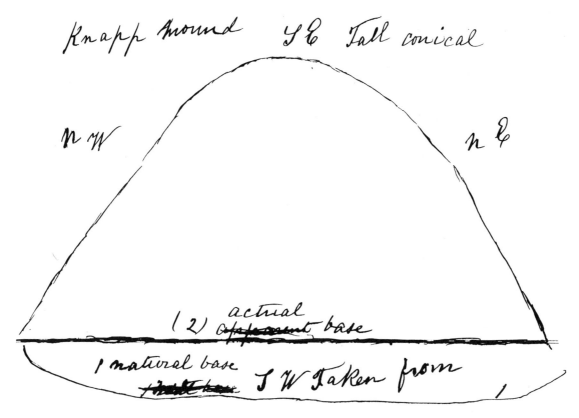

FIGURE 8.2

"Knapp Mound Tall conical" (Profile outline drawing of Mound A) by Edward Palmer, early July 1884. (National Anthropological Archives, Smithsonian Institution.)

> slope heights taken wil I think give the fair lope height of the mound
>> The second or large square mound [fig. 8.3] *of the Knapp group*
>> Length N. W. End *186 feet*
>>> "   S. E. Side *232 feet*
>>> "   N. E. End *192* "
>>> "   S. W. Side *235* " *4 inches*
>> Slope height South East side *71 feet*
>>> "   "   N. E. end *86 feet*. N. W. end same height
>>> "   "   S. W, side *86* "
>> Top measurement same mound
>> Length of N. E. end *71 feet*
>>> "   "   S. W. side *90* " *4 inches*
>>> "   "   N. W. end *76* "
>>> "   "   S. E. side *88* " *8 inches*
>> Diameter   *76 feet* " *5 inches*

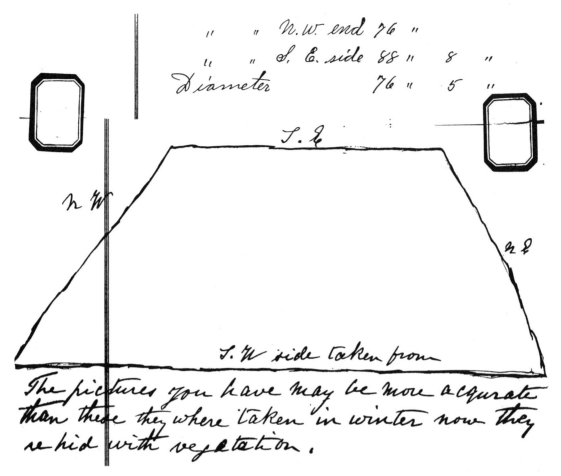

FIGURE 8.3

Profile outline drawing of Knapp Mound B by Edward Palmer, early July 1884.
(National Anthropological Archives, Smithsonian Institution.)

AHC Item 29 (1917:426)

Knapp Mounds—

July 1884—
    Tallest of the mounds is 813 ft. in circumference at the base, The S.E.
slope is 96 ft. with the base of 47 ft.
S.W. Slope is 102 ft.—base 57 ft. 5 inches.
Diameter of top = 50 ft.
Circumference on top 215 ft.
Second Large (square) mound
Length N.W. end = 186 ft.
    "   S. E. side = 213 ft. slope 71 ft.
    "   N.E. end. = 192 ft " height 86 ft.
    "   S. W. side = 213 ft. 4 inches slope 86 ft.
            Top measurements.

Length of N.E. end = 71 ft.
"   S. W. side = 90 ft. 4 inches
"   N.W. end = 76 ft.
                    " S.E. side = 88 ft. 8 inches
Diamter 76 ft. 5 inches .
The above are my own measurements—

————————

NAA BAE Letters

Cedar Keys July 13

Prof Thomas
          Dear Sir
          I forward the measurements you desired taken of the Salser-
town Mound and the two largest of the Knapp Group . with some additional notes . hope they wil be satisfactory—should there be any thing in
my notes needing change let me know and it shall be corrected if possible.
Have met with one Rail Road smash up escaped without injury . Failing to
make Rail Road connections has put me much behind
     Leave to morrow by Steamer for Key West
               Yours truly
               Edward Palmer
               Key West.
                    Florida .

PART THREE

Results

FIGURE 9.1

Page 224 from the May 26, 1883, issue of Frank Leslie's Illustrated Newspaper, *with engravings after Lewis's drawings of Arkansas mounds and related subjects. (Arkansas Archeological Survey Negative No. 872810)*

CHAPTER NINE

Publicity: *The Arkansas Press and* Frank Leslie's

MARVIN D. JETER AND MARY FARMER

For at least twenty-five years, Arkansas archeologists have been aware of the existence of an article entitled "Ancient Mounds in Arkansas," which had appeared in an 1883 issue of *Frank Leslie's Illustrated Newspaper*, a New York weekly with a tabloid format. The article featured a brief summary of Palmer's work in Arkansas, plus engravings of Arkansas mound sites and artifacts from them. In 1962 the University of Arkansas Museum obtained photographs of most of the engravings and a copy of the article's text. After the creation of the Arkansas Archeological Survey in 1967, copies were distributed to the Survey's relevant site files and research stations.

It was not until the 1980 discovery of the Lewis drawings in the Smithsonian's National Anthropological Archives that the originals from which most of the *Leslie's* engravings were made could be examined and compared to them. During the research for this volume, it was also learned that Palmer's explorations received some notice in the Arkansas press.

The Arkansas Press

The earliest mention of either Palmer or Lewis found in the Arkansas press so far is a brief item about Lewis in the *Pine Bluff Commercial* for October 25, 1882. It predates his association with this project and has been transcribed in chapter 2.

The earliest known article about the Mound Survey in Arkansas appeared in the December 5, 1882, issue of the Little Rock *Arkansas Gazette*. Under the heading "Pine Bluff Points" written by a correspondent called "Optic," the following paragraph appeared:

> Mr. Edwin Palmer, of the Smithsonian Institute, returned from Drew County Saturday. Near Tiller Station he uncovered a small mound, situated on Bayou Bartholomew, and exhumed seventy skeletons and about sixty vessels, of all shapes and sizes, such as were used by the mound-builders. They seem to have all been

359

buried at once, and without any system or design, as they were found in one confused heap. The skeletons and pottery, together with numerous sketches of this and other mounds in the vicinity, made by H. J. Lewis, have been forwarded to Washington. (Page 4, Column 5)

"Saturday" would have been December 2, 1882, which agrees perfectly with Palmer's letter to Powell, written in Pine Bluff on that date (see chapter 7). Aside from the exaggeration of the number of vessels, and perhaps of individuals, this is a generally accurate account of the Tillar finds.

Palmer's work was not welcomed by all Arkansawyers, however. On the day after the *Gazette* article appeared, the *Pine Bluff Commercial* featured the following anonymous article, which must have been inspired by the news of Palmer's finds at Tillar:

SAVE THE MOUNDS.

Arkansas is rich in archaeological remains and some provision ought to be made by the state, or by some rich private citizens towards gathering up and preserving these curious and interesting expressions of the past. Remains of monsters of the tertiary period have been found in several places in the western portion of the state. The mound-builders left their gigantic works and graves in our borders, and yet, year by year, these specimens and trophies are being gathered by foreign societies and transported to the large cities in the east where the citizen of this state will doubtless never see them again. These remains are of more value to our people, standing untouched in our midst than can be estimated or conceived of by the mind of the casual beholder. And if preserved, the day is not far distant when their value to our state in an educational and scientific point of view will be a thousand times greater than now. What is the use of building up large museums in Washington and St. Louis at an expense and deprivation of ourselves and from which we can never hope to derive any benefit?

There is now in this state a party of these relic hunters who are tearing to pieces every prominent mound they can find and shipping away the skeletons and patterns [*sic*; probably a misprint for "pottery"] there found. We are opposed to it and urge upon our people to save their mounds for our state museum which must soon be established either by public or private means. (December 6, 1882, page 1, column 2)

The next and last article by the Arkansas press on Palmer's work that has been found by the present research appeared in the *Arkansas Gazette* on January 27, 1883:

ANTIQUITIES FOUND
By an Agent of the Smithsonian Institute,
Near This City.

Dr. J. Palmer, agent of the Smithsonian Institute at Washington, D. C., was in the city a few days ago. While here he visited the Indian mounds on the Knapp place, sixteen miles southeast of the city, and made a more thorough investigation of them than has ever been made. He employed men to excavate the mounds, where they found Indian pottery of all sizes, shapes and states of preservation, arrow heads, and two magnificent crystals, as fine specimens as were ever seen. These were found ten feet below the surface of the earth. With them was found a brass image with the crucifixion on one side, with a Latin inscription below; on the other side was the letter "M." It was supposed to have belonged to more civilized Indians than those of the pottery age. The specimen was sent to the institute. Bones and other curiosities were found which the doctor had boxed up and sent to Washington. He paid a visit to Saline county and other parts of the state, in search of curiosities. His explorations will be of great interest to those who have any love for antiquities. (Page 4, column 2)

As previously noted, this article includes several inaccuracies, including the "association" of the crystals (found in Mound B, according to Palmer's notes) and the medal (from Mound D; cf. also Rolingson 1982:84–85). Also, given the article's emphasis on pottery, it is at least possible that the Knapp finds were conflated with the Tillar finds or donations from Mr. Thibault, whom Palmer had seen on January 20 (cf. also the apparent confusion in the *Leslie's* picture of Palmer, Lewis, and the "Knapp" artifacts; fig. 7.52; Rolingson 1982:74, 83–84).

The Leslie's *Article and Illustrations*

The May 26, 1883, issue of *Leslie's* carried a brief article on Palmer's and Lewis's work on page 222, followed by a full-page layout of nine engravings on page 224. Four of the engravings have already been reproduced above (figs. 7.34, 7.41, 7.48, and 7.52). Here, the entire page is shown (fig. 9.1). The article read as follows (cf. Palmer's notes and the discussions in chapters 6 and 7):

ANCIENT MOUNDS IN ARKANSAS.

The mounds raised long ago by the primitive inhabitants in various parts of the Western and Southern States still engage the attention of American archaeologists. The Smithsonian Institution at Washington devotes much attention to this subject, and Professor Edward Palmer, who has long been in its employ, has during the last year been making explorations in the Southwest, notably in the State of Arkansas. The region bordering the Arkansas River for many miles before its junction with the Mississippi is fruitful of ancient mounds, and the most important of these have been visited by the Professor in his recent trips.

The Knapp mounds are situated in Pulaski County on Mound Lake, about eighteen miles from Little Rock, and three miles from the Arkansas River, being not far from Reed's Landing. Professor Palmer found here a cluster of eight mounds, varying in height from four to one hundred and fifteen feet, the latter being the height of the one represented in the foreground of our illustration. This lofty mound is covered with a forest, which adds to the impressiveness of its appearance. To the left is another mound eighty five feet high, and the others represented in this sketch are thirty-five and twenty-five feet in height. On either side of the largest mound is a basin, which the Professor takes to have been the landing-place for the canoes of the builders. There is a faint outline of a levee running around the mounds and taking in about sixty-six acres, with an average height of about five feet. Many interesting relics were found in these mounds, among which were specimens of pottery of peculiar shape and style, and some unusually large skulls.

The Manard mound, which is near the Manard Bayou, about half a mile from the Arkansas River, in Desha County, resembles a huge pillar, rising almost straight from the surface of the surrounding country to the height of one hundred feet. It is twenty feet in diameter at the top, and seventy at the base, with an appendage on either side, the one twelve and the other twenty-five feet high. The side and top of the lofty mound are clothed with a fine growth of trees.

The Bradley mounds are situated on the Wapponapia, near the Mississippi, and range from five to eighteen feet in height, and are from fifteen to seventy-five feet in diameter at the base. There is here a cluster of five mounds, and a number of interesting relics were found near the base. The pottery appears to be made of clay and mussel-shells beaten up in small pits and mixed together, while the ornaments are of stone. The skulls and bones found in these mounds are remarkably large.

The Taylor mound-field is remarkable for the number grouped together, no less than thirty-seven in all, of which one is twenty-five feet in height and another eighteen, but the rest only from two and a half to five feet. These mounds were uncovered when the farm on which they were situated was opened up, and many interesting discoveries were made.

Professor Palmer had some novel experiences during this expedition, an ox or mule cart being often the only available vehicle. On one occasion, when crossing a bayou called by the sweet-smelling name of Skunk, the mule balked and fell in midstream, and after the driver had cut the animal free, the scientist and his associate had to tug the cart with its load of relics to dry land by hard pulling on a rope attached to the shafts. Professor Palmer entered upon archaeological work in 1867, and has visited all the principal mounds in the United States, besides exploring a number in Mexico.

The sketches which we present were made by the Professor's assistant, H. J. Lewis, a remarkably bright colored man, thirty years old, who was born a slave in Mississippi, and never had a day's schooling in his life, but has educated himself, and without any instruction has developed very promising ability as an artist.

In the best tabloid style, the *Leslie's* presentation seizes the reader's interest with sensational illustrations and leads the unwary toward romantic conjectures. The first site description, of the Knapp Mound, closes with remarks about "pottery of peculiar shape and style" and "unusually large skulls." The next, of the Menard Mound, emphasizes the impossibly steep "pillar," alleged to be one hundred feet high and only seventy feet across at the base. The third, of the Bradley Mound, returns to the theme of "remarkably large" skulls and bones. The last, of the Taylor Mound, merely closes with a vague reference to "many interesting discoveries."

Lurking behind all of this is the old theory of a lost race of non-Indian Mound-Builders. Indians are never mentioned in the article, although it does begin with a reference to "primitive inhabitants." Neither are Mound-Builders, although in the Knapp paragraph there is a reference to the "canoes of the builders." The main allusion to the lost race notion is that of unusually large skeletal remains (modern archeologists still occasionally hear such allegations from relic collectors, but the evidence somehow never materializes).

Two other aspects of this article are worth some brief comment. The episode about Skunk Bayou is nowhere mentioned in any of Palmer's surviving documents, although Palmer seems to have enjoyed recording his trials and tribulations in the field. An intensive effort to find such a stream, by focusing on old and modern maps of the localities visited by Palmer and Lewis, has been unsuccessful. This is not to conclude that the *Leslie's* writer made the incident up out of whole cloth, but it is possible. The function of a tabloid, after all, is as much to entertain as to inform.

Finally, the description of Lewis as "a remarkably bright colored man" in this New York publication simply reminds us that blithely unconscious (or semi-conscious) racism has never been confined to Arkansas or the South.

CHAPTER TEN

Aftermaths, Retrospects, and Prospects

The Mound Exploration Division really started winding down its overall field activities after 1886. In the specific case of Arkansas, Smith's table 1.2 shows that after Palmer left the project in mid-1884 (and effectively in late 1883, as far as this state is concerned), four other assistants worked between July 1884 and June 1885.

No detailed studies have been made of the notes and collections made by these other field assistants in Arkansas, but it is known that they concentrated their efforts in northeast Arkansas. For example, Norris followed Palmer at Tyronza Station, and Middleton worked extensively from a base at Jonesboro. They did venture into other parts of the state; Middleton's correspondence with Thomas indicates that he worked on the Ouachita River above and below Camden in March 1884 but was flooded out. His findings of Caddoan materials at the Piles Plantation (now known as the Kent site, 3OU6, not to be confused with the Kent site, 3LE8, near the mouth of the St. Francis), just north of Camden, represent the project's southernmost significant findings in the Arkansas portion of this valley (Thomas 1894:248–50). He also went as far southwest as the Red River valley in Miller County, near Texarkana, but his report of a mound site there was only catalogued (Thomas 1891:20), and no report on that county was made in Thomas's final report. As Smith's map (figure 1.6) indicates, the project was effectively concentrated in eastern Arkansas.

Little was done by the project in Arkansas after June 1885, and nothing after June 1886. However, in selected other portions of the country, work continued. During 1884 Thomas began to home in on the potentials of working in the Cherokee homeland of eastern Tennessee to establish a definitive connection between mounds and ethnohistorically documented Indians. Assistant J. W. Emmert, from Thomas's home town of Kingsport, Tennessee, worked productively in the Little Tennessee Valley from 1884 to 1889. During the final fiscal year of field work (ending in mid-1890), the last regular field assistant, Henry Reynolds, worked in five widely scattered states, and two others did limited work in Louisiana, a state that was definitely underrepresented because of the cluster-sampling strategy.

Publications

Ultimately, an archeological project is known by its fruits, in the form of publications. In this case, the process of publication began early. Holmes (1883) included some of Palmer's 1881 Tennessee finds in his study of ancient art in shell in the Bureau's *Second Annual Report*. The next year he described and illustrated the project's 1881 mound and artifact findings, with emphasis on Palmer's work in Tennessee and Arkansas, in the *Third Annual Report* (Holmes 1884). Again, in the *Fourth Annual Report* (Holmes 1886b), he essayed a preliminary synthesis of Mississippi Valley pottery, using some of Palmer's Arkansas materials. Only of trivial historical interest is Palmer's "Burnt Clay in the Mounds" note (1885), in which he once again misinterpreted the prehistoric structures of the Mississippi Valley on the basis of his mistaken analogy with Southwestern Pueblos.

Cyrus Thomas himself began publishing abstracts and brief notes in journals as early as 1883 and kept this up fairly steadily over the next decade (Brown and Williams 1980). His first major publication derived from this project, though, was "Burial Mounds of the Northern Sections of the United States" (Thomas 1887), in the *Fifth Annual Report*. This was followed by "The Problem of the Ohio Mounds" (Thomas 1889a), published as the Bureau's *Bulletin* 8, and "The Circular, Square, and Octagonal Earthworks of Ohio" (Thomas 1889b), published as *Bulletin* 10. Next came the "Catalogue of Prehistoric Works East of the Rocky Mountains" (Thomas 1891), published as *Bulletin* 12, followed by his *magnum opus* in the *Twelfth Annual Report*, the final 740-page "Report on the Mound Explorations of the Bureau of Ethnology" (Thomas 1894).

Thomas's final report was reprinted by the Smithsonian Institution in 1985, in a paperback edition which I have reviewed (Jeter 1986b). The report's coverage reflects several factors, including a general descriptive typology of mounds and other earthworks, availability of comparative ethnohistorical data, Thomas's own background, and perhaps choices made by Palmer. In terms of space allotted, the most intensively covered area was in fact east Tennessee, with some fifty-six pages, beginning with Sullivan County, where Thomas was born and raised, but emphasizing the Cherokee country. Next is Ohio, with fifty-three pages, emphasizing the Hopewell earthworks and summarizing Thomas's *Bulletin* 10 discussion (but not that of *Bulletin* 8, wherein he attributed the ancient Ohio works to the ancestors of the Cherokees); close behind, in a virtual third-place tie with fifty-two pages each, are Wisconsin (especially depicting the "effigy mounds") and Arkansas.

The great Mississippian and other mounds of Arkansas would probably have rated a fair amount of coverage in any event. It should be recalled, though, that before the project ever started in the field, Baird asked Palmer for a suggestion of a likely state for exploration, and Palmer apparently suggested Arkansas. It also seems likely that Lewis may have influenced Palmer to visit the southeast Arkansas localities near Lewis's home in Pine Bluff.

Despite the presence of numerous mounds, Louisiana only got three pages of coverage in the final report. It may have been believed that the Arkansas coverage adequately represented the types of mounds that Louisiana had to offer, although we now know that significant cultural differences were present during most of prehistory (cf. Phillips 1970). Another neighboring state, Mississippi, got some twenty-five pages of coverage, most of it in the Mississippi Valley. The intensive work done by the Lower Mississippi Survey in the Yazoo Basin makes it clear that much more mound work could have been done here, too (Phillips, Ford and Griffin 1951; Phillips 1970; Williams and Brain 1983). Perhaps flooding was a factor in both Mississippi and Louisiana.

In his final chapter, Thomas (1894:595–730) first cleared the air with a critical discussion of the various lost race theories, unwarranted assumptions, circular reasoning, and fraudulent finds. (Some of this material repeated verbatim his statements in the *Fifth Annual Report*.) He then systematically demonstrated that, when first contacted if not later, the Indians of the various eastern U.S. regions resembled the Mound-Builders (insofar as the latter's lifeways could be inferred from the Division's investigations), in terms of subsistence, settlement patterns, house construction, artifacts, burial customs, and not only the use but also the construction of mounds.

Thomas's discussions suffer mainly from lack of chronological control, and some of his arguments now seem strained or even dead wrong. But the subsequent century of archeological research has clearly sustained his main conclusions and bolstered them with great improvements in recovery and analytical techniques. He emerged from it all as the quintessential organizer, big-picture synthesizer, and hard-nosed doer and finisher. It was a remarkable performance by a man who had come into the project believing in the Mound-Builder myth (Willey and Sabloff 1974:49). As previously noted, he did not rest on these laurels but went on to outstanding achievements in Mesoamerican archeology.

Thomas's final report did not conclude the use of Mound Survey data by Bureau archeologists. As he stated in his preface (1894:19, 25), he downplayed analyses of the artifacts, deferring this task to the work of other specialists. Bureau reports that dealt with the two major artifact classes, lithics and ceramics, eventually appeared but did not restrict themselves to the Division's collections.

The least satisfactory is Fowke's "Stone Art" (1896), which appeared in the *Thirteenth Annual Report*. As Palmer had complained to Safford, his and other collections were used "without indication of the exact locality of their origin" (Safford 1926:480–81). Fowke generally provided provenience information only in terms of counties or "districts," remarking that "space would be needlessly occupied by attempting to name each county" (1896:60).

Much more significant is Holmes's "Aboriginal Pottery of the Eastern United States" (1903), which appeared in the *Twentieth Annual Report*. Although it was originally intended to accompany Thomas's 1894 final report, its publication was delayed and its scope was expanded to include not only the Division's collections but also some of those of the Peabody Museum, the Davenport Academy, the Academy of Natural Sciences of Philadelphia (from the recently begun explorations of C. B. Moore), and others (Holmes 1903:15–16). It is also lacking in specific provenience information but, unlike Fowke's study, makes up for this by presenting an effective synthesis of large-scale geographic patterning. It was in this work that the term "Middle Mississippi" first gained widespread archeological usage (1903:21, 80–104), evolving into the names of the Mississippian culture and the Mississippian culture period.

This study, in effect, ended the Bureau's work on the Mound Survey, some twenty-two years after the project had begun. The major publications had already turned to an emphasis on various other aspects of ethnology under Powell (see Judd 1967:78 for a listing), and as he left the scene this trend was increased under the influence of Franz Boas and the weaker administration of Holmes (Hinsley 1981:265–85). Archeology continued to be done and reported under the Bureau's auspices, but it was done in other areas for other reasons (cf. Judd 1967:78).

Although C. B. Moore continued to ply the Southern waters in his productive search for relics for his Philadelphia Academy, no real progress beyond Thomas's and Holmes's findings was made in and near Arkansas until the 1930s. At that time, James A. Ford and his associates, including Winslow Walker of the Bureau, and later Gordon Willey, Philip Phillips, and James B. Griffin, began to make relative chronological sense out of the artifacts and the mounds (Ford 1935, 1936; Ford and Willey 1940, 1941; Phillips, Ford, and Griffin 1951; Walker 1936).

Palmer's Contributions

As McVaugh emphasized (1956:11–12), Edward Palmer was simply not in the same league intellectually with the likes of Baird, Powell, Thomas, and Holmes, or his botanical and natural history patrons. He was first and foremost a man who for some reason had "a liking for travel and strange places" rather than any love of collecting for its own sake (1956:5–6). Another strong motivation was clearly his devotion to his own ideal of contributing to science, as expressed in his first letter of June 13, 1855, to Joseph Henry. As Hinsley has emphasized, "Movement was the key to Palmer and his science" (1981:71).

Palmer as Archeologist

McVaugh's (1956:85) assessment that Palmer "had neither the strength for excavation nor the patience and technical skill required for the meticulous dismemberment of the mounds" is accurate as far as it goes, but more should be said. It has already been seen that, at the beginning of the Mound Survey, Palmer was at the very front rank of archeological field workers in the Americas, having done pioneering work in Arizona, Utah, Maine, Mexico, and Texas. Unlike the other permanent field assistants, who were basically Midwesterners and Tennesseans, he had worked in areas where Native Americans were still practicing at least some of their traditional lifeways. As Meltzer has remarked about some of the Bureau's major figures,

> Most BAE archaeologists had earned their scientific credentials on geological and natural history expeditions to the deep canyons and vast Plains of the American West. . . . The result was an innovative and highly nationalistic archaeology, with the American Indian as its centerpiece. BAE archaeologists, who had encountered first-hand surviving American Indians, brought the knowledge gained in that encounter to their archaeology. In the BAE, American archaeology was but one aspect of a holistic study of the American Indian. (1985:251)

While Palmer probably could not have expressed this very well, he nevertheless tried to put it into practice in his Mound Survey work. But, like many if not most archeologists, Palmer arrived on the scene a century or two too late. The Quapaw, Caddo, and Tunicans were long gone from Arkansas when he arrived at the remains of their sites.

This is unfortunate, for here was a man whose real strength was in recording the lifeways and in-context material culture of living Native Americans, especially their uses of plants. He had done this over and over again in the Southwest, Great Basin, California, and Mexico with outstanding success in description, if not always in interpretation. He had also done some work along these lines among the Cherokees remaining in western North Carolina at the very beginning of the Mound Survey, again with notable success. And, after effectively closing his Arkansas field work, he made a few ethnological collections from Choctaws near Mobile, Alabama (McVaugh 1956:255). But in Arkansas he had to content himself with conjectures and analogies, some of them inappropriate.

He misinterpreted the details of house construction by carrying ethnographic analogy much too far, but at least he recognized that he was encountering the ruins of the upper portions of houses, over ashes and other materials on the floors, and then the hearths and floors themselves. He even recognized instances of superimposed houses, both in his western work and at sites such as Tyronza Station. Such recognition is not always automatic, even in supposedly more enlightened times (cf. Flannery 1976:13–23).

Where Palmer—and virtually all of his contemporaries—fell far short of modern archeological field techniques was in the establishment of horizontal and vertical controls. While it is true that reports are written about the mounds, houses, pits, and other prehistoric features and their associated materials rather than about grid systems, nevertheless grids are necessary as organizing devices for good field notes. Palmer was especially deficient in all aspects of quantitative control, from compass directions to distance measurements to height estimates. His notes are fair to good for their day in qualitative terms (recognition of kinds of features, or at least different kinds of deposits), but generally dreadful when they come to numbers—if they come to them at all.

More should also be said about stratigraphy. Although the real stratigraphic revolution in American archeology did not occur until about 1914 (Willey and Sabloff 1974: 88), Palmer and some of his more illustrious colleagues were at least aware of stratigraphy, probably through their contacts with geologists. As seen earlier, Baird's letter of April 12, 1881, to Palmer, based in part on discussions with Powell, suggested that Palmer should make "diagrams illustrating the relative positions of the relics, & of the different strata,—being careful to note their relation to the remains you may detect." Palmer did this much more in terms of notes than in diagrams, though. The only explicitly stratigraphic diagram produced by his Arkansas work is in Lewis's "Plate 3" (fig. 7.37) in the Menard series.

Palmer and the Arkansas Scene

From Palmer's first foray into the field, the expedition from Osceola to Pemiscot Bayou in late October 1881, we are in the company of a man who has pronounced opinions about right and wrong and at least an understated sense of humor (despite allegations to the contrary; McVaugh 1956:11). There are two major threads that hold his nonarcheological comments together: the work ethic and a general sense of racial justice.

Palmer's basic attitudes toward hard work, thrift, and other virtues must have been formed in his English homeland of Norfolk. They were deeply ingrained and stayed with him throughout a long and productive life. A number of both negative and positive comments that he made about the Arkansas scene of the 1880s were derived from this source. Over and again, he deplored idleness, drunkenness, and slothfulness, not to mention incompetence as manifested by bad hotels and worse meals. He also had some feelings against "progress" in its destructive aspects, as seen in his November 1, 1882, comment at the new town of Cherry Valley: "a fine timber country but they are getting ready to waste it."

On the other hand, he was willing to praise hard work, enterprise, and general competence. Examples of people starting with little and building good lives for themselves clearly appealed to him, as did the "hotel kept by colored men—very good fare & lodging" at Newport in late October 1883. There are also occasional wistful comments by this bachelor traveler about happy home life, as in the case of Mr. Thibault and his harmonious family or in the "pleasant, old fashioned hospitality" of Captain Morris and his family at Pacific Landing.

As for the race question, Palmer would have had little in the way of direct contact with blacks or Indians in his native England. But his first real employment in America probably gave him his basic orientation. He worked in Cleveland from 1849 to 1852 as an attendant to the crippled former Speaker of the House, John W. Taylor, who had been active in the anti-slavery movement. When the Civil War broke out, Palmer apparently felt strongly enough about some of the issues involved to leave far-away California and join the Union Army. After the war, in the Southwest in 1869, he was briefly associated with Vincent Colyer, a humanitarian who helped the causes of black soldiers and Indians. Whatever other influences may have affected Palmer, the result was an attitude of basic sympathy for blacks, but an ambivalent attitude toward Indians.

Palmer's Arkansas Delta experiences must have involved him in some of his most frequent and closest contacts with blacks and with white-black relationships. Again and again, his notes (although apparently not his speech or actions) deplore incidents of injustice to blacks. Although he referred to "darkies" on a couple of occasions and reported the use of the place name "Nigger Hill" in the White River valley, his own basic terms of reference were "colored," "black," or "negro." His employment of Lewis and their obvious good relationships, which may have extended beyond Lewis's official dismissal, speak for themselves.

Palmer's attitudes toward Indians are perhaps more complex. He did not contact living Indians in his Arkansas mound work, but his ideas about them are relevant to understanding some aspects of that work. His basic relationship toward Indians, living or dead, was that of a collector obtaining specimens. At least some of the time, he had a curious air of detachment from them as living, full-fledged humans, as evidenced by the incidents in Paraguay and the Apache country (McVaugh 1956:11, 30). He seems to have ignored his Indian patients to concentrate on collecting specimens in Oklahoma and to have infuriated them enough to have brought about a plot to kill him, but his life may have been saved by another Indian named Black Beaver (McVaugh 1956:36–37).

Palmer definitely believed in some kind of cultural-evolutionary "stage" scheme, perhaps influenced in his later years by the savagery-barbarism-civilization sequence of Lewis Henry Morgan (1877), which John Wesley Powell accepted (Hinsley 1981:133–40). However, it seems that his may have been a rather static two-stage scheme as applied to

Indians, a dichotomy between relatively civilized (or at worst, upper barbaric) "Toltecs" and relatively savage (or at best, lower barbaric) "Aztecs" (Palmer 1877b).

Despite this explanatory effort, Palmer was not really a theoretically oriented anthropologist. He was a collector who had grown up on the rural agricultural outskirts of Victorian civilization and was unable to overcome the "culture shock" of contact with Indian hunter-gatherers to the extent that John Wesley Powell, who had seen Indians camping near his Wisconsin childhood farm, did. He appears to have made a clear-cut contrast between the hunter-gatherers and the settled Indian agriculturalists and included it within the already extant Aztec-Toltec dichotomy, flavored by his English dislike for the Spanish and his willingness to doubt the significance of the Spanish conquest of the Aztecs. The ultimate result of all this, as far as Arkansas archeology is concerned, may have been the misnomer of the "Toltec" site. Another of Palmer's biases appears to have been in favor of Indian women, whom he regarded as generally industrious, and against Indian men, in whom he found less evidence of the work ethic.

With regard to blacks, though, it is likely that Palmer saw them as people who had been unjustly enslaved, freed by one means or another, and were now part of (or trying to gain admission to) American civilization. Here there was no relationship of collector and source of specimens. Instead, for Palmer there were the myriad relationships of people, some of whom happened to be black, in various occupations, within various levels of contemporary American society. In reading through the late 1880s and early 1890s issues of *The Freeman*, the "national colored illustrated newspaper" that Lewis worked for in Indianapolis, a modern reader would be struck not by a "black" style, but by a Victorian style of expression. Equal opportunity and full participation in American-Victorian society were clearly the ideals expressed in that paper and in Lewis's editorial cartoons for it, and Palmer was clearly in sympathy with such ideals. Perhaps his observations of situations and incidents and his reactions to them will be of some interest to students of Arkansas race relations.

Palmer, the Mound Survey, and Modern Arkansas Archeology

"Save the Mounds"

A point of departure for connecting Palmer's Mound Survey work to modern archeology in Arkansas is provided by the *Pine Bluff Commercial* article of December 6, 1882, which was transcribed in chapter 9. The article, headlined "Save the Mounds," was inspired by Palmer's work at Tillar and protested against "relic hunters who are tearing to pieces every prominent mound . . . and shipping away the skeletons and [pottery] there found." The writer called upon the people of Arkansas to "save their mounds for our state museum which must soon be established. . . ."

Palmer and his crews were indeed gutting sites by their excavations, which, from a modern (or even a 1930s) archeological standpoint, were very inadequately controlled. But, by the archeological standards of a century ago, Palmer was doing about as well as anyone else and even doing some innovative things, such as saving—in addition to the whole pots—items such as potsherds, lithic materials, fragments of burnt daub and floors, human and animal bones, and plant materials and keeping fairly detailed if not always clear and accurate records. The Mound Survey destroyed mounds, or portions of them, but at least preserved information about them.

As Palmer repeatedly noted, even then the sites were being ravaged by real relic hunters who, like today's, robbed the Indian graves and mounds of their contents and kept no records at all. The haul of Arkansas artifacts by these uncontrolled diggers—who often sell their finds to out-of-state or foreign collectors—dwarfs the combined well-documented collections of museums or other institutions made by painstaking professional and amateur archeologists. And, even though some of these artifacts, such as Palmer's, are removed to "foreign" institutions such as the Smithsonian, at least they are curated there in perpetuity and are ultimately accessible for study by archeologists or for exhibit to the general public. A number of Palmer's Arkansas artifacts have in fact been on exhibit at the Smithsonian before and during the period of research for this volume, and the Smithsonian does loan such artifacts to other museums for exhibits.

Analyses of Mound Survey Collections

The study of Palmer's and other collections made by Mound Survey agents in Arkansas has been quite limited but does have definite potentials. A major factor has been the simple one of physical distance; another has been that of the difficulty of dealing with old records and questionable proveniences. Yet it is possible to decipher Palmer's notes enough to correct some past misinterpretations as to site locations and even to find some intra-site provenience information.

The first real reuse of Palmer's collections was by Philip Phillips in his 1940–41 study of the Menard site; this was followed by Ford's (1961:160–66) more intensive restudy. The next opportunity for new reanalyses came at the January 1980 conference at the Smithsonian, when five Arkansas Survey archeologists and a number of others gathered on the eve of the centennial of the founding of the Mound Exploration Division. Two brief single-site studies based on that experience have been published (Jeter 1981; Rolingson 1982:71–86), clearly demonstrating the potentials of more detailed work. Palmer's collections and notes have also been used in a culture-historical synthesis and a methodological study (Jeter 1986a, 1989).

Mound and Site Destruction

How have the mounds and other sites been "saved" during the past century? Not very well. In one study, Ford and Rolingson (1972:28) reported that eighty-five percent of the known mounds in southeast Arkansas had been totally or substantially destroyed (1972:28). More recently, W. Fredrick Limp studied the Arkansas Archeological Survey's AMASDA data base, which indicated that "only 8% of the state's mounds are not damaged. Conversely, 68% have either major damage or are destroyed" (1987:17). His study took in many areas that had not been subjected to intensive construction and agricultural land-leveling, accounting for the difference from the earlier study, which was dominated by Delta farmlands. Limp also found that more than fifty percent of all known sites in northeast Arkansas have been largely or totally destroyed (1987:7).

The agents of destruction have by no means been confined to agriculture, construction, and natural processes such as erosion. All over Arkansas, mound and burial sites have been ravaged over the years and decades by recreational and commercial relic collectors, and the process has intensified in recent years. Sites are being leased and "mined" by commercial operators using heavy machinery (House 1987:48–49), as the value of artifacts soars on the national and international antiquities markets.

Public Archeology

In the face of this assault, professional archeologists have looked increasingly to the public for support. The Arkansas Archeological Society, an organization of professionals and amateurs, was founded in 1960. Its members were instrumental in the passage of a state antiquities law and the legislation that established the Arkansas Archeological Survey in 1967. The Survey's director, Charles R. McGimsey III, called national and international attention to the activities of the Society and Survey with his book, *Public Archeology* (1972). Scheibel and Early have summarized the first fifteen years of professional-amateur cooperation in Arkansas, focusing on the amateur certification program and the annual Society/Survey Summer Dig and training session (1982:310). The 1989 program at the Toltec (Knapp) Mounds was the twenty-seventh consecutive one and, like its recent predecessors, attracted well over one hundred participants and a great deal of favorable public attention.

Arkansas Museums

As for "our state museum which must soon be established," more than a century later it still has not been established. The enduring problem has been that despite its universally acknowledged archeological richness, Arkansas has been and is a poor state, and the establishment of such a museum has never been a high-priority item. This niche has been filled to some extent by the University of Arkansas Museum in Fayetteville.

The *Commercial's* 1882 outcry against the removal of Arkansas artifacts to distant cities and institutions was echoed a half-century later by Samuel C. Dellinger (1892–1973), the first director of the University Museum, with his famous remark about such institutions "skimming off the cream" of Arkansas archeology. Phillips, Ford, and Griffin (1951:40) replied that "the cream . . . had long ago been skimmed" by the pot hunters. During the late 1920s and 1930s, Dellinger's crews excavated numerous sites, not only in the northwest Arkansas Ozarks near the Museum, but also in northeast Arkansas, the Arkansas Valley, and (under WPA auspices) the Ouachita Valley (Jeter 1989). Many museum-quality specimens were obtained and kept in Arkansas. In recent years the University Museum occupied a rather out-of-the-way location on the third floor of one of the Fayetteville dormitories, but it finally was moved to a former field house in the middle of the campus, with more accessible exhibit space, in 1986.

The Arkansas Archeological Survey and Arkansas State Parks have also partially fulfilled this function, with exhibits at various university campus museums and parks around the state. The crown jewel of the system, of course, is the cooperative Survey/Parks program at Toltec Mounds State Park (Palmer's Knapp Mounds), which is in effect a combined indoor and outdoor museum, with occasional opportunities for participation by the general public in the Society/Survey Summer Digs, which have also been conducted at other State Parks and elsewhere.

A Retrospect and Prospect

Hinsley has summarized the early Smithsonian's anthropology as "leaving us finally with only rich images to ponder," such as "Palmer, fifty years old, after thirty years in the field, digging unnoticed in the mounds of Tennessee and Arkansas . . . " (1981:77). At least, we have noticed—and pondered.

Some of us literally, and others literarily, have walked a few miles along Palmer's and Lewis's trails. At the end of this particular trail, we might pause for a moment and think about what our efforts at "preserving the past for the future" (the Survey's motto) will look like in another century.

Notes

Chapter 6

1. Big Lake is widely (and wrongly) believed to have been formed by the 1811–12 New Madrid earthquake. Geologists and archeologists say it developed around A.D. 800, as a result of riverine processes (Morse and Morse 1983:9). It is now the site of a national wildlife refuge and an Arkansas wildlife management area.

2. While working in this same region for the Mound Survey in 1882, Col. P. W. Norris contracted malaria, which ultimately led to his death (Perttula and Price 1984:11).

3. For a humorous account of a comparable reaction to WPA archeological research in north Georgia in the 1930s, see Wauchope (1966:xiv-xv).

4. The Chickasawba Mound is actually only about 150 meters (or 500 feet) from Pemiscot Bayou. This entry should have said "north of Osceola," to which Palmer had returned before setting out for Chickasawba; in fact, he did say "24 miles North of Oseola" in his monthly report filed on December 6, 1881. The airline distance from Osceola is about seventeen miles.

5. Both figures are greater than the mound's present size, especially the top area.

6. These "water vessels" could only have been bottles, a diagnostic Mississippian vessel form. In the monthly report, Palmer only called them two pieces of pottery but did refer to their necks, implying that they were indeed bottles.

7. Unskilled Chinese laborers were brought into the Delta country of Arkansas, Mississippi, and Louisiana during the 1870s and 1880s, to replace freed slaves on the plantations, but the experiment was a failure. Most of these Chinese left Arkansas after a few years for the west coast or China (Tsai 1981). Palmer's notes also speak of the hiring of young Irish women and German men as replacement laborers.

8. Palmer returned to Pecan Point in July (and possibly October) 1882 and thanked Mrs. McGavock for a contribution (see chapter 7).

9. This would have been a bottle of the Nodena Red and White type, which dates to the Late Mississippi and Protohistoric periods (Phillips 1970:141–44).

10. These depressions and elevations may instead have been partly filled pits and eroded backdirt piles from relic hunters' digging, although Palmer should have been able to recognize such evidence.

11. The 1811–12 New Madrid earthquakes did not involve a volcano in the usual sense of above-ground ash and lava, but did include "vented-sand volcano" activity (Saucier 1989:104).

12. The scribe's version (published in Palmer 1917:410) says "50 feet across," which if taken literally would result in a circumference slightly over 150 feet.

13. The scribe's version adds the comment, "Probably some of the pieces may belong to some of the other bundles from this mound." As noted in chapter 5, the 1917 publication presented this entry in a way that made the specimen numbers appear to be counts of bundles.

14. This curious specimen number was entered, then lined out on the scribe's copy, and was not followed by any descriptive summary comments.

15. Dr. Lindsley also presented Palmer with "8 fine potts" for the Smithsonian in July 1882; see chapter 7.

16. This and the next two specimen numbers are entered in the margins, in Palmer's handwriting, in his report manuscript. The present transcription brings them into the text for clarity.

17. The scribe's version indicates that there were four crania (or packages of crania, which still might mean only four skulls).

18. The scribe's version indicates that there were five stones or packages of stone artifacts.

19. Here, Palmer exaggerated slightly. William Penn established Philadelphia in 1682, following a previous settlement in that vicinity by Delaware Swedes.

20. Thomas Nuttall (1786–1859) was a pioneering naturalist whose *A Journal of Travels into the Arkansa* [sic] *Territory, During the Year 1819* (1821; reprinted 1966) is a valuable and readily available resource for modern students of the early American settlement of Arkansas. On the pages cited by Palmer, Nuttall's text is essentially the same as the version given here by Palmer, who made only a few minor changes.

21. Peter Kalm (1716–1779), a Swedish clergyman and naturalist, traveled in the northeastern United States and adjacent Canada from 1748 to 1751. He had frequent personal contacts with Benjamin Franklin. His *Travels* were originally published in Swedish in three volumes, 1753–61; an English translation appeared in 1770–71, and a French translation, which Palmer could possibly have seen (and misunderstood?) was published in Canada in 1880 (Benson 1937:viii–xi).
    Whichever source he used, Palmer clearly misrepresented Kalm here. In 1749 Kalm had interviewed a ninety-one-year-old descendant of the earliest Delaware Swedes. After noting that "during the younger years of this old man, the Indians were everywhere in the country" (Benson 1937:268), Kalm stated, "As to their religion the old man thought it very trifling, and even believed that they had none at all" (1937:270).

22. During his return visit to Menard, Palmer estimated the height of Mound A as seventy feet, with other measurements also not in agreement with the first impressions given here. Thomas, perhaps attempting a weighted average of Palmer's figures, stated that the mound was, "according to Dr. Palmer's measurement, fifty feet high" (1894:229). Moore gave the height of this mound as only 34.5 feet (1908:487). Ford listed it as 35 feet (1961:148), and quoted the unpublished 1941 manuscript by Phillips which described Palmer's reports as "remarkably confusing and contradictory" (Ford 1961:160).

23. Phillips (quoted by Ford 1961:160) stated that the cross had been kept for many years by a member of the Menard family, but that it had been lost, possibly during a fire.

24. A perceptive comment by Palmer. Holmes (1884:476–77) listed thirty-six bowls as having come from this cache and also noted their differences from those found with burials, but Thomas (1894:229–31) did not comment on them. He did, however, publish two paragraphs of summary "remarks" by Palmer about the site in general and this find in particular.

   In his 1941 manuscript, Phillips echoed Palmer and Holmes by stating, "We have, then, an indication that there was on the site a special class of pottery, differing not only in type from the prevailing mortuary ware, but also differing in its manner of occurrence" (quoted by Ford 1961:161). Ford examined twenty-seven of the vessels and concluded that all fourteen decorated specimens "conform to one type, Wallace Incised. For some reason, this type is missing from Palmer's, and Clarence B. Moore's, as well as our cemetery collections" (1961:163). He went on to speculate about possible relationships to protohistoric Oneota pottery of the upper Mississippi Valley and possible Caddoan and Mexican connections.

   However, I would contend that there are close relationships, and even overlaps, between Wallace Incised and varieties of an indigenous type, Winterville Incised, which is very common in adjacent regions south of the Arkansas River. Indeed, by the sorting criteria of Brown (1978b:16), most of the so-called Wallace vessels illustrated by Ford (1961:Figures 11, 12) would have to be classed as Winterville Incised (cf. *var. Belzoni*), because their decorations are on the body rather than the rim. Also, Winterville-Wallace vessels have been found with burials, at the Kinkead-Mainard site on the Arkansas River above Little Rock (Hoffman 1977: Figures 5:9A, 6:45B, 9:33A, 33B, 10:54C, 11:44A) and at three sites in the Saline River valley of southeast Arkansas: Gee's Landing (3DR17; White 1970: Figures 6k, 9b, 9f, 9k), Gordon (3AS152; White 1987:40, 48, Figure 27b), and Fraser (3BR40; Jeter, notes on file at AAS-UAM station).

25. Here, an insertion by Palmer, possibly reading "with anything that [illegible]," was heavily lined out by the unknown editor.

26. Ford stated that "the classification in many instances must remain in some doubt, for the vessels have been reconstructed by the assembling of sherds from different vessels and fitting them by drastic trimming of the edges. Even where the fragments appear to have come from the same vessel, they appear to have been misfitted so that the design is thoroughly scrambled" (1961:161). He illustrated several examples (1961: Figures 11d, 11f, 12a, 12b).

   Safford quoted a communication from Palmer that expressed dissatisfaction with Thomas's practice of having Palmer's shipping cases opened before Palmer could return from the field and help with the cataloging (1926:480–81). In the same quotation, however, Palmer spoke approvingly of the "admirable paper" that Holmes had published in 1884 on these 1881 collections. Also, Palmer does not seem to have complained about Baird's letter of December 3, 1881, which spoke of unpacking Palmer's boxes.

27. This probably refers to small, hollow ceramic effigy heads of animals, broken off the rims of effigy bowls, which are fairly common on Quapaw phase sites. Ford illustrated one such vessel from Palmer's Menard collection (1961: Figure 13d), several from Moore's collections from Menard and Old River Landing (1961: Figures 15, 16, 18), and several broken-off heads from his own excavations (1961: Plate 25a–h).

   Palmer's field specimen number "134" given here for these items is out of sequence and incorrect, as it was already used at Pecan Point. It is repeated incorrectly in the NAA "2400" file scribe's copy of this report but was corrected to "139" in the scribe's copy that found its way to Arkansas. That version was published on pages 446–47 of the 1917 volume.

28. Compare an example to the contrary found at the Tillar site by Palmer himself in late November 1882 (Jeter 1981; see chapter 7).

29. Various burial positions have been found at Menard and other Quapaw phase sites (Moore 1908; Ford 1961:156, Table 3; Hoffman 1977).

30. John R. Maxwell was described by Goodspeed (1890:660–61) as a native of Arkansas County, born in 1829, who had attained the rank of captain in the Confederate army and subsequently farmed for a year before starting a mercantile business. He was said to be "a leading merchant of De Witt," nearly twenty miles due north of Arkansas Post, and to be "recognized as one of the most influential men of this locality."

31. Edward Foreman (1808–1885) was a medical doctor and college professor who became a "meticulous" museum naturalist. He recorded some forty-five thousand incoming specimens at the Smithsonian from 1867 to 1884, often making careful drawings (Hinsley 1981:71–77). Unfortunately, he does not seem to have made any drawings of Palmer's Mound Survey specimens.

32. Control of eastern Arkansas changed hands frequently during the Civil War. The "headquarters" would have been a minor one (William Shea, 1983 personal communication; Bearss 1962).

33. This historic building is known as the Old Belknap House (site 3AR51 in the AAS files). It was built by slave labor in 1843, using walnut timbers and an adobe plaster (the source of its nickname, "Dobe House") both inside and outside. The roof shingles and doors were of cypress. It had about twenty rooms and at least eight fireplaces and was indeed used as a Confederate hospital during the Civil War. It was hit by Union gunfire, including a cannonball that went through three rooms.

    The adobe has largely eroded away in recent decades, but the cellar pit remains, and the site has been declared eligible for the National Register of Historic Places (Hester A. Davis, 1986 personal communication).

34. This letter and Baird's of December 3 were received by Palmer on January 10, 1882. In his reply of that date, Palmer acknowledged receipt of a letter from "Mr. J. M. Null." No copies of the letter from Hull or Null have been found. The locality in question must have been the St. Francis River valley, which was scarcely undisturbed by the 1880s (see note 41).

35. In his January 10 reply, Palmer seized upon this opportunity to try to better his situation.

36. The hard-fired nests of mud-daubers or dirt-daubers are fairly frequently found in excavations of burned prehistoric houses. Palmer also recovered such nests at several other sites, including the Wildy site (then owned by B. F. Jackson) west of Osceola in October 1882, and at the Carpenter Mounds near Arkadelphia in February 1883.

37. Palmer was probably accustomed from childhood to the English tradition of quiet observance of Christmas. More extravagant German customs were brought to England and popularized there by Queen Victoria's husband, Prince Albert. The German customs also found fertile ground in the U.S. (John Solomon Otto, 1985 personal communication).

38. Several contemporary maps show Holly Grove in Monroe County between Indian Bay and Clarendon, but no Holley Wood.

39. A narrow-gauge railroad boom in Arkansas began in 1871 as construction started on the Arkansas Central Railway. By 1872 its first fifty miles, from Helena to Clarendon, were operating. This company was reorganized as the Arkansas Midland Railroad in 1878 (Dew and Koeppe 1972:277). The Texas and St. Louis Railway, organized in early 1882, became "the greatest of the narrow-gauge lines in Arkansas" (1972:279).

40. The 1884 Frank Gray map of Arkansas shows a Jonestown in Mississippi, about fifteen miles southeast of Helena, on a railroad spur leading to the Mississippi River opposite Helena. The Alcorn estate is about five kilometers (or three and a half miles) south-southeast of Jonestown and includes the Alcorn Mound (22CO508). James Lusk Alcorn (1816–1894)

was prominent in Mississippi and national politics from about 1843 to 1890. He had retired in 1877 to this plantation (McVaugh 1956:234). He is buried in the Alcorn Cemetery, atop the mound (John Connaway, 1985 personal communication).

Thomas (1891:123; 1894:253–58) did not mention the Alcorn Mound by that name in his sections on Coahoma County, but in the earlier publication did mention the "Roselle Mounds" as having been visited by Palmer.

41. Edwin Curtis (1830–1880) was another energetic archeological collector employed by the Peabody Museum. He had been hired by Putnam, while the latter was excavating mounds and "stone box" graves in the Nashville, Tennessee, vicinity in 1877. A brief obituary summarizing his life was published by Putnam (1881:12). He was two years ahead of Palmer in northeast Arkansas, having worked there in 1879 (Putnam 1880b:717–19; 1881:12), and his success may have inspired Palmer to suggest to Baird that Arkansas would be a good place to explore mounds.

Morse and Morse (1983:19) credited Curtis with "the first well-documented archeological excavations in northeast Arkansas" and noted that he spent the winter along the St. Francis River making collections from the Rose Mound, Fortune Mounds, Stanley Mounds (Parkin), and the Halcomb Mound. They remarked that he had problems in reaching the area, having to bring camping equipment and a "corpse of laborers," and that although no detailed report was ever published on his work, he "left a brief diary, and the materials recovered, including over 900 pots, are still available for study at Harvard."

42. Palmer was somewhat overenthusiastic. Later, in a February 18, 1883, letter to Thomas (see chapter 7), he suggested extending his mound investigations into Arizona.

43. Baird wrote Powell again on February 9, 1882, after Palmer had returned to Washington, and enclosed a list of expenses compiled by Palmer. Apparently Palmer received sufficient compensation for these expenses to keep him on the Mound Survey team. But he probably did not receive similar compensation from the economy-minded Cyrus Thomas.

44. John A. Murrell (1806–1845), originally from Tennessee, was a minor criminal and counterfeiter who enjoyed a glamorized image but was definitely overrated, according to a recent biographer (Penick 1981). He was one of a number of outlaws and pirates who lurked in the bottomlands along the Arkansas side of the Mississippi River, especially in the morass of eastern Crittenden and Mississippi counties above Memphis (1981:60).

45. The airline distance is only about ten miles.

46. Moore (1909:11) remarked upon "the great flood of 1882" in Arkansas (1909:11). See also Palmer's October 13, 1882, remarks on floods, in chapter 7.

47. This apparently refers to the vessels from the ceramic cache at the Menard site. The "peculiar figuring" would then refer to the Winterville-Wallace incised decorations.

48. The "Museum at Pumpilla" is apparently Baird's slang term for Putnam's Peabody Museum at Harvard, or at least for that museum's activities in conjunction with the expeditions of Dr. Raphael Pumpelly (1837–1923). Since 1866, Pumpelly had served informally as professor of mining geology at Harvard, among numerous other activities in geology and related fields, including ethnology and archeology. During late 1881, Putnam had tried to get a position for Palmer on Pumpelly's survey of resources in the Lake Superior vicinity (Palmer's letter of January 10, 1882, to Baird alluded to Putnam's efforts). On the same date, Palmer wrote to Putnam from Helena, stating "As soon as I hear from [Baird], will answer your letter regarding the position . . . I think it would be a delightful trip and Prof. Pumpelly has great experience and there would be no military about it" (Dexter 1987). In the event, though, Palmer continued working for the Bureau of Ethnology.

Chapter 7

1. The editors of the 1917 publication misread Palmer's "8" as a "5" (Palmer 1917:410).

2. The other scribe's copy of Palmer's monthly report gives the date as October 18. The name "Fishmouth Highlands" is not presently known for this vicinity, but the nearby community of Etowah was formerly known as Jackson's Island (Mrs. Charles Wildy, 1983 personal communication). Records observed through the courtesy of Lillian B. Florida of the Osceola Abstract Company show that in 1882, Benjamin F. Jackson owned the property which now includes the Wildy site.

3. This wording, in the 1917 *Arkansas Mounds* publication, may have misled previous investigators. In his previously unpublished report to the Smithsonian for the month of October 1882, however, Palmer stated that the locality was "sixteen miles by township lines, and north of west from Osceola." The site is actually 14.5 miles due west, then 1.5 miles due north, from Osceola by township lines.

4. The community of Louise is shown in extreme southeast Mississippi County, about thirty kilometers (or twenty miles) south of the Wildy site, on the 1883 Cram map of Arkansas, but does not appear on the 1882 Colton or 1884 Gray maps.

5. This probably does not refer to examples of the famous northeast Arkansas "head pots," but might well instead refer to small appliqued human faces on the bodies of ceramic vessels, or even to "rim rider" human head effigies on bowls, or human effigy hooded bottles, all of which have been found in this region (Phillips et al. 1951: Figures 102i–p, 107; Morse 1973: Figures 5, 18).

6. The Golden Lake community is shown on maps of the 1880s and still exists, but no site answering this description is known.

7. Big Bottom is shown on the 1882 Colton and 1884 Gray maps, about three miles north of Oil Trough and just north of a meander loop of the White River, approximately at the Akron Cemetery location. The Newark 1962 USGS quadrangle map shows Big Bottom Slough flowing beside the Akron Cemetery.

8. The other scribe, in the monthly report, rendered this as "unimportant," which seems more likely.

9. Information provided by Shirley Gardner of the Poinsett County Abstract Company in Harrisburg reveals that in 1879 Samuel G. (not T. G.) Stone purchased land located about three miles east of Harrisburg. He sold it in 1887. The name appears as "S. G. Stone" in Palmer's "entitled to thanks" statement and in his monthly report.

10. The gravels that Palmer encountered at the bases of this mound and the Brookfield Mound are consistent with the geology of Crowley's Ridge, a Pleistocene-age erosional remnant (House 1975; Morse and Morse 1983:7).

11. The abstract records furnished by Gardner indicate that Joshua Brookfield purchased land in 1872, immediately east of that later acquired by S. G. Stone. It was sold in 1900. The AAS site files do not include a site in this location.

12. From time to time, claims have been made about ancient seeds found in archeological sites having sprouted and produced unusual plants. Nabhan (1977) has reviewed the evidence from the American Southwest, where preservation of perishable materials is generally much better than in the Mississippi Valley, and concluded that claims of ancient viable seeds are "rich in folklore, but poor in facts." In general, he notes, domesticated plants, including maize or corn, have relatively short viability spans in storage (cf. Justice and Bass 1978), on the order of three to fifteen years. A few crop species have seeds that typically remain viable

for fifteen to one hundred years. Experiments on seed viability are in progress around the world (e.g., Darlington and Steinbauer 1961), but all of these projects are less than three hundred years old. The longest documented period of viable seed preservation, as of 1977, was 237 years, for Indian lotus (Nabhan 1977:145). There are many ways that modern seeds can be intruded into the depths of archeological deposits, and a number of claims of relatively great age for archeological maize specimens have been disproved by the new technique of accelerator radiocarbon dating (Conard et al. 1984).

13. This is obviously a slip of the pen; "poles" must have been intended.

14. The Webb Mounds site (3CG29), at the community of Bay, is actually about eight miles southeast of Jonesboro. Although Palmer did not visit the site, it was tested in February 1883 by another Mound Survey investigator, L. H. Thing, and in early 1884 (and/or late 1883) by yet another, James D. Middleton. Their findings were summarized by Thomas (1894: 201–03), and their collections are sufficient to identify it as a fairly important Middle Mississippian center, with the principal occupation assignable to the Cherry Valley phase (Morse and Morse 1983:246, 250, Figure 11).

15. This is undoubtedly an erroneous reference to Theodore Hayes Lewis. He was born in Virginia in 1856 but grew up near Chillicothe, Ohio, in the vicinity of the famous Hopewell earthworks. About 1880 he moved to St. Paul, Minnesota, where he met Alfred James Hill (1823–1895), an engineer and antiquarian. Hill hired Lewis to conduct archeological surveys and excavations, beginning in 1881. Lewis, an outdoorsman, spent most of the winter months working in southern states. This collaboration, which emphasized Minnesota and nearby states plus Manitoba, became known as "the northwestern archeological survey" and continued until Hill's death. The collections and notes are curated by the Minnesota Historical Society in St. Paul. Lewis lived in that city until 1905, when he went west (possibly to Colorado), and he seems to have disappeared from the historical record (Winchell 1911:vi–x, 78; Keyes 1928, 1930). I am grateful to Patricia Harpole, chief reference librarian of the MHS, for the above information. She also informed me that no one named A. L. Lewis is listed in the Society's records (1986 personal communication).

16. This is clearly a slip of the pen and should be "410".

17. The destruction of the east Arkansas Delta wetlands and associated woodlands has been summarized by Holder (1970).

18. Camp Butler was adjacent to Springfield, Illinois, and is now the site of a National Cemetery. It was the second largest prison camp in Illinois during the Civil War (Sheppley 1933:287).

19. Burnt Mill is shown on the modern quadrangle map, about nine airline miles northeast of Forrest City.

20. Again Palmer was barely beaten by T. H. Lewis. Since Lewis was apparently also an accomplished site-mapper (Keyes 1928, 1930), it might be worthwhile to examine the unpublished Hill-Lewis documents and collections related to Cherry Valley and other Arkansas and Louisiana sites. These non-Minnesota materials were transferred during the 1960s from the Minnesota Historical Society to the Science Museum of Minnesota in St. Paul (Patricia Harpole, 1986 personal communication). No attempt to follow this trail has been made during this research.

21. The correct name is Tuni Creek, as given by the other scribe.

22. This is obviously a slip of the pen by a weary scribe. The other scribe said "75 yards".

23. Despite Palmer's statement, this is obviously not a view of the same mound. Perhaps he intended to say "from" the same mound.

24. Lewis's drawing shows a house and outbuildings on the mound numbered 4.

25. Palmer returned to Bradley on February 16, 1883. The cotton had been picked, but floods and bad weather prevented further work.

26. This must be a slip of the pen for a number in the "71000" series, perhaps 71101.

27. Captain Morris was also mentioned by Palmer during his 1883 visit to Gilmore Station, Pacific Place, and Tyronza Station (see chapter 8).

28. *Pyracanthus* is still commonly used as an ornamental plant around homes in Arkansas. It normally blooms in the springtime (Eric Sundell, 1983 personal communication).

29. This is of course Palmer's artist-assistant, who lived in Pine Bluff. Perhaps he also donated an artifact, as the phrase "entitled to thanks" seems to have been used mainly in that context.

30. Dr. J. M. Taylor owned the Hollywood Plantation, which included the Taylor Mounds site, nearby in northeast Drew County. Palmer went there on November 22. He may have met Dr. Taylor in Pine Bluff while waiting for the weather to clear (see his letter of November 29 to Powell) and gotten "leads" on sites in that part of Drew and adjacent Desha and Lincoln counties from him and others. The remark about the photographs demonstrates that this document was rewritten by the scribe after May 17, 1883.

31. According to a classic study of southern black folklore, "The tools used in digging a grave are left on the site for a day or so after burial, the spades being, in certain localities, laid across the grave. The Negroes say that it is bad luck (or death) to move them, the idea no doubt being that the ghost of the dead remained in that locality for a definite period of time" (Puckett 1926:94–95). Puckett also noted that a wide variety of items, especially broken crockery and glassware, were often placed on the graves of Southern Blacks during the nineteenth and early twentieth centuries (1926:104).

32. Puckett reported,

> The New Orleans voodoos today, so I am told, use the snake in the main, only to work harm—to put people out of this world. To do this they get a poisonous snake and kill him . . . hang the head up in the chimney until it is perfectly dry, powder very finely, and slip into a person's food or drink. The powder inside the person will finally develop into full-grown snakes, which will destroy him unless removed. (1926:249)

33. The "dry communication" from the Walnut Lake-Choctaw Bayou locality to Heckatoo would have followed the drainage divide traversed by the L.R.,M.R.&T. Railroad most of the way. But Wells Bayou is on the east side of Bayou Bartholomew, and Star City is west of the latter stream. After Bayou Bartholomew and the backswamps that parallel it are crossed, an upland divide leads to Star City.

34. Bayou Bartholomew is an underfit stream occupying the last channel of a meander belt that was abandoned by the Arkansas River around two thousand years ago (Roger Saucier, 1987 personal communication; cf. Saucier 1974: Figure 1 for a geological map, but the chronology in that report is outmoded). The distance from the bayou's present source near Pine Bluff to its juncture with the Ouachita River in northeast Louisiana is only about 150 miles. The bayou meanders tortuously, so the actual distance by water may well be more than four hundred miles. Rolingson (1976a:106; 1976b) has documented the relative freedom from flooding of the old Arkansas River natural levees along the bayou, even during severe floods like that of 1927 (1976a:106; 1976b).

35. This artificial levee along the Arkansas River broke during the great 1927 flood (Daniel 1977).

36. This may be a slip of the pen for a number in the "71200" series.

37. Although Palmer did not include this "Plate C" in his instructions for making a panoramic view of the site (see his remarks under "Plate E" and "Plate F"), its right portion can be joined to the left portion of "Plate E" to continue the panorama. The anonymous engraver

for *Frank Leslie's Illustrated Newspaper* used a great deal of artistic license, but his "Taylor Mounds" illustration (fig. 9.1) appears closer to this "Plate C" drawing than to any of Lewis's other drawings of this site.

38. Palmer or the scribe may have moved these "Plate E" remarks ahead of those for "Plate D" because "D" was the central panel in the "E-D-F" panorama. The lower "1" over the house at the right margin of "Plate E" should be matched with the low "1" over the same house in "Plate D" and not with the higher "1" at the left margin of "Plate D," despite Palmer's remark about "margin of plates."

39. The correct spelling is Tillar, not "Tiller" as mistakenly rendered by Palmer, or "Filler" as the misspelling was compounded by the scribe and the editors of the 1917 publication.

40. This and the following remarks and Lewis's "Plate C" appear to describe a charnel house situation, with a mixture of articulated skeletons and disarticulated bones accumulated over a generation or so (Jeter 1981).

41. Lewis's "Plate A" has been lost.

42. This must refer to Lewis's "Plate B" (fig. 7.15) rather than "Plate C," since the site is east of Bayou Bartholomew. This would imply that "Plate B" was drawn looking southward. Lewis must have used some artistic license of his own here, if Palmer's earlier statement that the mound was 450 feet from the bed of the bayou is correct. A bit of licentiousness is also evident in Holmes's (fig. 7.17) redrawing of "Plate B," although his (fig. 7.18) version of "Plate C" is quite close to Lewis's original.

43. Palmer also mentioned the November 1882 report in his letter of December 2. However, it has not been found, although the drawings that he was going to send with it are in the Smithsonian.

44. There is no indication that another mound was visited before Palmer returned to Pine Bluff. Perhaps he was rained out again.

45. The promise was kept; see note 30.

46. The former junction of Opossum Fork (now interrupted by the artificial levee along the Mississippi River) and Cypress Creek was just north of the latter stream's confluence with the Mississippi River and about 7½ miles just west of due north from Arkansas City. Desha County land ownership records on file at Desha Abstract and Title Co. in McGehee, examined with the invaluable assistance of Susan Cash and Dolores Poe (the records before 1903 were written in a cryptic code), indicate that in the 1880s, one Benjamin Franklin owned most of the land in the north half of Section 29, T 11 S, R 1 W, which would have been very near this former stream junction.

    It is perhaps possible that Palmer's Franklin Mounds site is the one now listed as 3DE24 in the AAS files. That site has been given the name "De Soto Plantation" but should not be confused with Palmer's De Soto or De Priest Mound, which is definitely the site now called Cook Mound (3DE5), located nearly four miles north-northwest of 3DE24.

    Site 3DE24 was first definitely visited by C. B. Moore (1911:391), who did not find the kinds of artifact-rich burials he specialized in. It was recorded by the AAS in May 1970 as having four plowed-down mound remnants, the largest only about four feet high, and some village debris. It was recently visited by AAS Station Archeologist H. Edwin Jackson (1987), who found evidence of occupations during the Marksville, Baytown (especially), Coles Creek, and Mississippi periods. However, his accurate remapping of the site's location places it well to the west of the land known to have been owned by Benjamin Franklin, and of the stream junction. Palmer's site may yet await rediscovery.

47. This is another indication that Palmer's site was not 3DE24, which yielded fairly abundant artifactual evidence during Jackson's 1987 visit.

48. Palmer's caption on Lewis's Plate B (fig. 7.26) placed this mound "at the 9 mile post on the old line of the L. R., M. R. & T. Rwy." The 1880s maps contemporary with Palmer's visit show this railroad leading only west from Arkansas City, but the 1878 Colton map shows the old route. Judge Jim Merritt of McGehee, Arkansas (1986 personal communication), a charter member of the Desha County Historical Society, has summarized the history of early railroads in the county in a unpublished manuscript.

The Little Rock, Pine Bluff, and New Orleans merged with the Mississippi, Ouachita, and Red River in 1873. The new line was called the Texas, Mississippi, and Northwestern Railroad, and Powell Clayton was its president. However, it defaulted on its bonds, and in 1875 its assets were sold to the newly chartered Little Rock, Mississippi River, and Texas Railroad. The new company soon decided to abandon the tracks from Chicot City through Watson to Varner, because of difficulties in maintaining the roadbed due to Mississippi River floods. This abandoned track was the one noted by Palmer in his "Plate B" caption. It is not clear what the "9 mile post" was nine miles from, but it may have been Watson.

The new route followed higher ground, farther from the river, from Varner through Dumas, and southward to McGehee, thence eastward through Trippe Junction to Arkansas City. Chicot City and Eunice, which were in imminent danger from the river, were to be abandoned. The relocated line was completed in 1878; this was the "L.R.,M.R.&T." route, which Palmer and Lewis rode into southeast Arkansas, as depicted in Lewis's "Mound at Walnut Lake Station" drawing (fig. 7.7). It went bankrupt a few years after Palmer's visit, and its assets were sold. The major intersection of southeast Arkansas rail routes is now in McGehee and bypasses Arkansas City.

49. The Desha County land-ownership records show that during the 1880s James P. Clayton owned the west half of the southwest quarter and the northeast quarter of the southeast quarter of Section 31, T 10 S, R 1 W. This property is northeast of the De Soto Mound, as Palmer stated for the Clayton Mound, though the straight-line distance is somewhat less than his "2½ miles" (he could well have been estimating by section lines again).

Until recently, though, there were no recorded mound sites in the appropriate vicinity northeast of Cook. However, in 1986, Jackson (personal communication) inspected a map of Desha County site locations given to me in 1982 by the late Gerald Hobson, an amateur archeologist who lived in the nearby Kelso community. Hobson's map indicated a mound about two airline miles northeast of Cook, on the eastern parcel of the old J. P. Clayton property. Jackson made a field visit and was told by local informants that a mound had indeed been in that location but that it had been destroyed, probably before 1950. My subsequent field visits have produced vague recollections by an elderly informant that this mound was rather small, though, and its location seems to be too far east, away from the old State Levee, railroad line, and Cypress Creek. It is more likely that the mound seen by Palmer and Lewis was on the western parcel of Clayton's land, which is traversed by the creek and old levee, and that the mound was destroyed during major levee construction after the great 1927 flood or even incorporated into the new levee.

50. The records show that "Hy. De Priest" bought the northeast quarter of Section 12, T 11 S, R 2 W, on June 31, 1880, and lost it to the state of Arkansas on May 28, 1884, due to delinquent taxes. The Cook Mound, on some modern maps, overlaps into the northwest quarter of that section (but is mainly in Section 1 to the north), and is about an eighth of a mile from the De Priest quarter-section. However, Mr. Gibbs Ferguson of McGehee, an attorney experienced in such matters, advises that modern quadrangle maps are often quite inaccurate in such cases (1988 personal communication). Even if De Priest did not own the Cook Mound, he might well have farmed it and rented a house on it, especially since the land he owned to the east is relatively low and flood-prone.

51. According to the Colton 1882 map and an 1883 Mississippi River Commission map (exam-

ined through the courtesy of Gibbs Ferguson, Esq.), at that time Cypress Creek flowed into the Mississippi River directly opposite the west-southwest terminus of Catfish Point, Mississippi, near the southeast corner of Section 21, T 11 S, R 1 W. It is indeed about eight miles along the winding course of Cypress Creek from its mouth upstream to the Cook Mound.

52. The airline distance from the Cook Mound to the 1880s mouth of Cypress Creek is indeed five miles.

53. The soil composing the Cook Mound is indeed a dark gray, heavy clay or clay loam.

54. Palmer's measurements are, as usual, somewhat exaggerated, but the Cook Mound is a large one. Its actual height is at least twenty-five feet above the surrounding lowlands.

55. These "floating sidewalks" were still in use as late as about 1916 (Judge Jim Merritt, 1986 personal communication). Arkansas City was severely affected by the great Mississippi River flood of 1927 (Daniel 1977). Not only was the town inundated, but the river abandoned the meander loop adjacent to the waterfront, now known as Kate Adams Lake in honor of the steamboat *Kate Adams*, which formerly landed there.

56. Two building foundations on the east margin of the Mississippi River levee, at short distances north and south of Arkansas City, were shown to me in 1979 by one of the twentieth-century archeological pioneers of southeast Arkansas, George P. Kelley (Jeter 1979). According to Judge Jim Merritt (1986 personal communication), the northern foundations are the ruins of this cottonseed oil mill.

57. The correct name of the species is *Ailanthus altissima*. I visited this site with Dr. Eric Sundell of the University of Arkansas at Monticello, a botanist, on August 20, 1983. *Ailanthus* trees were present in abundance on the north slope of the mound. This species is almost legendary for its adaptability to unusual microhabitats, including parking lots in New York City, (Sundell, 1983 personal communication). A "voucher specimen" of *Ailanthus* from 3DE15 was taken by Sundell for the UAM Herbarium, annotated with the common botanical statement, "observed by Palmer."

   Ailanthus altissima was imported from the Orient and is also known as "tree of heaven," which may account for its presence in a cemetery despite the notoriously unpleasant smell of its flowers. Another possible explanation for its presence in this flood-prone region is that, "In the early 1800s, the tree was believed to absorb malarial poisons" (Krochmal and Krochmal 1973:31; I am indebted to Leonard W. Blake for finding this quotation.)

58. Luna (not Lunar) Landing is shown on maps of the 1880s on the Mississippi River in Chicot County, about two miles north of Lake Chicot. This is the southernmost Arkansas locality mentioned by Palmer in the surviving notes, which do not indicate any site visits in the vicinity. However, Thomas (1891:16) reported briefly: "Chicot County. Mound at Lake Village. Reported by Dr. Palmer." He also indicated a mound on Lake Chicot, opposite Lake Village (1891: Plate III). This was not mentioned in his later publication (Thomas 1894), and no such site is on record in the AAS files.

59. Hoffman (1975:12) found that there were doubts as to specific site proveniences in the Smithsonian's Desha County collections (1975:12). He stated that the catalog card indicated that the coin was not authentic. The pistol was described by Thomas as "a toy pistol of stone" (1894:239). Despite the provenience problems, it might be worthwhile to examine the collection to see if there are any historic Native American artifacts that might be the "broken articles of Indian origin" mentioned by Palmer as having been found at this 1756–79 French site.

60. As discussed in chapter 5, the field work reported here must have taken place in early to middle December 1882; "1883" probably indicates the year in which the scribe made this transcription.

61. The Menard site is actually about eight airline kilometers (or five miles) east-southeast of Ecores Rouges, which was the location of Arkansas Post from 1749 to 1756 and again after 1779 (Arnold 1983), including the time of Palmer's visits. Palmer got the direction more or less right in his November 29, 1881, report but gave the distance as eight miles.

62. This drawing is not really a bird's eye view—at least not that of a high-flying bird.

63. As previously noted, the actual height of the mound was about thirty-five feet (Moore 1908:487; Ford 1961:148).

64. Compare a 1941 photograph from a similar angle (fig. 7.36).

65. This is the beginning of the passage that was so badly misinterpreted in the 1917 publication. See chapter 5 for discussion and correction.

66. Again, the field work must have been done in 1882.

67. This must refer to "Plate I" (fig. 7.25).

68. This is a reference to "Plate 3" (fig. 7.29).

69. The Gardener or Wallace site is actually about three quarters of a mile northeast of Menard Mound A.

70. This obviously should be "Menard"; this is indirect evidence that these notes, and perhaps Palmer's originals from which they were taken, were written well after the Menard field work, probably in 1883, since Palmer did not arrive at the Knapp site until December 25, 1882.

71. This plan view map is basically an expanded and elaborated version of the one in figure 7.40.

72. This supposition is almost certainly wrong. Ford called this stream, adjacent to the Wallace site, "Deep Bayou" and distinguished it from Menard Bayou, adjacent to the Menard site (1961: 140–42, Plate 20). He suggested that Deep Bayou and Menard Bayou, in that order, had occupied former channel bends of the Arkansas River rather than the White. This definitely appears to be a correct interpretation of the geomorphological evidence.

    Ford also suggested that the Arkansas River was still in the "Menard course" when Arkansas Post was established in 1686, and that this was the key to his identification of Menard, rather than Wallace, as Osotouy (1961: 141–42). This should be rechecked by a professional geomorphologist.

73. The county lines changed shortly after Palmer's visit, and the Knapp or Toltec site is now in Lonoke County.

74. Despite Palmer's statement, it appears that at the time of his visit, the site was not owned by Gilbert Knapp, but by Eustis Feild Officer (b. 1849), the son of William Officer and Mary Officer, who had been married to Gilbert Knapp since 1857.

75. The lake, now known as Mound Pond, is indeed an abandoned meander of the Arkansas River. The Plum Bayou meander belt, north of the present Arkansas River course, was apparently continuous with the Bayou Bartholomew belt south of the modern river (Saucier 1974; Kaczor 1982:17). It is believed that the Mound Pond oxbow had already been abandoned when the site was occupied (1982:27). It was also formerly believed that this meander belt was still active until about A.D. 1000, i.e., while the Knapp site flourished, but it now appears that this meander belt was abandoned for the modern one around A.D. 1 (Saucier, 1987 personal communication), well before the time of the Plum Bayou culture.

76. This is now known as Mound A. Palmer's figures would convert to about thirty meters high; however, at present the mound is about fifteen meters high, as indicated by Holmes and Thomas, and it is believed that erosion has not significantly modified the major mounds (Rolingson 1982:1,74). No controlled excavations have been made into Mound A since Palmer's day.

77. "Levee" was Palmer's term for the prehistoric embankment that encloses the site (cf. Rolingson 1982:1; Miller 1982:41–42, Figures 28–30). Mary Eliza Knapp also compared the embankment to levees, in an 1876 letter to Joseph Henry at the Smithsonian (Rolingson 1982:71).

78. This is Mound B. Palmer's figure for the height converts to about twenty-three meters, but the present height is about 12.5 meters (Rolingson 1982:1,74). There was a minor erosional gully in the southeastern edge of this mound when the site became a state park. Before it was stabilized by the Arkansas Division of Parks in 1979, a stepped profile was cut along one edge of the gully, exposing a stratified sequence of occupational surfaces and intervening loads of fill and producing a radiocarbon sample that yielded a date of A.D. 805 ± 71 (Miller 1982:36–41, Figures 25–27).

79. The January 27, 1883, *Arkansas Gazette* article (see chapter 9) described these as "magnificent crystals, as fine specimens as were ever seen." It also asserted, incorrectly, that the Catholic medal (see note 83) was found with them.

    The use of quartz crystals, as raw materials for chipped artifacts including arrow points, as unmodified tools, and perhaps as scrying devices or for ceremonial purposes, is one of the distinguishing characteristics of Plum Bayou culture at the Toltec site and in adjacent regions (Hoffman 1982; Rolingson 1982:89, 93).

    Small quartz crystals are readily available from a number of localities in the Ouachita Mountains (specifically, from the Jackfork sandstone formations and some shales), including the Little Rock-North Little Rock vicinity. One of the best-known sources is Crystal Hill on the northwest edge of North Little Rock, but it does not appear at present to yield crystals as large as some from prehistoric contexts, i.e., longer than ten centimeters (or five inches). Other potential sources include another Crystal Hill adjacent to the Arkansas River between North Little Rock and Maumelle, a "Crystal Mountain" south of Pinnacle Mountain and about six kilometers (or four miles) southwest of the Arkansas River but accessible via tributaries, and yet another Crystal Hill near a small stream which drains through Crystal Valley into Fourche Creek. The latter is a relatively large stream, draining northeast from the Ouachita Mountains through the Little Rock vicinity into the Arkansas River a short distance above the Toltec site.

80. This probably should read "150 ft. long." That would be more in line with the shape of this depressed area, as portrayed in sketches and aerial photos.

81. This mound (Palmer's Mound 3) is now known as Mound C. In a rare reversal of form, Palmer underestimated its height; his "12 ft." converts to 3.65 meters, but the present height is about 4.2 meters (Miller 1982:30; Rolingson 1982:83). Lewis's drawing shows an abrupt change in contour atop this mound, as if a large amount of dirt had been removed fairly recently. It presently has a low, rounded, conical profile (Miller 1982:30, Figure 17). It was tested by the Arkansas Archeological Society in 1966 and appears to have been a burial mound (Davis 1966; Anderson 1977b; Rolingson 1982:5; Miller 1982:30, Figures 18–19).

82. This (Palmer's Mound 4) is now known as Mound D. Palmer noted some disturbance from deep plowing here, and since his visit it has been virtually leveled by construction and agriculture. Nevertheless, excavations by the University of Arkansas field school and the Arkansas Archeological Survey and Society in 1977–79 have documented the presence of undisturbed lower-level mound fill and a sub-mound midden. It probably was a substructure mound (as Palmer concluded), with at least four fairly complex, asymmetrical, largely lateral stages of construction (Rolingson 1982:5, 7, 89; Miller 1982:30–36, Figures 20–22). On the basis of these stratigraphic data, preliminary studies of ceramics and lithics from Mound D (Stewart-Abernathy 1982; Hoffman 1982) have provided an initial framework for definition of the site's cultural sequence (Belmont 1982a; Rolingson 1982:87–93).

83. This has been identified as an example of the "Miraculous Medal" or "Medal of the Immaculate Conception," commemorating a vision by a woman in France in 1830. The first such medal was struck in 1832 (Rolingson 1982:85).

84. The smallest mound on Plate 3 (Palmer's Mound 5) is now known as Mound E (Rolingson 1982:74, Figure 44). From surface indications, it now appears to have been completely leveled by agriculture, but when it was tested by the Arkansas Archeological Survey and Society in 1979, remnants of undisturbed loaded soils and a sub-mound midden were found beneath the plow zone (Miller 1982:36, Figure 23).

85. These are probably the mounds now designated as F and P. Due to erosion and concealment by vegetation, Mound P had been considered "part of the ridge that has been identified as Mound F" in recent years (Rolingson 1982:73).

86. This may refer either to the low rise now called Mound Q or the one now called Mound R.

87. The "large pond" is indicated by the cluster of trees immediately to the left of Mound B.

88. The "caves" do not appear to have had true cave-like ceilings, and Palmer probably should have called them "artificial inlets." Perhaps the overhanging trees, which Palmer stated had been purposefully "left from off" the drawing, gave them a cave-like appearance. Rolingson noted that the borrow pit ponds were largely filled in by agricultural leveling, and the "caves" or inlets had been completely filled in (1982:83). The 1979 test excavations confirmed their former presence in historic times; historic artifacts were found in the fill.

89. Beneath this date someone else penciled in "1883," but that is definitely not the year in which the letter was written. It is contained in an official Bureau of Ethnology "Letters Received" folder, signed by James C. Pilling, chief clerk, indicating that it was received January 3, 1883, and written December 29, 1882.

90. Palmer did not return to the St. Francis Valley.

91. Palmer did visit the Mayberry Mounds site in the Cache River valley near Cotton Plant, Woodruff County, in October 1883 (see chapter 8).

92. Palmer's surviving notes do not mention a visit to the Old Town site (3PH20 or 15-N-3) on the Mississippi River in Phillips County, a few miles downstream from Helena, but Thomas did state that a "Bureau assistant" had been there (1894:234–35). The investigation was thorough enough to produce a site map (1894:Figure 142) and some Late Mississippian vessels, one of them illustrated (1894: Figure 143). It is fortunate that this visit was made, as this important late prehistoric and protohistoric site was later completely destroyed by the river (Phillips 1970:940).

93. The correct legal description is Township 7 S, Range 5 W. The land in this vicinity has long since been cleared for the Cummins State Prison Farm.

94. This land also has been cleared for the prison farm, and the modern (Cades 7.5') quadrangle map shows only an intermittent stream in leveled land in what may have been the vicinity of the bayou noted by Palmer.

95. The aboriginal territories of the Choctaws were in east-central Mississippi and adjacent Alabama (Swanton 1946:32, Map 11; Blitz 1985), but in the 1830s they were removed to Oklahoma (DeRosier 1970). In December 1831 and January 1832, some twenty-five hundred Choctaws were stranded at Arkansas Post in bitter winter weather, with great suffering, sickness and death (1970:144–45). This may have been the episode reported as hearsay oral history to Palmer some fifty-one years later, although Garretson's Landing is about forty airline kilometers (or twenty-five miles) from Arkansas Post. Subsequent Choctaw groups took a more northerly route through Arkansas (1970:152–62). Alternatively, Palmer's informant may have confused the Choctaws with the Quapaws. The lower Arkansas Valley

was Quapaw territory at the time of European contact in the late seventeenth century and remained so until the removal of the Quapaws during the 1820s (Baird 1980).

96. Land ownership records indicate that Spellman family members owned land near Garretson's Landing. Possibly, a site on their property might have been the subject of a lost drawing by Lewis.

97. The 1905 Jefferson County plat map shows an L. D. Smuggs (not Snuggs) owning property extending to about a mile south of Garretson's Landing, but apparently not quite far enough south to include 3JE34, which at that time was on a quarter-quarter section owned by M. A. Conrad. However, the next quarter-quarter section to the south was owned by an E. D. Smuggs, so it seems likely that Conrad's land had indeed been owned by the estate of Palmer's "late Mr. Snuggs" in the 1880s. "Snuggs Byou," indicated on Lewis's drawing, was apparently a local name for a segment of Long Lake.

98. Land ownership records indicate that before 1884 Charles Howson had bought land that adjoined the road from Garretson's Landing to Linwood. This is southwest of Garretson's Landing, not northeast as indicated by Palmer; northeast would have been across the river, rather than near Linwood. A site on record in the AAS files, Blankenship (3JE20), is between the Linwood road and a small bayou, on the property that was owned by Howson, about two miles from the Garretson's Landing location; it matches Palmer's description in all of these respects.

99. The correct spelling of the landowner's name was probably Waldstein; the 1905 Jefferson County plat map shows members of this family still holding land slightly more than a mile east of 3JE63. Palmer's surviving notes do not state how many mounds were here, but Thomas referred to "three" mounds "covered with graves" and "about 1 mile north" or "something over a mile north" of Linwood Station (1891:19; 1894:242).

100. Palmer had just arrived at Arkansas City on the Mississippi River, but Garretson's Landing was on the Arkansas River. This mistake is also repeated in the text of this entry.

101. The newspaper article is still in the "2400" file in the December 23, 1882, issue of *The Weekly Times-Democrat*, a New Orleans paper that Palmer probably found in the lobby of the hotel at Arkansas City. It is entitled "An Old Louisiana Town," by J. H. Cosgrove. The article mentions Natchez in passing but is mainly about Natchitoches, in the Red River valley of northwest-central Louisiana. Inquiries at Northwestern State University and its Watson Memorial Library in Natchitoches (Hiram F. Gregory, Carolyn M. Wells, and Mildred Lee, 1987 personal communications) revealed that Cosgrove was a well-known regional historian in northwest Louisiana and adjacent Texas.

102. This must refer to the drawings of the sites in eastern Desha County, which were made in early December and may have been sent in the "Express" package mentioned in Palmer's December 29 letter. Several of the mounds in that region were indeed in use as cemeteries, for orchards, house sites, and cattle refuges—and still are.

103. McVaugh misinterpreted this ambiguous passage, concluding that Palmer had been in "Woodson, Saline County, Jan. 15, 1883, to take steamer to Reed's Landing" (1956:294). The correct interpretation is Rolingson's "he took passage on the steamer, *Woodson*, for Reed's Landing" (1982:72). The town of Woodson is now in Pulaski County, downvalley from Reed's Landing, and is almost seven airline kilometers (or four miles) from the present Arkansas River. The 1884 Gray map shows Woodson about three miles west of the western margin of a meander loop that is indicated as "Cut Off" on the 1882 Colton map, which does not show Woodson. The *Woodson*, on the other hand, was a real Arkansas steamboat; a photograph of it at a White River landing in the early 1900s has been on display in the Old State House Museum in Little Rock.
    Reed's Landing is shown on the 1882 Colton map and the 1884 Gray map as being on

the south margin of an Arkansas River meander loop that was in the process of being cut off. This process was soon completed, as the former loop is shown on the USGS Little Rock 1891 map as an oxbow lake (now called Old River Lake; cf. Rolingson 1982: Figure 3). Reed's Landing would have been about six kilometers (or four miles) west-southwest of the Knapp (Toltec) site.

104. The correct name is probably J. K. Thibault, as given in most of the subsequent statements about him. Although Holmes referred to him as "J. R. Thibault" (1886b: 382), he probably misread Palmer's handwriting; Palmer's "R" is clearly an "R" and not mistakable for a "K," but his "K" looks very much like an "R."

105. This probably refers to similar prehistoric vessels, rather than plaster casts. There are several more or less standard vessel forms in Quapaw phase (and other late) assemblages, such as "helmet" bowls and bottles with "hourglass" necks, which are represented in the Thibault collection.

106. The Thibault collection includes some Nodena Red and White vessels.

107. This could refer either to engraved "Caddoan" or to appliqued decorations. Several examples of the former, and one of the latter, are present in the Thibault collection.

108. Palmer could have been referring here to a double (horizontal compound) bottle and/or some of the shapes mentioned in note 105. Holmes (1886b:382, Figure 373) discussed and illustrated an unusual "oblong, trough-like vessel with projecting flat wings at the ends" and "head-shaped" vessels (1886b:410–11, Figure 424) from Thibault.

109. This might be the "spatulate celt" illustrated by Thomas (1894: Figure 150) as having come from the Knapp Mounds (coincidentally, Thomas's illustration is placed in the midst of the Thibault Mounds discussion). Rolingson also attributed this artifact to Knapp/Toltec (1982: 85), as it would seem from its specimen numbers, but noted that similar celts had been found at Quapaw phase and Caddoan sites. Given the mixups that occurred (1982:83–84), this is at least a possibility.

110. None of the quadrangle maps in the Arkansas Archeological Survey's files show Mills Bayou or a Galloway Lake near the location designated by Palmer, but the 1880s maps do show a Galloway community on the railroad about nine miles east-northeast from Little Rock, and the modern quadrangle maps show a Hill Bayou in this vicinity. The 1855 General Land Office map calls this Hills Bayou and shows it draining from Hills Lake into Horseshoe Lake, another old Arkansas River cutoff. An 1891 map of the Little Rock vicinity indicates the same drainage sequence.
   On the ground, Hill Bayou does have the appearance of a canal even today, because of its relatively straight channel, and it does empty into the "old Arkansas River" as Palmer said, but it is of natural rather than cultural origin.

111. The alleged "buried" (or "sunken") city was also mentioned in Palmer's letter of January 31, 1883, to Thomas. The *Arkansas Gazette* of March 1, 1882, had carried (on page 5) an article headlined "Indian village site near Benton may have Aztec origin," which apparently reported the uncovering of the Chidester site by the Saline River flood. Palmer had been gone from Arkansas for more than a month by then, driven out by excessive rains; apparently rumors about the site had become even more exaggerated by the time of his January 1883 work in nearby Little Rock.

112. The photograph has not been found. Palmer was again attempting to compensate for the loss of Lewis. An engraving of the mound, perhaps derived from the photograph or perhaps from the pencil drawing (also missing) mentioned by Palmer, was published by Thomas (1894: Figure 151) and is reproduced here as figure 7.61.

113. Unfortunately, Palmer's January 1883 report from the field has not been found.

114. Here and in the next two datelines, Palmer or the scribe erroneously lapsed back to the previous year.

115. This is undoubtedly an allusion to Cyrus Thomas. Palmer must have been still smarting from the letters he received in Arkansas City on January 10.

116. Palmer gave a more detailed description of what are today known as prairie mounds or pimple or mima mounds at the beginning of his "2400" file notes on these explorations around Arkadelphia. There are hundreds of thousands, perhaps millions, of these mounds, all west of the Mississippi River, in Arkansas, Louisiana, and portions of adjacent states. They occur only on landforms more than about three thousand or four thousand years old. They may have been formed in a relatively brief period, geologically speaking, between about 4000 and 1000 B.C. (Cain 1974; Saucier 1978:35–36), and would have been available for occupation by Late Archaic peoples (Jeter 1982a:92). Their mode of formation is uncertain, and numerous conjectures have been made; Palmer suggested that they were erosional remnants, an explanation favored by Cain (1974), but others prefer a depositional formation (Saucier, 1979 personal communication). The most optimistic attempt at explanation, popular around the south Arkansas oil fields, is that they were formed by natural gas bubbles underground. Although Palmer's experience of finding nothing in them is the most common, some of the mounds definitely were used prehistorically. Based on my experience with reports of such mounds in southeast Arkansas, it appears that they were much more likely to have been occupied if they were located near water.

117. Phillips, who had apparently not seen this remark of Palmer's, stated, "Archeologists since Holmes (1903) have been aware of some sort of cultural divide about the middle of the Lower Mississippi area. It cannot be localized, of course, but the indicators of change are usually somewhere in the section lying between the mouths of the Arkansas and Yazoo rivers" (1970:968). Holmes had defined several regional ceramic subgroups (1903:81); one of his distinctions was between "eastern Arkansas and western Tennessee" and "the lower Mississippi region."

Moore observed:

> As a boundary line between the Lower and Middle Mississippi Valley regions has not as yet been definitely determined, we would suggest that the Arkansas River and an imaginary line extending eastward from its mouth be considered as such, not only because the geographical position of the river fits it to serve as the basis of such a division, but for the reason that the aboriginal pottery of the Arkansas River possesses the distinctive features belonging to the ware of both the region above and the region below that stream. North of the Arkansas River incised decoration on earthenware is comparatively seldom encountered, and when it is present . . . it as a rule, of inferior execution . . . On the other hand, south of that river engraved, incised and trailed decoration on pottery is the rule rather than the exception . . . In the Middle Mississippi Valley region, north of the Arkansas, pottery with decoration in color—solid red or polychrome—is often found. South of the Arkansas, however, the use of pigments for decoration of pottery was rather infrequently resorted to . . . There can be no question that north of the Arkansas the average quality of the ware and the character of the modeling are inferior to those of the region to the southward. (1911:370–71)

Moore, like Palmer, did not really make a distinction between the Caddoan and true Lower Valley decorated wares below the Arkansas. The cultural divide that Phillips spoke of is not restricted to the late prehistoric and protohistoric remains that Moore and Palmer emphasized. It generally fluctuated above and below the present Arkansas-Louisiana state line, with plainwares more common to the north. This contrast goes back at least to the Marksville period (Belmont 1983:274, 276, Figure 2). It is also reflected in the Baytown-Troyville distinction (Belmont 1982b:78–79, Figure 2) and in Rolingson's (1982) Plum Bayou-Coles Creek distinction.

118. Palmer changed his mind about going to New Orleans during this field season (see the letter of February 18, 1883). Although his next job after leaving the Mound Survey in July 1884 was collecting specimens for the upcoming World's Fair in New Orleans, there is no record of his attending that exposition. He apparently did not see New Orleans until June 1910, less than a year before his death, on a return trip from Mexico to Washington (McVaugh 1956:262).

119. This is a reference to the site now known as the Anna Mounds (22AD500 or 26-K-1), known in the older literature as "Seltzertown mounds . . . 6 miles from Washington [Mississippi] and 11 miles [north-] northeast of Natchez" (Thomas 1891:123) or "the noted Selsertown group . . . 7 miles a little west of north from Washington" (Thomas 1894:263–64). In his March 19, 1883 letter to Thomas, Palmer referred to this site as "the so called Saltzertown Mound" and noted that he had collected some potsherds from it. Thomas stated that "Dr. Palmer made a hasty visit to them in 1884 [sic]; subsequently, in 1887, Mr. Middleton made a careful survey of them" (1894:263).

 This site consists of four mounds arranged atop a huge artificial platform at the margin of the loess bluff overlooking the Mississippi River, apparently to accentuate its height (Brain 1978:345–47, Figure 12.6). The dropoff from the summit to the valley floor is actually on the order of two hundred feet. Thomas stated that "Although the term 'platform' has been used here to indicate this somewhat remarkable elevation on which the mounds are placed, Mr. Middleton and Dr. Palmer express the opinion very confidently that it is chiefly a natural formation" (1894:264–65). They were wrong, though (cf. Brain 1978).

120. This may have been done in December 1883, when Palmer briefly visited Washington for the first time since August 1882 (McVaugh 1956:345).

121. Palmer seems to have had just about enough of river work (cf. the February 16 letter). He probably preferred working in the arid Southwest, which was the scene of his most significant botanical collecting (McVaugh 1956). The Bureau of Ethnology showed more restraint, by restricting the Mound Survey to "works east of the Rocky Mountains" (Thomas 1891; 1894: Plate XX).

 The "mounds" that Palmer had observed in Arizona were probably mainly rubble of relatively late prehistoric pueblos or pueblo-like structures. Peacock Springs is about 140 kilometers (or 85 miles) northwest of Prescott, in northern Mojave County, Arizona, in territory aboriginally occupied mainly by the Walapai Indians. Neither Henry F. Dobyns nor Robert C. Euler, archeologists and ethnographers with a great deal of experience in these regions, knew of any significant mound-like remains in this locality (1985 personal communications). Dobyns had been told by informants that this was a prime antelope hunting area for Pai Indians, using blinds that were made by stacking stones. Such features might deteriorate into mounds of rubble, but he did not observe any such evidence during his field work in the mid-twentieth century. He also stated that no stone habitation structures are known this far west.

122. The archeology of the Prescott region, a west-central Arizona upland that drains from its western portions into the Colorado River system and from its other portions ultimately into the Salt-Gila system, has been summarized by myself (Jeter 1977). Chino Valley drains the northern portion of the Prescott region in a generally southeastward direction into the Verde Valley, which then trends southeastward into the Salt River Valley above Phoenix. The major excavated site in the Chino Valley is King's Ruin (Spicer 1936), a pueblo-like structure.

 The Verde Valley and portions of the Prescott region were explored for the BAE by Jesse Walter Fewkes (1912). The major excavated site in the Verde Valley is Tuzigoot (Caywood and Spicer 1935), another pueblo-like ruin. The famous cliff dwelling Montezuma's Castle (a misnomer derived from the same notion as the name of the Toltec site in Arkansas) is also in this valley but has never been adequately reported. Palmer's work in these regions has been summarized in chapter 2 of this volume, and recent work in the Verde Valley has been cited in a review (Jeter 1982c).

123. The Salt and Gila valleys of southern Arizona were the heartland of the prehistoric Hohokam (Haury 1976), who did have mounds, including not only trash mounds but also purposefully constructed platform mounds (1976:80–102). Hayden's Ferry is now known as Tempe, the site of Arizona State University. On the Phoenix side of the Salt River, a short distance downstream from Tempe, is the classic Hohokam site of Pueblo Grande, now a city museum that features a mounded mass of structural rubble. Current issues in Hohokam archeology have been discussed in several recent publications (Doyel and Plog 1980; Doyel 1981; McGuire and Schiffer 1982; Dittert and Dove 1985; Doyel and Elson 1985).

124. Friar's (or Friars) Point is on the Mississippi River in Coahoma County, Mississippi, about fifteen miles north-northwest of Clarksdale and twelve miles west of Jonestown, which Palmer had already visited on January 3, 1882. According to Thomas (1891:123), Palmer had visited the Roselle Mounds, six miles east of Friar's Point. However, he did not mention the site in his (1894:253–58) section on this county, dealing instead with sites visited by Col. P. W. Norris in 1884 and by W. H. Holmes on his 1890 trip.

The Roselle mound site is now known as the Parchman Place (22CO511 or 15-N-5; John Connaway, 1985 personal communication). It was reported but not visited by Calvin Brown (1926:107) and summarized by Phillips, Ford, and Griffin as a "large village site with large and small platform mounds and small mounds in plaza arrangement" (1951:51). Phillips made it the type site for his Parchman phase, which he compared to Late Mississippian phases such as Kent and Walls (1970:939–40). Information about this phase was updated by Starr (1984), who revisited this site (1984:185–88), along with several others.

125. Palmer revisited the Arkadelphia locality in September 1883. One of the sites spoken of here must have been the Carpenter Mounds, where he worked extensively. He visited several other sites in the Okolona vicinity south of Arkadelphia.

126. This passage was paraphrased by Thomas (1894:252). The drawing referred to by Palmer has not been found, but Thomas (1894: Figure 156) did publish a Holmes engraving. It was probably not a revision of a Lewis drawing, as it shows leaves on trees and no sign of flooding (as noted in chapter 2, Lewis made a drawing of the Troyville site and town during the March 1883 flood).

Walker (1936) conducted salvage excavations at Troyville, where the final destruction of the remarkable Great Mound was taking place. This mound was said to have been eighty feet high, including a steep conical cap that was destroyed during the Civil War. Walker reported that George Beyer of Tulane University had worked at Troyville in 1896 and confirmed Palmer's descriptions, including laminated masses of cane and wood "in some places 12 to 14 inches in thickness" (1936:12–13). Walker also found a great deal of cane, including some thick sections (1936: Plate 9c). He noted that it was greenish-yellow when the heavy clay covering was removed but quickly turned black on exposure to the air, and he suggested that this "probably accounts for its charred appearance according to Palmer and Beyer" (1936: 13–14).

Chapter 8

1. Neither Major Davis nor the two mounds have been identified, though it would appear that this was the return to the Arkadelphia vicinity that Palmer had spoken of in his March 19 letter. Yet it seems odd that he would then go to Little Rock, only to turn around and go back to Arkadelphia. The "accompanying accounts" spoken of by Palmer at the end of this paragraph have not been found.

2. This appears to refer to a company, not to Desha County.

3. Palmer went to the Cotton Plant vicinity in Woodruff County in October 1883.

4. September 16, 1883, was a Sunday.

5. This final version omits a statement made by Palmer in his original notes, which read, " . . . some mussel shells burnt allso peices of broaken potts was found these are somewhat seperated they are sent under letter C in different packages but need resorting."

6. This specimen list is on a separate sheet of paper but is inserted here to follow Palmer's account of work at these mounds. His actual notes go directly from the Carpenter Mounds account to the Okolona Mound account.

7. Here the original notes state "It is situated in a rather broaken spot which was formerly covered with timber." This statement was omitted in the final version presented here.

8. Palmer's original wording was "These conditions was rejected by me."

9. The original wording was "A yarn goes that . . ."

10. The original wording was " . . . came to house sight consisting of a quantity of ashes . . ."

11. The original wording was " . . . or the surrounding surface which is not a favorable sight besides there is no permanent natural water during wet times water is in bottom places."

12. In the original, the name is given as J. E. Gibson.

13. This does not appear to have been done.

14. Again a specimen list is inserted after the site notes that it should accompany. Palmer's actual final version of his site notes goes directly from the Clem Mounds notes to those on the house sites in Independence County, near Batesville, but that document is definitely out of chronological sequence.

15. The Arkansas History Commission has an incomplete scribe's version of this letter, which was published on pages 393–94 of the 1917 volume. It is not transcribed here, as it does not differ significantly from the relevant portion of Palmer's original.

16. Mann Satterwhite Valentine II (1824–1892) was the eldest son of a wealthy merchant in Richmond, Virginia. He continued his father's business and spent the latter years of his life studying ethnology and corresponding with scientists and others about archeology, especially that of Virginia. He left a portion of his estate for the founding of a museum. The Valentine Museum was incorporated in 1894, opened in 1898, and continues today, with its primary emphasis being "the life and history of Richmond." Unfortunately, it appears that none of Valentine's posters that Palmer mentioned later in this letter have survived (Edie Jeter, Valentine Museum, 1985 personal communication).

17. The wording of this final version does not differ significantly from that of Palmer's original version, except that here Palmer cautiously changed "famous Choctaw crossing" to "so called Choctaw crossing" and inserted "so called Choctaw" before "burying ground." His caution was probably warranted. During the removal of the Choctaws from Mississippi to Oklahoma in the 1830s, many of them passed through this portion of Arkansas (DeRosier 1970:152–62). However, Palmer's second-hand information about "many choice things" having been found at this burial site sounds more like a description of a Late Mississippian, Protohistoric, or Early Historic period situation. Sites, including burial sites, of Late Mississippian and possibly Quapaw phase affiliation are known in this vicinity (Figley 1964, 1966; cf. Morse and Morse 1983:301, Figure 12.1).

18. The scribe, or possibly Palmer's original, must have omitted "not" here.

19. Palmer's original version has some different wordings but no significant differences from this final version.

20. This list was on a separate sheet of paper but is inserted into this appropriate place, between site summaries in Palmer's final version.

21. Palmer's original version again has some different wordings, none of them significantly different.

22. The only significant difference in the original version was that Palmer had written "Woodrough Co Tenn" at the top; someone, possibly Palmer, had scratched out "Tenn" and written "ruff" under "Woodrough."

23. Here Palmer drew a line in the margin, connecting the specimen number to the paragraph above in which the implement was first mentioned.

24. The correct spelling is Des Arc. Palmer's "Desarc" looks something like "Desaic" without a dot over the "i."

25. The correct spelling is "Tate"; Palmer's rendering in the next entry was right. Land ownership records show that Andrew J. Tate purchased the land containing this site in 1877 and still owned it in 1883.

26. The implement mentioned has not been examined during this research. Hoffman (1975:17) reported nothing more peculiar than a stone earspool in the Smithsonian collection from this site; it might be the artifact in question. The donor's name was probably spelled Carlee, as in the next scribe's entry. Her home town of DeValls Bluff is more than fifty kilometers (over thirty miles) northeast of this site. But there is a Carlee Brake, an old Arkansas River cutoff, less than ten kilometers (about five miles) west of the site; perhaps she was visiting relatives living near the site at the time of Palmer's visit.

27. Palmer's combination of "diameter" and "long" measurements is confusing at best. Recent research at this site indicates that this mound is about 15 feet high and 110 feet in diameter (Michael Nassaney, 1988 personal communication). The shape is difficult to ascertain due to disturbances and erosion.

28. In June 1988 Nassaney cleared the profiles of a deep pot-hunter's pit and encountered a burned floor about eight feet below the top surface of this mound. An archeomagnetic dating sample was obtained by Daniel Wolfman (personal communication).

29. This specimen number list, like the preceding one, is on a separate sheet of paper but is inserted into this relevant place in the sequence.

30. Palmer seems to have left Arkansas by early November and not to have revisited Indian Bayou. This seems to be a past-tense entry covering several days. Perhaps Palmer had his interesting finds at Indian Bayou on his mind after writing it at the beginning of this note and incorrectly wrote that place name here instead of another, such as Newport; he had visited that vicinity in October 1882 with some promising results and immediately caught a train for Newport after receiving this letter.

31. "Sunday" would have been October 28. "Jefferson Co" is another indication of carelessness in writing this entry and a suggestion that it was written some time after the fact. Batesville is in Independence County. After visiting that locality, Palmer went by train to Little Rock, thence apparently to two sites near Pine Bluff in Jefferson County.

32. Palmer got the county right in this final version but in his original version, he wrote both "Jefferson" and "Jackson" and scratched them out. Newport is in Jackson County, across the White River from Independence County.

33. In the original version, Palmer wrote "a space of about thirty acres."

34. In the original version, Palmer added "At one time many entire specimens could be found but now that is impossible."

35. In the original, the name is spelled "Fesmire."

36. Here the original version added "The fragmentary specimens gathered up was sent appropriately marked."

37. Again the specimen number list is on a separate sheet of paper and inserted after the relevant site description.

38. Newport is actually in Jackson County, just downstream from Independence County. Palmer had previously visited Newport and had gotten the county right, in October 1882.

39. It is assumed here, perhaps incorrectly, that Palmer changed his plans and did not go immediately to Helena. He does not seem to have gone to a place fourteen miles from there, either, though he did visit a site six miles from Helena. Also, he apparently never got to Delhi, Louisiana (see the following note). In the reconstruction proposed here, he instead went from Little Rock by rail to two sites near Pine Bluff, then by rail to northeast Arkansas, and proceeded down the Mississippi Valley to Helena and out of the state. This at least has the benefit of arranging his site visits within relatively neat regional clusters.

40. Delhi is near the famous Poverty Point site, a unique Late Archaic manifestation which features several mounds, one of them about seventy feet high (Webb 1977). There is no indication that Palmer ever got there. Poverty Point only got a passing mention in Thomas's catalog (1891:104), and none at all in his final report, which only allotted portions of three pages to Louisiana (1894:250–52).

41. Palmer must have visited Jackson briefly, if at all; it is not mentioned in McVaugh's (1956: 132–352) list of localities he visited. The Mississippi state collections have been curated by the Mississippi Department of Archives and History in Jackson since 1902 (John Connaway, 1985 personal communication).

42. Thomas reported an old Creek settlement at Cragdale, Alabama, about four miles southeast of Talladega (1891:15; 1894:290). This is in the east-central portion of that state, in the former Upper Creek territory, but the cultural and temporal relationships among late prehistoric and protohistoric sites in this region are unclear (Knight 1980:22–23). Early maps show "Eufala Old Town," a Creek town site, in the Cragdale vicinity (Knight, 1988 personal communication).

43. The few alternative wordings in Palmer's original version are not appreciably different from those in this final version.

44. Powell Clayton (1833–1914) owned several sections of land in this vicinity during the time of Palmer's visit. He was an extremely controversial figure in Arkansas politics during his lifetime and remains so as a historical figure. As a colonel in the Union army during the Civil War, he occupied Pine Bluff in 1863. He was Reconstruction governor of Arkansas from 1868 to 1871, a U.S. senator from 1871 to 1877, leader of the Arkansas Republican party from 1877 through 1896, and U.S. ambassador to Mexico from 1897 to 1905 (Burnside 1978:1–2, 24; 1981).

   After retiring, Clayton did not return to Arkansas, but lived out his days in Washington, D.C. He was the author of a book entitled *The Aftermath of the Civil War in Arkansas*, published posthumously (Clayton 1915), which aroused the indignation of "traditional" Southerners. He was buried in Arlington National Cemetery with military honors, and his obituary in the *New York Times* referred to him as "a distinguished statesman, diplomat, and soldier" (Burnside 1978:215–17).

   Palmer's and Clayton's paths could have crossed on several occasions both before and after Palmer's Arkansas visit. As previously noted, Palmer lived in Leavenworth, Kansas, from early 1858 until the summer of 1859. Clayton was stationed there as a U.S. Army officer from 1855 to 1861 (Burnside 1978:1). Palmer made numerous trips to Mexico between 1885 and his death in 1911 and made his home in Washington during that time. But I have found no indication of any such meetings in Palmer's writings nor in McVaugh's 1956 biography.

45. Glen Lake is known today as Glen Brake. Clifton Breckinridge was born in Kentucky in 1846 and joined the Confederate army at the age of fifteen. After the war he worked three years and saved enough money to complete college in Virginia. Upon graduation he was in poor health and joined an older brother who was a cotton planter near Pine Bluff. He was elected to the U.S. House of Representatives in 1882, about the time of Palmer's visit, and served in Congress from 1883 to 1894, when he resigned to become the American ambassador to Russia, a post he held until 1897.

46. In his original version, Palmer had written, "as if on top of house at the time of the distruction," using the false analogy with Southwestern Pueblo structures and lifeways as he had done in several earlier cases.

47. This specimen list is on a separate sheet of paper and is inserted here after the notes on the site it refers to.

48. Some readers have found this description ambiguous, but upon examination of old maps it is clear that it was Tyronza Station that was on the railroad, not Roman's farm. The railroad ran northwest to southeast, and a location six miles southwest of the station would also be about that far from the railroad.

49. This sounds very much like Ford's description of "typical clinkers formed by burning concentrated piles of grass, such as haystacks," which he found at several places on the Menard site and interpreted "as evidence that at least some of the structures had thatched roofs" (1961: 156). Palmer's comparison to lava must have been made with vesicular basalt in mind. This lightweight, frothy-looking but hard and abrasive rock is common in a number of Western locations that Palmer had frequented, especially in southern Arizona, where it was used prehistorically to make *manos* and *metates* (grinding stones), and for other uses.

50. Palmer's wording in the original version was somewhat different here: "only one or two small pieces of plain pottery was found besides the ashes under the brick material . with the exception of the two opened, the others where a mile away from any permanent water."

51. In the original Palmer added "The soil is black sandy" after this sentence.

52. This is one of Palmer's original notes about Roman; it was not transcribed into his final version.

53. Thomas (1891, 1894) did not list any site at Scanlon's Landing.

54. The site, of course, is east of the Arkansas River, another example of Palmer's "directional dyslexia."

References Cited

Akridge, Scott
  1986   De Soto's route in north central Arkansas. Arkansas Archeological Society Field Notes
          211:3–7.
Anderson, David G.
  1977a   Postdepositional modification of the Zebree behavioral record. In Excavation, data
          interpretation, and report on the Zebree Homestead site, Mississippi County, Arkan-
          sas, edited by Dan F. Morse and Phyllis A. Morse, Chapter 8. Report submitted to
          Memphis District, U.S. Army Corps of Engineers, by Arkansas Archeological Survey,
          Fayetteville.
  1977b   Archeological investigations at the Knapp (Toltec) mound group: 1966 test excavations
          at Mound C. Manuscript on file, Arkansas Archeological Survey, Fayetteville.
Anonymous
  1876   Exploration of a mound in Utah. [Based on notes by Edward Palmer.] American Natu-
          ralist 10:410–14.
  1883   Ancient mounds in Arkansas. Frank Leslie's Illustrated Newspaper 56:222, 224.
  1910   Cyrus Thomas. American Anthropologist (new series) 12:337–43.
Arnold, Morris S.
  1983   The relocation of Arkansas Post to *Ecores Rouges* in 1779. Arkansas Historical Quar-
          terly 42:317–31.
Atwater, Caleb
  1820   Description of the antiquities discovered in the state of Ohio and other western states.
          Transactions and Collections of the American Antiquarian Society 1:105–267.
Bahr, Donald M.
  1983   Pima and Papago social organization. In Handbook of American Indians, Vol. 10:
          Southwest, edited by Alfonso Ortiz, pp. 178–92. Smithsonian Institution, Washing-
          ton, D.C.

Baird, Spencer F.

1859   Mammals of North America; the descriptions of species based chiefly on the collections in the Museum of the Smithsonian Institution. J. B. Lippincott, Philadelphia.

1884   Report of the Secretary. In Annual report of the Board of Regents of the Smithsonian Institution for the year 1882, pp. 1–56. Smithsonian Institution, Washington, D.C.

1885   Report of the Secretary. In Annual report of the Board of Regents of the Smithsonian Institution for the year 1884, pp. 1–98. Smithsonian Institution, Washington, D.C.

Baird, W. David

1980   The Quapaw Indians: a history of the Downstream People. University of Oklahoma Press, Norman.

Baird, W. David (editor)

1977   Years of discontent: Doctor Frank L. James in Arkansas, 1877–1878. Memphis State University Press, Memphis.

Barnhart, Terry A.

1983   A question of authorship: the Ephraim George Squier-Edwin Hamilton Davis controversy. Ohio History 92:52–71.

Bearss, Edwin C.

1962   The White River expedition, June 10–July 15, 1862. Arkansas Historical Quarterly 21:305–62.

Belmont, John S.

1982a   Toltec and Coles Creek: a view from the southern Lower Mississippi Valley. In Emerging patterns of Plum Bayou culture: preliminary investigations of the Toltec Mounds Research Project, edited by Martha Ann Rolingson, pp. 64–70. Arkansas Archeological Survey Research Series, No. 18.

1982b   The Troyville concept and the Gold Mine site. Louisiana Archaeology 9:65–98.

1983   A reconnaissance of the Boeuf Basin, Louisiana. Louisiana Archaeology 10:271–84.

Benson, Adolph B. (editor)

1937   Peter Kalm's travels in North America. Wilson-Erickson, New York. Reprinted in 1966 with minor revisions by Dover Publications, New York.

Binford, Lewis R.

1964   A consideration of archaeological research design. American Antiquity 29:425–41.

1968   Archeological perspectives. In New perspectives in archeology, edited by Sally R. Binford and Lewis R. Binford, pp. 5–32. Aldine, Chicago.

1972   An archaeological perspective. Academic Press, New York.

1983   In pursuit of the past: decoding the archaeological record. Thames and Hudson, New York.

Blitz, John Howard

1985   An archaeological study of the Mississippi Choctaw Indians. Mississippi Department of Archives and History Archaeological Reports, No. 16.

Bohannon, Charles F.

1973   Excavations at the Mineral Springs site, Howard County, Arkansas. Arkansas Archeological Survey Research Series, No. 5.

Brain, Jeffrey P.

1978   Late prehistoric settlement patterning in the Yazoo Basin and Natchez Bluffs regions of the Lower Mississippi Valley. In Mississippian Settlement Patterns, edited by Bruce D. Smith, pp. 331–68. Academic Press, New York.

1985   Introduction: update of De Soto studies since the United States De Soto Expedition Commission report. In "Classics of Smithsonian Anthropology" reprint of Final report of the United States De Soto Expedition Commission, by John R. Swanton, pp. xi–lxxii. Smithsonian Institution Press, Washington, D.C.

Brain, Jeffrey P., Alan Toth, and Antonio Rodriguez-Buckingham
    1974   Ethnohistoric archaeology and the De Soto *entrada* into the Lower Mississippi Valley. Conference on Historic Site Archaeology Papers 7:232–89.

Breternitz, David A.
    1966   An appraisal of tree-ring dated pottery in the Southwest. Anthropological Papers of the University of Arizona, No. 10.

Brose, David S.
    1973   The northeastern United States. In The development of North American archaeology, edited by James E. Fitting, pp. 84–115. Anchor Press, Doubleday, Garden City, New York.

Brown, Calvin S.
    1926   Archeology of Mississippi. Mississippi Geological Survey, University, Mississippi.

Brown, F. Martin
    1967   Dr. Edward Palmer's collecting localities in southern Utah and northwestern Arizona. Journal of the Lepidopterists' Society 21:129–34.

Brown, Ian W.
    1978a   James Alfred Ford: the man and his works. Southeastern Archaeological Conference Special Publications, No. 4.
    1978b   Decorated pottery of the Lower Mississippi Valley: a sorting manual. Avery Island Conference Document, Lower Mississippi Survey, Peabody Museum, Harvard University.

Brown, Ian W., and Stephen Williams
    1980   Cyrus Thomas, eastern North American bibliography. Document of the Smithsonian Institution-Lower Mississippi Survey Conference on the Mound Exploration Division of the Bureau of (American) Ethnology, January 9–11, Washington, D.C.

Bruce, Robert V.
    1987   The launching of modern American science, 1846–1876. Alfred A. Knopf, New York.

Burnside, William H.
    1978   Powell Clayton: politician and diplomat, 1897–1905. Ph.D. dissertation, Department of History, University of Arkansas.
    1981   Powell Clayton. In The governors of Arkansas: essays in political biography, edited by Timothy P. Donovan and Willard B. Gatewood, Jr., pp. 43–54. University of Arkansas Press, Fayetteville.

Bye, Robert A., Jr.
    1972   Ethnobotany of the Southern Paiute Indians in the 1870s: with a note on the early ethnobotanical contributions of Dr. Edward Palmer. In Great Basin cultural ecology: a symposium, edited by Don D. Fowler, pp. 87–104. Desert Research Institute Publications in the Social Sciences, No. 8.
    1979a   An 1878 ethnobotanical collection from San Luis Potosi: Dr. Edward Palmer's first major Mexican collection. Economic Botany 33:135–62.
    1979b   Hallucinogenic plants of the Tarahumara. Journal of Ethnopharmacology 1:23–48.
    1980   Ethnobotanical collections of Dr. Edward Palmer from southern California and vicinity, 1875–1876. Manuscript in possession of the author, Jardín Botánico, Universidad Nacional Autónoma de México, Mexico City.
    1985   Botanical perspectives of ethnobotany of the Greater Southwest. Economic Botany 39:375–86.

1986   Medicinal plants of the Sierra Madre: comparative study of Tarahumara and Mexican market plants. Economic Botany 40:103–24.

Cain, Robert H.
1974   Pimple mounds: a new viewpoint. Ecology 55:178–82.

Caywood, Louis R., and Edward H. Spicer
1935   Tuzigoot: the excavation and repair of a ruin on the Verde River near Clarkdale, Arizona. Field Department of Education, National Park Service, Berkeley, California.

Chapman, Carl H., and Leo O. Anderson
1955   The Campbell site: a Late Mississippi town site and cemetery in southeast Missouri. The Missouri Archaeologist, Vol. 17, Nos. 2–3.

Chapman, Jefferson
1985   Tellico archaeology: 12,000 years of Native American history. University of Tennessee Press, Knoxville.

Clayton, Powell
1915   The aftermath of the Civil War in Arkansas. Neale Publishing Co., New York. Reprinted in 1969 by Negro Universities Press, New York.

Clinch, George
1901   Early man. In The Victoria history of the counties of England: Norfolk, Vol. I, edited by H. Arthur Doubleday, pp. 253–78. Archibald Constable & Co., London. Reprinted in 1975 for the University of London Institute of Historical Research by William Dawson & Sons, Kent.

Conard, Nicholas, et al.
1984   Accelerator radiocarbon dating of evidence for prehistoric horticulture in Illinois. Nature 308:443–46.

Conner, Daniel Ellis
1956   Joseph Reddeford Walker and the Arizona adventure. University of Oklahoma Press, Norman.

Culin, Stewart
1907   Games of the North American Indians. Twenty-fourth Annual Report of the Bureau of American Ethnology, pp. 3–846.

Curren, Caleb
1984   The protohistoric period in central Alabama. Alabama-Tombigbee Regional Commission, Camden, Alabama.

Dall, William H.
1915   Spencer Fullerton Baird: a biography. J. P. Lippincott, Philadelphia.

Daniel, Pete
1977   Deep'n as it come: the 1927 Mississippi River flood. Oxford University Press, New York.

Darlington, H. T., and G. P. Steinbauer
1961   The eighty-year period for Dr. Beal's seed viability experiment. American Journal of Botany 48:321–25.

Darrah, William C.
1951   Powell of the Colorado. Princeton University Press, Princeton, N.J.

Davis, Hester A.
1966   Nine days at the Toltec site: the Society's third successful dig. Arkansas Archeological Society Field Notes 20:2–5.

DeRosier, Arthur H., Jr.
1970   The removal of the Choctaw Indians. University of Tennessee Press, Knoxville.

De Voto, Bernard
  1954   Introduction. In Beyond the hundredth meridian: John Wesley Powell and the second opening of the West, by Wallace E. Stegner. Houghton Mifflin, Boston. Reprinted in 1982 by Bison Books, University of Nebraska Press, Lincoln and London.

Dew, Lee A., and Louis Koeppe
  1972   Narrow-gauge railroads in Arkansas. Arkansas Historical Quarterly 31:276–93.

Dexter, Ralph W.
  1987   The F. W. Putnam-Edward Palmer relations in the development of early American ethnobotany. Paper presented at the tenth annual conference of the Society of Ethnobiology, Gainesville, Florida.

Dickinson, Samuel D.
  1980   Historic tribes of the Ouachita drainage system in Arkansas. The Arkansas Archeologist 21:1–11.
  1986   The River of Cayas, the Ouachita or the Arkansas River? Arkansas Archeological Society Field Notes 209:5–11.

Dittert, Alfred E., Jr., and Donald E. Dove (editors)
  1985   Proceedings of the 1983 Hohokam Symposium. Arizona Archaeological Society Occasional Papers, No. 2.

Doyel, David E.
  1981   Late Hohokam prehistory in southern Arizona. Gila Press, Scottsdale, Arizona.

Doyel, David E., and Mark D. Elson (editors)
  1985   Hohokam settlement and economic systems in the central New River drainage, Arizona. Soil Systems Publications in Archaeology, No. 4.

Doyel, David E., and Fred T. Plog (editors)
  1980   Current issues in Hohokam prehistory: proceedings of a symposium. Arizona State University Anthropological Research Papers, No. 23.

Dyer, Frederick H.
  1909   A compendium of the War of the Rebellion, Vol. 3: regimental histories. Torch Press, Cedar Rapids, Iowa. Reprinted in 1959 by Thomas Yoseloff, New York.

Early, Ann M.
  1982   Caddoan settlement systems in the Ouachita River basin. In Arkansas Archeology in Review, edited by Neal L. Trubowitz and Marvin D. Jeter, pp. 198–232. Arkansas Archeological Survey Research Series, No. 15.
  1986   Dr. Thomas L. Hodges and his contributions to Arkansas archeology. The Arkansas Archeologist 23–24:1–8.
  1988   Standridge: Caddoan settlement in a mountain environment. Arkansas Archeological Survey Research Series, No. 29.

Euler, Robert C., George J. Gumerman, Thor N. V. Karlstrom, Jeffrey S. Dean, and Richard H. Hevly
  1979   The Colorado plateaus: cultural dynamics and paleoenvironment. Science 205:1089–1101.

Fagan, Brian M.
  1984   The Aztecs. Freeman, New York.

Faulk, Odie B.
  1970   Arizona: a short history. University of Oklahoma Press, Norman.

Fewkes, Jesse Walter
  1907   The aborigines of Porto Rico and neighboring islands. Twenty-fifth Annual Report of the Bureau of American Ethnology, pp. 3–220.

1912 Antiquities of the upper Verde River and Walnut Creek valleys, Arizona. Twenty-eighth Annual Report of the Bureau of American Ethnology, pp. 181–220.

Figley, Charles A., Jr.
1964 How not to dig—a horrible example. The Arkansas Archeologist 5:109–10.
1966 Westward ho! in 3WH4. The Arkansas Archeologist 7:41–52.

Flannery, Kent V. (editor)
1976 The early Mesoamerican village. Academic Press, New York.

Ford, James A.
1935 Ceramic decoration sequence at an old Indian village site near Sicily Island, Louisiana. Louisiana Geological Survey Anthropological Studies, No. 1.
1936 Analysis of Indian village site collections from Louisiana and Mississippi. Louisiana Geological Survey Anthropological Studies, No. 2.
1961 Menard site: the Quapaw village of Osotouy on the Arkansas River. Anthropological papers of the American Museum of Natural History, Vol. 48, Part 2.
1963 Hopewell culture burial mounds near Helena, Arkansas. Anthropological Papers of the American Museum of Natural History, Vol. 50, Part 1.

Ford, James A., and Gordon R. Willey
1940 Crooks site: a Marksville period burial mound in La Salle Parish, Louisiana. Louisiana Geological Survey Anthropological Studies, No. 3.
1941 An interpretation of the prehistory of the Eastern United States. American Anthropologist 43:325–63.

Ford, James A., Philip Phillips, and William G. Haag
1955 The Jaketown site in west-central Mississippi. Anthropological Papers of the American Museum of Natural History, Vol. 45, Part 1.

Ford, Janet L., and Martha A. Rolingson
1972 Site destruction due to agricultural practices in southeast Arkansas. Arkansas Archeological Survey Research Series, No. 3.

Fowke, Gerard
1896 Stone art. Thirteenth Annual Report of the Bureau of American Ethnology, pp. 47–178.

Fowler, Catherine S., and Don D. Fowler
1981 The Southern Paiute: A.D. 1400–1776. In The Protohistoric period in the North American Southwest, A.D. 1450–1700, edited by David R. Wilcox and W. Bruce Masse, pp. 129–62. Arizona State University Anthropological Research Papers, No. 24.

Fowler, Don D., and Jesse D. Jennings
1982 Great Basin archaeology: a historical overview. In Man and environment in the Great Basin, edited by David B. Madsen and James F. O'Connell, pp. 105–20. Society for American Archaeology SAA Papers, No. 2.

Fowler, Don D., David B. Madsen, and Eugene M. Hattori
1973 Prehistory of southeastern Nevada. Desert Research Institute Publications in the Social Sciences, No. 6, Reno, Nevada.

Fowler, Don D., and John F. Matley
1978 The Palmer collection from southwestern Utah, 1875. University of Utah Anthropological Papers, No. 99 (Miscellaneous Papers, No. 20).

Gatewood, Willard B., Jr. (editor)
1979 Slave and freeman: the autobiography of George L. Knox. University Press of Kentucky, Lexington.

Geldart, Herbert D.
1901 Botany. In The Victoria history of the counties of England: Norfolk, Vol. 1, edited by

H. Arthur Doubleday, pp. 39–55. Archibald Constable and Co., London. Reprinted in 1975 for the University of London Institute of Historical Research by William Dawson and Sons, Kent.

Gibson, Jon L.
    1979   Review of Archaeology and ceramics at the Marksville site, by Alan Toth. Louisiana Archaeology 4:127–37.

Gifford, Edward W.
    1932   The southeastern Yavapai. University of California Publications in American Archaeology and Ethnology 29(3).
    1936   Northeastern and western Yavapai. University of California Publications in American Archaeology and Ethnology 34(4).

Goetzmann, William H.
    1966   Exploration and empire. W. W. Norton, New York.

Goodspeed Publishing Co.
    1889   Biographical and historical memoirs of Pulaski, Jefferson, Lonoke, Faulkner, Grant, Saline, Perry, Garland, and Hot Spring counties, Arkansas. Goodspeed Publishing Co., Chicago. Reprinted in 1978 by Southern Historical Press, Easley, S.C.

Goodwin, Grenville
    1942   The social organization of the western Apache. University of Chicago Press, Chicago. Reprinted in 1969 by University of Arizona Press, Tucson.

Griffin, James B.
    1967   Eastern North American archaeology: a summary. Science 156:175–91.

Hale, Kenneth, and David Harris
    1979   Historical linguistics and archeology. In Handbook of North American Indians, Vol. 9: Southwest, edited by Alfonso Ortiz, pp. 170–77. Smithsonian Institution, Washington, D.C.

Hallowell, A. Irving
    1960   The Beginnings of anthropology in America. In Selected papers from the American Anthropologist, 1888–1920, edited by Frederica de Laguna, pp. 1–90. Row and Peterson, Evanston, Illinois.

Hansen, Marcus Lee
    1940   The Atlantic migration, 1607–1860: a history of the continuing settlement of the United States, edited with a foreword by Arthur M. Schlesinger. Harvard University Press, Cambridge.

Harrington, Mark R.
    1927   A primitive Pueblo city in Nevada. American Anthropologist 29:262–77.
    1930   Archeological explorations in southern Nevada. Southwest Museum Papers 4:1–25.

Harris, Marvin
    1968   The rise of anthropological theory: a history of theories of culture. Thomas Y. Crowell Co., New York.

Haury, Emil W.
    1976   The Hohokam, desert farmers and craftsmen: excavations at Snaketown, 1964–1965. University of Arizona Press, Tucson.

Haven, Samuel F.
    1856   Archaeology of the United States. Smithsonian contributions to knowledge, Vol. 8, Article 2.

Hayden, Irwin
    1930   Mesa House. Southwest Museum Papers 4:26–92.

Heizer, Robert F.

1954   Notes on the Utah Utes by Edward Palmer, 1866–1877. University of Utah Department of Anthropology Anthropological Papers, No. 17.

Hemmings, E. Thomas, and John H. House (editors)

1985   The Alexander site, Conway County, Arkansas. Arkansas Archeological Survey Research Series, No. 24.

Herber, Elmer C. (editor)

1963   Correspondence between Spencer Fullerton Baird and Louis Agassiz—two pioneer American naturalists. Smithsonian Institution Press, Washington, D.C.

Hinsley, Curtis M., Jr.

1981   Savages and scientists: the Smithsonian Institution and the development of American anthropology, 1846–1910. Smithsonian Institution Press, Washington.

Hoffman, Michael P.

1975   Prehistoric archeological material from Arkansas at the Smithsonian Institution: an inventory and assessment. Manuscript on file, University of Arkansas Museum and Arkansas Archeological Survey, Fayetteville.

1977   The Kinkead-Mainard site, 3PU2: a late prehistoric Quapaw phase site near Little Rock, Arkansas. The Arkansas Archeologist 16–18:1–41.

1986   The Protohistoric period in the lower and central Arkansas River valley in Arkansas. In The Protohistoric period in the Mid-South: 1500–1700, edited by David H. Dye and Ronald C. Brister, pp. 24–37. Mississippi Department of Archives and History Archaeological Reports, No. 18.

Hoffman, Teresa L.

1982   Lithic technology at Toltec: preliminary results from Mound D. In Emerging patterns of Plum Bayou culture: preliminary investigations of the Toltec Mounds Research Project, edited by Martha Ann Rolingson, pp. 54–59. Arkansas Archeological Survey Research Series, No. 18.

Holder, Trusten H.

1970   Disappearing wetlands in eastern Arkansas. Arkansas Planning Commission, Little Rock.

Holmes, William Henry

1878   Report on the ancient ruins of southwestern Colorado, examined during the summers of 1875 and 1876. Tenth Annual Report of the United States Geological and Geographical Survey of the Territories, pp. 381–408.

1883   Art in shell of the ancient Americans. Second Annual Report of the Bureau of Ethnology, pp. 179–305.

1884   Illustrated catalogue of a portion of the collections made by the Bureau of Ethnology during the field season of 1881. Third Annual Report of the Bureau of Ethnology, pp. 427–510.

1886a Pottery of the ancient pueblos. Fourth Annual Report of the Bureau of Ethnology, pp. 257–360.

1886b Ancient pottery of the Mississippi Valley. Fourth Annual Report of the Bureau of Ethnology, pp. 361–436.

1891   Aboriginal novaculite quarries in Garland County, Arkansas. American Anthropologist (old series) 4:313–15.

1903   Aboriginal pottery of the eastern United States. Twentieth Annual Report of the Bureau of American Ethnology, pp. 1–237.

Horn, Pamela

1981   The rural world, 1780–1850: social change in the English countryside. St. Martin's Press, New York.

Hough, Walter
   1911   Edward Palmer. American Anthropologist 13:173.

House, John H.
   1975a   Prehistoric lithic resource utilization in the Cache Basin: Crowley's Ridge chert and
           quartzite and Pitkin Chert. In The Cache River archeological project: an experiment in
           contract archeology, assembled by Michael B. Schiffer and John H. House, pp. 88–91.
           Arkansas Archeological Survey Research Series, No. 8.
   1975b   Summary of archeological knowledge updated with newly gathered survey data. In The
           Cache River archeological project: an experiment in contract archeology, assembled by
           Michael B. Schiffer and John H. House, pp. 153–62. Arkansas Archeological Survey
           Research Series, No. 8.
   1987   Kent phase investigations in eastern Arkansas, 1978–1984. Mississippi Archaeology
           22:46–60.

Howard, Robert W.
   1975   The dawnseekers: the first history of American paleontology. Harcourt Brace Jovano-
           vich, New York and London.

Hudson, Charles
   1985   De Soto in Arkansas: a brief synopsis. Arkansas Archeological Society Field Notes
           205:3–12.

Hughes, Langston, Milton Meltzer, and C. Eric Lincoln
   1983   A pictorial history of Blackamericans. Crown, New York.

Igoe, Lynn M.
   1981   250 years of Afro-American art: an annotated bibliography. R. R. Bowker, New York.

Jackson, H. Edwin
   1987   The De Soto Plantation site (3DE24), Desha County, Arkansas. Arkansas Archeologi-
           cal Society Field Notes 218:3–8.

Jennings, Jesse D.
   1974   Prehistory of North America, second edition. McGraw-Hill, New York.

Jeter, Marvin D.
   1977   Archaeology in Copper Basin, Yavapai County, Arizona: model building for the pre-
           history of the Prescott region. Arizona State University Anthropological Research
           Papers, No. 11.
   1979   George P. Kelley and the development of archeology in southeast Arkansas. Arkansas
           Archeological Society Field Notes 169:12–16.
   1981   Edward Palmer's 1882 excavation at the Tillar site (3DR1), southeast Arkansas. South-
           eastern Archaeological Conference Bulletin 24:57–59.
   1982a   The archeology of southeast Arkansas: an overview for the 1980s. In Arkansas arche-
           ology in review, edited by Neal L. Trubowitz and Marvin D. Jeter, pp. 76–131. Arkan-
           sas Archeological Survey Research Series, No. 15.
   1982b   The protohistoric "Tillar complex" of southeast Arkansas. Paper presented at the
           forty-seventh annual meeting of the Society for American Archaeology, Minneapolis,
           Minnesota.
   1982c   Review of "Archaeological investigations at the confluence of the Verde River and West
           Clear Creek," by S. Stebbins, D. E. Weaver, Jr., and S. G. Dosh. The Kiva 47:293–96.
   1986a   Tunicans west of the Mississippi: a summary of archeological and early historic evi-
           dence. In The Protohistoric period in the Mid-South: 1500–1700, edited by David H.
           Dye and Ronald C. Brister, pp. 38–63. Mississippi Department of Archives and His-
           tory Archaeological Reports, No. 18.
   1986b   Review of 1985 reprint of "Report on the mound explorations of the Bureau of Eth-
           nology," by Cyrus Thomas. Southeastern Archaeology 5:148–50.

1989   Methods of relating historical collections of artifacts and associated records to known sites and current research. Chapter 15, in Tracing archaeology's past: historiography of archaeology, edited by Andrew L. Christenson. Southern Illinois University Press, Carbondale, in press.

Jeter, Marvin D., David B. Kelley, and George P. Kelley
1979   The Kelley-Grimes site: a Mississippi period burial mound, southeast Arkansas, excavated in 1936. The Arkansas Archeologist 20:1–51.

Jeter, Marvin D., Jerome C. Rose, G. Ishmael Williams, Jr., and Anna M. Harmon
1989   An archeological and bioarcheological overview of the Lower Mississippi Valley and Trans-Mississippi South in Arkansas and Louisiana. Arkansas Archeological Survey Research Series, in press.

Judd, Neil M.
1919   Archeological investigations at Paragonah, Utah. Smithsonian Miscellaneous Collections, Vol. 70, No. 3.
1926   Archeological observations north of the Rio Colorado. Bureau of American Ethnology Bulletin 82.
1967   The Bureau of American Ethnology: a partial history. University of Oklahoma Press, Norman.
1968   Men met along the trail: adventures in archaeology. University of Oklahoma Press, Norman.

Justice, Oren L., and Louis N. Bass
1978   Principles and practices of seed storage. U.S. Department of Agriculture, Agriculture Handbook No. 506.

Kaczor, Michael J.
1982   Preliminary report on the soils and geology at the Toltec Mounds site. In Emerging patterns of Plum Bayou culture: preliminary investigations of the Toltec Mounds research project, edited by Martha Ann Rolingson, pp. 17–29. Arkansas Archeological Survey Research Series, No. 18.

Kaczor, Michael J., and John Weymouth
1981   Magnetic prospecting: preliminary results of the 1980 field season at the Toltec site, 3LN42. Southeastern Archaeological Conference Bulletin 24:118–23.

Keel, Bennie C.
1970   Cyrus Thomas and the Mound Builders. Southern Indian Studies 22:3–16.

Keyes, Charles Reuben
1928   The Hill-Lewis archeological survey. Minnesota History 9(2):96–108, June 1928.
1930   A unique survey. State Historical Society of Iowa Palimpsest 11(5):214–26, May 1930.

Knight, Vernon J., Jr.
1980   Culture complexes of the Alabama Piedmont: an initial statement. Journal of Alabama Archaeology 26:1–27.

Krochmal, Arnold, and Connie Krochmal
1973   A guide to the medicinal plants of the United States. Quadrangle/The New York Times Book Co., New York.

Laurin, Ronald
1981   1981 controlled surface collections at the Toltec site (3LN42). Arkansas Archeological Society Field Notes 182:3–8.

Leslie, James W.
1981   Pine Bluff and Jefferson County: a pictorial history. Donning Co., Norfolk, VA.

Lewis, Thomas M. N., and Madeline Kneberg
  1946   Hiwassee Island: an archaeological account of four Tennessee Indian peoples. University of Tennessee Press, Knoxville.

Limp, W. Fredrick
  1987   Archeological site destruction in Arkansas. Arkansas Archeological Survey Technical Papers, No. 6.

Little, Elbert L., Jr.
  1950   Southwestern trees: a guide to the native species of New Mexico and Arizona. U.S. Department of Agriculture Handbook No. 9.

Lockett, Samuel H.
  1873   Mounds in Louisiana. Annual report of the Smithsonian Institution for 1872, pp. 429–30.

Marshall, William
  1795   The rural economy of Norfolk, 2nd edition. G. Nicol, London.

Mason, Otis T.
  1884   The Mound-Builders. American Naturalist 18:745–46.
  1896   Primitive travel and transportation. United States National Museum Report for 1893–94, pp. 237–593.

McClurkan, Burney B.
  1971a   Fort Desha, the location of Arkansas Post ca. 1735–1750. Conference on Historic Site Archaeology Papers 6:32.
  1971b   The search for Fort Desha. Arkansas Archeological Society Field Notes 77:5–6.

McGimsey, Charles R. III
  1972   Public archeology. Seminar Press, New York.

McGuire, Randall H., and Michael B. Schiffer (editors)
  1982   Hohokam and Patayan: prehistory of southwestern Arizona. Academic Press, New York.

McVaugh, Rogers
  1956   Edward Palmer: plant explorer of the American West. University of Oklahoma Press, Norman. Reprinted in 1977 by Theophrastus Publishers, Little Compton, Rhode Island.

Meltzer, David J.
  1985   North American archaeology and archaeologists, 1879–1934. American Antiquity 50:249–60.

Miller, John E. III
  1982   Construction of site features: tests of Mounds C, D, E, B and the embankment. In Emerging patterns of Plum Bayou culture: preliminary investigations of the Toltec Mounds research project, edited by Martha Ann Rolingson, pp. 30–43. Arkansas Archeological Survey Research Series, No. 18.
  n.d.   The Washington Mounds, Hempstead County, Arkansas: results of 1981 excavations. Manuscript on file, Arkansas Archeological Survey, Fayetteville.

Moore, Clarence B.
  1908   Certain mounds of Arkansas and of Mississippi. Journal of the Academy of Natural Sciences of Philadelphia 13:480–600.
  1909   Antiquities of the Ouachita Valley. Journal of the Academy of Natural Sciences of Philadelphia 14:1–170.
  1910   Antiquities of the St. Francis, White and Black rivers, Arkansas. Journal of the Academy of Natural Sciences of Philadelphia 14:255–364.

1911   Some aboriginal sites on Mississippi River. Journal of the Academy of Natural Sciences of Philadelphia 14:367–480.

1913   Some aboriginal sites in Louisiana and in Arkansas. Journal of the Academy of Natural Sciences of Philadelphia 16:1–98.

Morgan, Lewis Henry
  1877   Ancient society, or, researches in the lines of human progress from savagery through barbarism to civilization. Henry Holt and Co., New York.
  1881   Houses and house-life of the American aborigines. U.S. Geological Survey Contributions to North American Ethnology, Vol. 4. Reprinted in 1965 by University of Chicago Press, Chicago.

Morse, Dan F. (editor)
  1973   Nodena: an account of 75 years of archeological investigation in southeast Mississippi County, Arkansas. Arkansas Archeological Survey Research Series, No. 4.

Morse, Dan F., and Phyllis A. Morse
  1983   Archaeology of the Central Mississippi Valley. Academic Press, New York.

Morse, Phyllis A.
  1981   Parkin: the 1978–1979 archeological investigations of a Cross County, Arkansas site. Arkansas Archeological Survey Research Series, No. 13.

Nabhan, Gary Paul
  1977   Viable seeds from prehistoric caches? Archaeobotanical remains in Southwestern folklore. The Kiva 43:143–59.

Newell, H. Perry, and Alex D. Krieger
  1949   The George C. Davis site, Cherokee County, Texas. Society for American Archaeology Memoirs, No. 5.

Nuttall, Thomas
  1821   A journal of travels into the Arkansa Territory, during the year 1819. Thomas H. Palmer, Philadelphia. Reprinted in 1966 by University Microfilms, Ann Arbor, Michigan.

Palmer, Edward
  1871   Food products of the North American Indians. U.S. Department of Agriculture Annual Report for 1870, pp. 404–28.
  1873   Indian rope and cloth. American Naturalist 7:755.
  1874a   The manufacture of pottery by the Indians. American Naturalist 8:245–47.
  1874b   The berries of Rhamnus croceus as Indian food. American Naturalist 8:247.
  1875a   Clay-balls as slung shot or cooking stones. American Naturalist 9:183–84.
  1875b   An Indian mill seen in the Museum of Nassau, New Providence. American Naturalist 9:248–49.
  1875c   The starch of Zamia. American Naturalist 9:509–11.
  1877a   Manufacture of pottery by Mojave Indian women. Proceedings of the Davenport Academy of Natural Sciences, Vol. 2, Part 1 (January 1876–June 1877), pp. 32–34.
  1877b   Remarks concerning two divisions of Indians inhabiting Arizona, New Mexico, Utah, and California. American Naturalist 11:735–47.
  1878a   Cave dwellings in Utah. Eleventh Annual Report of the Peabody Museum: Reports of the Peabody Museum 2(2):269–72.
  1878b   Notes on Indian manners and customs. American Naturalist 12:308–13.
  1878c   Indian food customs. American Naturalist 12:402.
  1878d   Fish-hooks of the Mohave Indians. American Naturalist 12:403.
  1878e   Plants used by the Indians of the United States. American Naturalist 12:593–606, 646–55.
  1880   A review of the published statements regarding the mounds at Payson, Utah, with an

account of their structure and origin. Proceedings of the Davenport Academy of Natural Sciences, Vol. 2, Part 2 (July 1877–December 1878), pp. 167–72.

1881 The sacrificial stone of the city of Mexico, is it genuine or not? American Naturalist 15:752–54.

1882 Mexican caves with human remains. American Naturalist 16:306–11.

1885 Burnt clay in the mounds. American Naturalist 19:825.

1887 Ornaments on pottery. American Naturalist 21:97–98.

1917 [Posthumous] Arkansas mounds. Publications of the Arkansas Historical Association 4:390–448.

Parry, Charles Christopher
1877 Exploration of a mound near Utah Lake, Utah. Proceedings of the Davenport Academy of Natural Sciences, Vol. 2, Part 1 (January 1876–June 1877), pp. 28–29, 82.

Peet, Stephen D.
1883 [Editorial] Explorations of mounds. The American Antiquarian 5(4):332–40.

Penick, James L., Jr.
1981 The great Western land pirate: John A. Murrell in legend and history. University of Missouri Press, Columbia.

Perino, Gregory
1967 The Cherry Valley mounds and Banks Mound 3. Central States Archaeological Societies Memoirs, No. 1.

Perttula, Timothy K., and James E. Price
1984 The 1882 investigations by Colonel P. W. Norris at the Powers Fort site, 23BU10, southeast Missouri. Tennessee Anthropologist 9:1–14.

Phillips, Philip
1970 Archaeological survey in the Lower Yazoo Basin, Mississippi, 1949–1955. Papers of the Peabody Museum, Harvard University, Vol. 60.

n.d. Ouachita River survey, 1939. Field notes on file, Arkansas Archeological Survey, Fayetteville.

Phillips, Philip, James A. Ford, and James B. Griffin
1951 Archaeological survey in the Lower Mississippi Alluvial Valley, 1940–1947. Papers of the Peabody Museum, Harvard University, Vol. 25.

Poinsett, Joel R.
1841 Discourse, on the objects and importance of the National Institution for the Promotion of Science, established at Washington, 1840, delivered at the first anniversary. P. Force, Printer, Washington, D.C.

Powell, John Wesley
1875 Report on the exploration of the Colorado River of the West and its tributaries. Washington, D.C.

1876 Report on the geology of the eastern portion of the Uinta Mountains. Washington, D.C.

1878 Report on the lands of the arid region of the United States, with a more detailed account of the lands of Utah. Forty-fifth Congress, second session, House of Representatives Executive Document 73, Washington, D.C.

1881a Report of the director. First Annual Report of the Bureau of Ethnology, pp. xi–xxxiii.

1881b On limitations to the use of some anthropologic data. First Annual Report of the Bureau of Ethnology, pp. 71–86.

1894 Report of the director. Twelfth Annual Report of the Bureau of Ethnology, pp. xix–xlviii.

Puckett, Newbell Niles
1926 Folk beliefs of the Southern Negro. University of North Carolina Press, Chapel Hill.

Reprinted in 1969, as The magic and folk beliefs of the Southern Negro, by Dover Publications, New York.

Putnam, Frederic Ward
1875a   The pottery of the Mound Builders. American Naturalist 9:321–38.
1875b   Report of the Curator [for 1874]. Eighth Annual Report of the Peabody Museum: Reports of the Peabody Museum 1(8):7–55.
1876   Report of the curator [for 1875]. Ninth Annual Report of the Peabody Museum: Reports of the Peabody Museum 1(9):7–23.
1878   Report of the curator [for 1877]. Eleventh Annual Report of the Peabody Museum: Reports of the Peabody Museum 2(2):191–220.
1880a   Report of the curator [for 1878]. Twelfth Annual Report of the Peabody Museum: Reports of the Peabody Museum 2(3):466–96.
1880b   Report of the curator [for 1879]. Thirteenth Annual Report of the Peabody Museum: Reports of the Peabody Museum 2(4):715–51.
1881   Report of the curator [for 1880]. Fourteenth Annual Report of the Peabody Museum: Reports of the Peabody Museum 3(1):7–38.
1882a   Report of the curator [for 1881]. Fifteenth Annual Report of the Peabody Museum: Reports of the Peabody Museum 3(2):55–82.
1882b   Notes on the copper objects from North and South America, contained in the collections of the Peabody Museum. Fifteenth Annual Report of the Peabody Museum: Reports of the Peabody Museum 3(2):83–148.
1886   Report of the curator [for 1884 and 1885]. Eighteenth and nineteenth Annual Reports of the Peabody Museum: Reports of the Peabody Museum 3(5–6):401–32.

Putnam, J. A.
1966   Commentary on Dr. Edward Palmer—food products of the North American Indians. Washington Archaeologist 10(1):2–4.

Ramenofsky, Ann F.
1985   The introduction of European disease and aboriginal population collapse. Mississippi Archaeology 20(1):2–19.

Rhees, William Jones (editor)
1901   The Smithsonian Institution: documents relative to its origin and history, 1835–1899: Vol. 1—1835–1887. Government Printing Office, Washington, D.C.

Rolingson, Martha Ann
1976a   The Bartholomew phase: a Plaquemine adaptation in the Mississippi Valley. In Cultural change and continuity: essays in honor of James Bennett Griffin, edited by Charles E. Cleland, pp. 99–119. Academic Press, New York.
1976b   Forests and floods: clues to the Mississippi Valley floodplain environment in southeastern Arkansas and significance for prehistoric settlement. Paper presented at the Southeastern Archaeological Conference, Tuscaloosa, Alabama.

Rolingson, Martha Ann (editor)
1982   Emerging patterns of Plum Bayou culture: preliminary investigations of the Toltec Mounds Research Project. Arkansas Archeological Survey Research Series, No. 18.

Safford, William E.
1911a   Edward Palmer. Popular Science Monthly 78:341–54.
1911b   Edward Palmer. Botanical Gazette 52:61–63.
1911c   Edward Palmer. American Fern Journal 1:143–47.
1926   Edward Palmer: botanical explorer. Unpublished manuscript, on file at Division of Plant Exploration and Introduction, U.S. Department of Agriculture, and National Anthropological Archives, U.S. National Museum, Smithsonian Institution, Washington, D.C.

St. Louis Republic

    1906   The book of St. Louisans: a biographical dictionary of the leading living men of the city of St. Louis. The St. Louis Republic, St. Louis, Mo.

    1912   The book of St. Louisans: a biographical dictionary of the leading living men of the city of St. Louis and vicinity, 2nd ed. The St. Louis Republic, St. Louis, Mo.

Saucier, Roger T.

    1974   Quaternary geology of the lower Mississippi alluvial valley. Arkansas Archeological Survey Research Series, No. 6.

    1978   Sand dunes and related eolian features of the lower Mississippi alluvial valley. Geoscience and Man 19:23–40.

    1989   Evidence for episodic sand-blow activity during the 1811–1812 New Madrid (Missouri) earthquake series. Geology 17:103–06.

Schambach, Frank F.

    1970   Pre-Caddoan cultures in the Trans-Mississippi South: a beginning sequence. Ph.D. dissertation, Department of Anthropology, Harvard University.

Schambach, Frank F., and John E. Miller III

    1984   A description and analysis of the ceramics. In Cedar Grove: an interdisciplinary investigation of a late Caddo farmstead in the Red River valley, edited by Neal L. Trubowitz, pp. 109–70. Arkansas Archeological Survey Research Series, No. 23.

Scheibel, Russell G., and Ann M. Early

    1982   The productive partnership: amateur and professional in Arkansas archeology. In Arkansas archeology in review, edited by Neal L. Trubowitz and Marvin D. Jeter, pp. 310–15. Arkansas Archeological Survey Research Series, No. 15.

Schoolcraft, Henry R.

    1851–57   Historical and statistical information respecting the history, condition, and prospects of the Indian tribes of the United States, Vols. 1–6. Philadelphia, Pennsylvania.

Sealey, Neil E.

    1985   Bahamian landscapes: an introduction to the geography of the Bahamas. Collins Caribbean, London.

Sheppley, Helen Edith

    1933   Camp Butler in the Civil War days. Journal of the Illinois State Historical Society 25:285–317.

Sherrod, P. Clay, and Martha Ann Rolingson

    1987   Surveyors of the ancient Mississippi Valley: modules and alignments in prehistoric mound sites. Arkansas Archeological Survey Research Series, No. 28.

Shutler, Richard, Jr.

    1961   Lost City, Pueblo Grande de Nevada. Nevada State Museum Anthropological Papers, No. 5.

Silverberg, Robert

    1968   Mound Builders of ancient America: the archaeology of a myth. Greenwich, New York.

Smith, Bruce D.

    1986   The archaeology of the Southeastern United States: from Dalton to De Soto, 10,500–500 B.P. Advances in World Archaeology 5:1–92.

Spaulding, Albert C.

    1957   Review of "Method and theory in American archaeology" articles by Gordon R. Willey and Philip Phillips. American Antiquity 23:85–87.

Spicer, Edward H.

    1936   King's Ruin. In Two pueblo ruins in west central Arizona, by E. H. Spicer and L. R.

Caywood, pp. 5–85. University of Arizona Bulletin, Vol. 7, No. 1 (Social Science Bulletin No. 10), Part 1.

Spradling, Mary M. (editor)
1980   In black and white. Gale Research Co., Detroit.

Squier, Ephraim G., and Edwin H. Davis
1848   Ancient monuments of the Mississippi Valley. Smithsonian Contributions to Knowledge, Vol. 1. Washington, D.C.

Starr, Mary Evelyn
1984   The Parchman phase in the northern Yazoo Basin: a preliminary analysis. In The Wilsford site (22CO516), Coahoma County, Mississippi, by John M. Connaway, pp. 163–209. Mississippi Department of Archives and History Archaeological Reports, No. 14.

Stegner, Wallace E.
1954   Beyond the hundredth meridian: John Wesley Powell and the second opening of the West. Houghton Mifflin, Boston. Reprinted in 1982 by Bison Books, University of Nebraska Press, Lincoln and London.

Steward, Julian H.
1937   Ecological aspects of Southwestern society. Anthropos 32:87–104.
1938   Basin-Plateau aboriginal sociopolitical groups. Bureau of American Ethnology Bulletin 120.
1955   Theory of culture change. University of Illinois Press, Urbana.

Stewart, Kenneth M.
1983   Mohave. In Handbook of North American Indians, Vol. 10: Southwest, edited by Alfonso Ortiz, pp. 55–70. Smithsonian Institution, Washington, D.C.

Stewart-Abernathy, Judith C.
1982   Ceramic studies at the Toltec Mounds site: basis for a tentative cultural sequence. In Emerging patterns of Plum Bayou culture: preliminary investigations of the Toltec Mounds Research Project, edited by Martha Ann Rolingson, pp. 44–53. Arkansas Archeological Survey Research Series, No. 18.

Story, Dee Ann, and Samuel Valastro, Jr.
1977   Radiocarbon dating and the George C. Davis site, Texas. Journal of Field Archaeology 4:63–89.

Studley, Cordelia A.
1884   Notes upon human remains from caves in Coahuila. Sixteenth Annual Report of the Peabody Museum: Reports of the Peabody Museum 3(3):233–59.

Sturtevant, William C.
1969   History and ethnography of some West Indian starches. In The domestication and exploitation of plants and animals, edited by P. J. Ucko and G. W. Dimbleby, pp. 177–99. Aldine-Atherton, Chicago.

Swallow, George C.
1858   Indian mounds in New Madrid County, Missouri. Transactions of the Academy of Science of St. Louis 1:36.

Swanton, John R.
1939   Final report of the United States De Soto Expedition Commission. House Document 71, 76th Congress, 1st Session, Washington, D.C. Reprinted in 1985 by Smithsonian Institution Press, Washington, D.C.
1946   The Indians of the southeastern United States. Bureau of American Ethnology Bulletin 137.

Tanselle, G. Thomas
    1981   Literary editing. In Literary and historical editing, edited by George L. Vogt and John B. Jones, pp. 35–56. University of Kansas Publications, Library Series, No. 46.

Thomas, Cyrus
    1873   Ancient mounds of Dakota. Sixth Annual Report of the U.S. Geological Survey of the Territories, for the year 1872, pp. 655–58.
    1887   Burial mounds of the northern sections of the United States. Fifth Annual Report of the Bureau of Ethnology, pp. 3–119.
    1889a   The problem of the Ohio mounds. Bureau of Ethnology Bulletin 8.
    1889b   The circular, square, and octagonal earthworks of Ohio. Bureau of Ethnology Bulletin 10.
    1891   Catalogue of prehistoric works east of the Rocky Mountains. Bureau of Ethnology Bulletin 12.
    1894   Report on the mound explorations of the Bureau of Ethnology. Twelfth Annual Report of the Bureau of Ethnology, pp. 3–742. Reprinted in 1985, as No. 7 in the "Classics of Smithsonian Anthropology" series, by Smithsonian Institution Press, Washington, D.C.

Trubowitz, Neal L., and Marvin D. Jeter (editors)
    1982   Arkansas archeology in review. Arkansas Archeological Survey Research Series, No. 15.

Tsai, Shih-shan Henry
    1981   The Chinese in Arkansas. Report submitted to Arkansas Endowment for the Humanities by the University of Arkansas, Fayetteville.

Vogt, George L., and John B. Jones (editors)
    1981   Literary and historical editing. University of Kansas Publications, Library Series, No. 46.

Walker, Winslow M.
    1936   The Troyville Mounds, Catahoula Parish, Louisiana. Bureau of American Ethnology Bulletin 113.

Walker, Winslow M., and Robert M. Adams
    1946   Excavations in the Matthews site, New Madrid County, Missouri. Transactions of the Academy of Science of St. Louis 31(4).

Wauchope, Robert
    1966   Archaeological survey of north Georgia, with a test of some cultural hypotheses. Society for American Archaeology Memoirs, No. 21.

Webb, Clarence H.
    1977   The Poverty Point culture. Geoscience and Man, Vol. XVII.

Weber, J. Cynthia
    1973   The Hays Mound, 3CL6, Clark County, south central Arkansas. Report submitted to National Park Service by Arkansas Archeological Survey, Fayetteville.

White, Leslie A.
    1942   The Pueblo of Santa Ana, New Mexico. American Anthropological Association Memoirs, No. 60.
    1943   Energy and the evolution of culture. American Anthropologist 45:335–56.
    1949   The science of culture. Grove Press, New York.
    1959   The evolution of culture. McGraw-Hill, New York.

White, Patsy
    1970   Investigation of the cemetery at the Gee's Landing site. The Arkansas Archeologist 11:1–20.

1987   The Gordon site: a Middle Coles Creek to Late Mississippi period occupation in Ash-
        ley County, southeast Arkansas. The Arkansas Archeologist 25–26:1–51.

Wilcox, David R.
1981   The entry of Athapaskans into the American Southwest: the problem today. In The
        protohistoric period in the North American Southwest, AD 1450–1700, edited by
        David R. Wilcox and W. Bruce Masse, pp. 213–56. Arizona State University Anthro-
        pological Research Papers, No. 24.

Wilcox, David R., and Lynette O. Shenk
1977   The architecture of the Casa Grande and its interpretation. Arizona State Museum
        Archaeological Series, No. 115.

Willey, Gordon R.
1966   An introduction to American archaeology, Vol. 1: North and Middle America. Pren-
        tice-Hall, Englewood Cliffs, N.J.

Willey, Gordon R., and Philip Phillips
1958   Method and theory in American archaeology. University of Chicago Press, Chicago.

Willey, Gordon R., and Jeremy A. Sabloff
1974   A history of American archaeology. W. H. Freeman, San Francisco.
1980   A history of American archaeology, second edition. W. H. Freeman, San Francisco.

Williams, Stephen
1980   Wills de Hass and how it all began. Paper presented at the Southeastern Archaeologi-
        cal Conference, New Orleans, La.

Williams, Stephen, and Jeffrey P. Brain
1983   Excavations at the Lake George site, Yazoo County, Mississippi, 1958–1960. Papers
        of the Peabody Museum, Harvard University, Vol. 74.

Winchell, N. H.
1911   The aborigines of Minnesota: a report based on the collections of Jacob V. Brower,
        and on the field surveys and notes of Alfred J. Hill and Theodore H. Lewis. Minnesota
        Historical Society and The Pioneer Co., St. Paul.

Wolfman, Daniel
1982   Archeomagnetic dating in Arkansas and the border areas of adjacent states. In Arkan-
        sas archeology in review, edited by Neal L. Trubowitz and Marvin D. Jeter, pp. 277–
        300. Arkansas Archeological Survey Research Series, No. 15.
1984   Geomagnetic dating methods in archaeology. In Advances in archaeological method
        and theory, Vol. 7, edited by Michael B. Schiffer, pp. 363–458. Academic Press,
        New York.

Wood, Robert D.
1985   The voyage of the Water Witch: a scientific expedition to Paraguay and the La Plata
        region (1853–1856). Labyrinthos, Culver City, California.

Woodward, H. B.
1901   Geology. In The Victoria history of the counties of England: Norfolk, Vol. 1, edited by
        H. Arthur Doubleday, pp. 1–29. Archibald Constable and Co., London. Reprinted in
        1975 for the University of London Institute of Historical Research by William Dawson
        and Sons, Kent.

General Index

Index of Places and Archeological Sites